PC Upgrade and Repair Bible: Desktop Edition

PC Upgrade and Repair Bible: Desktop Edition

Barry Press and Marcia Press

WILEY

Wiley Publishing, Inc.

PC Upgrade and Repair Bible: Desktop Edition

Published by
Wiley Publishing, Inc.
10475 Crosspoint Boulevard
Indianapolis, IN 46256
www.wiley.com

Published by Wiley Publishing, Inc., Indianapolis, Indiana
Published simultaneously in Canada

Library of Congress Control Number: 2004103150

ISBN: 0-7645-5731-9

Manufactured in the United States of America

10 9 8 7 6 5 4 3

1B/SQ/QU/QU/IN

For general information on our other products and services or to obtain technical support, please contact our Customer Care Department within the U.S. at (800) 762-2974, outside the U.S. at (317) 572-3993 or fax (317) 572-4002.

Wiley also publishes its books in a variety of electronic formats. Some content that appears in print may not be available in electronic books.

WILEY

About the Authors

Barry Press has designed leading-edge computer hardware, software, and networks for over 30 years, including a unique cable television modem, campus-wide ATM networks, a desktop computer capable of analyzing adverse drug interactions, and an artificial intelligence planning system. He has programmed Windows since Version 1.0 and has taught as an adjunct professor of computer science at the University of Southern California.

Marcia Press worked in public accounting as a tax CPA for what was then one of the Big Eight, moving later to her own practice. She handles the administrative part of the work for the Presses' computer books — the tracking, calls, follow-ups, and research — and does the sanity checks on their initial drafts. She's a fan of good wine, gardening, reading, and shopping, and is a serious gourmet cook.

The Presses are the authors of *PC Upgrade and Repair Bible*; *Networking by Example*; *Teach Yourself PCs*; and *PC Toys: 14 Cool Projects for Home, Office, and Entertainment* and coauthors of *Building the Power-Efficient PC: A Developer's Guide to ACPI Power Management*.

Credits

Acquisitions Editors
Katie Mohr
Katie Feltman

Senior Development Editor
Kevin Kent

Production Editor
Gabrielle Nabi

Technical Editor
Bill Karow

Copy Editors
Susan Hobbs
Anne Owens

Permissions Editor
Carmen Krikorian

Editorial Manager
Mary Beth Wakefield

Vice President & Executive Group Publisher
Richard Swadley

Vice President and Executive Publisher
Bob Ipsen

Vice President and Publisher
Joseph B. Wikert

Executive Editorial Director
Mary Bednarek

Project Coordinator
Erin Smith

Graphics and Production Specialists
Kelly Emkow
Heather Pope

Quality Control Technicians
John Greenough
Susan Moritz

Proofreading and Indexing
TECHBOOKS Production Services

For Ping and Crash.

And Al Gore, who apparently invented the Internet.
That one's still too good to give up on.

Preface

PCs have evolved from obscure kits built by hobbyists to something found in every part of people's lives. PCs are now used for much more than office automation, but those applications require that you know something about the inner workings of your computer to get the best results. The *PC Upgrade and Repair Bible* will tell you about the computer hardware you need to run today's personal computer operating systems and Internet software, and help you to figure out what configuration of hardware is best for your computing needs. The information inside will help you evaluate what you need to run Windows or UNIX and what you need to access the Internet.

Tuning your hardware configuration using the ideas in this book will help you get more out of your computer. The current generations of Windows (Windows 2000 and Windows XP) can do more for you than their predecessors, but place greater demands on your computer than those predecessors. Similarly, UNIX (be it Linux, FreeBSD, or another version) can be a wonderfully low-cost and stable network platform, but the resources it needs to respond well to an onslaught of network traffic can be large, too.

Whether you have thousands of machines on a corporate network, a few machines in a small office, or a machine at home shared between work and family, a computer sized for what you do will give you the power you need to get your work done. Using the latest operating systems, you can run more programs at once, access a greater variety of networks, and use new kinds of hardware to the fullest extent. For most users, this increased capability will expand what you do with your computer, which in turn might require more hardware than before. Doing more with your computer makes you more productive, but makes the computer hardware work harder.

Is This Book for You?

This book provides the information you need to make effective hardware choices, including coverage of system components, upgrades, and new systems. It covers hardware for current and emerging technologies, including wireless LANs, ADSL (Asymmetric Digital Subscriber Line) and cable TV networks, and digital video.

This is a book both for people who will be opening up and working on their computers and for people who want to understand what goes on inside a computer. You'll see what's inside, what the pieces do, how they work, and how they're connected. You'll learn what determines the performance of your computer, what your options are for more performance, and how to add new capabilities to your computer.

This book is for you if you want to

+ Evaluate the suitability of upgrading an existing computer

+ Determine the upgrades needed to make an underpowered machine suitable for your specific purposes

+ Specify an effective new configuration of an existing machine to meet your requirements

+ Buy the right new machine

+ Build a new machine from components that precisely meet your needs

+ Integrate your PCs into local area networks and the Internet

+ Tune your computer system for peak performance

+ Install upgrades into an existing machine

There's no real magic to working on the insides of your computer. However, it can be complex, and you might encounter odd results that you have to diagnose and correct. If you're comfortable working with Windows or UNIX when things go wrong, you've got the most important prerequisite. If in addition to that you can work successfully on small, delicate mechanical parts, this book can teach you how to work inside your computer.

It's not mandatory that you take apart your computer to get the most from this book. If you understand how to use your computer but want to know what goes on behind the scenes, read this book. We'll show you what's inside and how it works.

What's in This Book

We've organized this book into seven parts and a glossary:

+ **Part I: Introduction (Chapters 1–3)** — It seems obvious that not everyone needs the same computer, but it takes some analysis to see the details behind why that's true. You don't have to settle for a hobbled machine — not with the cheap, screamingly fast ones on the market now — but you get the most value by thinking through what you'll really benefit from. This part of the book looks at the problem from high altitude: What can you tell about what you need from the outside?

+ **Part II: Processors and Motherboards (Chapters 4–5)** — Part II teaches you about the core of your computer, the processor chip and the electronics that surround it. Everything you do with your computer depends on and plugs into this core.

+ **Part III: Video (Chapters 6–7)** — Part III starts the explanations of the key subsystems in your PC, covering your video card and monitor. Nearly all your interaction with your PC is through the display, and good display performance is critical for much of what you'll do with your PC.

✦ **Part IV: Storage (Chapters 8–10)** — Seemingly a dull area of computer design a decade ago, the sizes of and options for computer storage have exploded. Part IV covers how disks work and how to integrate them, what you can do with CD and DVD, and the latest in USB-attached external storage.

✦ **Part V: Networks and Communications (Chapters 11–15)** — Part V looks at networking, both LANs and the Internet. You'll learn the ways your PC communicates and how networks of computers work, and understand how to set up wireless networks that give you flexibility while protecting your security.

✦ **Part VI: Multimedia and Peripherals (Chapters 16–20)** — Part VI covers one of the best outcomes from the amazing performance and capacity you'll get in even the least capable PC being made today, which is what you can now do with sound, pictures, and video.

✦ **Part VII: Integration (Chapters 21–25)** — Parts I to VI cover the individual technologies and components surrounding your PC. In Part VII, you'll read about what's involved in integrating those together, including cases and power supplies, mobile computing, unusual applications, diagnosis, and repair. With all that in hand, you'll see how to build your own quiet, very high performance PC.

You'll find a lot of black and white drawings and photographs throughout the book. In addition, we've printed key photos in color toward the back of the book so you'll be sure to see what you need to.

Although later chapters do build on earlier ones, you don't have to read the book in sequence from cover to cover — you can dive into the parts that most interest you. If you find you're not understanding what's there, go back to the relevant earlier chapters.

Navigating Through This Book

Every chapter in this book opens with a quick look at what's in the chapter and closes with a summary of the most important points in the chapter. You'll find icons in the margins of the text to draw your attention to specific topics and items of interest. Here is what the icons mean:

Caution The *Caution* icon points out a common problem you'll want to know about, along with suggestions for what to do to avoid or fix the problem.

Cross-Reference The *Cross-Reference* icon indicates references to more information or more detailed discussion elsewhere in the book.

Note The *Note* icon points out additional important information or an insight related to the topic at hand.

 Tip The *Tip* icon highlights things you'll want to do to make sure you get the most out of your computer.

One further informational point: Throughout the book, we talk about both bits and bytes (a byte is 8 bits), and about thousands, millions, and billions of those. We use the notation in Table P-1 consistently. Lowercase *b* stands for "bits," and uppercase *B* stands for "bytes."

Table P-1
Bits/Bytes Measurements Used in This Book

Symbol	Definition
Kb	Kilobit — 1,024 bits
KB	Kilobyte — 1,024 bytes
Mb	Megabit — 1,048,576 bits
MB	Megabyte — 1,048,576 bytes
Gb	Gigabit — 1,073,741,824 bits
GB	Gigabyte — 1,073,741,824 bytes

Don't be surprised if we've added terabytes — 1,024 gigabytes — to the table in the next edition.

About the Fourth (Desktop) Edition

We've slimmed down this version of the *PC Upgrade and Repair Bible* to a smaller, less expensive book, targeting it specifically at home, home-office, and small-office users. What we eliminated was specifically the topics useful only in large companies, along with some of the specific product photos and specifications. What's left is what you need to work with the current generation of technology and systems, to upgrade and repair them as necessary, or to make the decision to replace a PC with a more suitable system. In these pages, we give you the essentials of PC upgrade and repair.

When we wrote the first edition of the *PC Upgrade and Repair Bible,* many people were still running computers based on the Intel 486 processor, and upgrades to those systems were an important topic. When we wrote the *PC Upgrade and Repair Bible,* Professional Edition, the Pentium and Pentium Pro were thoroughly entrenched; the Intel Pentium II and AMD K6 were just starting to penetrate the market. The third edition saw the obsolescence of the Intel Pentium and its predecessors, as the Pentium II and K6-2 processors owned the industry.

The lifetime of products in the personal computer industry is often as short as six months, so four years after the third edition, everything has changed once again. The Intel Pentium 4 and AMD Athlon processors own the market, RAM-BUS memory had its day and has been eclipsed by faster, less expensive products, Windows 9X is history, and Linux is important enough to be the subject of questionable lawsuits about its ownership.

Still, our overall goal remains unchanged: to give you an understanding of what the best of the industry has to offer and how to exploit it.

Acknowledgments

We gratefully acknowledge the assistance of the following people and companies in the development of this book:

Antec Incorporated; American Power Conversion Corporation; ATI Technologies Incorporated; Belkin Corporation; Cisco Systems; Cyber Acoustics LLC; DeLorme; Eagletron Incorporated; Eastman Kodak; Edelman; ESC Technologies; Hewlett-Packard Development Company, L.P.; HomeSeer Technologies LLC; Ideazon Incorporated; Intel Corporation; Ketchum; Logitech Incorporated; Microsoft Corporation; Pinnacle Systems Incorporated; Porter Novelli; Samsung Electronics Company Limited; Seagate Technology LLC; Ultra-X Incorporated; and Voyetra Turtle Beach

Alex Alexander, George Alfs, Derek Baker, Abby Bliss, Melody Chalaban, Courtney Coe, Jolene Cramer, Debbie DeFreece, Ingrid de la Fuente, Seth Dotterer, Katie Feltman, Karen Franz, J R Fuller, Will Gaerlan, Kelly Gordon, Christine Goutaland, Lora Heiny, Bill Karow, Kevin Kent, Aimee Leclerc, Caleb Mason, Mike McDougall, Patti Mikula, Paul Millsap, Katie Mohr, Aaren Muhleman, Joe Paglia, Nathan Papadopulos, John Paulson, Jen Press, Katie Press, Joe Runde, Billy Rudock, Paulien Ruijssenaars, John Swinimer, Manny Vara, Dr. Gilbert Verghese, Matt Wagner, and Colin Wu

Thanks to all of you.

Contents at a Glance

Preface ix
Acknowledgments xiii

Part I: Introduction 1
Chapter 1: Getting Ready 3
Chapter 2: Why Isn't the Same Computer Right for Everyone? 13
Chapter 3: PC Overview 27

Part II: Processors and Motherboards 43
Chapter 4: Processors, Cache, and Memory 45
Chapter 5: Buses, Chipsets, and Motherboards 65

Part III: Video 77
Chapter 6: Video 79
Chapter 7: Monitors and Flat Panels 93

Part IV: Storage 109
Chapter 8: Hard Disks and Disk Arrays 111
Chapter 9: CD and DVD 129
Chapter 10: Removable Storage 145

Part V: Networks and Communications 155
Chapter 11: Modems 157
Chapter 12: Wired and Wireless Networking 175
Chapter 13: Hubs, Switches, Routers, and Firewalls 193
Chapter 14: Configuring a Windows Network 211
Chapter 15: Internet Services, Antivirus, and Anti-Spam 225

Part VI: Multimedia and Peripherals 249
Chapter 16: Sound Cards, Speakers, Microphones, and MP3 Players 251
Chapter 17: Digital Cameras, Video Capture, and DVDs 275
Chapter 18: Keyboards and Game Controllers 289
Chapter 19: Mice, Trackballs, and Tablets 301
Chapter 20: Printers, Scanners, and All-in-One Units 311

Part VII: Integration **327**

Chapter 21: Cases, Cooling, and Power 329

Chapter 22: Laptops and Handheld Computers 347

Chapter 23: You're Going to Put That Where? 359

Chapter 24: Diagnosis and Repair 375

Chapter 25: Building an Extreme Machine 395

Glossary 421

Index 447

Contents

Preface ix

Acknowledgments xiii

Part I: Introduction   1

Chapter 1: Getting Ready 3

You Can Do What You Can Imagine 3
What do you do with your computer? 4
Which operating system do you want, and why? 5
Should you upgrade your computer? 6
What new computer should you buy? 6
What about support and maintenance? 7
What about future upgrades? 7
Basic Techniques 8
Static electricity 8
Tools 9
Summary 11

Chapter 2: Why Isn't the Same Computer
Right for Everyone? 13

Buying into a Moving Target 16
Choosing an Operating System 19
Windows 19
Linux and UNIX 20
What You Need to Run Windows 21
Support and Maintenance Service 25
Summary 26

Chapter 3: PC Overview 27

What's Inside Your Computer? 27
Processors and instructions 30
Buses 32
Memory 34
Disk drives and I/O channels 36
Video cards and monitors 39
What's Outside Your Computer? 42
Summary 42

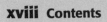
Part II: Processors and Motherboards 43

Chapter 4: Processors, Cache, and Memory 45

Executing Instructions 45
Cache Memory 48
Big, Fast Memory 50
Motherboard Choices 51
Intel: Celeron and Pentium 4 Processors 53
    Pipelining and superscalar execution 53
    Dynamic branch prediction 54
    Dynamic execution 55
    Extensions to the instruction set 56
    Hyperthreading and multiprocessors 57
    Expected performance gains 58
AMD 60
Power Management 62
Summary 63

Chapter 5: Buses, Chipsets, and Motherboards 65

The ISA Bus: It's Old and Slow, and (Finally) Almost Gone 67
PCI 69
PCI Express 70
Chipsets 70
Motherboards 72
External Buses 75
    Universal Serial Bus 75
    IEEE 1394 (FireWire) 75
    PC Card 75
Summary 76

Part III: Video 77

Chapter 6: Video 79

A Computer Monitor Is Not the Same as a Television 79
    The Video data path 81
    Sixteen million is a whole lot of colors 81
Video Buses 83
What a 3D Video Accelerator Does 83
Video Compression 87
Television in a Window 90
Choosing a Video Card 91
Video Drivers 92
Summary 92

Chapter 7: Monitors and Flat Panels 93

Flat Panel Displays 94
  LCDs and active matrix technology 94
  Keeping the LCD image sharp 94
CRT Specifications and Measurements 97
  Focus and convergence 97
  Color balance, tracking, purity, and saturation 99
    Incident static magnetic fields 100
    Incident dynamic fields 101
  Ghosting 101
  Geometric distortion 102
Controls 102
Multimedia Monitors 104
Display Data Channel 105
Choosing a Monitor 106
Summary 107

Part IV: Storage   109

Chapter 8: Hard Disks and Disk Arrays 111

Disk Drive Performance 113
Disk Drive Reliability 115
Redundant Array of Inexpensive Disks (RAID) 117
  What RAID does 117
  RAID levels 118
    RAID level 0 118
    RAID level 1 119
    RAID level 2, level 3, and level 4 120
    RAID level 5 121
Adding a Disk Drive 122
Top Disk Support Questions 124
Summary 128

Chapter 9: CD and DVD 129

What Is a CD-ROM? 129
Bootable CD-ROM 135
Recordable CD-ROMs 137
DVD 137
Recordable DVD 140
Top Support Questions 142
Summary 143

Chapter 10: Removable Storage 145

Floppy Disks and Competitors 145
Universal Serial Bus 147
External USB Storage 149
Small Scale File Transfer and Backup 150
Backup with External Disk 152
Summary 153

Part V: Networks and Communications 155

Chapter 11: Modems 157

Signals and Very Long Wires 158
Dial-up Analog Modems 159
DSL 164
Cable Television 165
Fixed Wireless and Satellite 168
Choosing Your Internet Access 170
Choosing a Modem 172
Choosing a dial-up modem 172
Choosing an internal or external modem 173
Summary 174

Chapter 12: Wired and Wireless Networking 175

Network Characteristics 176
Point-to-point or shared media 176
Baseband or modulated 176
Full- or half-duplex 177
Access methods 177
Network Technologies 179
Ethernet 179
Wireless transmission 184
Choosing Your Network Technologies 191
Summary 191

Chapter 13: Hubs, Switches, Routers, and Firewalls 193

Designing Small Local Area Networks 193
Ethernet Switches 195
Expanding Your Network 196
Routers 198
Transmission Control Protocol 201
User Datagram Protocol 203
Domain Name Service 203
Network Security and Firewalls 204
Packet filters 205
Network Address Translation 206
Standalone firewalls 207
On-computer firewalls 209
Summary 210

Chapter 14: Configuring a Windows Network 211

Network Protocols 211
Inside the Network Pipes 212
Media and network addresses 213
Domain Name Service and Address Resolution Protocol . 215
Dynamic Host Configuration Protocol (DHCP) 215
Configuring TCP/IP 218

Configuring File Sharing 219
    Windows 2000 and Windows XP 220
    Windows 98 222
Configuring Printer Sharing 222
Summary 223

Chapter 15: Internet Services, Antivirus, and Anti-Spam 225

Internet Services 225
    Ping 225
    World Wide Web 226
    File transfer 228
    Electronic mail 229
    Telnet 231
    Newsgroups 232
    Time 233
    Instant messaging 234
        Internet Relay Chat 234
        Proprietary messaging 234
Viruses and Worms and Trojans, Oh My! 234
    Viruses 235
    Worms 238
    Trojans 240
    Cracks 241
    Antivirus and anti-adware software 242
Dealing with Spam 245
Summary 248

Part VI: Multimedia and Peripherals   **249**

Chapter 16: Sound Cards, Speakers, Microphones, and MP3 Players 251

What Is Sound? 251
Analog Audio 254
Waveform Audio 255
    Waveform audio hardware 257
    Audio compression 259
Musical Instrument Digital Interface 262
CD Audio and Line Interfaces 263
USB Audio 264
Choosing Speakers 264
MP3 Players 267
Working with Microphones 268
    Voice annotation 269
    Speech recognition 269
    Voice over IP and Internet phones 270
Picking a Sound System 271
Top Support Questions 272
Summary 273

Chapter 17: Digital Cameras, Video Capture, and DVDs 275

Still Image Photography 276
    Image resolution and memory 277
    A darkroom on your desk 280
    Choosing a digital camera 281
Video 283
    Video capture and editing 284
    Making DVDs from video 286
Summary 288

Chapter 18: Keyboards and Game Controllers 289

Keyboards 289
    Switches and tactile feedback 289
    Keyboard layouts 293
    Ergonomics and repetitive stress 293
    Impaired access 296
Game Controllers 296
    Joysticks 297
    Game pads 299
    Wheels 299
Summary 300

Chapter 19: Mice, Trackballs, and Tablets 301

Mice 302
    Mouse cursors 304
    Microsoft Intellimouse 304
Trackballs 306
Tablets 308
Top Support Questions 309
    Mouse 309
    Tablet 310
Summary 310

Chapter 20: Printers, Scanners, and All-in-One Units . . . 311

Printers: Getting the Ink (Only) Where It Belongs 311
    Ink jet printers 312
    Laser printers 314
    Page description languages 315
    Choosing a printer 317
Scanners 319
    Mechanisms 320
    Number and accuracy of colors 321
    Resolution 321
    Interfaces 324
    Software 324
All-in-One Units: Combining Printing, Fax, and Copying 325
Summary 326

Part VII: Integration 327

Chapter 21: Cases, Cooling, and Power 329

Cases, Fans, and Cooling 329
    Airflow and heat buildup 333
    Cooling 333
    The ATX form factor 337
    Choosing a case 339
Power Supplies 340
    Selecting good power supplies 341
    Uninterruptible power supplies 341
External Connectors 343
Summary 346

Chapter 22: Laptops and Handheld Computers 347

What's in Your Laptop? 347
    Processor, memory, and bus 348
    PC Card and PC CardBus 350
    Laptop displays 351
    Disk 351
    Communications and ports 351
Batteries 352
Docking Stations 353
Handheld Computers 354
Global Positioning System 355
Communications Security 356
Upgrades 357
Summary 357

Chapter 23: You're Going to Put That Where? 359

Never Be Out of Reach 360
Sensors and Alerts 360
Building and Using Your Surveillance System from Kits 361
    Parts list 361
    Working with the TrackerCam software 364
    Live Internet surveillance 365
    Recorded Internet surveillance 368
    Motion detection and tracking 369
    Videoconferencing 371
Building a Surveillance System to Your Own Design 372
    Multiple cameras 372
    Long cables and wireless cameras 373
        Long cables 373
        Wireless 373
    Integrated home automation 373
    Archiving to removable storage 374
Summary 374

Chapter 24: Diagnosis and Repair **375**

Basic Techniques 376
Mechanical Procedures 376
Disassembly tips 378
Which slot is the board in? 378
What cables connect to the card? 378
Where is pin number one? 379
Top-level disassembly 380
Isolation Procedures 381
Rules of thumb 381
Observation and low-level isolation 382
System unresponsive 383
Monitor unresponsive 384
Video operational during boot 384
Memory failures 386
Diagnostics 386
Problems in Functioning Machines 387
Configuration problems 387
It doesn't work right 388
Network Diagnosis 389
Viruses 390
Case Study: A Dead Machine 390
Summary 393

Chapter 25: Building an Extreme Machine **395**

Hardware Planning 395
Preliminary Mechanical Assembly 398
Chassis layout and assembly 398
Mounting the drives 400
Installing the Motherboard 402
Installing the processor 404
Inserting the memory 407
Cabling in the power supply 409
Wiring the chassis to the motherboard connectors 411
Final Cabling 413
Installing Adapter Cards 415
Planning Your Software 416
Configuring BIOS 417
Configuring the Disk and Installing Windows 418
Checking Your Configuration 419
Installing Applications 419
Summary 420

Glossary **421**

Index **447**

Introduction

P A R T

I

♦   ♦   ♦   ♦

In This Part

Chapter 1
Getting Ready

Chapter 2
Why Isn't the Same
Computer Right for
Everyone?

Chapter 3
PC Overview

♦   ♦   ♦   ♦

Getting Ready

Computers are indispensable for much of the work and play people do. After years of stagnation during which people focused on office automation and business applications and asked where the value was in the ever faster parade of new systems, PCs have crossed a price and performance threshold. Systems you can buy today for hundreds of dollars, not thousands, have the power to make home movies, store and play your music, serve as your home darkroom, and enhance a home theater.

They still do office automation, too.

As recently as when we wrote the third edition of this book, a computer with that kind of power cost thousands of dollars, and most people used a single PC. Four years later, a PC costing less than $500 can handle almost everything you might do, and a surprisingly large number of homes have three or more computers on a local area network. People's priorities have shifted to put stability and capability on par with minimum cost and maximum value.

You Can Do What You Can Imagine

Everyone does something different with their computer, or does similar things in different ways. These differences lead to different answers to the question of what's the best computer for you.

You can start the analysis to answer that question by thinking about these issues:

- ✦ What do you use the computer for? What programs do you use, and how?

- ✦ What are the benefits you expect from your computer? Will achieving those benefits alter the ways you use the computer?

- ✦ If you upgrade, what will limit the performance of your computer?

✦ If you buy new equipment, how much and what kind of equipment do you need? What are the options in choosing that equipment? How are you likely to want to upgrade that equipment in the future, and what should you do now to make that easier?

✦ For both upgrades and new purchases, what are the support and maintenance requirements, and how can your decisions make getting support easier when something goes wrong?

✦ After you select a hardware configuration, what are the growth options during the life of the equipment, and what are the benefits those options can provide? What choices can you make early on to reduce the cost of future growth?

The following pages expand on each of these questions to explain why they're important and how your answers affect your choices.

What do you do with your computer?

Different things you do create different amounts of work for your computer. The typist using an ancient DOS version of WordPerfect places relatively small demands on a computer. The host for a network game tournament needs some memory, a decent *processor* (also called a *central processing unit*, or *CPU*), and high-speed communications. The game player needs screamingly fast CPU and video. The publisher assembling books from text, photographs, and graphics needs it all — lots of memory, a fast CPU, high-resolution video, voluminous storage, and good communications capabilities if files are transmitted electronically.

How you use your computer determines how great a workload you impose on it, so we'll discuss not only what you use the machine for, but also what programs you use and in what combinations you use them. These factors affect how powerful a machine you need. For example, suppose you're still running the computer you bought in 1998. You might have an old version of Microsoft Word on a machine with a Pentium II processor clocked at 266 MHz, 16 megabytes (MB) of memory, and a 4 gigabyte (GB) disk. You're still running Windows 95 on the machine, but your partner says that you'll be fantastically better off with Windows XP and the improved reliability of the more recent versions of Windows. She convinces you to upgrade your software, but now you ask "Will I have to upgrade my computer to run that new software?"

With a computer like that, the answer is Yes. You'll need more memory, more disk space, and a faster processor. We'll look at how you can upgrade your machine, and examine the possibility of replacing the main processor board — the *motherboard* — as an alternative to piecemeal upgrades. We'll also talk about whether or not upgrading this machine makes sense compared to purchasing a new computer — sometimes it's far less expensive to get the same capabilities with a new machine than by upgrading one you have.

We want to caution you to be hardnosed about upgrades because much of the hype and noise you hear that computers are obsolete six months after you buy them is driven by the notion that people always need the fastest, latest hardware. That's absurd. If your computer does what you want the way you want, nothing forces you to upgrade your hardware or software. You may need

Less Than the Sum of the Parts

We recently decided to upgrade our daughter's old computer because the old 600 MHz Pentium III in it was too slow to support the programming and other schoolwork she was doing. We targeted a Pentium 4 at 2.4 GHz or faster, 512MB or memory or more, and at least 40GB of disk, and we planned to install the upgrades in her existing case.

Much to our surprise, that's not how it played out. We check the Dell site now and then to keep track of what's new and where current prices are, and stumbled across a configuration that was both significantly faster than what we'd planned and — including shipping — was about a hundred dollars less than we would have paid for upgrades. That deal went away in a matter of days, but not before we snapped one up. We couldn't buy the upgrade parts for the same price at which Dell could sell and ship the complete machine. It doesn't happen often, but it's worth remembering.

upgrades to do new things, or to do the same things with new software, but that's an explicit choice you get to make.

Which operating system do you want, and why?

Upgrades that let you do more with your computer always seem better than ones required just to run new versions of the same programs the same way as before. Upgrades that increase capabilities and productivity create added value; ones that just maintain existing functionality are little more than a surcharge on the cost of the software upgrade.

The hardware upgrades you need also reflect the operating system you decide to run. For example, Windows 2000 and Windows XP are free from the resource restrictions that plagued Windows 95 through Windows Me. Windows 2000 and Windows XP can run more programs at the same time than their predecessors. If you take advantage of this — say by keeping your e-mail, word processing, and fax software open while you run a corporate order-entry application — you will use more memory than before. You may also find that you need higher resolution on your display to keep all those windows visible at once. Greater display resolution may in turn make you want to replace a 14- or 17-inch monitor with a 19-inch one to keep the text legible.

If your computer is on a home or office network, you may find Windows' improved capabilities invaluable when handling multiple forms of network communication. You can work with file servers, printers, cameras, and other devices at the same time that you search the Internet for the latest news. You can let your coworkers pull files off your disks to combine with their own work. As easy as this can now be, though, it means your computer is doing more work. That means memory and processor resources are being used to service the networking load. If you don't have enough of those resources, you'll need to upgrade to keep working at full speed while these features run behind the scenes.

If you're deploying an Internet server, you'll want to choose between Unix and Windows NT. Both can host a full suite of services, but you'll have to choose among a wide range of choices that affect the hardware you need, the available support, and the cost of software.

Gaining an understanding of your hardware requirements begins by estimating the basic hardware you need to maintain your current capability. This book shows you how to make those estimates and how to achieve a complete understanding of your growth options.

Should you upgrade your computer?

The starting point for upgrades is always the existing computer. We'll discuss how to characterize the performance you can expect from that machine and how to identify the components that limit the performance of your applications. Knowing that will let you predict if the machine's performance needs to be improved. You'll see how to identify the "choke points" that limit performance, how to eliminate them, and how to decide which upgrade options make sense. You'll learn how to identify when it's better to replace the entire computer than to make incremental upgrades.

For example, suppose your company's standard user workstation is a Pentium III processor running at 933 MHz, hosting Windows 2000 in 256MB of memory. You've been using desktop videoconferencing to talk to your children at college, but the video quality isn't very good. Can you afford to fix this? Perhaps. You might need faster communications, might need more memory, or might simply need to drop in a faster video card.

Or, suppose you have a Celeron 1 GHz processor with 128MB of memory, and you want to know if you can use it to process photos from your new digital camera. The analyses you'll do with this book will show you that you can, but you'll want to upgrade memory to 256MB or 512MB, and may need to add disk space too.

The process of analyzing upgrade options is very much like that of selecting options to include in a new machine. We'll look at a wide range of computer components from the point of view of what each can do for you, examining the characteristics of each and looking at how those characteristics affect the performance you can expect. We'll look at relative advertised prices to show the relative cost of features and performance. The prices you'll pay for equipment changes as technology evolves, so we'll use the comparisons to illustrate the analysis rather than as the rigid basis for choice.

What new computer should you buy?

Buying a new computer is very much like a 100 percent upgrade of an old computer; in fact, new computers are often bought as replacements for older ones. Upgrading a machine constrains the choice of components in order to remain compatible with surviving components, while configuring a new computer opens up all the technology options. The decision of what to buy is therefore more complex for new computers, requiring you to weed through more choices.

For example, suppose you've narrowed your selection to two models, one of which uses what the vendor calls a 533 MHz front side bus and the other of which offers an 800 MHz front side bus. The 800 MHz bus machine is more expensive, so you want to know if the extra money is worth it. We'll give you the tools to decide by showing you what a front side bus is, why its speed is important for some processors but not for others, and how to decide which choice is your best option.

What about support and maintenance?

Whatever your demands on a computer, you'll want to carefully consider the support available from the suppliers you choose and the options you have for maintenance when something fails. Both hardware and software are constantly changing, and new versions will at times offer dramatically better performance or brand-new capabilities. Different manufacturers have very different track records for supporting their products as operating systems and hardware evolve. Some vendors position their products for specific markets, and offer support for some configurations but not others. We'll look at what's required to support hardware and software fully and examine the issues of manufacturer support.

There's a wide range of utilities specific to Windows that help automate some of the critically important periodic maintenance items. We'll look at what problems these tools can solve and what you need to do to be ready for disasters beyond their reach.

What about future upgrades?

Knowing the relative costs and benefits of upgrade options can help you make new equipment choices that extend the equipment's operating life. Choosing technologies and components that allow low-cost, high-payoff upgrades later requires some thought, but can help you use minor upgrades to put off the next major upgrade for years. We'll configure several sample systems and look at what the options and costs are for future increased capability.

For example, the Universal Serial Bus (USB) can interface many different types of equipment to your computer. You can connect disks, CD-ROMs, scanners, cameras, speakers, and networks to a USB port without adding new cards inside the computer. If you'll be hooking in network, modem, videoconferencing, and sound cards later, saving slots (the places you put cards in a computer) like this can be critical. Choosing whether to upgrade with USB 1.1 or USB 2.0 becomes an important decision because some applications won't run with the older USB 1.1 hardware.

The organization of this book follows the ideas above. We'll start by discussing ways to understand how you use your computer and how much work you make it do. A look at your operating system and what it can do for you helps you expand your understanding of what you need from your computer. We'll take a computer apart after that, looking at all the pieces inside to understand what they do. We'll examine the features and characteristics of each element, learning to read manufacturers' descriptions with an eye to making smart decisions. We'll look at how to decide what components can be upgraded to solve performance problems, and make comparisons among competing upgrades. We'll use the same ideas to decide when a completely new computer is the right idea. Finally, we'll look at how to evaluate the growth left in a computer and how to get the most out of what you have.

Basic Techniques

You have to do a few things right if you're going to work on computer hardware effectively. Here they are:

✦ **Control static electricity.** You absolutely have to control static electricity (also called *electrostatic discharge*, or *ESD*). Voltages you can't see or feel can kill the chips in your computer.

✦ **Follow careful, well-defined procedures.** You get nowhere ripping hardware or software apart and making random changes hoping something will work. You have to have a carefully thought-through sequence in mind. You'll want to change only one thing at a time (and test the result) so you can isolate what causes different results.

✦ **Use the proper tools.** We're as guilty as anyone of using vise grip pliers as a universal tool, but that's not the right way to go about working on computer hardware. The parts are relatively small and fragile, so you must have tools appropriate to the job.

Static electricity

The hundreds of millions of transistors inside the chips in your computer are fantastically small. Although the small size of the transistors makes the speed and functionality those chips offer possible, that same small size reduces the voltage the transistors can withstand. Here's a typical warning about the maximum ratings on chips:

> Operating the device beyond the "Absolute Maximum Ratings" may cause permanent damage. Exposure to stress beyond the "Operating Conditions" limits specified for the device may affect reliability.

Typical signal and power level operating conditions for the largest chips in new computers are no more than 3 volts, down from the 3.3 volts and 5 volts used just a few years ago. You can't feel static electricity at much below 30 volts, and you can easily generate thousands of volts without intending to. The absolute maximum voltage rating for most chips is 6.5 volts; some are even less. Because you're not likely to feel less than 30 volts, you can destroy a chip without even feeling a tingle. What's worse is that you can weaken a chip (priming it to fail a little later), damaging it just short of complete failure. Ultimately, your feet scuffing on the ground, clothes rubbing on you, and a multitude of other small things can generate the ammunition that kills a chip.

Here's the no-compromises plan to prevent static electricity problems:

✦ **Ground everything, including you.** It's not enough to simply touch a piece of metal — static electricity can build back up simply from your moving as you work. The best way to prevent a static electricity discharge is to not let any charge build up to begin with. Grounding everything — connecting you, your tools, and the equipment to a good ground — takes care of this. A proper anti-static workstation includes not only a grounded workbench, but also a ground mat, a grounded wrist strap (which fastens securely around your wrist), and foot straps. Grounds should connect through an unbroken wire to a secure cold-water ground. (Be sure the pipe into the ground is an unbroken length of metal, with no plastic sections.) If you're going all out, consider grounded tools and a humidifier. Increased water in the air helps static charges bleed off.

✦ **Avoid materials that build up static charges.** Workbench tops should be a conductive, anti-static material. Under no circumstances should you work on a plastic, vinyl, carpeted, cloth-covered, finished, or waxed surface. Parts should be stored in plastic bins or bags made of conductive, anti-static material. Check bins and bags for extraneous material that could cause static buildup.

✦ **Floors should be conductive tile.** Avoid vinyl, carpet, finished wood, sealed or dusty concrete, and floor wax. You can get carpet spray to minimize static buildup, but it's not really the right answer.

You'll also want to keep static-building material out of your work area. This includes most plastics, nylon, polyethylene, Styrofoam, vinyl notebooks, cellophane, and adhesive tape. Clothing often includes static-building material, so your best bet is to wear a conductive smock.

✦ **Avoid other people.** Onlookers are inevitable, but without their own anti-static protection, they can destroy in a second what you've worked to protect. Keep people without appropriate anti-static protection at least 3 feet away from the work area so they can't touch anything.

Obviously, you can work in a less protected environment, and realistically, a work area like that is more than most homes and offices can afford. Many service centers, operations that *should* take careful precautions, do with less protection than we've recommended above. Simplifying the protections increases your risk, especially in a dry atmosphere, so we'll cover what you should do for sufficient protection with minimum fuss.

Tools

Almost everything you need to do to a personal computer can be done with just a few simple tools, such as screwdrivers, socket drivers, and pliers. You'll need some more-sophisticated tools if you're making cables. (Of course, if you're making cables, you might need to have your head examined. Making cables takes lots of time, saves very little money — if any, and may actually cost more — and is one of the most error-prone assembly jobs there are. If we had a dollar for every screwed-up cable we've had foisted on us. . . .)

✦ **Screwdrivers** — You'll need both slotted and Phillips screwdrivers. You'll want a range of sizes from small to medium.

✦ **Socket drivers** — Many of the screws used in personal computers have heads that fit hex drivers, which lets you avoid stripped heads and makes it less likely that you'll drop the screw where it doesn't belong. The most common sizes are 3/16, 7/32, and 1/4 inch. We've seen Torx heads on screws in a few computers, but only rarely.

✦ **Pliers** — The ones we use the most are a pair of very long needle-nose pliers. They won't exert much force, but they'll handle small parts and get into tight places.

✦ **Flashlight** — You'll want one of the compact, halogen bulb flashlights so you can get a lot of light in a small place. One you can make stay put in small places is even better.

✦ **Mirror** — You can't always see what you need to directly. A small mirror on a long handle can solve a lot of problems that otherwise require you to disassemble more than necessary.

✦ **Multimeter** — Some failures are best diagnosed with a multimeter. We have a portable one from Heath we bought many years ago, but you can get multimeters anywhere. You don't need extreme accuracy (which is expensive), but you'll want to look for one that's durable. They have a habit of falling off workbenches and other places.

✦ **Soldering iron** — If you know what you're doing to the point where you want to be able to repair connectors or remove and replace components from circuit cards, you'll need a soldering iron. Not a soldering gun, and not the sort of iron Grandpa used to make tin cans with. If you're working on circuit card components, you want a grounded, temperature-regulated unit that protects components from overheating and static electricity. If the cost of one of those seems too high, think twice about whether you can afford to be without one, and think three times about why you need to be soldering on a circuit board at all.

You'll find most of these tools, if not all, in a compact tool kit for PC service. They're sold by a lot of companies. You don't need the super-spiffy giant size. Look for good quality tools, however — junk is too frustrating to bother with.

As important as these tools are, the most important tools you'll have are your eyes and ears, and some programs you'll keep on disk. You provide the eyes and ears; we'll cover some of the programs later in the book.

Summary

✦ This book can help you decide on the computer configuration or upgrade that is best for you.

✦ The computer that's best for you depends on what you do with it.

✦ The computer you need may be the one you already own after some upgrades.

✦ Understanding what's in computer hardware gives you the tools to choose upgrades or a new computer to meet your needs and budget.

✦ You can simplify support and maintenance and reduce your future computer costs by choosing hardware effectively now.

Why Isn't the Same Computer Right for Everyone?

✦ ✦ ✦ ✦

In This Chapter

Realizing there's always a faster computer coming

Examining why faster may not be better

Exploring what more current versions of Windows can do for you

Comparing minimum and real-world Windows hardware requirements

Choosing support and maintenance

✦ ✦ ✦ ✦

Your computer has about a dozen components you need to consider, including the processor, memory, at least three buses, power supply, case, hard disk, optical drive, display, network, modem, sound, and printer. (Don't panic — we'll explain what each of those is in later chapters.) Each of these components has a handful of defining characteristics, with each characteristic having a range of choices. The result is hundreds of possibilities for configuring your computer, and a lot of confusion for novices trying to figure out how to upgrade or what to buy.

The performance you can get for each of those components increases constantly, while the price of any given performance level decreases at the same time and the technology changes at a breathtaking rate. In the fall of 1995, for instance, a 133 MHz Intel Pentium was a very fast processor for desktop computers. In spring of 1999, a top-end processor was a 450 MHz Intel Pentium II. In summer of 2003, the top-end processor was a 3.2 GHz Intel Pentium 4. The MHz (megahertz) unit means millions of clock ticks per second, and GHz (gigahertz) means billions of clock ticks per second, so, ignoring the significant internal changes between those processors, there's been a phenomenal increase in the rate at which they work. Figure 2-1 compares the clock rates for these three processors, normalizing the rate against that of the 133 MHz Pentium. The relative clock rate of the Pentium is 1; the Pentium II is over 3 times faster than the Pentium, and the Pentium 4 is over 24 times faster.

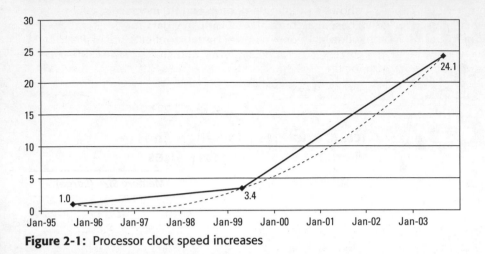

Figure 2-1: Processor clock speed increases

The dashed trend line in Figure 2-1 emphasizes the fact that speed increases aren't constant. The rate at which computer speed increases is itself increasing — something that will continue for years to come.

The underlying engine powering improvements in all electronic devices is Gordon Moore's empirical observation, validated over more than 30 years, that the number of transistors in the highest density chips will double every couple of years. The nearly straight line on the logarithmic plot in Figure 2-2 shows how closely the prediction has come true.

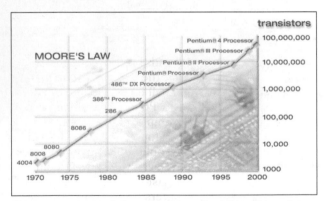

Figure 2-2: Moore's Law predicts a doubling of transistor density every couple of years.
Courtesy Intel Corporation

Memory chips are the first kinds of devices to benefit from nearly every advance in semiconductors because they have a highly repetitive internal structure that makes them easier to make than less-regular designs such as processors. Table 2-1 shows a prediction of high-end PC memory sizes by the Open Source Initiative based on fundamental industry data for the number of transistors on a chip following Moore's Law. The table reflects history rather accurately, including current-generation systems, and so is a reasonable estimate of memory size for the next six years.

Table 2-1
Actual and Predicted High-End Mainstream PC Memory Sizes

Year	Memory Size (Small)	Memory Size (Large)
1980	8KB	32KB
1983	32KB	128KB
1986	128KB	512KB
1989	512KB	2048KB
1992	2MB	8MB
1995	8MB	32MB
1998	32MB	128MB
2001	128MB	512MB
2004	512MB	2048MB
2007	2048MB	8192MB
2010	8192MB	32768MB

Source: Open Source Initiative

Not everyone needs the fastest computer available, and the consequence of the constant increases in top-end performance is that the low end of the market ratchets up, too. That causes computer prices to fall for a machine of constant features and performance; the least capable new PC you can buy now is nevertheless capable of a great many things. (For example, at the same time we drew Figure 2-1, the slowest desktop processor we found on the Dell Web site was a 2.2 GHz Intel Celeron, which in Figure 2-1 would plot at over 16 times the clock rate of the 133 MHz Pentium.) The power of even the slowest computers now being sold, and of computers sold in the last few years, is so great that they can do most of what people do with computers — word processing, spreadsheets, e-mail, and simple photos. Because they're so capable, it's important that you don't overvalue change in computer technology. If the machine you have does what you want, you can expect to use it until your needs change, or until added features in new versions of your software are compelling enough to make you upgrade to a version that no longer runs well on your machine. When you become dissatisfied with the machine you have, you'll do the necessary upgrades and keep on working.

Tip

If you haven't already, you'll soon find that different people hold very different opinions on what constitutes good computer hardware and on what should be in a computer, holding those opinions with an intensity that easily approaches that of religious wars. We're not as radical as that suggests, but a number of our opinions are in this book. Most of our opinions are based on the idea of computer upgrade and repair by mystic incantation — that is, remember what worked well for you in the past and, unless you have a good reason not to, keep doing it.

For example, we're partial to certain products from Intel, Crucial, Seagate, Kodak, and a number of other companies. Conversely, we won't buy anything made by some other manufacturers because we know from both experience and insight into their operations that their products are bug-ridden and not likely to get better soon. The end result of focusing on quality and weeding out the garbage has been that we spend less time fixing our computers than some otherwise very competent people we know.

We suggest that you adopt the same approach — when you identify a quality manufacturer, stick with them. If it becomes clear to you that a manufacturer's products are not well engineered and manufactured, shun them. Do this for complete systems you buy as well as for upgrades.

Buying into a Moving Target

The wide range of possible options for configuring computers is one reason manufacturers offer preconfigured systems — standard system packages meet the needs of most customers, and serve as a baseline the sales staff (or Web site) can use to focus on the needs of customers with unique requirements.

How you use a computer and what you do with it, as well as what combinations of technology make sense, will determine the choices you make. For example:

✦ A great machine for gamers would combine high-end video with a fast processor and lots of memory.

✦ A good configuration for economy word processing would combine a low-end machine with a midrange-capacity disk, a sharp monitor, and a good quality ink jet printer.

Depending on your objectives, high-end performance may not require the most expensive equipment. For example, 3D accelerated video cards can provide blazing frame-update rates (the speed at which the game can update the screen), but by avoiding the latest high-end versions, you can get good performance at midrange cost.

Table 2-2 shows a range of complete, new desktop systems representative of what you could buy in the spring of 2004. If the computer industry continues at its current rate, the table will be obsolete before the next edition of this book can be published. Laptop and handheld computers present a whole other set of issues that we'll talk about later. Our strategy for categorizing the columns in Table 2-2 is to examine what's in new computers selling for under $500 (low-end), approximately $1,000 (midrange), and $2,500 (high-end) or more. We've indicated our minimum recommendations in boldface. The low-end category in the table is above the minimum configuration required to run Windows and Linux. The features shown in the midrange and high-end columns are representative of what you will want if you're working with photos or video, or if you're playing games. Any specific system configuration is likely to have components from all three columns.

Table 2-2
Computer Configuration Options (Spring 2004)

Category	Low-End	Midrange	High-End
Case	Desktop or smaller	**Mini-tower** or Tower	Tower or Rackmount
Display Bus	Built into motherboard	**8X AGP**	**8X AGP**
Display Resolution	800×600	**1280×1024**	1600×1200 and up
Hard Disk Access Time	13 ms	10 ms	9 ms
Hard Disk Capacity	40GB	**80 to 120GB**	120 to 500GB
I/O Bus	ATA	ATA	Serial ATA
Local Bus	PCI	PCI	PCI
Memory Interface	PC2700 DDR SDRAM	PC3200 DDR SDRAM single or dual channel	PC3200 DDR SDRAM dual channel
Memory Size	128MB	**256 to 512MB**	1GB and up
Modem	56 Kbps V.92	**Broadband**	Broadband
Monitor Size/Type	17-inch CRT	**19-inch CRT** **17-inch LCD**	21-inch CRT 20-inch LCD
Network Cabling	Switched 100Base-T	**Switched 100Base-T and/or IEEE 802.11b**	Switched Gigabit Ethernet and/or IEEE 802.11g
Optical Drive Transfer Rate	CD-ROM 7200 Kbps (48X)	DVD-CD/RW (Mbps) DVD-R: 21.6 (16X) CD-R: 7.0 (48X) CD-W: 7.0 (48X) CD-RW: 3.5 (24X)	**DVD-RW (Mbps)** **R: 10.8 (8X)** **W: 5.4 (4X)** **RW: 3.2 (2.4X)**
Power Supply	250 watts	**300 to 350 watts**	450 watts and up

Continued

Table 2-2 *(continued)*

Category	Low-End	Midrange	High-End
Printer Interface	USB	USB	USB or Network
Printer Resolution and Technology	2400×1200 dpi color ink jet	**2400×1200 dpi color ink jet and/or 600 to 1200 dpi laser**	600 to 1200 dpi color laser
Processor Type and Speed	2.5 GHz Intel Celeron or AMD XP2400+ Athlon	2.8 GHz Hyperthreaded Intel Pentium 4 or AMD XP2800+ Athlon	**3.4 GHz Hyperthreaded Intel Pentium 4 Extreme Edition or AMD XP3200+ Athlon**
Scanner Optical Resolution	None	1200 dpi	2400 dpi and up

Although it's the term used by manufacturers, the term *low-end* at the top of the second column in Table 2-2 is incredibly misleading. A machine with a 2.5 GHz Celeron processor, 128MB of memory, a 17-inch monitor, and a 40GB disk is classed as a low-end machine, but is terrific for significant word processing and spreadsheets, and even for some games. You can buy a system like that, with monitor, for around $500. It's quick, if not fast, and very capable. To give you an idea of how capable, consider that we chose to write this entire book on a lesser machine, one with a 933 MHz Intel Pentium III, 512MB memory, and 80GB of disk. We didn't give up anything important with that choice; a machine with those specifications really can do a lot.

It's because some configurations fit certain applications better than others that we chose the Pentium III computer over another PC we have, one with a 2.53 GHz Pentium 4, 512MB memory, and 60GB disk. The Pentium III machine has two very large monitors — 21 and 19 inches — each running at 1600×1200 resolution, versus a single 21-inch monitor on the Pentium 4. The additional screen space on the second monitor makes it possible to put reference material and calculations on one screen while keeping the chapter we're writing visible on the other. Working that way with two screens is far more efficient for us because the dual screen configuration eliminates flopping between programs.

Don't infer, however, that ancient computers are just as useful as new ones, because the minimum useful machine specifications do creep up over years. That obsolescence happens both because new hardware doesn't support the older interfaces and because new, more powerful software runs too slowly without increases in computing power. The machine on which we originally started writing books was a 50 MHz Intel 486 with 16MB memory, 2GB disk space, 1280×1024 resolution display on a 17-inch monitor, modem, and scanner. You can't load current versions of Windows on that machine anymore, much less run a current-day word processor, causing more than a few people to pine for the slimmer, more compact designs of yore, and ooze disdain for modern bloated software. Our view is that the payoffs we realize from the newer machines, such as being able to keep our e-mail program open while we write, access files on our file server and on Internet servers maintained by our publisher, and compress an edited video stream to DVD in the background while we work, is an enormous gain in productivity, one easily worth the few hundred dollars the newer machine costs now. We used to have to mail chapter text and drawings to the publisher; the advent of broadband networks and more-capable software lets us now do all our work through the Internet. We get work done faster, and with less effort.

You will make your own choices about your computer configuration based on your situation. A cramped office or kitchen counter offers little room for a full-size case. A two-machine network isolated from the Internet is simple to set up with cables, while a wireless network lets you sit out on the deck while you work and remain connected to both your other computers and the Internet.

Configuring a machine to your exact specifications requires detailed research and understanding; buying a prepackaged configuration lets you choose based on top-level parameters. Integrating a machine yourself lets you pick the exact components it will contain; buying from a major vendor makes onsite service available. Buying a complete machine from a vendor eliminates the headaches of putting it together yourself.

Choosing an Operating System

Counting both systems and versions, you have many operating systems to choose from. If you're planning to run Microsoft Windows, you have to choose which version, a choice with significant technical and performance implications. If you're planning to run Linux on your PC, you still have to choose which distribution (essentially, which company's enhancements to and packaging of the standard Linux) and which version of that distribution. Linux isn't yet suitable for a beginner who doesn't have a captive expert nearby, but it's made great strides in the last few years, and the day when a beginner can succeed unaided with Linux isn't far off.

Windows

There are two technically distinct Windows architectures. One — what we'll call Win9X in this book — originated with Windows 95, a successor to Windows 3.1 and ultimately DOS, and inherited both compatibility benefits and reliability problems from its parents. The other architecture originated with Windows NT, and is available today as Windows 2000 or Windows XP. Windows 2000 and Windows XP are the most reliable versions of Windows, but are not necessarily compatible with all the software and hardware built for Win9X.

Practically, however, there are only three useful versions of Windows: Windows 98 Second Edition (Win98 SE), Windows 2000, or Windows XP. No version of Windows prior to Windows 98 Second Edition (Win98 SE) is more stable, and SE includes Universal Serial Bus (USB) support without additional patching. Windows Millennium Edition came after Win98 SE, but introduced many reliability problems.

Our bias is to run Windows 2000. Windows XP is technically superior to Windows 2000 and offers some very nice added features, but we prefer not to deal with Microsoft's Windows Product Activation (WPA). We properly license every copy of all the software we run — it's the right thing to do, and intellectual property is what keeps authors fed — but there are enough documented cases of WPA failing and shutting down properly licensed machines that we choose not to deal with it. The machines we do work on run Windows 2000.

However, choosing between Windows XP and Windows 2000 is far less significant than choosing one of them over Win9X. Win9X is far less secure, and its fundamental design creates inherent stability problems. Windows XP and Windows 2000 are more secure, more robust, and more stable than any version of Win9X can ever be. Unless you *must* run software that operates only under Windows 98, you should use Windows XP or Windows 2000. Most software that runs under Windows 98 will run under Windows XP or Windows 2000, even if not explicitly labeled and supported by the manufacturer. If you can, try the software to see. The most common limitation preventing you from using software on the newer operating systems is hardware the manufacturer supports only for Windows 98, in which case you might be stuck.

Linux and UNIX

The many varieties of UNIX are mostly used to run *servers*, computers used to perform tasks remotely for you across a network. Of the nonproprietary versions of UNIX, the two best known are Linux and FreeBSD. Both are available from a variety of companies; we use the Linux versions from Red Hat or Mandrake, and the FreeBSD version from FreeBSD Mall (formerly Walnut Creek CD-ROM). Linux is the most widely used version, but all versions of UNIX are less common than Windows on desktop computers because of these factors:

✦ **Limited device support** — Device drivers are not as widely available for UNIX as for Windows. Manufacturers usually write Windows drivers for new hardware first and may never write drivers for any version of UNIX. Independent programmers are typically left to write those drivers, often without support from the hardware developer.

✦ **Relatively complex administration** — Installing and configuring UNIX is more of a manual process than that for Windows, requiring more knowledge of the operating system's internal design. Users without support from knowledgeable system administrators may not be able to make the system do everything they want without investing a lot of time and effort. Linux developers in particular have invested a great deal of effort in simplifying system administration in recent years, but the task remains harder than it is for Windows.

✦ **Limited training** — Windows has been the dominant operating system for so long that nearly all computer users know something about how to use it. Until recently, versions of UNIX — although similar in some ways to Windows — were different enough that untrained users would not be successful using the operating system. Realizing that massive retraining is unlikely, Linux developers have attacked that problem by leveraging Windows know-how, writing software to make Linux system administration tools and application programs more like their Windows equivalents.

The UNIX community is investing a lot of effort into improving the tools for managing and configuring systems, to the point where it's possible that within a few years a naïve computer user will have the ability to successfully choose UNIX instead of Windows or Macintosh.

What You Need to Run Windows

One of the most frequently asked questions about Windows is "What are the minimum machine requirements?" As shown in Table 2-3, Microsoft says you need a fairly minimal machine for Windows 98.

Table 2-3
Stated Minimum Requirements for Windows 98

Status	Component
Required	Intel 486DX processor or better
	16MB of memory, with more recommended to improve performance
	120 to 295MB available hard disk space
	VGA or higher resolution display
	CD-ROM or DVD drive
	Mouse or other pointing device

Windows 2000 has larger stated requirements, shown in Table 2-4.

Table 2-4
Stated Minimum Requirements for
Windows 2000 Professional

Status	Component
Required	133 MHz Intel Pentium processor or better
	64MB of memory, with more recommended
	2GB hard disk with at least 650MB space available
	VGA or higher resolution graphics card and monitor
	CD-ROM or DVD optical drive
	Keyboard

The requirements in Table 2-4 are for Microsoft Windows 2000 Professional. Windows 2000 Server minimum requirements increase the minimum memory and free disk space. Microsoft also states that system requirements for Windows-based programs may exceed the Windows system requirements themselves.

Table 2-5 shows the stated minimum requirements for Windows XP.

Table 2-5 Stated Minimum Requirements for Windows XP Home or Professional	
Status	**Component**
Required	233 MHz Intel Pentium or Celeron, or AMD K6/Athlon/ Duron processor or better
	64MB of memory, with more recommended
	1.5GB available hard disk space
	Super VGA (800×600) or higher resolution graphics card and monitor
	CD-ROM or DVD optical drive
	Keyboard and mouse

In reality, the stated requirements are very low and, perversely, are more suited for PCs running Linux. Windows will install and run minimally with these resources, but unless you're an extremely patient person, the performance will be unacceptably slow. Many of the features that would make you want Windows in the first place — great networking, multitasking, and multimedia, for example — require additional resources. And, as Microsoft notes, any major application you would want to run requires yet more resources.

You'll see later in the book that the realistic minimum computer you need really depends on what you want to do with the computer. Before that, though, look at each of Microsoft's recommendations.

✦ **Processor** — Microsoft states that Windows 98 requires at least an Intel 486, while Windows 2000 and XP require Pentium-class processors. Considering that processors as slow as the 233 MHz Pentium II were introduced in 1997 and made obsolete by the Pentium III in 1999, the computers you're likely to work with will be far faster than the minimums.

✦ **Memory** — As Microsoft notes, the minimum memory requirement is for Windows by itself. Table 2-6 shows the minimum available memory required for a number of Windows programs under Windows XP.

Table 2-6
How Much Memory Do Programs Need?

Program	Available Memory Required (MB)	Available Memory Recommended (MB)
Adobe Illustrator 10	128	
Adobe Photoshop 7	128	
Broderbund 3D Home Architect Deluxe 5	96	128
Broderbund 3D Home Landscape Designer Deluxe 5	64	128
CorelDRAW! Version 11	128	
DeLorme Street Atlas USA 2004	64	128
Funcom Anarchy Online	128	512
LucasArts Star Wars Galaxies	256	
Microsoft Encarta 2004 Reference Library Plus DVD	128	
Microsoft Halo	128	
Microsoft Internet Explorer 6	32	
Microsoft Office 2003	128	Add 8MB for each running Office application
Microsoft Visual Basic .NET 2003	160	
Microsoft Visual C++ . NET 2003 Standard	160	
Netscape 7.1	64	
Sony Online Entertainment EverQuest Lost Dungeons of Norrath	256	512
Square Enix USA Final Fantasy XI	128	

If anything, the numbers shown in Table 2-6 are low and count only the memory required by the application, not by other programs and not by Windows itself. In practical terms, you'll want more than the minimum stated memory requirement. Our general total installed memory recommendations are shown in Table 2-7. Specific applications can increase these numbers (for example, the Windows 2000 machine we use for image editing with Adobe Photoshop has 512MB; the Windows XP machine you see how to build in Chapter 25 has 1GB).

Table 2-7
How Much Memory Do You Need?

Operating System	Minimum PCURB Recommendation	General PCURB Recommendation
UNIX	128MB	256MB
Windows 98	64MB	256MB
Windows 2000	256MB	512MB
Windows XP	256MB	512MB–1GB

The numbers in Table 2-7 incorporate the observations that memory is incredibly cheap and that more memory drastically improves performance on many systems.

✦ **Hard Disk** — The performance and size of the disk in your computer are critical. If you're still running drives smaller than 10GB, they're probably full, causing you to have to juggle what you store and what you delete. If so, replace those disks because larger, faster disks are low cost, and it's not worth the time to agonize over what you can afford to delete. Your Windows folder alone can be huge — the folder holding Windows 2000 on the Pentium III PC we write on is 1.42GB. Application software has grown in size, too. Our installation of Microsoft Office 2000 Professional plus Visio 2000 is 400MB, and doesn't include all the options.

If you upgrade a desktop computer, 40GB is the smallest disk you should consider, and then only for cost-constrained situations. In the summer of 2003, Seagate Technology offered only one drive as small as 10GB. Half of the models they offer are 40GB or larger. The ready availability and relatively low cost of large, high-performance drives makes it impractical to waste time fighting a too-small disk.

Table 2-8 shows, based on program size alone, why it's so easy to consume enormous amounts of disk space, listing the available disk space requirements for the same programs listed in Table 2-6.

Table 2-8
How Much Hard Disk Space Do Programs Need?

Program	Available Hard Disk Space Required
Adobe Illustrator 10	180MB
Adobe Photoshop 7	280MB
Broderbund 3D Home Architect Deluxe 5	100MB
Broderbund 3D Home Landscape Designer Deluxe 5	100MB

Program	Available Hard Disk Space Required
CorelDRAW! Version 11	200MB
DeLorme Street Atlas USA 2004	580MB (approx. 1GB including data disk)
Funcom Anarchy Online	700MB
LucasArts Star Wars Galaxies	2GB
Microsoft Encarta 2004 Reference Library Plus DVD	2.9GB
Microsoft Halo	1.4GB
Microsoft Internet Explorer 6	12MB
Microsoft Office 2003	500MB
Microsoft Visual Basic .NET 2003	2GB
Microsoft Visual C++ .NET 2003 Standard	2GB
Netscape 7.1	52MB
Sony Online Entertainment EverQuest Lost Dungeons of Norrath	500MB
Square Enix USA Final Fantasy XI	6GB

✦ **Display** — Windows runs at either 640×480 or 800×600 resolution with a basic Video Graphics Array (VGA) display adapter, although 640×480 is not supported beginning with Windows XP. No acceleration is necessary to get instantaneous screen updates at those resolutions unless you are playing 3D video games or doing real-time video editing. You can work with a 14-inch monitor at 640×480 resolution, but you'll be more productive with a bigger one. We don't recommend anything smaller than a 17-inch monitor now, and suggest 19- or 21-inch units or LCD flat panels, if possible.

Support and Maintenance Service

Computers break and have problems, so one way or another you'll want support and maintenance service. If you have the know-how and the time (and have that time no matter when things go wrong!), you may want to consider doing support yourself or within your company; otherwise, you need to consider where and how you get service and support.

✦ The original manufacturer of your hardware may offer service and support. Most manufacturers will refer you to the software publisher for support on programs you installed yourself. They may also decline to support hardware additions to the machine you make yourself. This is particularly true for the large nationwide computer manufacturers.

✦ Many nationwide vendors offer you the choice of doing repairs your-self according to their instructions (with component exchange by mail), opting for mail-in repairs, or having onsite repairs performed. Local stores generally offer a choice of walk-in or onsite repair.

✦ Third-party repair companies flourished and then died out in the mid-eighties. The industry trend of outsourcing support operations has once again created third-party companies that, if your business or need is big enough for them to care, will contract with you for service and support operations.

✦ Many people have friends with good computer experience. If your friends are sufficiently experienced, and are willing, they may be able to do upgrades and repairs for you.

What you support yourself and what you support with outside help isn't an all-or-nothing decision. Many companies do in-house computer upgrades, leaving repairs to others. Choosing your approach for maintenance and support need not be a complex process — figure out what your choices are, weigh those choices by your past experience and any current information you can get, and pick. Don't forget to account for the value of faster service (whether it's in-house or outside).

Summary

✦ No matter what computer you buy, there's a faster one coming soon.

✦ The fastest computer might not be the one you need — you need the one that does your work well at a price that fits what you want to invest.

✦ The minimum requirements Microsoft states for Windows are unrealistically low.

✦ Virtually any computer still running meets the minimum requirements for Windows and UNIX, but you may need more speed for specific applications.

✦ You'll end up wanting at least 20GB or more of hard disk space, and probably much more.

PC Overview

Your computer looks like a box accompanied by a screen, keyboard, and mouse, but there's a lot hidden inside that box. You choose many components located in the box when you buy a new computer, but too many people do so based on specifications without understanding what those components are and what the specifications mean. This chapter is a tour of your PC with the covers off, identifying the components inside, what they do, and what their important characteristics are.

What's Inside Your Computer?

Figure 3-1 shows the inside of a typical computer, and identifies each of the core components: processor, memory, bus, input/output (I/O), disk, display, and power supply. The minimum set of components you need to run instructions is a processor supported by memory and a power supply. A power supply is necessary to make the electronics work at all; the memory holds instructions and data while the processor works executing instructions. The chassis holds all the components together, protects them from damage, and provides shielding to prevent interference with radios, televisions, and other electronic devices.

In This Chapter

Examining processors, memory, and buses

Understanding disk drives and input/output (I/O) channels

Exploring video cards and monitors

Fitting components into the whole

Power supply

Processor (under fan)

I/O   Memory   DVD writer

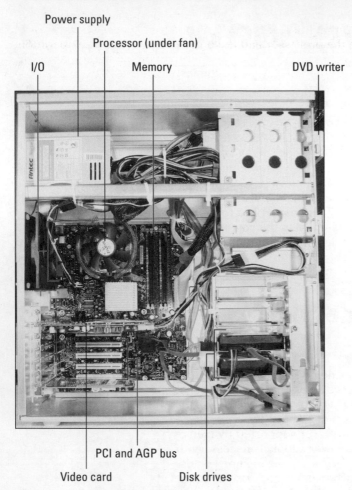

PCI and AGP bus

Video card   Disk drives

Figure 3-1: Components inside a computer
©2004 Barry Press & Marcia Press

A computer with nothing but a processor, memory, and power supply isn't very useful because it can't communicate with you or with other computers. Each of the other core components exist to either store information or let the processor communicate:

✦ **Bus** — Connects the processor to the memory, I/O channels, and display

✦ **I/O channels** — Connects the bus (and therefore the processor) to the disk, keyboard, mouse, network, and any other devices

✦ **Disk** — Stores large amounts of information, retaining that information even when the power is off

✦ **Display** — Draws images and characters on a monitor, giving programs a way to output in a way you can read

These components connect together through the bus as shown in Figure 3-2. The bus stars out from the processor to everything else because all the information flows between the processor and the other components. The operation of the components in your computer is very repetitive: the processor grabs an instruction from memory, and decides what the instruction says to do. Based on what the instruction requires, the processor grabs more information from memory or disk, operates on it if ordered to by the instruction, and then stores the data back in memory, on disk, or in the display card. The processor does this basic cycle billions of times every second it's turned on. Little besides turning the computer off stops the repetitive sequence.

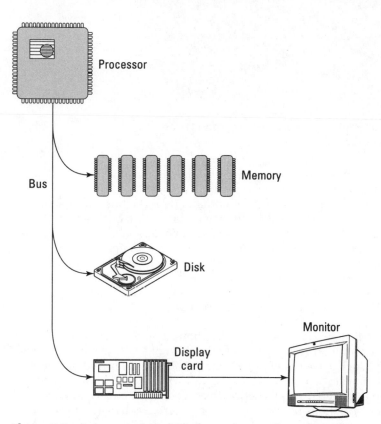

Figure 3-2: A computer consists of a processor plus components to store and communicate information.

A special signal inside the computer, called the *clock signal* (or just the *clock*), synchronizes components in the computer, providing the cadence to which the entire assembly marches. The clock times every action by the processor and sets the synchronization requirements for all the other components. Every instruction executed by the processor starts on the beginning of a clock cycle and lasts for one or more clock cycles.

Processors and instructions

Figure 3-3 shows what a processor looks like, while Figure 3-4 shows what the chip inside the package looks like.

Figure 3-3: An Intel Pentium 4 processor packaged for use
Photo courtesy Intel Corporation

When programs run, their instructions are stored in memory. An instruction execution cycle starts when the processor reads the next instruction from memory. The memory receives the read command over the bus and then one or more clock cycles later returns the requested instruction back across the bus to the processor. The processor decodes the instruction and decides what has to be done to carry it out. If the instruction requires an operand from memory, the processor calculates the address of the operand and commands the memory to fetch the operand. The processor completes gathering the necessary data after some number of clock cycles, computes the result, and if necessary stores it back to memory, disk, or the display.

The length of each instruction execution cycle determines the performance of the computer. If a computer running at a clock speed of 4 GHz can complete an instruction every clock cycle (including reading the instruction and data, computing the result, and storing back to memory), it will execute 4 billion instructions per second. If the average instruction takes two clock cycles, it will execute 2 billion instructions per second, and no more. Each instruction operates on one or more pieces of information, the *operands* of the instruction. An instruction might add or compare two numbers or might search a set of numbers for a specific value.

Executing instructions is the work the processor does. The tasks the processor carries out — tracking actions you take with the keyboard, joystick, or mouse; rendering and presenting the graphics on the display; moving information from disk to memory and back; communicating with your network; running your desktop accessories; or keeping the current print job going — each require some number of instructions to complete. The number of instructions required divided by the number of instructions per second determines how long each task takes.

Figure 3-4: The chip inside an Intel Pentium 4 processor
Photo courtesy Intel Corporation

The actual number of instructions the processor executes per second is determined by a lot of factors, including:

✦ How big the instruction is in memory, which in turn determines how many clock cycles it takes for the memory to deliver the instruction to the processor. Not all instructions are the same size.

✦ How many operands the instruction has, and where they are located.

✦ How long it takes the memory or I/O channel (and therefore the disk) to deliver those operands to the processor.

✦ How long the processor actually takes to manipulate the operands and complete the instruction.

✦ How long it takes to put the result where it belongs.

Adding the time each of a program's instructions takes then tells us how long the program takes to run, which is a measure of performance.

Buses

Buses are wires that computer chips operate according to an agreement (called a *protocol*) for how every chip connected to the bus must behave. A bus connects the processor to each of the other components, but there are other buses elsewhere in your PC.

The bus wires themselves carry signals among the chips, communicating what the other component should do, an address for where within the component the function should be carried out, and the information being transferred. Because bus cycles move information from one place to another, there are always two players in every bus cycle, and the cycle itself is very much like a conversation. Let's listen in on one conversation between your processor and memory:

```
Processor: Memory, I'd like the number at address 77349.
(Pause while the memory works.) * * *
Memory: Here it is. The number stored there was 42.
```

That conversation represents the processor reading memory. The processor can also write to memory, which involves a conversation like this:

```
Processor: Memory, store a number at address 77349.
Processor: Memory, the number to store is 100250.
(Pause while the memory works.) * * *
```

The memory is silent throughout that last conversation, never replying that it has actually received the information and completed its work. The buses in PCs rely on the *assumption* that the source will get the data there in time. If not, the destination picks up garbage. Your computer crashes at best, but at worst silently corrupts some calculation or stored value.

There are several distinct buses inside your PC, not just one, each designed for a particular purpose:

✦ **Front side bus** — The front side bus (FSB) connects the processor to a *chipset*, one or two chips responsible for joining all the different buses together. The two major processor manufacturers, Intel and AMD, each use a different design for the FSB. Because of that, you can't directly plug an Intel chip into an AMD socket, and vice versa.

✦ **Memory bus** — The memory bus connects the chipset to the memory modules. Current technology memories use bus designs called

Double Data Rate (DDR) Synchronous Dynamic Random Access Memory (SDRAM) or RAMBUS; somewhat older designs use Single Data Rate (SDR) SDRAM.

✦ **Graphics bus** — All high performance graphics chips interface to the chipset through an Accelerated Graphics Port (AGP) bus.

✦ **Expansion bus** — The expansion bus connects adapter cards and I/O buses to the chipset. As of late 2003, all PCs used the PCI bus to implement the expansion bus, but within a few years, the newer PCI Express bus will replace PCI.

Figure 3-5 shows how the buses connect. The chipset in Figure 3-5 is a composite of what's labeled the Northbridge and Southbridge chips, a common PC design. There's another bus between the Northbridge and Southbridge chips, one typically proprietary to the chipset manufacturer.

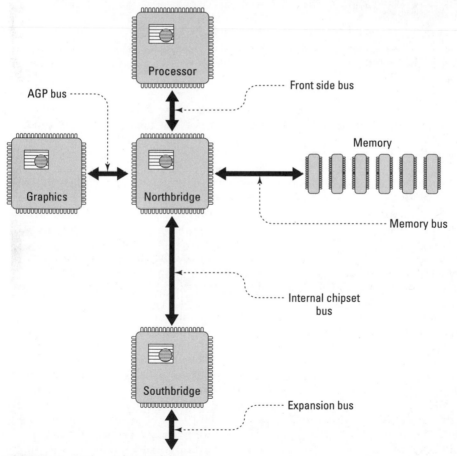

Figure 3-5: PC bus interconnections

Memory

PC memory comes mounted on printed wiring modules, as shown in Figure 3-6.

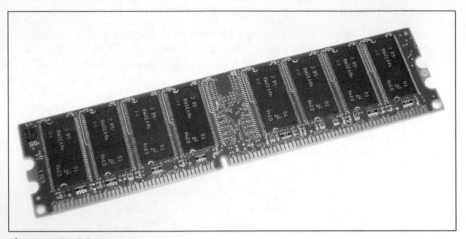

Figure 3-6: PC memory
©2004 Barry Press & Marcia Press

If you've ever seen one of the old pigeonhole desks with rows of compartments to sort letters into, you've got a picture of how memory is organized in your computer. Figure 3-7 shows the idea — a memory in a PC is a collection of places to store numbers, each with its own unique address. Although everything stored in memory is just a number, the interpretation of each number depends on the program that owns the information. The number 42 stored in address 3 in Figure 3-7 could be part of an instruction to the processor, part of your address on a network, part of your address at home, a count of eggs you own (meaning that you likely have more than enough in the refrigerator), part of a bigger number that's the cost of last night's pizza, one dot in a drawing, the character *B* in "HAPPY BIRTHDAY," or a lot of other things. Memory locations don't care what the meaning of the number they store is, only that the number needs to be faithfully stored and retrieved on request.

Numbers stored in individual bytes in memory range from 0 to 255 (which is what can be represented by the 8 bits in each byte). That's not enough to do everything you use a computer for. If the computer has to remember that you have thousands of paper clips in inventory, it has to store that number in at least two memory locations. Most PC processors are designed to operate on 4 bytes (32 bits) at a time, so programs for those processors store most numbers as 32-bit values. If the first byte holding your paper clip inventory is at address 102916, locations 102916 through 102919 hold the entire number. The same idea is true for instructions, which can require 1, 2, or more bytes to hold. Any time the processor references the first byte of a number or instruction, it references all of them.

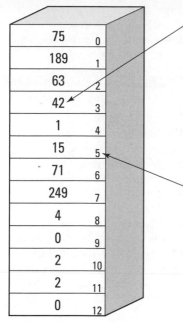

75	0
189	1
63	2
42	3
1	4
15	5
71	6
249	7
4	8
0	9
2	10
2	11
0	12

Memory is a collection of places to store numbers. Each place, called a memory location, is one byte. One memory location stores one value. That value can be anything in the range from 0 to 255.

Each memory location stores a physically different number, although the same value can be stored in different locations any number of times.

Every memory location has an address, which is a unique number assigned to it and no other location. When the processor wants to read or write the value in a specific location, it tells the memory the address of the location. Addresses usually start at zero and continue up from there.

Figure 3-7: Memory is a bunch of compartments. Each one stores a number.

Making the bus wider improves performance because the processor is likely to read all 4 bytes of a number if it reads any of them. *Strings* — a group of characters in order, one following another — are common exceptions to storing information in 32-bit chunks, but because strings are so often at least several characters long, very little of the effort in retrieving four characters (4 bytes) at a time goes to waste.

Your PC uses memory modules made from several memory chips. It's built that way because memory chips themselves are commonly only a few bits wide. The memory module operates the individual chips in parallel. The key parameters defining a memory module are these:

✦ **Capacity** — A memory module holds a specified number of bytes, with one address corresponding to each byte. The capacity of a memory module is the number of bytes it holds.

✦ **Width** — A memory module built from multiple chips in parallel can be as wide as the module designer wants, with the width being the number of bits (8 to a byte) that the memory accesses at one time. Common widths for memory modules used in current computers are 32, 36, 64, and 72 bits, depending on whether or not your computer checks data transfers from memory for reliability. Don't confuse the bit width of memory with the number of pins on the module because there are also pins for power and control. Common pin counts are 30, 72, and 168.

✦ **Access time** — There is a minimum interval the memory requires from the time it's told to read a number to the time when the number is available for the processor to use. Smaller access times mean the memory is faster and more expensive, but faster memory does not make your computer run faster. The memory has to be fast enough to keep up with the processor, but because the clock and the processor control speed, not the memory, faster memory than the system is timed for has no value.

✦ **Cycle time** — Another interval, the cycle time, specifies the minimum time from one memory operation to the next. The memory requires a small delay for it to recover between when it transfers data on the bus and when it starts the next operation. The cycle time is the access time plus that small recovery delay.

The volume of information a memory can read and write per second — its *bandwidth* — depends on its width, access time, and cycle time. Greater width and faster times result in greater memory bandwidth. Memory width is relatively easy to come by because all the engineer has to do is put more chips in parallel. Access time and cycle time can be reduced by building faster chips, but the cost of the memory goes up dramatically.

Disk drives and I/O channels

Disk drives are rectangular metal bricks with connectors at one end, as in Figure 3-8. The photo shows a disk drive with the cover off, exposing the internal mechanism.

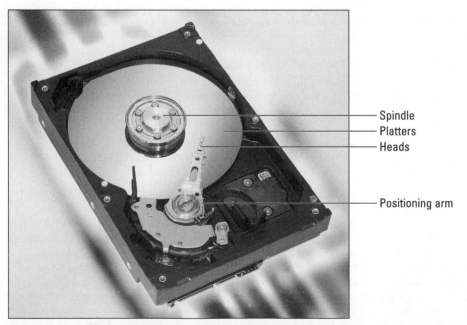

Spindle
Platters
Heads

Positioning arm

Figure 3-8: Seagate Barracuda disk drive
Photo courtesy of Seagate Technology

Memory costs 150 to 200 times as much as the equivalent disk capacity, which is why common memory sizes are 128MB to 1GB, while disks (also called fixed disks, hard disks, and hard drives) are commonly in the 40 to 250GB range. This huge difference in size means that you can afford to store far more on disk than in memory. Disks also have the nice characteristic of remembering what you wrote to them after you turn off the power. There are computer memories that can do that, too — the *flash memory* you find in cameras and MP3 players — but it is significantly more expensive than conventional computer memory.

Although disks are inexpensive, they're far slower than memory. Disk access times are about 100,000 times slower than memory, far too slow for processors to use for storing the instructions and data they are working on and still give you good performance. That's why your computer uses the disk for storing programs and data when you're not using them, but loads them into memory when you're actively working with them.

An *I/O channel* connects your disk (and other attached devices) to the computer's bus. We'll use the more common term *I/O bus* later in the book instead of I/O channel, but we've used I/O channel here to be sure that when we refer to a bus there's no confusion between the computer bus and the I/O bus. The I/O channel receives requests from the processor over the bus, rearranges the request if it needs to, and hands it off to the disk.

Disk is not only slower than memory, but it's also harder to talk to. Instead of having an array of electronic storage locations that are all equally accessible (as a memory does), the physical construction of a disk has distinct major structures that let a magnetic head move over a rotating magnetic platter. The callouts in Figure 3-8 identify the parts inside a typical disk, including the spindle, platters, heads, and positioning arm. The more complex characteristics of these structures cause a disk to be much more complicated to use.

The disk is built from one or more *platters*, flat metal or glass plates coated with a magnetic oxide (like on video tape) that rotate on the spindle. Both sides of the platter are used. Information is read and written on the platters by *heads*, which are mounted on arms. The platters spin under the heads, so for a given head position each head traces a circle over the platter beneath it. The heads move together on the arm, so the set of heads traces a cylinder over the platters. Each circle on one side of a platter under a head is called a *track* and is divided into chunks called *sectors*. The sector is the smallest addressable unit on the disk, specified by the combination of cylinder, head, and sector. All the bytes in one sector get read or written at once.

Although PCs used to transmit the cylinder, head, and sector addresses to disk drives directly, there were compatibility problems with that approach as disks grew from the 10MB capacity of the original IBM PC/XT to the monster drives of today holding 200GB or more. Computers now just send block numbers (sometimes called sectors numbers), where the block number for a specific sector is as follows:

```
Block number = cylinder number * head number * sector
number
```

The total capacity of a disk is the number of sectors times the sector size, or

```
Total size = Total sectors * 512
```

For example, suppose you have a disk guaranteed to have 234,441,648 sectors. Multiplying times 512 bytes per sector shows that the disk contains 120,034,123,776 bytes. Disks are sold as if 1 gigabyte contains 1,000,000,000 bytes, so your 120,034,123,776-byte disk is sold as having 120GB capacity. In Windows, however, 1 gigabyte contains 1,073,741,824 bytes, so in Windows Explorer the disk is shown with a capacity of 111.79GB.

Aside from its capacity, the important characteristics of a disk all relate to performance. The key disk performance characteristics are:

✦ **Rotation rate** — Rotation rate is the speed at which the disk platters turn under the heads, measured in revolutions per minute (RPM). Rotation rates presently run from 5,400 to 15,000 RPM. Faster rotation rates are better because they reduce the access time, and because they increase the sustained data transfer rate.

✦ **Access time** — Access time is how long it takes from when the processor requests data from the disk until it's available. The position of the heads over the tracks and the current sector under the heads is likely to be different than the processor requests, with larger differences causing larger access times because there's more physical distance to cross getting to the destination. The variability of access times means access time specifications are necessarily averages. Access times are typically from 14 milliseconds (ms, one thousandth of a second) down to 8 ms. Smaller access times are better.

✦ **Sustained transfer rate** — The data transfer rate a disk can sustain is the rate at which the combination of disk and I/O channel can, over a period of time, maintain a data transfer. The transfer rate is typically limited to the rate at which sectors sweep under the heads because that determines how much data can actually be transferred onto or off of the platters.

The rotation rate is set by the speed of the motor turning the disk. The faster it turns, the faster sectors fly past the heads. More sectors past the heads means more bytes, so (assuming the data density is comparable) the sustained transfer rate for a disk with a higher rotation rate will be higher. A higher rotation rate also means that when the sector your processor wants is not right under the head at the time of the request, less time will be required before the sector rotates around to be read. Faster rotation rates, therefore, improve access times, although head seek times are the major component of access times. Faster rotation rates are more expensive, partly because the electronics needed to handle the higher data rates on and off the disk are more expensive.

Access time is primarily determined by the speed with which the arms can move the heads from one cylinder to another. A head positioning motor moves the arms back and forth. Lower access times require more power and greater accuracy from the head positioning motor, increasing its cost.

Sustained transfer rates of 40MB per second are standard today. Rates of 100MB per second are possible with excellent equipment.

Video cards and monitors

A *video card* is a memory with some surrounding electronics. Figure 3-9 shows what's inside a video card from that point of view. Your monitor requires three signals, one each for red, green, and blue. These signals are analog signals, like what goes to the speakers in your stereo, not numbers. The digital-to-analog (D/A) converters do the work of changing the numbers the processor puts in the video memory into the signals the monitor needs. Your PC's processor works with the video memory and the graphics acceleration processor to put the information in the memory that will result in the proper picture on the monitor.

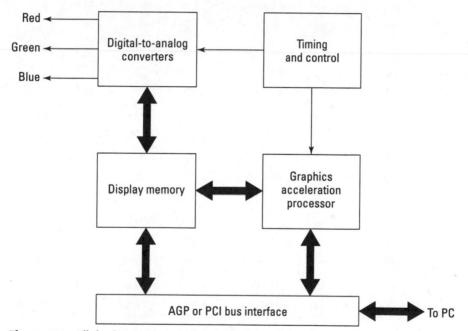

Figure 3-9: All the interesting work in a display card centers around the memory.

If you look very closely at your monitor, you see thousands of tiny dots. Each one of these dots is called a *pixel* and is represented by a number in the video memory. The size of the pixel in video memory, ranging from 1 to 4 bytes, determines how many different colors the pixel can display. More bytes per pixel gives you more colors, but also requires more video memory and makes the processor work harder to move more information into video memory.

Table 3-1 shows the minimum display memory your video board has to have for many of the video resolutions supported by Windows. The resolution and number of colors you use directly determine your minimum display memory size. Video memory is relatively large — the table shows that the maximum possible memory in the original IBM PC, 640KB or 0.625MB, would be enough only for video memory in the smallest size, lowest number of colors mode in the table. If you've ever wondered why a graphical operating system like Windows or Linux with X Windows needs more power to run than DOS, here's a clear example how much more resources and work are involved.

Table 3-1
Resolution, Colors, and Display Memory Size

	Display Characteristics			Display Memory Size (Megabytes) vs. Color Depth			
Width	Height	Aspect Ratio	Pixels	8 Bit	16 bit	24 bit	32 bit
800	600	1.333:1	480,000	0.458	0.916	1.373	1.831
1,024	768	1.333:1	786,432	0.750	1.500	2.250	3.000
1,152	864	1.333:1	995,328	0.949	1.898	2.848	3.797
1,280	720	1.778:1	921,600	0.879	1.758	2.637	3.516
1,280	768	1.667:1	983,040	0.938	1.875	2.813	3.750
1,280	960	1.333:1	1,228,800	1.172	2.344	3.516	4.688
1,280	1,024	1.250:1	1,310,720	1.250	2.500	3.750	5.000
1,360	768	1.771:1	1,044,480	0.996	1.992	2.988	3.984
1,600	900	1.778:1	1,440,000	1.373	2.747	4.120	5.493
1,600	1,024	1.563:1	1,638,400	1.563	3.125	4.688	6.250
1,600	1,200	1.333:1	1,920,000	1.831	3.662	5.493	7.324
1,920	1,080	1.778:1	2,073,600	1.978	3.955	5.933	7.910
1,920	1,200	1.600:1	2,304,000	2.197	4.395	6.592	8.789
1,920	1,440	1.333:1	2,764,800	2.637	5.273	7.910	10.547
2,048	1,536	1.333:1	3,145,728	3.000	6.000	9.000	12.000

Aspect ratio is the ratio of the display width in pixels to the height. The standard PC aspect ratio is 1.333:1, also expressed as 4:3. HDTV monitors use an aspect ratio of 1.778, more commonly expressed as 16:9.

As the information to be displayed changes, your processor has to update the contents of the video memory. How much work the processor does to do the update is determined by how much video memory it has to update. Updating every pixel of a display set for 1280×1024 resolution and 8-bit pixels (256 colors) requires that the processor move 1.25MB of data into the display memory. The processor executes a lot of instructions for every pixel, so in redrawing the screen it executes hundreds of millions of instructions. If all the data the processor needs is in memory, and if you're running a processor capable of billions of instructions per second, the update is done in between flickers of the monitor, and you never see it.

As computer capabilities go up, so do the computing requirements. Updating a display set for 1600×1200 resolution and 32-bit pixels (about 4.3 billion colors) requires that the processor move 7.32 MB of data to refresh the screen. That same processor executing billions of instructions per second may now take enough time that a slight flicker is noticeable.

Display update performance is critically important to game players, particularly those playing action games where the screen changes continuously, and 3D computer-aided-design (CAD) designers doing three-dimensional fly-throughs of their design. Your eye sees motion on the display because it fills in the differences between the successive images (frames) it sees. As long as the frame rate is high enough, you remain unaware of that process and perceive smooth motion. If the frame rate gets too low, you become aware of successive frames and the motion becomes jerky. Video update rates that are too slow give some people headaches or make them dizzy, and many people complain about flicker on the screen at update rates of 60 times per second or less. A decade ago, games used video resolutions of 320×240 at 256 colors to limit the work to update the screen to what the processor, bus, and video card could achieve and keep refresh rates up. Game designers today assume fast processors, fast buses, and hardware acceleration in the video board, making it common to see games running at 1024×768 or higher in 32-bit color. Table 3-1 shows that a refresh rate of 70 frames per second at that resolution requires moving 3 × 70 = 210MB per second into the video memory. Not only is that 100 times faster than the bus in the original IBM PC, it's 3 times faster than what the PCI bus in every PC built today can sustain, even though it can go faster for short bursts.

That level of required performance is why designers have created new buses for video cards and why video cards themselves have onboard accelerators.

Ultimately, the rate at which information flows into the display memory determines how happy you'll be with video performance. Technologies that increase that rate make motion-intensive programs work better and make other graphic applications snappier, too. The approaches engineers use to get better display performance include:

✦ **Get a bigger hammer** — Increasing the performance of the path into the display memory means you get more information in and out. The highest-performance display cards today are ones using the 8X AGP bus, which at peak rates can transfer a whopping 2133MB per second. The 8X AGP standard replaced the 4X (1066MB per second), 2X (533MB per second), and 1X (266MB per second) versions of AGP, which in turn replaced the PCI bus (133MB per second peak) for video cards.

✦ **Delegate** — All the performance numbers above assume that the processor does all the work. For example, when a line has to go from one place to the other, the processor has to individually draw every dot that makes up the line into pixels in the video memory. The alternative is to put a specialized chip, called an *accelerator*, on the card that can be told to do things the processor needs done. Instead of drawing every pixel in a line, for instance, the processor can simply tell the accelerator to draw the line. Instead of transferring hundreds of thousands of bytes to draw all those dots, the processor transfers a few bytes that give the accelerator the command.

What's Outside Your Computer?

The key characteristic separating what's outside your computer from what's inside is your need to access the elements outside the case. Components inside the case don't provide their own protection from handling, making them less expensive but more fragile. Components outside the case have their own cases, making them heavier and more expensive, but durable enough for you to work with.

The distance separating components outside the computer from the processor, memory, and internal bus also limits the speed at which external devices can communicate. The fastest connections inside your PC, those between processor and memory, are at least 50 times faster than the fastest connections to the outside, those to an external disk or camcorder. The fastest connections inside the PC can't be longer than inches; the fastest ones outside the PC can be several feet long.

Fortunately, most external connections don't need the highest speeds. No matter how fast you type, for example, you'll never type faster than the relatively slow speeds of your keyboard cable.

Summary

✦ The speed at which your computer performs a task depends on the amount of information the computer has to handle and the rate at which it can process that information.

✦ The core of your computer includes the processor, bus, memory, disk, video card, and monitor.

✦ You can evaluate the performance of each of the core elements by looking at how much information is handled, and how often.

Processors and Motherboards

P A R T

In This Part

Chapter 4
Processors, Cache,
and Memory

Chapter 5
Buses, Chipsets,
and Motherboards

Processors, Cache, and Memory

✦   ✦   ✦   ✦

In This Chapter

Exploring what the
processor does

Explaining cache and
main memory

Examining Intel and
AMD processors

Considering
multiprocessors

✦   ✦   ✦   ✦

The first step in understanding the performance you
get from a processor and how the processor
relates to the bus and to memory is to look closely at
what the processor does, which is to execute instructions. Understanding the instruction execution cycle
leads to understanding what engineers have done to
speed up processors and to understanding why you
would choose one processor over another.

Executing Instructions

If you had an assistant who scrupulously carried out
your instructions but had no ability to think independently, you might give that person tasks by writing out
detailed lists of instructions. Each instruction would
have to be quite simple and would have to completely
specify what you want done. For example, a list of tasks
might include the following instruction:

```
Pick up the green box and put it on the
top shelf.
```

The microprocessor in your computer is very much like
this imaginary assistant. It carries out sequences of
instructions — programs — accurately, but without
understanding. Each instruction clearly and precisely
specifies an action the processor is to take, leaving
nothing undefined.

Here's an instruction that might be executed on an *x*86-
architecture machine:

```
c7 05 42 01 15 71 01 00 00 00        mov
a,1
```

The instruction does a very simple thing — it takes the number 1 and stores it in a chunk of memory. The portion of the instruction that you or I would be most likely to understand is the part that says mov a,1. The same instruction in a form the processor understands (obeying conventions defined by Intel when they created the 386 processor) is the sequence of numbers c7 05 42 01 15 71 01 00 00 00. Even the c7 value is a number to the computer. It looks funny because it's not in base 10; it's in base 16 (where the digits are 0 through 9 and a through f).

The machine version of the instruction has the same three components as the readable version, as shown in Table 4-1.

Table 4-1
Machine Instructions to Processors

Machine Version	Readable Version	Description
c7 05	mov	The operation code (opcode) for the instruction is mov. The mov opcode tells the processor to read a chunk of information from one place and write it to another. The c7 05 code also tells the processor that the chunks of information it should move are 4 bytes long.
42 01 15 71	a	The destination for the move operation is a location in memory we've named a. The processor doesn't know or understand that name — instead, it knows that the memory location we want to store into has the address 42 01 15 71.
01 00 00 00	1	The operand for the move — the value we want to store in a — is the number 1. That value is stored directly in the instruction in the 4 bytes 01 00 00 00.

The processor does a lot of work to execute this simple instruction. Broken down into the small steps that together store the number 1 into a, here's what happens:

1. **Fetch the opcode from memory.** This happens by telling the memory the address of the instruction, commanding a read cycle, waiting, and pulling the memory result off the bus.

2. **Examine the result from the memory (c7 05).** Upon examination, the processor decides that it needs to execute a move of a 4-byte operand to a memory location. It also determines from that value that the operand will immediately follow the instruction.

3. **Ask the memory for the 4 bytes following the instruction** (42 01
   15 71). After those bytes are returned, the processor sets itself up to
   use that value as the address where the result is to be stored.

4. **Ask the memory for the 4 bytes** (01 00 00 00) **following the result
   address.** The processor stores those bytes in a temporary operand-
   holding place inside the processor.

5. **Tell the memory to store the operand in the destination.** After all
   that setup, the intended action finally happens.

6. **Advance the next instruction pointer.** The next instruction starts at
   the first byte past the operand fetched in Step 4. After advancing the
   pointer, the processor starts the cycle again.

Done in the most straightforward way, the preceding sequence takes a long
time because the processor is idle while the memory works, and the memory
is idle while the processor works. Early microprocessors, such as the Intel
8088 used in the original IBM PC, operated just this way, but newer designs do
better. Seeing how those newer processors improve execution performance
requires that we look at a slightly more complicated program:

```
mov   a,1
mov   b,35
```

This program is almost the same. All we've done is to add a second instruction
that stores the value 35 into the memory location named b. The important characteristic of the new program is that all of the steps the processor carries out to
execute the second instruction are independent of what it must do to execute
the first instruction. The instructions are so completely independent that the
order in which they are executed makes no difference, which means that a smart
enough processor could choose the order itself. Nor does the processor have to
be constrained to execute one of the instructions first — it works out the same if
the processor executes both instructions at the same time.

Overlapping operations, such as by running multiple instructions at the same
time or cycling the memory while the processor works, is at the core of how
processors gain speed beyond simply running at faster rates. The arithmetic-
logic unit (ALU) in the processor does the computational work, adding, sub-
tracting, multiplying, and dividing numbers, and carrying out other operations
required by programs. The bus interface communicates with the rest of the
computer through the bus, fetching and storing information as directed by the
ALU and control sections. The control section decodes instructions and tells
the other sections how to carry out the work each instruction requires.

Processors implementing parallel execution are designed like the drawing in
Figure 4-1. The functions of the processor are implemented by multiple units,
each of which operates independently. Several copies of the most common
units exist to allow multiple operations at the same time. An execution control
unit coordinates the operation of all the units.

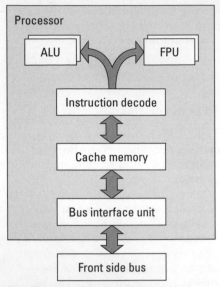

Figure 4-1: Cooperating units in a current-generation processor

The point of adding all this hardware and complexity is speed. Adding parallel hardware, increasing the clock rate, and requiring fewer clock cycles to execute each instruction all contribute to increased speed. In the process, however, the demands on the bus and memory for increased performance have increased sharply.

Cache Memory

A Pentium 4 processor clocking at 3.2 GHz (gigahertz, or a billion cycles per second) starts a clock cycle every 312.5 ps (picoseconds, trillionths of a second). The memory technology that provides the hundreds of megabytes of memory needed to run programs returns values nanoseconds after the processor makes the request, 10 to 100 times slower than the instruction issue rate. The ability of the processor to execute so many instructions while waiting for one value from memory means that, without some help, these screamingly fast processors will do nothing but spend all their time waiting for data.

PCs do use the fastest memory technology available at a reasonable cost, but in addition use these ideas to increase the volume of data available to the processor:

> ✦ **Improve the combined interaction of the processor, bus, and memory.** Changing the basic operation of the bus cycle allows the next memory access to start while the prior one is still wrapping up and runs the memory and processor in lock step, increasing the effective rate at which the processor can access the memory.

✦ **Don't access the memory so often.** Inserting a smaller, faster memory —
a *cache memory* — between the processor and main memory to
remember what's stored in memory locations the processor is likely
to need in the future reduces the rate at which the processor wants
memory access.

✦ **Organize the memory physically to allow parallel operation.** You
can build more than one bank of memory, arranging the memory
banks so that they are accessed in rotation. This idea, called *interleaving*, allows separate values to be returned to the processor at the
speed of the memory divided by the number of banks. For example,
if you have 10 banks of memory that can each be accessed every 100
ns, interleaving can provide a memory access as often as every 10 ns.
Interleaving requires that the order of access to memory — such as
always wanting the next higher address location — be known when
the memory is designed. Addressing the next sequential location is
very common for computer programs, but is not always the case.

When computer scientists look at the behavior of computer programs, they
find that programs do not access all of memory equally often. Instead, locations in memory that the program has accessed recently are far more likely to
be accessed again in the near future. The processor can use a local, cached
copy of those recent instructions, in which case main memory accesses are
needed only the first time the instructions are referenced. Much less storage is
required for this local copy than for main memory, and if the local copy is fast
enough, the processor never has to wait for memory.

Designers used to build cache memory from separate static random access
memory (SRAM) chips, but that approach isn't fast enough any more. Memory
directly inside the processor chip can be made fast enough to keep up with
the processor, though, and the massive increase in number of transistors possible on the chip has let processor designers put two levels of cache onboard
with the processor:

✦ **L1 cache** — The first-level cache memory, internal to the processor,
is called Level 1 (or L1) cache. It is faster than all other memory, but
smaller — typically 8KB or 16KB. It handles very recently used values, as found in small, tight program loops.

✦ **L2 cache** — The second-level cache memory, also internal to the
processor, is called Level 2 (or L2) cache. It handles values less
recently used than L1 cache.

Some systems use a third level of cache external to the processor. Multiple levels of cache memory reduce the demand on main memory created by the
fastest processors to the point where affordable memories can be used and
record values being written by the processor to memory, delaying writing
them until some later time when the memory is not busy. Cache memory that
delays memory writes is called *write-back* cache, in contrast with *write-through*
cache, which simply handles read access but forces the processor to wait
while writes complete.

Big, Fast Memory

Computer memory chips have a very simple, direct function — they remember information you write to them and let you read it back later. Giving them a huge capacity, good speed, and a low price, however, makes memory design so difficult that the newest chip technology almost always shows up first in new memory designs. All main memory uses dynamic random access memory (DRAM) technology; the original IBM PC used chips holding 16 kilobits (Kb), while chips holding a gigabit (Gb) are now available. Changes in the way the processor and bus control the memory have at the same time increased the effective speed, although not as dramatically as size has increased. There has been an exponential growth in memory capacity, as shown in Figure 4-2.

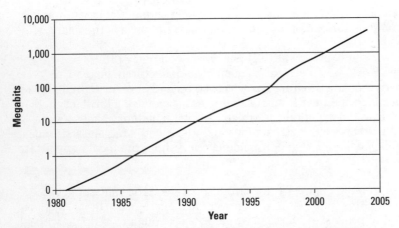

Figure 4-2: Exponential growth in per-chip memory capacity

The inside of a DRAM chip is a square array of storage locations, as shown in Figure 4-3. The memory breaks the address your processor passes it into two halves, called a *row address* and a *column address*. Together, the two half-addresses identify one bit in the memory.

The actual memory performance you get in a system results from the combination of how fast the chip itself responds and how the chip interacts with the processor and bus. Nearly all PCs now use synchronous DRAM (SDRAM) memory. SDRAM technology couples the operation of the memory tightly to the processor clock, reducing the timing tolerances necessary to coordinate the operation of the processor and memory and increasing performance. Enhancements to the basic SDRAM technology include double data rate (DDR) SDRAM, which transfers two data cycles per clock, and dual channel architectures, which interface two memory banks to the processor in parallel.

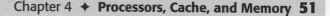

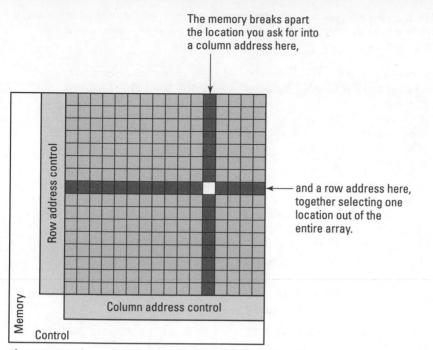

Figure 4-3: The memory is a square array inside the chip.

The driver behind these and all the other memory technologies PCs have used has been the need to provide faster and faster memory access to increasingly powerful processors. Memory access wasn't much of a problem for the slow 8088 processors in the original IBM PCs, but as processor width went from 8 to 32 bits (with 64-bit processors now available), and processor speeds went from 4.77 MHz to 3.2 GHz (with 4 GHz coming), change had to happen. The inability of any memory technology to survive much more than 5 years has been a measure of how fast processor design changes.

Motherboard Choices

Because it contains the processor, bus, and memory, the motherboard is the core of your computer. All the parts of your computer need to be in balance. If any one component is significantly slower than the rest, it can slow down the entire system, forming what's called a *choke point*. Similarly, a component significantly faster than the rest of the machine will be restricted by choke points elsewhere in the system and might not be able to deliver the performance it is capable of.

Dire as that sounds, however, current-generation PC components are typically so fast that you really need to think through only a few key issues to avoid choke points in all but the most specialized systems:

✦ **Processor and front side bus speed** — The processor communicates with memory through a data path called the front side bus (see Chapters 3 and 5). Faster processors require faster memory access, and therefore a faster front side bus. The motherboard limits the maximum front side bus speed (and determines whether you'll be using an Intel or AMD processor), so you want to choose a motherboard with enough room to grow.

✦ **Amount, type, and configuration of memory** — Motherboards have only so many slots in which to plug memory modules. If you fill them, adding more memory to the system requires that you remove some of the memory you bought previously. Faster processors also benefit from motherboards supporting multiple memory channels and faster memory technologies.

Some motherboards limit the amount of memory you can install, even if installing the additional memory is physically possible. Check the manufacturer specifications.

✦ **Adapter card bus type** — All PC motherboards built today provide PCI bus slots, and provide one AGP slot unless the graphics functionality is built onto the motherboard. Having no AGP slot means you can't upgrade the system's graphics performance. The PCI Express bus will replace PCI within several years, but isn't a factor in the market yet.

✦ **Internal I/O ports** — Parallel ATA (AT Attachment, for disk drives) and floppy disk controller ports are universal on motherboards. Some now provide Serial ATA ports.

✦ **External I/O ports** — The Universal Serial Bus (USB, Chapters 5 and 10) is so widely used now that it's very convenient to have many, many USB ports built into the system. The PC you'll see how to build in Chapter 25 has eight USB 2.0 ports, six in back and two in front, convenient for temporarily attaching USB flash memory disks and cameras. IEEE 1394 (FireWire, Chapter 5) is less common, but nice to have on the front panel if you have a camera using that interface.

Motherboards also commonly offer options for audio and Ethernet. Both can be added using separate PCI adapter cards.

Given that you make these choices well, most of the other choices you make configuring a PC are simple and much less expensive to change. Faster video is a one-card change if you have an AGP slot, but impossible if you don't. Greater disk capacity is a plug-in operation if you have a spare port, or requires an add-in controller if you don't.

Intel: Celeron and Pentium 4 Processors

Ignoring processors for servers, Intel offers two processor families — the Pentium 4 and the lower cost Celeron. Both families include lower power mobile versions for laptop and handheld computers. Processor prices decrease over time as new, faster ones come into production, so the important things to keep in mind when you're deciding what family and speed processor you should buy are these:

✦ You pay a definite premium for the bragging rights the fastest processors give you, with the price of newly-introduced high-speed chips relatively higher than the speed increase would indicate. The Celeron processors are less expensive than the Pentium 4, but offer somewhat lower performance. Celerons are also less demanding on the motherboard and memory.

✦ You pay a premium to upgrade. Replacing the processor to upgrade it may require replacing the motherboard and possibly the memory, and so may be more expensive than just swapping a chip.

Overall, you need to decide how much performance you need and what you're willing to pay for it. You'll use the processor for several years, and you can expect the demands your software will place on it to go up. Nevertheless, even the slowest processors now in production may be faster than what you'll ever need. What you're willing to pay should balance the immediate cost against the length of time the processor will meet your needs.

Pipelining and superscalar execution

Although early transistor radios needed only a few transistors to receive radio broadcasts, there are tens of millions of transistors in your PC's processor. The day isn't that far off when there will be over 100 million, yet it doesn't take that many transistors just to fetch instructions and add numbers. Instead, chip designers use the additional hardware to make processors faster in several ways.

Superscalar instruction execution is a way to get more work done at once by having more than one instruction in progress at any one time. The Pentium and Celeron processors implement superscalar execution using a *pipeline* in the chip, which is much like the old firefighter's bucket brigade. Figure 4-4 shows how pipelining works. When there's just one unit to do all the work — the equivalent of the top of the figure — it takes at least one clock tick to do each step, and nothing happens in parallel. Firemen get more buckets in motion with a bucket brigade, splitting the job up into multiple tasks that feed forward from one to another. That's what's going on in the bottom of the figure — the pipeline is the equivalent of a bucket brigade, where each row in the diagram represents a separate, parallel element in the processor. Having more parallel elements of the processor work on the job gets more work done every clock tick.

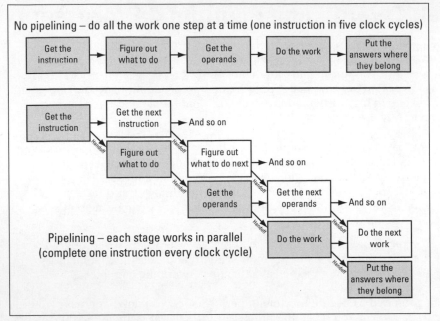

Figure 4-4: Pipelining for superscalar execution

Each of the units in a processor pipeline is called a pipeline *stage*. Each stage is specialized to the work it has to do. The total work the pipeline does is the same in every PC processor because they execute the same instructions, but processors with more stages have to do less work in each stage. Pipelines with stages that each do less work are simpler, which means they can run at higher clock rates, but take longer to restart (such as when a program takes an unexpected jump). Intel's designers have chosen to use simple, high-speed stages and long pipelines; AMD's designers have chosen more complex stages and slower clock rates (discussed later in this chapter). The choice between the two is so difficult that, in practice, there's no good way to know which will be faster for the programs you run other than to test your software.

Dynamic branch prediction

Programs jump around and loop to accomplish their tasks — they're not just straight-line sequences of instructions. For example, suppose the processor comes across an instruction sequence like this:

1. Load the value of COLOR.

2. Test if COLOR equals GREEN.

3. Store a new value in COLOR.

4. If the old value of COLOR was GREEN, the next instruction is number 1; otherwise, the next instruction is number 5. (An instruction like this one is called a branch.)

5. (Do whatever comes next. . . .)

Pipelining causes processors to load instructions well in advance of the current instruction being executed. At the time the processor is doing the work for instruction number one, for example, the pipeline might be loading instruction number four. The processor then does the work for instruction number two and simultaneously wants to fetch the instruction that will follow instruction number four. Because the processor can't know which instruction that is until it executes instruction number four and makes the branch decision, the pipeline doesn't know what to do.

Some older processors with very short pipelines solved this problem by doing nothing, allowing the pipeline to empty until they knew what instruction would be next. In our example, three cycles would pass with no instructions being executed (a *pipeline stall*) while the instruction after number four loads, is looked at, and gets its operands. Processors with long pipelines lose too much time during pipeline stalls for this approach to be workable, so instead they implement a technique called *branch prediction*. The idea is that the processor assumes that the next instruction is always the one immediately after the branch. If this assumption is true, the processor loses no time. If it's wrong, the processor stalls for a number of cycles while it loads the right instruction. A more sophisticated approach to branch prediction, however, is to recognize that many branches are there to make the code loop, and so will be executed over and over. This approach suggests that the most likely next instruction the second time the branch is seen is the instruction that followed the branch last time. The Pentium and Celeron processors all use this strategy and improve on it by fetching both the instruction immediately after the branch and the one that followed the branch the last time through the loop.

Dynamic execution

More than uncertainty, following a branch instruction can cause the processor pipelines to stall. For example, look at this sequence:

1. Load the value of COLOR.
2. Load the value of SATURATION.
3. Multiply COLOR times SATURATION.
4. Store the multiplication result in COLOR.

The first two instructions can be executed in parallel by the pipelines, but the third instruction has to wait for the first two, and the fourth has to wait for the third. Adding more pipelines or more pipeline stages to the architecture won't make this sequence faster because of the dependencies among the instructions that cause a conventional pipeline to stall, but more sophisticated analysis of the instruction stream — a technology Intel calls *dynamic execution* — will.

Figure 4-5 shows how dynamic execution works. Instead of the simpler linear pipeline structure in the bottom portion of Figure 4-4, dynamic execution uses a more complex structure centered around an *instruction pool*. The processor still executes instructions a pipeline stage at a time, but returns the result to the execution pool between stages. Stages take the next instruction they can work on at each clock cycle, even if the instruction taken is out of linear order.

Being able to work on any instruction that's ready to go means that the hand-off between pipeline stages doesn't have to be in rigid, linear lock step. The control circuits for the instruction pool ensure that necessary dependencies between instructions are observed, but otherwise allow for out-of-linear-order instruction execution.

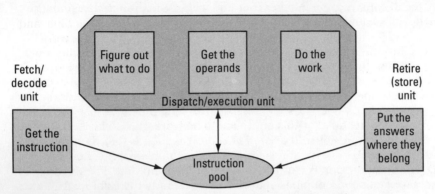

Figure 4-5: Dynamic execution centers on the instruction pool.

An extended version of the previous example illustrates the advantage of dynamic execution:

1. Load the value of COLOR.
2. Load the value of SATURATION.
3. Multiply COLOR times SATURATION.
4. Store the multiplication result in COLOR.
5. Load the value of CHANNEL.
6. Add 1 to CHANNEL.
7. Store the updated CHANNEL in SURFCHANNEL.

Even though the instructions at Steps 3 and 4 will stall briefly, the fetch/decode unit will continue to fill the instruction pool from Steps 5 through 7. At the point the dispatch execution unit stalls at Step 3, the instruction at Step 5 will be available. The dispatch execution unit picks up that instruction and its successors and keeps working. No cycles are wasted on pipeline stalls, so your program runs faster.

Extensions to the instruction set

Some of the most demanding PC applications involve signal processing, such as full-motion audio/video compression and decompression, speech recognition, videoconferencing, and image processing. Signal processing algorithms often have characteristics different than those of more general purpose computations, characteristics a processor can exploit for better performance.

Intel's first extension to the PC instruction set was the MMX technology, shipped in late 1996. Software for those applications using the new multimedia extensions (MMX) instructions registered performance gains of from 1.5 to 4 times the performance of a non-MMX processor. MMX provides additional instructions that give the processor the ability to process parallel streams of data, such as the values for left and right audio channels, with a single instruction stream. Combining stereo this way doubles the power of the individual instruction because handling more data streams (such as red, green, blue, and intensity for color images) with a single instruction stream gets more work done per instruction executed. The ability for one instruction to handle several data streams is called Single Instruction Multiple Data technology, or SIMD. The MMX SIMD instructions work on integers only, though, and switching between floating point operation and MMX operation is time consuming. The integer limitation is significant, so Intel later added the streaming SIMD extensions (SSE) and SSE 2, adding floating point capability similar to what MMX delivered for integers.

The new instructions do more than handle multiple data flows at once. Suppose the range of values a program is working on runs from 0 to 255. If the program scales a number up or down in that range, it's entirely possible that the value could go below 0 or above 255, creating what's called underflow or overflow, respectively. If you don't limit the value to the range 0 through 255, the results will be wrong. Without MMX or SSE, you'd have to test for over/underflow and do the correction in software, including a time-consuming jump around the instruction that corrects the error. With MMX or SSE, you just use the new instructions providing range limited arithmetic. The values get "clamped" at the extremes, and the program continues on — without a pipeline stall — as if nothing special had happened.

Hyperthreading and multiprocessors

Building clever, faster processors is not the only way to make a faster computer — adding multiple processors, called *multiprocessing*, is a relatively inexpensive way to get more speed. You don't need to add more disks or other peripherals when you add another processor; you just need the additional processor and its interface on the motherboard. You'll need UNIX or Windows NT/2000/XP to support multiprocessing. Windows 9X is exclusively a uniprocessor operating system and studiously ignores all those other processors.

The most recent Pentium 4 processors take multiprocessing one step further. Intel observed that although the massive number of transistors they can now fabricate in processors lets them build more functional units into the processor, creating the opportunity for more parallelism, those units are often idle while other units work. Intel observed, however, that if they let the one processor look like two to the software, they could exploit the fact that PCs running Windows or UNIX now run many programs at the same time. Arranging for multiple programs or multiple threads of execution in the same program to make use of those idle units, what Intel calls *hyperthreading,* incurs only a relatively small hardware cost and lets the processor exploit all the work developers have done supporting multiprocessor systems.

Expected performance gains

You don't get two times the performance from a two-processor system, or *n* times the performance from an *n*-processor system. The overhead of coordinating the operation of multiple processors, limitations on main memory, and limitations on your software's ability to keep multiple processors busy reduce the payoff you get. Figure 4-6 shows the idea, although the actual shape of the curve you get will vary depending on the system implementation and the software you run. In all likelihood, you will see performance less than shown in the figure. You'll get much less than shown from hyperthreading, where performance gains from the added processor are typically in the 10 to 30 percent range.

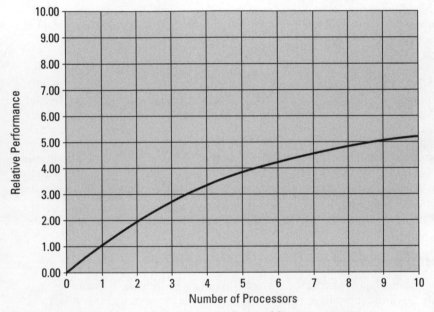

Figure 4-6: Illustrative performance gain from adding processors

The only reliable way you can know the performance gain you get from a particular multiprocessor or hyperthreaded system is to measure performance running your own workload. The behavior of multiprocessor systems is simply too complex to allow accurate prediction (other than, perhaps, through simulation). For example, consider the following factors:

✦ **Cache implementation and coordination** — Multiprocessor systems have to solve the problem of maintaining consistency among multiple copies of a single value that might be multiply stored in the caches. Figure 4-7 shows the problem.

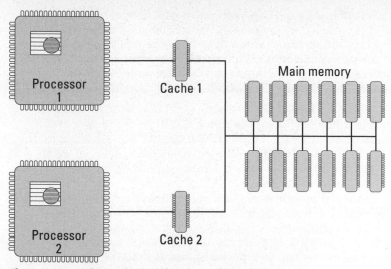

Figure 4-7: Independent caches in multiprocessor systems

Suppose Processor 1 reads the value of COLOR from main memory, and suppose the value is GREEN. A copy — GREEN — remains in Cache 1. Later, suppose Processor 2 sets COLOR to BLUE. Cache 2 will hold the value BLUE, and main memory will be updated to have BLUE in COLOR, as well. The problem is that, unless something specific happens, Cache 1 won't have the news and will store GREEN. This means that if a program runs on Processor 1, it will load the (incorrect) value GREEN from cache and not the (correct) value BLUE.

This problem is called the cache coherence problem. A cache coherence protocol solves the problem, ensuring that when Processor 2 changes the value of COLOR, Cache 1 marks its copy as invalid and throws it away. This process ensures that any later access to COLOR by Processor 1 retrieves the correct value from main memory.

✦ **Bus performance** — Although the front side buses in current-generation computers are fast enough for one processor, loading them with multiple processors can create bottlenecks. Hyperthreaded processors use faster front side buses, while multiprocessor systems use multiple bus architectures.

✦ **Multi-threaded software** — Multiple processors won't do you much good if you have only one program running at a time, particularly if the program does only one thing at a time. Server computers, such as the ones used to support access to World Wide Web pages across the Internet, can naturally have a copy of the server program running for each user accessing a page, and so can benefit from multiple processors. Depending on how you use it, the computer on your desk may not have much to do other than to run the program you're using. Unless that program breaks its work into several pieces that can be run in parallel, or you run more than one program at once, the second and other processors will sit idle. The most common example of applications that exploit parallelism is the more powerful image processing programs, which can dispatch processors to crunch on different parts of the image.

Windows NT/2000/XP has had the ability to let programs run parallel operations from the beginning. Windows 9X and its predecessors did not. Because the market for Windows 9X programs was far larger than that for Windows NT programs, software developers generally wrote for the larger market and did not implement parallel operations.

If you actively use several programs at once, and if those programs take signifi- cant time to do things, you'll also benefit from a dual processor or hyper- threaded system. In principle, a very fast processor can be shared among several programs transparently; in practice, multiprocessor systems using somewhat slower processors can feel more responsive than the faster uniprocessor.

AMD

The Intel-compatible processor market is so large that it was impossible for companies to resist building competitors to the Intel chips. AMD licensed designs from Intel for a while, but moved on to design and build its own inde- pendent designs. AMD has taken different design approaches than Intel, opting for more complex pipeline stages that do more work per clock cycle, and intro- ducing a 64-bit architecture extending the existing 32-bit standard. AMD's strat- egy results in processors that run at lower clock rates than the Intel ones, but not necessarily ones with lower performance. The value of the 64-bit architec- ture in anything but servers remains to be seen.

AMD has given its desktop Athlon processors, which compete with the Intel Pentium 4, names that include numeric designators intended to suggest the Pentium 4 clock speed at which the Athlon delivers equivalent performance. Whether the processor is faster or slower depends on what you're doing, so inevitably you'll want to research benchmarked performance or run your own. The AMD processors are highly compatible with the Intel ones; the only down- side you might see is that you'll likely use motherboards built from third-party chipsets. The rate of problems for those chipsets is somewhat higher, but if you research the specific chipset and motherboard you're looking at for reported problems and stick with proven motherboard manufacturers such as ASUS, you should be okay.

Courts have held that manufacturers can replicate Intel's instruction set (often called the *x86* instruction set), but have imposed difficult conditions for doing so. The competitor can't reverse engineer what Intel has done, taking apart the Intel product to replicate what it does. Instead, they have to start with a speci- fication of what the product has to do and create a new, independent design. Engineering in compatibility starts very early in the design cycle, well before first chip production. It's difficult and expensive.

Compatibility Above All Else

AMD has to provide complete compatibility with the Intel products because you, as a purchaser, have to know that your software runs without problems on their chips. If you couldn't be sure of that, no amount of improved performance or reduced cost could make the purchase worthwhile.

Compatibility is paramount. The old Intel 8080 processor, for example, did some odd things with the status flags that characterized the results of arithmetic instructions. Some time after the introduction of the Intel 8080, a competing manufacturer (not AMD) introduced an 8080 "replacement" that was significantly faster. Unfortunately, the manufacturer had "improved" Intel's design to correct the status flag "flaws." Somehow, it didn't seem important to the manufacturer that the change caused a lot of software programmed to work around the supposed flaws not to work. They probably sold some of those chips somewhere after this incompatibility came to light, but not very many. Speed always takes second place to compatible operation, and few chip manufacturers since then have dared to deviate from absolute equivalence to Intel's documented specifications.

In that light, AMD's strategy to bring the 64-bit Opteron processor to market is bold. The Opteron delivers excellent 32- and 64-bit performance, while Intel's 64-bit Itanium is barely useful in its 32-bit compatibility mode. The two 64-bit architectures are incompatible, too, so it will be interesting to see how the market develops and which 64-bit architectures finally prevail. Intel's announcement in February of 2004 that they would ship processors compatible with the AMD 64-bit extensions validates AMD's approach, but it remains an open question which 64-bit architecture will ultimately dominate the market.

AMD approaches strict compatibility this way:

✦ **High-level compatibility model** — Before AMD's engineers design the first circuit in a new processor, they look at the architectural features (like pipelines) they plan to use. The high-level compatibility model allows them to understand how those features will perform against the x86 instruction set. Design doesn't continue until they achieve a mix of features that in simulation provides the desired performance.

✦ **Register behavior model and logic model tests** — As designers work out finer and finer details of the design, these models help them verify that the design still meets the specification. Getting errors out of the design early is a big cost saver, so continuous modeling and simulation is essential to getting the product to market.

✦ **Hardware emulation** — This is the final verification before building chips. The actual chip hardware design is run on a computer designed to simulate chip operation. The combination is fast enough to make it practical to run real operating systems and application software, greatly increasing the visibility into the operation of the chip and helping to uncover subtle errors.

✦ **System-level tests** — Once chips come off AMD's line, they go into computers and begin an extensive test sequence to ensure that they run Windows and other PC operating systems and applications; and they also undergo a wide variety of specialized hardware and software tests (including tests by independent laboratories).

Power Management

Power management started as a way to extend the battery life in laptop computers because the less power the computer uses, the longer the battery lasts. The initial standard for how Windows and the BIOS interacted to do this was called Advanced Power Management (APM), but that approach has been replaced by the more capable and reliable Advanced Configuration and Power Interface (ACPI) specification. Power management reduces system-wide power consumption in one or more of these ways:

✦ **Slow down or stop the processor clock** — Because the power that all the chips in your computer draw depends on how fast the chips are running, slowing down or stopping the processor reduces not only the power consumption by the processor but also the power consumption of the cache and the main memory. You won't notice this happening — Windows knows when the processor is idle and runs the processor at full speed at all other times. The processor goes from stopped to full speed immediately, without a delay.

✦ **Set the display to low power or standby** — Whether you have a desktop or laptop computer, the display consumes a major portion of the total system power. The picture tube and its supporting electronics consume most of the power in a monitor, and the lights for the liquid crystal display (LCD) use most of the power in a laptop display. Screen savers don't affect power consumption directly; the display consumes almost the same power whether the screen is all black or all white.

The difference between low-power and standby modes in a monitor is in how much gets turned off. Standby takes less power, but takes a little more time to turn back on. LCD display lights are either on or off, and since they generate more light after they get hot, there will be some difference in the image you see when the lights go back on until they are hot again.

✦ **Spin down the disks** — The motor that rotates the disk spindle and platters consumes most of the power in a disk drive. By keeping the electronics alive but turning off the motor, disk drive manufacturers reduce power consumption when the computer is idle. There's an irritating delay to spin the disk back to operating speeds, though, so it's important to strike a balance between power savings and operating convenience.

Power conservation is part of desktop computers as well as laptops, providing features such as instant-on and making it ecologically reasonable to leave your computer on all the time. Microsoft argues that Windows computers need to be available on-demand — without a boot sequence — to do the work you want. The idea is that the PC should always be on and ready, but like a television, appear off when not in use. When you (or your network) want service, the computer should wake up immediately, do the work, and then automatically go back to sleep.

This isn't a small goal. We've seen a surprising number of manufacturers recommend turning off power management features in the BIOS and in Windows as one of their first steps in troubleshooting erratic problems. Stopping a computer in its tracks in a manner that lets it resume properly later is fiendishly difficult. If you have problems you can't isolate any other way, you might temporarily try turning off power management features yourself. You can always turn them back on if the problem lies elsewhere.

Summary

✦ Your processor executes instructions at a blindingly quick rate, but each instruction does one literal, simple thing. It takes a lot of instructions to do useful work.

✦ Every instruction requires one or more memory references, so cache memory that can provide high-speed memory access for some references lets the processor run without waiting.

✦ All of your computer components need to be in balance. Adding components that upset the balance gets you less performance than you paid for.

✦ Hyperthreaded systems are becoming more and more common on the desktop. You'll need Windows XP to fully exploit those processors.

Buses, Chipsets, and Motherboards

✦ ✦ ✦ ✦

CHAPTER 5

In This Chapter

Connecting chips together

What's on your motherboard

Connecting external devices to your motherboard

✦ ✦ ✦ ✦

If you're the type that takes apart electronic things to see what's inside, and if you've done that for the last 45 years or so, you've noticed a profound change in how electronic systems are built. Forty years ago and more, what you noticed first were the tubes, transformers, and other large components. Inside a box under those components were some other components and a whole lot of wires. Building anything this way took a lot of labor to screw things together, cut wires, and make connections, with a great deal of the labor simply in the process of connecting wires to terminals.

Not too much later, electronics manufacturers switched to using printed circuit boards, which are flat pieces of fiberglass or other stiff, non-conductive material. A printing and etching process places strips of copper (called *traces*) on and in the card, with areas at the end of the strips called pads to which the manufacturer attaches components. Printed circuits started out with traces on one side, but rapidly evolved to traces on both sides. Later versions laminated more than one card together, providing many layers to hold traces. The reason for adding layers to the boards was that the components had become more complex, with more connections, and simple one- and two-layer boards could not provide enough traces.

Every new layer on a printed circuit costs more money to design and build. As the cost to make connections grew, and as the number of connections outstripped even very expensive multilayer boards, designers started looking for ways to reduce the number of connections (and so the number of traces and layers). One very successful way has been to share wires among more than two devices. Figure 5-1 shows the idea, using the problem of connecting a processor to its memories as an example.

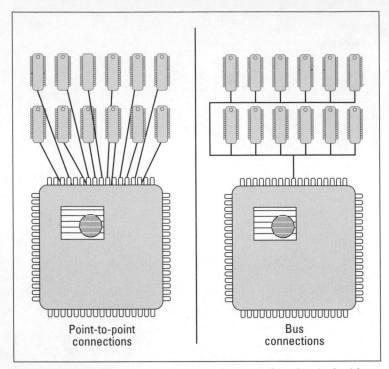

Point-to-point
connections

Bus
connections

Figure 5-1: Sharing wires to do more than one function is the idea
behind the buses in all computers today.

The most straightforward design for connecting a processor to its memories
uses a separate wire for every connection (this is the drawing on the left in
Figure 5-1). Suppose that every memory chip had its own set of wires to connect it to the processor. Using 512Mb (megabit) chips, a 1GB memory array
needs 16 chips. Each chip has in excess of 60 pins, so to connect up every chip
with its own wires, you need almost 1,000 wires. If you want to add memory,
you need over 60 more wires for every chip. You need even more wires to connect to your disk, video, and other components. The processor talks to only a
few of the memory chips at once, however, so most of these wires are doing
nothing while a few do useful work. The wires are functional duplicates of one
another, serving the same purpose (such as conveying data signals) except for
the fact that they connect to different memory chips.

As connections became relatively more expensive and the cost of circuits built
out of transistors became very much cheaper, changes in design to substitute
cheap transistors for expensive wires became possible. The idea of a bus grew
out of this substitution.

Instead of using point-to-point connections, suppose that every memory chip
connects to the same set of wires (so you use the same 60 wires with all chips,
not 60 for each chip). You have to add a few new wires to identify which chips
should be active at any instant of time because the processor doesn't talk to
every memory at once. The drawing on the right side of Figure 5-1 diagrams this

scheme, called a *bus*. A wire carrying a data signal, for instance, connects to the processor and equally to all the memory chips. Using the same wire across all the memory chips means that only one can use the wire at a time, but because that's how the processor works in the first place, there's no interference.

The ISA Bus: It's Old and Slow, and (Finally) Almost Gone

Buses have been in personal computers since the first 8080-based designs in the late 1970s. Computers prior to the PC used a variety of buses, with the most common one being called the S-100 bus (after the 100 pins on its connector); the IBM PC introduced the Industry Standard Architecture (ISA) bus. A bus is defined by a specification, which usually includes all the elements needed to ensure that products built to the specification fit into and work in a computer built to the same specification:

✦ **The physical specification** — A bus usually includes a *backplane*, which is the circuit card all the other cards plug into, and those other cards. If the base card has components on it, it's frequently called a *motherboard* rather than a backplane. The plug-in cards have shape and size specified so they fit into a standard-sized chassis. The physical specification details the connector(s) used between the backplane and the cards, the distance between cards, the maximum heat dissipation, and other mechanical issues.

✦ **The electrical specification** — Every active pin on a bus connector carries a signal, power, or ground. The electrical specification for the bus defines what signal is on each pin on the connector and the minimum and maximum specifications for each.

✦ **The bus timing and protocol** — The behavior and timing of the signals that control the bus have to be very precisely defined so that everything plays together properly. Figure 5-2 shows the simplified timing and protocol for the ISA bus. If this were the fully detailed drawing, the minimum and maximum times between events would be shown, and the exact signals making up each of the signal groups shown would be identified. The top two lines in the figure show how addresses go on the bus, the middle line the timing for read or write commands, and the bottom two the timing for data being read or written on the bus. The gray areas in the timing diagram represent times when the signals are allowed to be changing; the white areas are times when the signals must remain stable.

When a processor wants to communicate with memory or an input/output (I/O) device over the ISA bus, it goes through these steps according to the timing of Figure 5-2:

1. Output an address onto the bus ("Address lines") and assert the "Address enable" signal so that cards on the bus know that there is an address present they should look at.

2. If this will be a memory or I/O write, output the data to be written onto the bus ("Write data").

3. Output the command to be performed by the cards onto the bus ("Command"). The defined commands include memory read, memory write, I/O read, and I/O write.

4. If this is a memory or I/O read, wait the required amount of time, and after the data is stable, pull the data off the bus.

5. Remove the command from the bus.

6. Remove the address enable from the bus.

Amazing as it is that the ISA bus survived for nearly 20 years, there's no longer much of anything good to be said about the ISA bus. It's slow — orders of magnitude slower than the now-aging Peripheral Component Interconnect (PCI) bus. It's not as reliable as PCI because certain critical signals must be captured at the point they change from high to low or low to high. (More reliable buses allow devices to look for high or low status, not transitions.) It's terribly constraining for software and for system configuration because it can't address enough memory and doesn't provide enough interrupt control signals. It's difficult to work with because the vast majority of ISA cards and systems ever built required the user to manually set addresses and interrupts, and to know what addresses and interrupts will work.

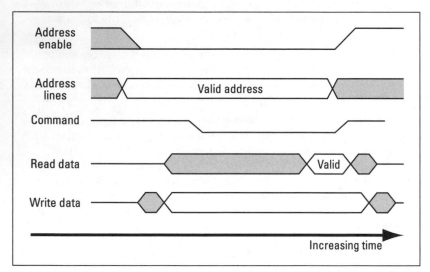

Figure 5-2: The operation of the ISA bus is defined by a simple set of signals and rules.

The one good thing to be said about the ISA bus was that, for a long time, nearly every PC — Windows or otherwise — had one, and building cards that work in an ISA bus machine was well understood. A manufacturer could sell a card for the ISA bus knowing there were a tremendous number of machines capable of hosting that card. A user could buy an ISA card and know that the chances are good that it can be made to work.

For all that, however, few computers or motherboards are now built incorporating the ISA bus. It's too slow for anything interesting any more, and caused too many conflicts and configuration problems.

PCI

Based on the experience of the ISA and several other less common buses, computer designers realized a new bus was needed and that the new bus had to meet these goals:

✦ **Provide increased performance** — Target performance was upwards of 100MB per second. Support for at least the full 32-bit address and data width of Intel-compatible processors was required.

✦ **Support multiple bus masters** — Allowing peripheral devices to control high-rate transfers independently offloads the processor, increasing net system performance.

✦ **Enable automatic system configuration** — Incorrectly assigned addresses and interrupts are the cause of far too many system problems. The bus had to establish the underlying structures and mechanisms to allow the computer to assist the user with this problem.

✦ **Be processor independent** — The cost of developing chips to support the bus and products that implement the bus is significant to manufacturers; the money spent on cards is of importance to users. The bus needed to preserve those investments across generations of processors.

✦ **Impose low implementation costs** — The PC market is extremely cost sensitive, so it was critical that the bus design not price systems or cards beyond what the market will accept.

The *Peripheral Component Interconnect* (PCI) bus accomplished all this. The PCI bus has supported the 486, Pentium through Pentium 4 and Celeron, Athlon, Opteron, and many non-Intel compatible processors using the three-tier structure shown in Figure 5-3. The fastest operations (including memory and the AGP card interface) are on the host (or front side) bus, connected through the Northbridge chip. The PCI bus once connected the Northbridge and Southbridge chips, but has now been replaced by a faster proprietary bus between the two, relegated to replacing the ISA bus for slower interfaces off the Southbridge.

Transfers to devices not on the front side bus are detected by the Northbridge chip and passed through the proprietary bus to the PCI bus below the Southbridge chip. Transfers on the PCI bus occur at rates up to 133MB per second, although sustained rates rarely go above 50 to 70 MB per second.

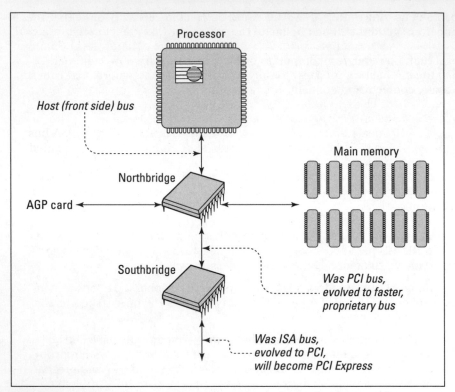

Figure 5-3: PCI implements a three-tier structure for performance and compatibility.

PCI Express

PCI itself will be replaced in a few years by PCI Express, a faster interface capable of operation over longer distances. PCI Express will make possible, for example, core processing boxes that reside on the floor out of the way and communicate at PCI or faster speeds with desktop display and interface units.

Chipsets

Early on, the chips surrounding the processor in a PC were there to help it run and to provide the minimal functions necessary for ISA bus support. The chips you found on the motherboard included a clock generator (which was the part of the processor that somehow never fit on the chip itself), a direct memory access (DMA) controller, an interrupt controller, a timer chip, the BIOS chips, and some other small stuff. All those circuits are still required in your computer, but (with the exception of the BIOS) they've been taken over by the chips that support the much faster structures you now use, including the host bus and the PCI bus.

Figure 5-4 shows how things started. Most of the chips on early motherboards had to do with the care and feeding of the processor (like the clock generator), and with helping the processor handle interfaces to the outside world (like the DMA, interrupts, and timer chips). The simplicity of the bus interface — not much more than chips to strengthen the signals from the processor — was possible because the speeds of the processor and memory (on the ISA bus) were reasonably closely matched. That match wasn't an accident because the ISA bus began as an extension of the bus on the Intel 8088 processor. The placement of added memory, video, disk, and sound functions on the ISA bus further simplified the motherboard design because all the complexity tended to be on plug-in cards.

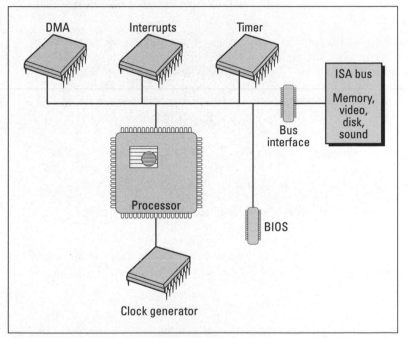

Figure 5-4: Chips on early motherboards

Processor speed increased faster than the speed of memory in the evolution of the PC. System and processor designers responded with faster, more complex designs that solved the resulting problems and exploited the additional power possible in larger, faster chips dedicated to specific functions. In the case of the logic that goes on a motherboard, the result was chipsets that encapsulate nearly all the circuits surrounding the processor and controlling the host and PCI buses.

The PCI bus is enormously more complex to implement than the ISA bus because the speed gain that PCI delivers requireed sophisticated system and processor designs. Bringing that complexity to market at a low price required that specialized chips encapsulate the complete front side bus and

PCI functionality. Elements of the chipset support the processor host bus, the cache and main memory, the PCI bus itself, and integrated peripherals including a PCI Integrated Drive Electronics (IDE) disk controller. Some of the features implemented in current motherboard chipsets include:

✦ **Synchronous dynamic random access memory (SDRAM) support —** The chipset provides the interface between the processor and main memory. The capabilities in the chipset determine what configurations your motherboard will handle.

✦ **IDE and Bus-mastering IDE —** Most chipsets implement a parallel IDE disk interface, enabling support for fast ATA disks using the *Ultra DMA* IDE interface. You won't see better disk performance from DMA on the IDE ports, but you will see lower processor usage during disk transfers.

✦ **Serial ATA —** The shortcomings in the IDE interface, including the lack of error checking and very limited cable lengths, lead to the creation of the faster, more reliable serial ATA specification. Serial ATA already runs at bus rates of 150MB per second, so it's faster than PCI. That speed mismatch makes it valuable to implement the serial ATA ports directly on the motherboard where they can be connected to a faster bus.

✦ **Peripheral support, including audio, USB, and Ethernet —** The newest chipsets add support for audio on the motherboard, eliminating the need for a sound card, and support for the Universal Serial Bus (USB) and Ethernet. Chipsets for low-cost machines include built-in video card functions, eliminating yet another separate card.

PCs support a variety of other buses, depending on their use, sometimes by additions to the chipset. The most common of those other buses are the PC Card and IEEE 1394 interfaces.

Motherboards

If you open your computer, you'll see a large board on the bottom or side of the case, into which other boards are plugged. That large board is called the *motherboard* and is the focus for the processor, memory, and buses. Many of the motherboard characteristics you need to consider are prominently featured in computer system advertisements, including processor type, clock speed, and bus. An equal number of key characteristics are often omitted, such as onboard peripheral support, the range of processor speeds supported, the maximum amount of memory, and the number of memory slots. These latter characteristics strongly affect your ability to upgrade the machine in the future. Figure 5-5 is a typical example, showing the Intel D875PBZ motherboard annotated to identify the major components. The features and layout of your motherboard will vary somewhat, but the ideas are similar and the parts tend to look much the same.

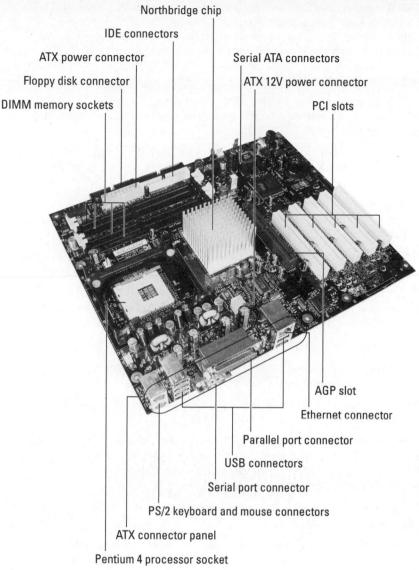

Northbridge chip

IDE connectors

ATX power connector

Serial ATA connectors

Floppy disk connector

ATX 12V power connector

DIMM memory sockets

PCI slots

AGP slot

Ethernet connector

Parallel port connector

USB connectors

Serial port connector

PS/2 keyboard and mouse connectors

ATX connector panel

Pentium 4 processor socket

Figure 5-5: The motherboard is the core of your computer.
©2004 Barry Press & Marcia Press

The components in Figure 5-5 are identified in the following list, starting with the processor socket and going clockwise:

✦ **Processor socket** — This motherboard accepts Intel Pentium 4 processors. The ZIF (Zero-Insertion Force) socket lets you easily insert and remove the chip. Be careful to seat the processor in the socket firmly before closing the clamp. If you don't, some of the pins may not make contact properly and the machine won't boot. The heat sink retention bracket surrounds the socket.

✦ **DIMM memory sockets** — This motherboard uses PC2700 or PC3200 SDRAM memory on dual inline memory module (DIMM) strips, depending on the speed of the processor's front side bus (533 and 800 MHz, respectively). The faster memory works with the slower bus, although the system won't be any faster, letting you prepare for future processor upgrades.

✦ **ATX power connector** — The ATX power supply output wires terminate in a single relatively large connector, plus a smaller connector for added 12 V power.

✦ **Floppy connector** — The floppy disk controller is on the motherboard. You run a standard cable from the floppy disk drive in the case to this connector.

✦ **Disk drive connectors** — If you use an IDE (parallel ATA) disk or CD-ROM, you'll plug those devices into the IDE connectors. Use the Serial ATA connectors for newer disk drives.

✦ **Northbridge chip** — Although small, the support chip comprises the bulk of the electronics surrounding the processor, including support for the AGP and PCI buses, the disk controller, and other functions.

✦ **PCI connectors** — Up to five PCI adapter cards plug in here and are secured to the back of the case with a screw.

✦ **AGP connector** — An AGP video card plugs in here.

✦ **Ethernet connector** — Plug the PC into your local area network (LAN) using this onboard RJ-45 connector.

✦ **Parallel port connector** — You'll plug an older printer into this connector. Newer printers use USB or Ethernet.

✦ **USB connectors** — Keyboards, mice, speakers, cameras, scanners, and other devices plug into the USB ports. Unlike the PS/2 mouse, keyboard, and parallel ports, you don't have to turn off the computer to attach and detach USB devices.

✦ **Serial port connector** — Serial ports let you plug in modems and other external devices.

✦ **PS/2 mouse and keyboard connector** — These are standard mini-DIN connectors that match the one at the end of your mouse or keyboard cable. Look for drawings near the connectors to determine which is for the mouse and which for the keyboard.

✦ **ATX connector panel** — All the external I/O connections from the motherboard, including sound, game, serial, parallel, USB, Ethernet, mouse, and keyboard ports, are directly attached to the motherboard and mounted on the ATX connector panel.

Also on the motherboard is the *basic input-output system* (BIOS), the program that starts up the computer when you turn on the power. A *flash memory* chip holds the BIOS code, even when the power is off. A special procedure allows you to update the BIOS in the flash with new code; you'll get both the update software and the new BIOS image from the PC or motherboard manufacturer's Web site.

External Buses

The external connections to your PC have evolved from simple single-point connections, such as serial and parallel ports, to high-speed external buses you can use to connect multiple devices.

Universal Serial Bus

The *Universal Serial Bus* (USB) is the most common external bus, used to connect mice, keyboards, cameras, GPS receivers, handheld computers, disk drives, serial and parallel ports, and more. We cover USB in Chapter 10 because one of its most exciting uses is for external, removable storage; however, you'll want to keep in mind that the most convenient way to have enough USB ports is for them to be provided directly by the motherboard. It's best to have USB 2.0 ports because they'll operate at the highest 480 Mbps rate, yet throttle down if you connect a slower USB 1.1 device.

IEEE 1394 (FireWire)

Another external bus is the one defined by IEEE specification 1394, popularly called FireWire. Like USB (Chapter 10), IEEE 1394 is a serial bus, transmitting 1 bit at a time over copper wire with multiple devices cabled into a tree. IEEE 1394 is as fast as USB 2.0, being capable of rates from 100 to 400 Mbps. IEEE 1394 supports far more connected devices than USB, too.

Nevertheless, few products use IEEE 1394. Typical products that do are digital movie cameras, digital still cameras, and digital VHS players.

PC Card

The PC Card (previously PCMCIA, or Personal Computer Memory Card International Association) bus originated as a way to plug in modules to laptop and smaller computers. PC Card devices are roughly the size of a credit card, and from 3.3 to 10.5 millimeters thick. The initial PC Card products were add-on memory and plug-in software, but manufacturers were quick to offer a wide range of products:

✦ Read/write and read-only memory

✦ Hard disk drives

✦ Modems (including Integrated Services Digital Network (ISDN) and Cellular data/fax)

✦ Network adapters (including wireless and adapters combined with modems)

✦ Small Computer System Interface (SCSI) adapters

✦ Sound adapters

PC Cards plug into a 68-pin host socket. Three PC Card sizes exist, with a fourth being debated.

✦ Type I cards (such as memory) are 3.3 mm thick.

✦ Type II cards (usually I/O devices such as modems) are 5 mm thick.

✦ Type III devices (typically data storage or radio devices) are 10.5 mm thick.

✦ Type IV was intended to be an 18-mm slot for large-capacity hard drives, but never made it to market.

A PC Card fits in any slot either its own size or a larger size. For example, a Type II modem fits into a Type III slot.

Summary

✦ Buses are fundamental to the organization of your PC's electronics.

✦ The primary buses inside your PC are PCI, AGP, and parallel or serial ATA. The primary external buses are USB, IEEE 1394, and PC Card (PCMCIA).

✦ The key decisions about your computer — processor, cache, and bus — primarily concern the motherboard. The choice of motherboard drives everything else you do.

Video

P A R T

III

◆   ◆   ◆   ◆

In This Part

Chapter 6
Video

Chapter 7
Monitors and
Flat Panels

◆   ◆   ◆   ◆

Video

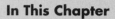

In This Chapter

Behind the screen

Getting images from
dots and numbers

Examining video
accelerators

Considering video
compression

Y our monitor and video display board work
together as a pair, much like a disk and its controller. The capabilities of the monitor must match the
needs of the display modes requested by your software
and output by your video card. To understand how the
monitor and video board work together and contribute
to the performance of your computer, we'll start at the
monitor and work inward through the functions of the
video board.

A Computer Monitor Is Not the Same as a Television

Although much of what a computer monitor does
appears similar to what a television does, the requirements on a computer monitor are much more stringent.
A television that meets the North American standard,
for example, displays roughly 525×700 pixels, with a
viewable area smaller than those numbers. The
European Phase Alternating Line (PAL) standard is a little different at 625×833 pixels, but close to the same
size. The most basic computer monitor meeting the
Video Graphics Array (VGA) standard, however, displays no fewer than 640×480 pixels — all viewable —
with very high-end monitors capable of resolutions of
2,048×1,536 pixels and more. It is for this reason that
products that display television in a window on the
computer screen are fairly inexpensive and work well,
but products that display computer images on televisions are limited to basic VGA resolutions — 640×480 is
common, although some products output up to
1,024×768 — and often smear the images.

If you look closely at the screen on a conventional monitor or liquid crystal display (LCD) panel, you'll see a
pattern of tiny colored dots that, when each is lit up at
the right brightness, forms the picture you see (monitors using the Sony Trinitron tubes have vertical lines of
color instead). These dots are called *pixels* (picture elements). The chain of electronics that delivers this image
to you runs from the face of the monitor's cathode ray

tube (CRT) or the LCD back through the display electronics to the video card, and from there into the rest of the computer.

Figure 6-1 shows in more detail the process of drawing a picture by sweeping the dots on the screen. One complete traverse of the screen starts at position **1** and moves to the right. At the end of the line (**2**) the beam turns off and rapidly moves down and to the left to **3** and the start of the next line. The sweep of the second line takes the beam to the right, ending at **4**. This process continues with the beam moving downward until the pattern finishes at **5**. The beam then turns off and moves back to **1** to repeat the process.

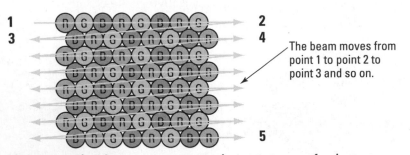

The beam moves from point 1 to point 2 to point 3 and so on.

Figure 6-1: The picture on your screen is a swept array of red, green, and blue dots.

The changes in brightness the beam delivers while sweeping over the dots determines the picture you see. For example, a completely blue screen results if the beam is off for the red and green dots but on for the blue ones. The brightness of the blue dots is controlled by the brightness of the beam when it's over blue dots. More complex pictures are simply combinations of red, green, and blue dots at the right brightness. Your eye sees not the individual dots but the composition of them into a complete image.

Because the timing of changes in brightness must be critically synchronized to the position of the beam on the screen, the video board timing controls the scan frequencies of the monitor as well as the operation of the board. All the signal timing is ultimately related to the dot clock, which is a signal within the video board that pulses once every time the beam on the screen passes a triangle of red, green, and blue dots (one pixel). For example, if the display is set to 640×480 resolution, the dot clock pulses 640 times as the beam traverses once from left to right on the screen over the visible part of the image. The dot clock continues to pulse as the beam makes its fast retrace from right to left and then repeats the cycle for the next line. Ignoring overscan and retrace, the dot clock frequency is the resolution of the screen times the number of frames per second. For a display at 1,280×1,024 at 75 Hz, the dot clock runs at slightly over 98 MHz.

Cross-Reference   There's more on monitors in Chapter 7.

The Video data path

A digital-to-analog (D/A) converter is a device that outputs a signal corresponding to the number fed to the converter. If the converter receives a zero value,
it outputs a zero signal. If it receives a large number, it outputs a large signal.
A video board has three D/A converters, one each for the red, green, and blue
signals sent to the monitor (Figure 6-2). The dot clock sets the timing of pixel
data from the display memory at the D/A converters, sending a new pixel value
for each clock pulse. At 1,600×1,200 resolution, there are (1,600 × 1,200) =
1,920,000 dots on the screen; if you configure the display for an 85 Hz refresh
rate, the dot clock runs at 1,920,000 × 85 = over 163 megahertz. In 32-bit color
mode, the display memory delivers over 622 megabytes per second in that
example, fetching 4 bytes per dot clock.

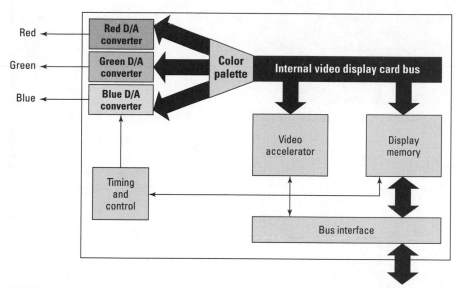

Figure 6-2: A video board lives or dies by how fast it moves data around.

The video bus delivers the data from video memory to the D/A converters.
Achieving a constant, high-speed flow of data to the D/A converters across the
video bus led designers to many of the same techniques used in processor
front side and memory buses, including making the bus wider to get more out
of each bus cycle and using optimized bus cycles to speed access. It's not marketing hype that drove video cards to a 256-bit internal bus — making the bus
wider reduces the bus cycle rate.

Sixteen million is a whole lot of colors

There are three common Windows color settings. One-byte pixels can specify
256 colors. Two-byte pixels — called High Color — can specify 65,536 colors.
Four-byte pixels — called True Color — can specify 16,777,216 colors plus a
brightness channel in the fourth byte. (A 3-byte, 24-bit format is also available.)

"When you're using 24 bits of color, most people can't see the difference between two adjacent colors. It also becomes hard to name them." — Microsoft Beta Tester T-Shirt

Each of the three D/A converters (one each for red, green, and blue) accepts 1 byte at a time, so some work is needed to be able to feed all three pixel formats to the converters. Figure 6-3 shows the options. In 24- and 32-bit display modes, 1 byte in a pixel goes to each of the three converters. In 16-bit modes, the 16-bit value is split into fields (usually 5 bits for red, 6 for green, and 5 for blue). The fields are extracted from the value and sent to the corresponding D/A converter. The only difference between the two modes is the number of bits used to store the color values.

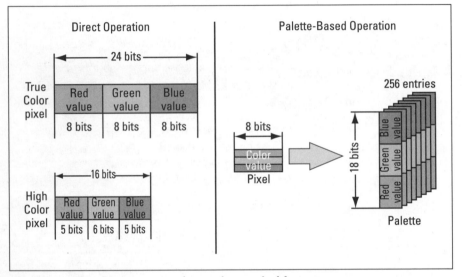

Figure 6-3: Windows supports three primary pixel formats.

The 256-color mode is different from the other two, using 8 bits to store each pixel. If the video card divided that 1 byte into fields as with High Color — say with 3, 3, and 2 bits per color — the card could not provide good rendition. Instead, the 8-bit value gets used as an index into a color palette with 256 entries, each holding a wider value that can be sent to the D/A converters. Every pixel is therefore one byte, and as bytes are read from the display memory, they go through the color palette shown in Figure 6-3. Each of the 256 possible values in the byte corresponds to one entry in the palette. Each entry in the palette contains a value for red, green, and blue, each of which are fed to the corresponding D/A converter. The overall structure permits programs to choose a set of 256 possible onscreen colors from a much wider range of colors, but creates problems when switching from one program to the next. The 256-color mode is a compromise for slow, limited capability computers, but isn't required any longer.

Video Buses

The enormous data rates between processor and video card required for high-resolution, high-performance graphics exceed what's possible with the Peripheral Component Interface (PCI) bus. That problem led designers to create the Accelerated Graphics Port (AGP), which started as a modified version of PCI, to provide greater data rates between system and video memory. Successive generations of the AGP specification — 1X, 2X, 4X, and now 8X — increased transfer rates to 2.1 gigabytes per second.

The 8x AGP technology will be the last revision. Succeeding generations will be based on the PCI Express serial graphics specification and should show up in PCs some time in 2004 or later.

For conventional 2D displays, the data rates AGP makes possible are enough to support several independent displays. ATI, nVidia, and Matrox all make video cards supporting multiple independent monitors from the same card, and if you're willing to add PCI cards alongside the AGP card, Windows supports up to nine monitors. Your desktop extends over all the monitors you have, creating a larger surface on which you can keep open applications.

What a 3D Video Accelerator Does

Three dimensional games, visualization, and virtual reality systems put you in a simulated first- or third-person world where you can move around in a highly detailed environment. These programs work by maintaining a "wire-frame" structure giving shape to the objects in the world (walls, floors, and ceilings), and by painting the surfaces of the objects with colored patterns called *textures*, a process called *texture mapping*. Figure 6-4 is a three dimensional view of a room; Figure 6-5 is the wire-frame view of the textured representation in Figure 6-4. Everything you see in Figure 6-4 is the result of textures painted on the floors, walls, and ceilings defined by the wire frame.

A lot of work is required to create a 3D image. Overall, the sequence is what's shown in Figure 6-6, with each step moving the program's model of what exists in an imaginary world further from that model and closer to dots on your screen. As the computations progress from left to right, there become more objects to do computations for — objects transition to polygons which then transition to texels — increasing the amount of work to be done in each block.

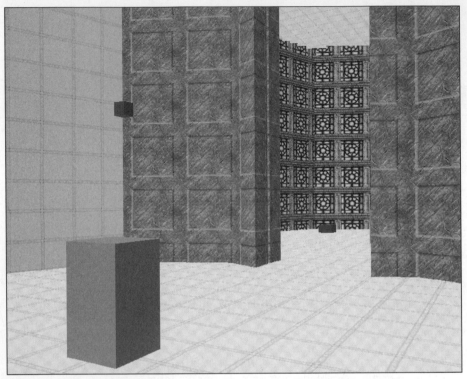

Figure 6-4: Textures rendered on a wire frame create a realistic image.

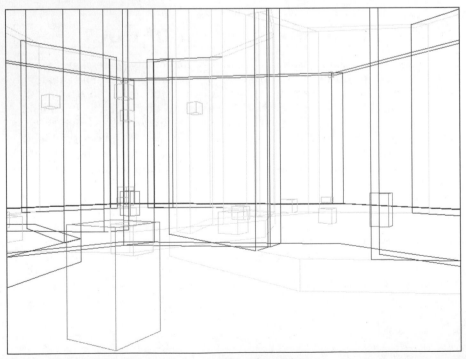

Figure 6-5: The wire-frame structures define the surfaces.

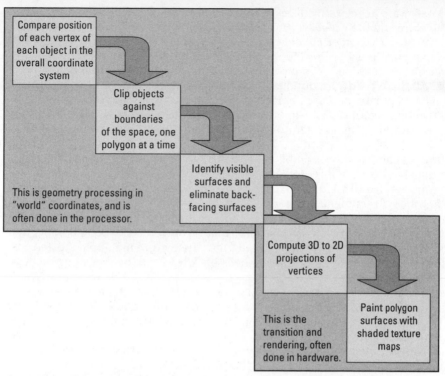

Figure 6-6: The 3D viewing and rendering pipeline transforms a program's model of what exists into the image you see.

The details of each step in Figure 6-6 are:

1. **Compute vertices** — The processor computes the position of each vertex of each object in the overall coordinate system.

2. **Clip edges** — Objects may extend past the edges of the visible area. The overhang has to be eliminated, so the processor clips the edges of objects against the drawing region boundaries, one polygon of an object at a time.

3. **Eliminate hidden surfaces** — You want the final display to omit hidden surfaces. The processor has to identify visible surfaces and eliminate back-facing surfaces.

4. **Compute projections** — The display is only 2D, as if a glass surface is interposed between your eye and a 3D scene. Simulating this in the computer requires computing 3D to 2D projections of the vertices of each polygon.

5. **Paint surfaces** — Once you have a set of 2D polygons, you can paint the surface of each one with a shaded, perspective-scaled texture map.

A 3D hardware accelerator takes over operations on the right side of the pipeline, freeing the processor for the work on the left. Simple accelerators do only the polygon rendering and texture mapping; more capable accelerators scoop up functions in prior blocks of the figure, such as by permitting the "Compute Vertices" block to pass floating-point coordinates into the next stage. All these hardware optimizations reduce the workload on the processor. The most sophisticated accelerators move processing at the vertices, such as lighting effects, into the accelerator by allowing the program to download simple programs into the accelerator that run for each vertex.

Texture mapping is more complicated than simply copying a patterned bitmap to the screen because it requires dealing with the perspective effects in the wire frame and with visibility of objects due to solid surfaces being in front of one another. A rectangular pattern bitmap has to be distorted to fit perspective changes. You can see this in Figure 6-4 on the walls that are not perpendicular to your point of view. Surfaces like that have to recede along perspective lines toward a vanishing point, requiring that the texture map be distorted to be shorter and shorter as your eye moves back towards the vanishing point.

The calculations to do texture mapping and to decide which parts of what surfaces are visible are computationally expensive — they require a lot of work by the processor. That's the basic reason why real-time 3D rendering requires a fast processor for good performance. Higher resolution screen formats require significantly more computation — 640×400 resolution takes 4 times the computation of 320×200, while 1280×1024 resolution takes over 16 times the computation of 320×200. That increased computational load is why the higher resolutions became common only with the more recent high-speed processors and high-performance 3D accelerators.

Another key 3D rendering operation is polygon drawing, which is the most common technique to represent moving objects. Textures drawn on the polygons give the object a realistic look while retaining the advantages of fast 3D views. Polygon drawing is similar to the process of covering arbitrary wire frames with texture maps, but is restricted to flat convex shapes to improve performance. A mesh of triangles can be used to approximate any 3D surface, which reduces the complexity of rendering the object onto the screen and makes the operation faster. Because you can make objects arbitrarily detailed by making the triangles smaller, there's no necessary loss of visual quality.

Because the two most important operations for high-speed 3D graphics are texture mapping and polygon rendering, you usually measure 3D software and hardware performance in textured pixels (*texels*) per second and filled polygons per second. Some of the most highly tuned 3D software is in games, so those that report rendering performance measures sometimes make excellent 3D video benchmarks.

Video Compression

The data rates for digital motion video can become high enough to stress your computer's performance and take up a significant amount of storage, as shown in Table 6-1, which shows how many minutes of video you can store on a 650MB CD-ROM. MPEG 1 video is equivalent to the quality you get from a VCR, which makes the most interesting point about the data in Table 6-1 — the fact that it's possible to compress video at a ratio of over 100:1 and still get useful images on playback.

Table 6-1 Digital Video Requires Compression to Be Useful in a PC Environment		
Content	*Mbps*	*Minutes per one CD-ROM*
Uncompressed video (CCIT-601 standard digital video is a little slower, at 167 megabits per second)	184.32	0.47
MPEG 1 compressed video	1.50	57.29
MPEG 2 compressed video (MPEG 2 supports variable data rates)	4.00 8.00	21.48 10.74

A variety of video compression technologies are used in personal computers today, but all are related to the framework established by the Motion Picture Experts Group (MPEG). The MPEG 1 and MPEG 2 standards define most MPEG applications, but MPEG 4 is becoming widespread because of its ability to store a full-length movie on a CD-ROM, albeit with quality less than that of a DVD.

The video you see on a television is really a high-speed succession of still frames, each slightly different from the next. MPEG video compression exploits the successive frame structure of video by using a combination of still image compression plus algorithms to exploit the interframe redundancy.

The MPEG still image compression technology uses what's called the Discrete Cosine Transform, or DCT, the same approach used in JPEG image compression. The DCT is based on the idea that a time-varying signal — the sequence of pixels in a line, for instance — can be represented by the sum of a number of signals at different frequencies. Figure 6-7 sketches that idea. The upper graph is a time-varying signal we made by adding two single-frequency signals together. We did a frequency analysis on the composite signal, which produced the lower graph. The two blips in the lower graph occur at the points corresponding to the two signals we added together, and show that one of the two signals was significantly stronger than the other.

Because you can reconstruct the time-varying signal (the image) from the decomposed frequencies, the frequencies (and their amplitudes) are equivalent to the image itself. You lose some still image quality if you omit the highest frequencies when you reconstruct the image, but omitting the highest-frequency information (as JPEG compression does) drastically reduces the size of the stored image, compressing it on disk or over a network.

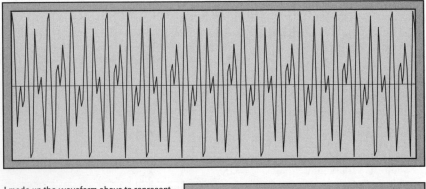

I made up the waveform above to represent a time-varying signal, such as we might see in an image. Although there's a certain regularity, it's not clear what that regularity is.

The frequency analysis at the right reveals that the time-domain signal is really made up of two specific frequencies (the blips in the graph), with one much stronger than the other.

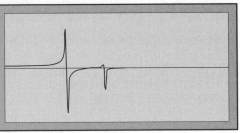

Figure 6-7: Decomposition of a signal into signals of different frequencies

Figure 6-8 shows the intraframe compression process implementing those ideas. The DCT algorithm compresses blocks in the image (rather than the entire image at once) to simplify the computations. After conversion of the image to DCT coefficients, quantization limits the number of bits, exploiting the fact that the eye is more sensitive to the effect of the low-frequency coefficients than the high-frequency ones.

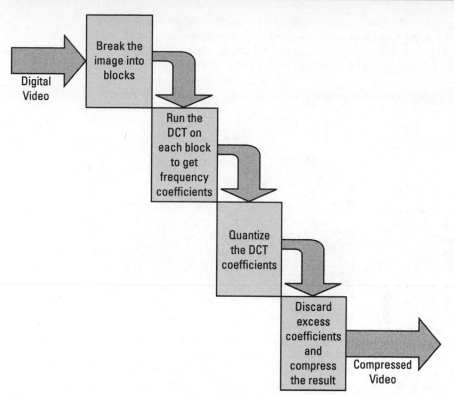

Digital Video

Break the image into blocks

Run the DCT on each block to get frequency coefficients

Quantize the DCT coefficients

Discard excess coefficients and compress the result

Compressed Video

Figure 6-8: MPEG compression discards high-frequency image information.

Manipulating the quantization process allows greater or lesser quality in the compressed image, and in the process requires more or fewer bits in the output data stream.

MPEG compression adds to the JPEG DCT compression by finding and storing just the differences between successive frames. Figure 6-9 shows what happens. The point of the frame structure shown in the figure is to allow the movement of blocks (the same ones that were DCT encoded by intraframe coding) to be specified. I-frames are completely intraframe coded. P-frames specify motion of blocks from the preceding I- or P-frame. B-frames specify motion of blocks from preceding or succeeding B-, P-, or I-frames.

It's possible that a block in a frame can't be found in a preceding or succeeding frame. If so, the block is individually DCT-coded and transmitted in the output sequence.

P-frames – interframes – code the differences from the previous frame, so they depend on the preceding frames. The differences are presented as motion of a coded block from the preceding I-frame or P-frame, so the motion coding process requires finding the best match block in the prior frame and describing how it has moved in the x and y directions. The arrows show the successive relations from I-frame to successive P-frames.

I-frames – intraframes – are ⟶ compressed as self-contained images using DCT techniques.

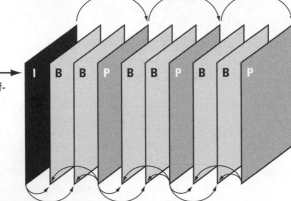

B-frames – bi-directional frames – code the differences from preceding or succeeding frames. The differences are presented as motion of a coded block from the referenced frame. These arrows show the possible B-frame dependencies. The precise I-/B-/P- frame sequence is determined by the encoder, and need not be the IBBPBBPBBP sequence shown here.

Figure 6-9: The frame structure in an MPEG file defines how motion estimation relates successive video frames.

Television in a Window

We have to admit that when we first saw a board that would let us turn part of a computer screen into a television, we didn't believe it. Fun's fun, but we figured we were better off working without television programs in the corner of the screen. In the same way that we didn't see the need to turn a computer into a several-thousand-dollar boom box that plays CDs, we didn't see any point in turning it into an expensive television. In both cases, we were wrong. We didn't anticipate the value of an MP3 library holding literally thousands or tens of thousands of songs, and didn't realize how useful replacing the tape in a VCR with the disk in your computer could be. Adding a TV tuner to your PC lets you create the equivalent of a TiVo personal video recorder, which is the best thing that happened to television since cable and satellite.

A TV tuner decodes the television signal to a video image, then overlays it onscreen in a window. The first TV tuner cards did this by overlaying the analog video signal from the television image on top of the computer display signal, but the products now on the market do the overlay work digitally, sending the television signal out to the video board as a digital pixel stream. The video board updates the video memory with the pixels from the television board. The usual output and digital-to-analog conversion circuits on the video board create the combined signal sent to the monitor. Compressing and writing the digital video to disk implements the video recorder function.

Choosing a Video Card

Choosing a video board is dependent on what you want from your computer and on which manufacturers you have confidence in. Even though video drivers come with Windows, you may still be dependent on the board manufacturer. (For example, we've seen a video board capable of 1600×1200 resolution that was supported only in 1280×1024 resolution by the standard Windows drivers. The manufacturer's enhanced drivers were required to realize the full capability of the board.)

Matching Video Hardware and Software

Many 3D video games use the Microsoft DirectX technology to work with the hardware on the video card. As of early 2004, the current version of DirectX was 9.0b, which was a significant advance over earlier versions. Most significant of the features in DirectX 9 is the ability for developers to create small programs that the video hardware executes for each vertex in the polygon model.

Not all video cards include the hardware and software drivers to support DirectX 9, but the most demanding PC video games (including Microsoft's Halo and Valve's Half-Life 2) require it for the best appearance and performance. Use a video card supporting only a lesser DirectX revision and you should expect poor graphics and slower display rates.

That said, don't forget that the PC video card market is intensely competitive, with both ATI and nVidia doing everything they can to be the leader. Not all those efforts work in your best interest. Manufacturers have been caught tuning their drivers for improved benchmark performance, which has no benefit for game play. Eidos and Ion Storm have explicitly tuned Deus Ex: Invisible War for the nVidia hardware, stupidly buying into an nVidia marketing program, and delivered a game that runs badly on ATI hardware. Worse, in the process, they failed to test their copy protection adequately, and as of patch level 1.1, Eidos admits they have bugs that cause the game to fail to run on the system that you see how to build in Chapter 25.

Keep anti-consumer practices like that in mind when you buy hardware and software.

Video Drivers

Most problems with video cards arise from incompatibilities between the drivers and your software. Although we strongly recommend not updating drivers unless you have a good need to, video drivers are among the most updated software there is.

The most direct way to get updated video drivers for Windows is on the Internet from the card manufacturer's Web site. There are many video card suppliers, but often they just manufacture standard designs by ATI or nVidia. If you have a card based on an ATI or nVidia design, you're probably better off getting drivers directly (www.ati.com and www.nvidia.com, respectively) than from the actual manufacturer.

Manufacturers often don't provide drivers for UNIX systems; contact your UNIX vendor or, if you use a UNIX system with the XFree86 X Window system, look at www.xfree86.org.

Because many video cards use their own specialized drivers, the first thing to do when you're upgrading a video card is to undo anything that's tied to your existing card. In Windows, that means you'll want to change your video driver to the Standard VGA driver, which should work with both your old and new cards. We've also seen driver updates that failed if the prior ones weren't uninstalled, so check that in the Add/Remove Programs applet in the Windows control panel.

Summary

✦ Video images are arrays of dots (pixels) output by the video board.

✦ Higher resolution — more pixels — means closer dot spacing on the monitor, and more work for the video board.

✦ You get more possible colors by using more bytes per pixel, which takes more memory and creates more work for the video board.

✦ Hardware accelerators that take over the work of software can improve video performance.

✦ Realistic 3D displays on your screen require enormous numbers of computations, leading to other opportunities for accelerators to improve performance.

Monitors and Flat Panels

◆ ◆ ◆ ◆

CHAPTER 7

In This Chapter

Understanding flat
panel displays

Examining CRT
specifications

Working with Display
Data Channel

◆ ◆ ◆ ◆

It's easy to say what you want in a monitor. You want
it to be sharp, with bright, clear color. You want what
you see to fill the screen, free of geometric distortions.
You want it to deliver all the capabilities of your
video card.

Getting what you want is more complex. The technical
characteristics of your monitor determine the limits of
the display modes you can get on the screen. Dot pitch
and the horizontal and vertical frequencies or resolution are readily evident, but sharpness, color balance,
distortion measurements, and the rest of the characteristics are harder to specify or measure. Some require
specialized test equipment or software to put up test
displays. Often you can find information on those technical characteristics in product reviews and sometimes
in manufacturer data.

In a dramatic change from the past, there are now two
viable technologies for desktop PC monitors. Cathode
ray tube (CRT) monitors have been the technology of
choice for decades, but are now rapidly being displaced
by the same liquid crystal display (LCD) technology
found in laptop computers. The significance of the
change in the market is so great that many companies
have completely abandoned manufacturing CRT monitors, which are now commodity products, in favor of
LCDs. In this chapter, we look first at the newer flat
panel technology, then cover the characteristics of the
older CRT monitors.

Flat Panel Displays

A flat panel display is the desktop version of the display you find in laptop computers. The advantages of a flat panel are as follows:

✦ Requires less space and less power than a CRT

✦ Has no geometric distortion

✦ May deliver a sharper image

You can build a flat panel display in several ways, of which the most common are plasma panels and liquid crystal displays (LCDs). Plasma panels are used in the relatively large flat televisions now available, while LCDs dominate computer applications.

LCDs and active matrix technology

Most LCD panels use the active matrix technology, with three transistors at each pixel to control colors and a backlight to illuminate the entire array. Figure 7-1 shows how the technology works. When the active matrix transistors are off, the liquid crystal material blocks the transmission of the incident light at the back of the cell (upper drawing). Each transistor in the cell (one per color) can be turned on independently. When a transistor is turned on, it reorients the liquid crystal material and allows white light to pass. A colored filter in front of the transistor blocks all but one color, creating the usual red-green-blue triad making up one pixel (lower drawing).

The LCD panel itself requires very little power, but the backlight requires enough power to be a significant drain in laptop applications. The LCD requires a backlight for operation, and the mean time between failures (MTBF) of the backlight is around 20,000 hours. Backlights are not generally replaceable by users. If you use a flat panel display for long periods, it's quite likely you'll have to have the light replaced.

Changing the image on the display requires physical changes in the cells controlled by the active matrix transistors, changes that slow down and ultimately stop if the panel gets too cold.

Keeping the LCD image sharp

Most desktop LCD panels come with a standard VGA port to interface to standard video display cards. The signals at the VGA port are analog, however, with their per-pixel timing implicit in the dot clock operating in the video card. That approach works relatively well for CRTs because mistiming simply spills the beam over into the next pixel, but can cause fuzziness on a LCD, which has to reconstruct the digital signal to switch the active matrix transistors.

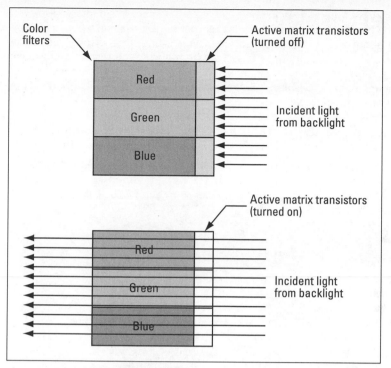

Figure 7-1: An active matrix LCD

Recognizing this limitation, Intel, Compaq (now HP), Fujitsu, Hewlett-Packard, IBM, NEC, and Silicon Image formed the Digital Display Working Group (DDWG) to standardize a digital interface between PCs, consumer electronic devices, and digital displays. The result of that work is the Digital Visual Interface (DVI) specification. DVI includes the Plug and Play features of the Display Data Channel (DDC) interface for analog monitors (see the section "Display Data Channel," later in this chapter) and can support flat panel resolutions up to 1920×1080 with the basic interface cable defined in the specification.

In a CRT, low-resolution formats simply extend the timing of each dot, allowing the beam to cover multiple pixels. In an LCD, however, the dots are in fixed positions, and digital processing is required to display an image of lower resolution than the panel's native size display. The two ways to do this are:

✦ **Use part of the panel** — You can display the smaller image using just part of the panel, centering the image with an unused border. Each dot occupies just one pixel on the panel, so the image is as sharp as possible, but many pixels remain unused.

✦ **Scale the image to fit the panel** — Alternatively, you can resample the image to create more pixels, interpolating between dots to generate the intervening pixel data. The resampling approach uses all the pixels on the display, but leaves the edges in the image somewhat fuzzy.

Tip

Either way, the image won't be as large and as sharp as an image displayed at the panel's native resolution. It's for that reason that some laptops warn you about a loss of sharpness when you change the display resolution down from its maximum setting. If you're reducing the resolution to make the text on the display larger, try using Windows' large fonts setting instead (Control Panel ➪ Display ➪ Settings ➪ Advanced ➪ General; it's the Font Size drop-down list).

DVI-enabled flat panels and video cards have connectors like that shown in Figure 7-2. If you have a choice between DVI and standard VGA, use the DVI connection.

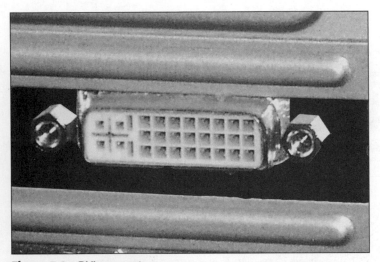

Figure 7-2: DVI connector
©2004 Barry Press & Marcia Press

LCD monitors are typically specified in terms of viewable diagonal, interfaces, brightness, contrast, and viewing angle. Buying an LCD panel is much like buying a monitor — see the unit in operation and (assuming they're all optimally adjusted) look for the ones that are sharp and bright, with good color and contrast. Software such as DisplayMate (www.displaymate.com) can help you evaluate LCDs (and CRTs) before you buy and help you tune your system for peak video quality.

The Samsung line of desktop LCDs illustrates what you can get as of late 2003. You can get LCD panels with both analog (VGA) and digital (DVI) inputs from 15 inches viewable diagonal measurement to 24 inches, and resolutions from 1024×768 to 1920×1200, respectively; and if you're not on a limited budget, they have a giant 40-inch model, too. LCD pricing is driven by the number of pixels in the glass more than the size of the panel; in late 2003, the sweet spot was the 17-, 18-, and 19-inch displays with 1280×1024 resolution. Street prices for those models at that time were from $580 to $610, which isn't much of a difference. Those prices will move down further, and as production methods and volumes improve, prices for even larger, higher resolution LCDs will come down, too.

CRT Specifications and Measurements

Although less expensive, CRT monitors are more complex than LCDs. The technical characteristics that define your monitor's performance are focus and convergence; color balance, tracking, purity, and saturation; ghosting; and geometry.

Focus and convergence

A CRT monitor uses triangles of three-color dots filling the screen (or lines grouped in tri-color sets in the case of monitors using the Sony Trinitron tube). How the beams inside the picture tube illuminate those dots determines how well the monitor can generate crisp edges on what it draws, rather than blobs with colored halos at the edges. Figure 7-3 shows how this works. The phosphors on the cathode ray tube (CRT) surface — the red, green, and blue dots — are in groups of three called triads. Each triad has one corresponding hole in the shadow mask. The hole keeps the beam from an electron gun from illuminating the wrong color phosphors.

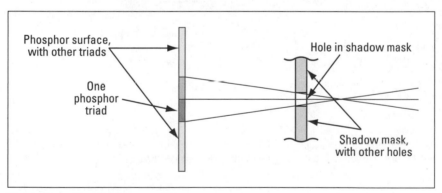

Figure 7-3: The shadow mask

Three separate electron beams exist: one for red, one for green, and one for blue. All three go through the same hole in the shadow mask for the same triad; but, because the electron guns are offset in a triangle around the centerline of the CRT, the pattern of the beams through the shadow mask — the "shadow" — is itself a triangle. If the beams from the electron guns are precisely focused, they project dots onto the phosphor layer no bigger than the dots themselves, and don't overlap onto adjacent triads. Lining up the individual beams through the shadow mask is called *convergence*. If the aim of the electron beams onto the phosphors, through the shadow mask, is precise, each beam illuminates only its own color dot. Misconvergence shows up as miscolored edges on lines and in areas.

You see poor focus on the screen as fuzziness because adjacent triads get some illumination from the beam and light up. A poorly focused monitor can't form a one-pixel edge.

Misconvergence and poor focus most often show up at the corners and edges of the screen, or in the center if the corners and edges are right. Figure 7-4 shows why this happens. The extensive bend required in the electron beam to reach the sides and corners of the tube tends to distort the beam, which in turn requires the electronics to adapt to correct the distortion. If the electronics do this badly, they distort the beam in the center and force you to compromise by setting the controls for a place between the center and the outside. As a result, neither area ends up in focus or well converged on the monitor.

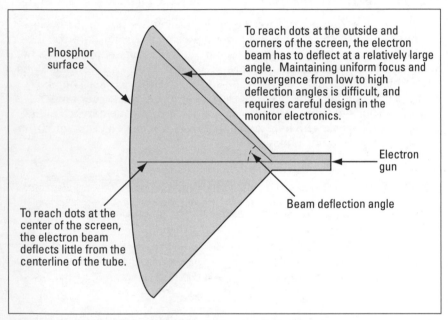

Figure 7-4: Shorter CRTs make the electronics design harder.

The flat-face CRTs now available further complicate the electronics because the focal length from the electron gun varies as the beam sweeps both vertically and horizontally, requiring additional controls to modulate the focus coils correspondingly.

Another cause of poor image quality can be poor design of the shadow mask. The electron beam carries a certain amount of power, some of which is absorbed by the shadow mask. The shadow mask heats up as a result, which can cause it to distort if it's not well constructed. This means you'll want to look at a monitor's performance after it's been on for a while as well as when it's cold, and also when you have the brightness and contrast cranked up (which increases the heat load on the shadow mask).

Tip

The brightness and contrast your monitor delivers is the result of a balancing act with the sharpness of focus and accuracy of convergence. A brighter image is the result of more power in the electron beam, which is harder for the electronics to control. This means that you should check focus and convergence with the brightness at its maximum useful setting. This doesn't mean all the way up; it means at the brightest point you'd actually set it to. For many monitors, that's the point just before the black areas start to turn gray, with the contrast adjusted to its maximum useful point. That's as difficult as it's going to get for the monitor, so if it handles well at that adjustment, it should be okay at lower levels as well.

Another important element to check on the monitor is its antiglare treatment because different monitors have different antiglare treatments. Some use coatings on the face of the CRT, some use lenses, and some roughen the face of the CRT. Most antiglare approaches degrade the sharp focus a little, so you'll want to see how the manufacturer balanced these elements.

Color balance, tracking, purity, and saturation

Your eye is sensitive to color relationships. Skin tones that are off-color draw your eye. A monitor needs to achieve good color balance to look right. It has to maintain the correct intensity relationship between red, green, and blue.

The characteristics of the electronics in the monitor are such that the color balance tends to vary with brightness. Having the monitor balance on a bright image doesn't mean that it will remain balanced on dark ones. The electronics may not maintain good color tracking as the brightness varies. Check for balance both on bright areas and in dark grays because of this limitation. Your video card may have adjustments for color balance, but overall you want the monitor to get the balance and tracking right. Color balance on the video card is most useful for adjustments to get screen and printer colors to correspond. If the monitor is off-balance, you may not have the necessary range of adjustments available.

Good color saturation means that colors are neither too strong, with similar colors being indistinguishable, nor washed out and faded. The difference is the same as when you run the color saturation control back and forth on a color television. At one end, colors wash out to black and white, while at the other end colors are sharply defined like those on a poster, with no intermediate color tones.

Color purity means that the colors on the screen are uniform everywhere, with no patches of odd color. The most common causes of purity problems are unwanted magnetic fields deflecting the beams on their way to the shadow mask, through the shadow mask, and to the phosphors. This can happen two ways: a device outside the monitor can create a magnetic field that reaches into the tube, or the shadow mask can become partially magnetized.

Incident static magnetic fields

A surprising number of things can create static magnetic fields, including power transformers, telephones, speakers, and (of course) magnets. Don't forget that magnets and power transformers can be inside other objects. Their magnetic fields can extend through an unshielded or poorly shielded equipment case and into your monitor. If they do, one of two consequences can happen: you get local discolorations, or you get a ripple in the image on the screen.

If the problem is a static magnetic field, such as from a magnet or a speaker (which contains a magnet), it can slowly magnetize the shadow mask (see Figure 7-5). The problem is that the permanent magnet must provide a strong, stable magnetic field for the voice coils to push against. If the speaker isn't shielded, or is shielded poorly, that magnetic field reaches outside the speaker. If the speaker is placed too close to your monitor, it can reach into the CRT. When that happens, it starts to magnetize the shadow mask. Magnetization of the shadow mask can distort the color and the focus in the affected parts of the tube.

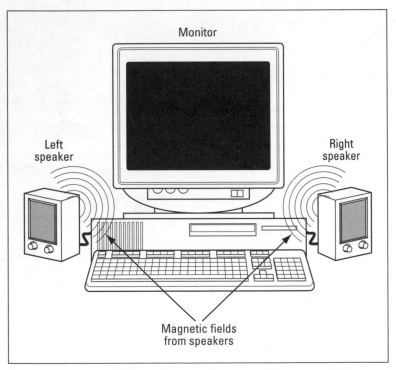

Figure 7-5: Magnets in speakers can discolor or blur your monitor.

A device called a degaussing coil inside the monitor is wound around the tube and activated every time you turn on the monitor. This device tries to neutralize residual magnetization of the shadow mask by these constant fields, but it's only so strong and can do only so much. Over time, the shadow mask can acquire a local magnetic field that discolors the display in that region. We've also had the combination of a field from speakers and the action of the degaussing coil combine to leave no residual field, so that when we removed the speakers, discolorations appeared in the corners of the display that had been near the speakers.

Your options are to use well-shielded speakers, or to keep the speakers well away from the front of the CRT. The safe distance depends on the speaker and on the shielding in the monitor itself. Moving the speakers to the back of the monitor helps, as well as spacing them laterally away from the monitor case.

> **Tip**
> You can check a monitor for color-purity problems by looking at a pure white screen. (For example, set the document background color to white, open an empty document in Word, and use the View ➪ Full Screen command. More comprehensive tests are available in DisplayMate.) If you see patches of faint color, the monitor may need to be degaussed with a strong degaussing coil. Degaussing is an operation involving passing a strong alternating magnetic field past the entire screen. Over tens of seconds, you slowly move the coil far away from the tube and then turn it off. You can get degaussing coils at larger electronics supply stores, or on the Internet — search Google for *degaussing coil*. Follow the directions that come with the coil carefully because you can make things worse if you use it improperly.

Incident dynamic fields

Varying magnetic fields too near your monitor can cause the image to be wavy. A common source of such fields is power transformers: devices that use magnetic fields to shift power from one form to another. If you find one part of the display vibrating back and forth on the screen, look for other electronic components (wall transformers, uninterruptible power supplies, boom boxes, neighboring monitors in a multiple-monitor setup, and so forth) that are close to the monitor and see what happens when you move them away.

Ghosting

As the electron beam sweeps along a line, the video amplifiers in the monitor have to pass an intensity signal to the beam so that each pixel is painted at the right intensity. If the bandwidth the video passes is too small, the intensity signal can't change fast enough, producing ghosts — shadows and streaking of the on-screen image. The strength of the ghost image depends on how intense the original image is. A small change may not create a noticeable ghost, but a black-to-white vertical edge can create highly noticeable shadows.

> **Tip**
> The relevant capability of the video amplifier is called the maximum video bandwidth and is typically in the range of 50 to 150 megahertz (MHz). An acceptable maximum video bandwidth is implied by a manufacturer specification that the monitor will handle the resolution you want. To be sure that it does meet your requirements, look at a maximum-resolution display with alternating black and white bars. If you see ghosting (and the monitor cable hasn't been extended), the video bandwidth is inadequate and you should find another monitor.

You can also cause ghosting by using a cable that's too long or is of poor quality. Capacitance in the cable slows the rise and fall of the video signals, leading to ghosts. Cables that are too long can have too much capacitance because the effect increases with the cable length; poor quality cables (even short ones) can have too much capacitance because every foot adds more capacitance than for high quality ones.

Geometric distortion

For the image you see onscreen to look right, it has to be geometrically correct, straight, even, and flat. Figure 7-6 shows the distortions CRT monitors are prone to creating. (LCDs have the pixels in physically fixed positions, so these distortions can't happen.) Each of the problems in Figure 7-6 can be corrected with the right electronics and adjustments on the front of the monitor, but if your monitor doesn't provide the controls you need, you're stuck with whatever it does on its own. Monitor test software like DisplayMate is useful for adjusting geometric distortions because it displays test patterns that allow you to see and remove these errors.

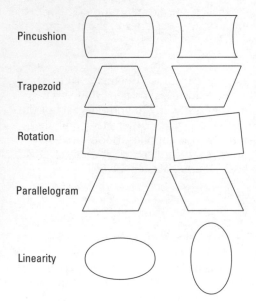

Pincushion — Pincushion distortion means the edges of the display image curve in or out, rather than being straight.

Trapezoid — Trapezoid distortion means that the top and bottom of the display widths are not the same.

Rotation — Rotational distortion means that the raster scan lines tilt up or down, rather than being flat.

Parallelogram — Parallelogram distortion causes the top and bottom edges of the raster to be laterally offset from each other.

Linearity — Linearity means that pixels are evenly spaced and in the proper proportion. Circles will be circles, not ovals.

Figure 7-6: Geometric distortion

Controls

There's no apparent consensus on what controls you really need on a monitor. Some monitors have only contrast and brightness controls, and others have a complete set of controls letting you adjust everything. You can find controls with simple, clear layouts, and ones that would leave a genius hard pressed to figure out how to use them. A great image is more important than great controls, but the controls may be what you need to get the image you want.

A good monitor stores control settings independently for each resolution, so you don't have to keep readjusting the controls. The typical controls you find on CRT monitors include:

✦ **Horizontal size and position** — This control adjusts the width of the raster on the screen and lets you center the image laterally. You'll find that both the horizontal and vertical characteristics of the image change as you change display resolution and refresh rate, so you need these controls to compensate. You'll also find that the horizontal and vertical settings interact with each other, so get them both close to right before trying to set them to their final positions.

✦ **Vertical size and position** — These controls are similar to the ones for horizontal size and position, letting you set the height and top-to-bottom position.

✦ **Pincushion** — A pincushion control lets you vary the bulge or tuck at the side of the raster. The setting applies to all resolutions and refresh rates. Be sure that you have the horizontal and vertical settings right before you adjust pincushion; otherwise, you're almost guaranteed to get the setting wrong.

Be careful how you decide if the edges are straight. The bezel of the monitor surrounding the tube is not always itself straight, so it may not work well for this process. What you use can be as simple as a piece of paper folded to make a straight edge. Be sure the image displayed on the screen completely fills the screen. A maximized window works because you can use the window frame as the reference line that should be straight.

✦ **Tilt, rotation, and trapezoid** — These controls work in the same way as the pincushion control, but they relate to other distortions. The same caution applies about getting the horizontal and vertical settings right first. You're also likely to notice that the four settings interact some, so you might have to adjust them several times before you get it right.

✦ **Color temperature** — If you've ever played with a light dimmer, you've probably noticed that as the light gets dimmer, it gets redder, and as it gets brighter, it gets bluer. This change in color, which affects the perceived color of objects illuminated by the light, corresponds to a change in the temperature of the filament in the light, or what's called the color temperature. Color temperature is measured in degrees Kelvin — relative to absolute zero — with lower temperatures giving redder colors. Monitors with color temperature adjustments provide settings for several standard temperatures, such as 9300 and 6500 degrees Kelvin, and may provide a user-defined setting. The color temperature interacts some with color balance (which you normally adjust on the video card, if at all) because the effect is to alter the balance between red and blue.

The color temperature can be very important if you're doing critical color matching to make sure that the results you get on the screen correspond to what you scan and what you print; otherwise, it's a matter of personal preference.

✦ **Brightness and contrast** — Although most of the other controls on a monitor correspond to those a service technician sets on a television, the brightness and contrast are exactly the same as you're used to. The two controls interact somewhat and have limited range on some monitors. It's common to adjust the contrast at around 80 percent of the full range (or more), with brightness just below the point where the raster outside the image appears, but many people find this setting too harsh. The setting you use is personal preference, influenced by the lighting and other characteristics of where you work.

✦ **Degauss** — In the same way that magnetic fields from speakers and transformers can leave the shadow mask with residual magnetism, so can other weaker fields. Most monitors have a coil wound around the tube near the front, called a degaussing coil, that is used to remove these effects. When you turn the monitor on, a strong alternating current in the coil produces a strong alternating magnetic field that penetrates the tube and slightly magnetizes the shadow mask, first one way and then the other. Over several seconds, the monitor reduces the current, reducing the field strength as it alternates back and forth. By the time the field reaches zero, the process leaves the shadow mask completely demagnetized.

There's a limit to the strength of the degaussing coil, partly due to the relatively large current flowing through it. That current generates a lot of heat, too much of which will destroy the coil. For this reason, if your monitor has a manual control to energize the coil, you don't want to use it too often. Waiting several minutes between activations should be long enough. If the built-in degaussing coil can't clear the problem after a few tries, you probably need to go get a stronger coil.

Another useful control feature is the capability for the monitor to display the current horizontal and vertical frequencies. Most current monitor designs will blank when they see an invalid signal. Many units will also blank when they see a signal they can't handle. You want that feature to make sure a misconfigured video card can't damage the monitor.

Multimedia Monitors

It's become fashionable to build speakers into monitors and offer them at higher prices as multimedia products. The same strategy seems to apply to power controllers (devices you put under the monitor that have switches to control the power for different peripherals) and keyboards.

We don't recommend buying these products. Packaging the speaker into the monitor ensures that its magnetic field is as close to the display tube as possible. Even if the manufacturer shields it well, you're starting out with a difficult problem. Speakers in monitors tend to use smaller magnets and amplifiers, and so have limited bass response. Speakers in power controllers and keyboards suffer from limited size, making it hard to get good sound, too.

You can also get speakers that are designed to hang from either side of your monitor. Mounting them there ensures they're right where they can cause the most trouble, up near the shadow mask and as close as possible to the tube. If you need that arrangement to maximize desk space, make sure you choose units that move the low-frequency drivers into a subwoofer you can put some-where else. If you can't do that, it's better to space your speakers somewhat away from and toward the back of the monitor (or on the wall).

Display Data Channel

The Display Data Channel (DDC) is a way for your computer to get information about your monitor — CRT or LCD — and its capabilities. DDC-compatible monitors can feed that information to a DDC-capable video card, which in turn forwards the information to your operating system. Windows knows how to use DDC information if you set up your monitor as Plug and Play compatible; Linux may not. Plug and Play software can detect and configure your monitor automatically, simplifying setup.

There are three levels of DDC implementation, DDC1, DDC2B, and DDC2AB, as shown in Figure 7-7A through 7-7C, respectively. All three let the monitor send data in a specific format to the computer, making it possible for Plug and Play software to detect what the monitor is and configure the video card appropri-ately. The DDC2AB version also lets the computer send commands to the mon-itor, allowing software to set the monitor controls just as you would from the front panel controls.

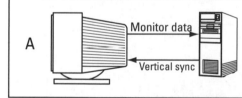

A — Monitor data → / Vertical sync ← : The DDCI interface lets the monitor continuously transmit information about its capabilities. The data always comes in a specific format — the computer can't stop it or control it.

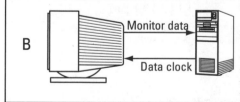

B — Monitor data → / Data clock ← : The DDC2B interface can't control the monitor, but it allows the computer to request one of two data formats for the information continuously transmitted by the monitor. The data clock signal adds this capability, and allows the computer to control the data transmission from the monitor.

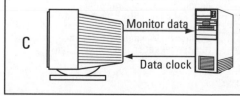

C — Monitor data → / Data clock ← : The DDC2AB interface creates a two-way control interface between the monitor and the computer, allowing the computer to request specific information and to send commands to the monitor.

Figure 7-7: The three levels of DDC implementation

Making DDC work requires both the monitor and video card to be DDC-capable, but results in a fully Plug and Play video subsystem.

Choosing a Monitor

We recommend monitors 17 inches or larger. LCDs should have native resolution no less than 1280×1024; CRTs should have a dot pitch no greater than 0.28 millimeters. The added screen space you get from the higher resolution those monitors provide lets you work more effectively. You can find CRT monitors with worse dot pitch, such as the 0.31 millimeter dot pitch 20-inch unit we once saw advertised as a "corporate grade" unit. If you do the side-by-side comparison with higher-quality monitors, you'll quickly see the loss of sharpness and understand why working with one of these units can be uncomfortable.

Tip
People with vision impairments that require they use large screens in the minimum possible resolution should use CRT monitors, not LCDs, because a CRT gives you a sharper image at low resolutions.

Glare off the screen and directly in your eyes can make an image hard to look at no matter how you adjust the display. Try to avoid the situations illustrated in Figures 7-8A and 7-8B to keep glare to a minimum. Light shining directly on the screen or in your eyes reduces contrast and can make working very uncomfortable. Figure 7-8C shows more desirable arrangements.

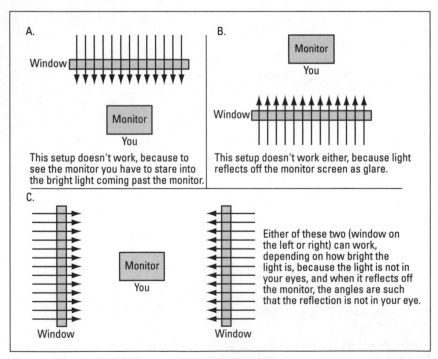

Figure 7-8: Placing the monitor to minimize glare

Summary

✦ LCD monitors need fewer adjustments than CRT monitors, but can lose quality at lower image sizes than the native display panel size.

✦ A monitor with a comprehensive set of controls can be made to perform better than the same monitor with few controls.

✦ Most users will do well with a good quality 17- to 19-inch monitor. Some types of work benefit from larger monitors and, therefore, benefit from the added cost.

Storage

◆   ◆   ◆   ◆

In This Part

Chapter 8
Hard Disks and
Disk Arrays

Chapter 9
CD and DVD

Chapter 10
Removable Storage

◆   ◆   ◆   ◆

Hard Disks and Disk Arrays

◆   ◆   ◆   ◆

In This Chapter

Estimating disk
performance — transfer
rate and latency

Understanding disk
reliability — Mean time
between failures (MTBF)

Redundant Array of
Inexpensive Disks (RAID)

◆   ◆   ◆   ◆

Many technologies go into building the high-performance disk drives we use. They include the
magnetic effects that pack data onto the platters, the
design and construction of the heads themselves, the
precision with which the platters themselves are built,
and the electronics that turn small signals off the disk
heads into data for your computer.

As interesting as they are, however, these don't matter
from the standpoint of choosing the disk products you'll
put in your computer. What you really care about are
capacity, performance, reliability, and price. The large
volume of disks manufactured and sold to the personal
computer market ensures that you can base your buying decisions on actual field experience, not projections,
so the underlying technology is less important than
what's being delivered in users' machines.

Disks all use a common geometrical layout, as in Figure
8-1. They record data on magnetized platters at precisely defined head positions. At each position, each
head traces out a *track* as the disk rotates. Tracks are
divided into units of data, called *sectors*, that can be
individually read and written. All the tracks at a single
head position collectively form a *cylinder*.

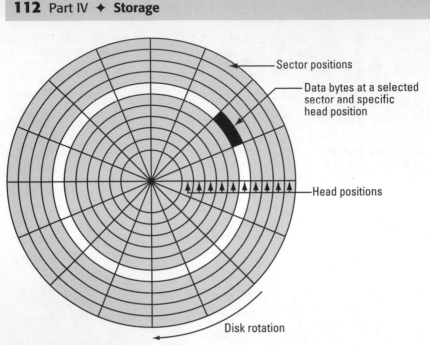

Figure 8-1: The data in one pie-shaped cut under one head position is a sector on a disk.

Capacity is reasonably straightforward: It's how many gigabytes the disk holds. You have to be careful to look at the capacity of the drive after it's been formatted (which is what most drive manufacturers specify). The formatting operation eats up space for sector addresses, space between sectors, and the like, and that's space you can't get at or use. Disk manufacturers most commonly specify capacity as the formatted capacity of the drive, but divide by 1,000,000,000 to convert to gigabytes, not 1,073,741,824 (1,024×1,024×1,024) as do Windows and UNIX. A 200GB drive sold by the manufacturer will report as 186.26GB when you look at it through the operating system.

 Note In case you're wondering, the number 1,024 shows up in a lot of computer-related places because it's the power of 2 closest to 1,000.

Table 8-1 shows Seagate's estimates of how much storage you need for different things you'll do with a PC.

Table 8-1
PC Storage Requirements

Application	*Average Storage Required*
1 minute standard definition-quality TV video clip	10MB
1 full CD-ROM	700MB
12 hours of MP3 audio files	1GB
62 rolls of low-resolution digital film	2GB

Application	Average Storage Required
Installation of Windows XP, Microsoft Office, Quicken, Netscape Navigator	2.5GB
Audiophile digitized music library	6GB
6 feature-length video movies	12GB
1,800 digital images, 4 hours digital video, 40 hours MP3 music, 15 games, 25 applications	100GB

Table courtesy of Seagate Technology

Disk Drive Performance

The most important factor in disk drive performance is throughput on and off the disk, as measured in your PC. That's not possible for manufacturers to measure, so they specify a number of parameters you can use to estimate the performance you'll see:

✦ **Sustained throughput** — For reasonably large transfers, such as loading programs from disk or reading/writing the swap file, disk performance is limited by the sustained throughput onto or off the disk itself. The rotation rate of the disk times the number of sectors per track determines the sustained throughput.

✦ **Seek and rotational latency** — For short transfers of data not in the disk cache, the performance you get is determined by the time it takes to move the head to the right cylinder and for the right sector to rotate under the heads. A faster rotation rate reduces the rotational latency.

✦ **Cache buffer size** — The cache buffer on the drive can strongly affect the performance you get. Predicting the effect of different cache sizes is hard, but you can assume in general that a bigger cache is better as long as you remember this is not always true.

The sustained throughput in bytes per second is the number of bytes in a sector times the number of sectors per track times the track rotations per second. The data sheet for the 200GB Seagate Barracuda (which spins at 7,200 RPM) explicitly specifies the average sustained transfer rate, listing it as greater than 58 megabytes per second. That number is amazing when you consider that only a few years ago you had to exercise care to get a disk fast enough for video recording at 4 to 8 megabytes per second.

Disk manufacturers sometimes don't specify the sustained throughput of the disk explicitly, but if some other specifications are available, you can calculate it. The average sustained transfer rate equals the rotation rate times average sectors per track times 512 bytes per sector. Disk manufacturers put more sectors on the outer tracks of the platter (because they're larger and have more space), so there's no one number for sectors per track. You can use the minimum number, the maximum, or the average. As long as you compare rates you compute consistently, it doesn't matter.

For small transfers, the time to get the heads positioned over the right sector is much larger than the time to actually transfer the data. The drawing in Figure 8-2 shows the timeline for a disk access and, by the length of the segment, indicates that the positioning time can be enormously longer than the actual transfer time. The average seek time is commonly specified by the disk manufacturer and depends on the physical design of the heads and the actuator mechanism that mounts and moves the heads. The lighter (and by implication smaller) the heads and mechanism, the faster they can start and stop moving, and the smaller the seek time will be.

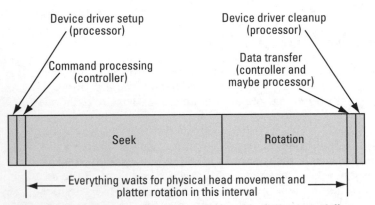

Figure 8-2: The time to transfer small data blocks is essentially the time to position the heads over the data.

The rotational latency isn't always specified, but if you know the rotation rate, you can calculate the delay. On average, the disk is positioned one half of a revolution away from the data you want, in which case the average rotational latency is one half of the rotation time. For a typical 7,200 RPM drive, the rotation time is about 8.3 ms (calculated as the reciprocal of the rotation rate), so the average rotational latency is half the rotation time, or about 4.2 ms in our example. If the average seek time is 9 ms, the total average access time — the time it takes from when the drive gets the command to read to when it starts delivering data — is the sum of the two, or 13.2 ms.

The access time is a useful number because it lets you predict the random access performance of the drive. The 13.2 ms access implies that you can do about 76 random transfers per second because you have about 76 13.2 ms intervals in 1 second, and you're assuming all the time is taken by the seeks. If you're transferring single sectors at 512 bytes per transfer, that's a transfer rate of only 38KB per second, which is pretty awful. Even though Windows transfers a cluster at a time, which would typically be 4KB on a drive like this, a database program might use only one sector in the cluster. If that's true, the additional data transferred is wasted, and the 38KB per second represents usable data transfer.

This analysis shows why the operating system disk cache is so critical and why the value of a disk cache goes up as the size of the reads your programs do goes down. Operating systems dynamically size the disk cache in memory based on disk activity and on how much memory your programs need. If programs need all the available memory, the cache can get too small, and performance can drop precipitously. You have to have more memory than just what your programs are specified to require if there's going to be room for the cache — that's part of why more memory can provide a significant performance boost to machines with limited memory.

Disk Drive Reliability

If you go looking at disk drive data sheets, you'll see that manufacturers no longer boast Mean time between failures (MTBF) specifications in the product data sheets. Nevertheless, if you search their Web sites, you'll see more detailed product specifications and find MTBF values from 500,000 to 1,500,000 hours. If you leave the drive powered up and running all the time, this is between 57 and 170 years.

No one is likely to use the same disk that long, so it's worth asking why anyone worries about disk failures. MTBF is really only a measure of the probability that a device will fail, one you can use to estimate how likely it is that the device will run for a specified amount of time without failure. The conversion from MTBF to probability of failure is not an obvious computation; Figure 8-3 shows the probability a device will survive a stated length of time for different MTBF values. For example, the probability that a disk with an MTBF of 1,200,000 hours will go 5 years without a failure is over 96 percent. Said differently, if you have a large number of these drives, after 5 years you can expect nearly one drive in 25 to have failed. In practice, you'll probably do better than that because these calculations assume the drive is powered on 24 hours a day.

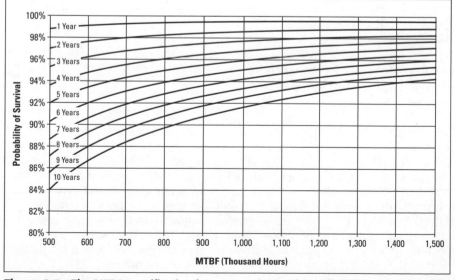

Figure 8-3: The MTBF specification lets you estimate the probability a device will last a specified lifetime.

If you conclude from this analysis that eventually you're going to see a hard disk failure, you're undoubtedly right. (Yes, now might be a good time to go back up your computer if you can't remember when you did it last. Check that your restores work, too.) Rare as they are, disk failures are some of the worst computer failures from a lost time standpoint, because in addition to the time it takes you to diagnose the problem and replace the drive, you have to find the backups, restore them, and worry about the data that wasn't backed up.

If you knew a drive was going to fail, though, you could grab the important files before it died. The Self-Monitoring Analysis and Reporting Technology (SMART) helps you do that, monitoring critical drive performance parameters in the disk's controller. When one of the parameters degrades past a threshold, the drive reports out to your computer that a failure may be pending. That report is your warning to back up data carefully and replace the drive. Figure 8-4 shows how a drive that monitors the height the head flies above the platter responds to variations in flying height. If the height gets too high, the signal the head generates weakens and the error rate off the drive skyrockets. If the head gets too low, it hits the surface and damages the drive. The dotted lines in the figure represent the alert thresholds, at which the drive reports it has a problem.

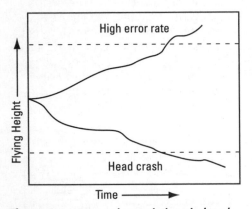

Figure 8-4: Measuring variations in head flying height helps predict disk failures.
Drawing courtesy of IBM

Other typical characteristics SMART watches include data throughput of the drive; time for the drive to spin up to operating speed; the number of sectors declared defective during operation and remapped to other, good sectors; and the frequency with which errors occur while the heads are seeking a new position. SMART is not infallible — disk failures can occur on a SMART drive without warning because there are both predictable and unpredictable failures. Predictable failures are preceded by gradual degradation of some parameter before the failure and are more common for mechanical failures in the drive. According to Seagate, 60 percent of drive failures are for mechanical reasons, so in practice, SMART gives good coverage of coming trouble.

Redundant Array of Inexpensive Disks (RAID)

Capacity, reliability, and performance are important for file servers or other machines where you're storing large or important files. Disk drives are vulnerable to failure, though, and when they do fail, data written since the last backup is lost. Disks have limitations on how fast they can go, although disk speed is only a limitation for heavily loaded servers.

Suppose you, like us, make DVDs instead of video tapes of your favorite shows. We record uncompressed video at about 13.5GB per 1-hour show, editing it down to 9.5GB before compressing it onto DVD. The total space is therefore 23GB per hour. The biggest drives available always come at premium prices, but you can buy 80GB drives readily at good prices. Unfortunately, you'll get less than 4 hours on an 80GB drive before you have to start making DVDs.

You can get much greater capacities, avoid losing data from disk failure, and do all that at reasonable cost using a technology called Redundant Array of Inexpensive Disks (RAID), invented at the University of California at Berkeley by D. A. Patterson, G. Gibson, and R. H. Katz. The industry also uses the phrase Redundant Array of Independent Disks, so you'll probably see both. RAID uses conventional disks with specialized host adapters to change how data goes onto your disk.

What RAID does

The idea behind RAID is to take the conventional disks in personal computers and gang them together in parallel. The resulting assembly gives you the low cost of disks manufactured in high volume plus good reliability and a multiplier on the performance of individual disks. Figure 8-5 shows how this works. The host adapter (frequently called a controller in RAID systems) sits between one high-rate data stream (on the computer side) and several lower-rate streams (on the disk side). When the computer writes to the disk, the host adapter takes high-rate data and breaks it into multiple synchronized streams, one for each disk, in a process called striping. Reads by the computer cause the host adapter to take a data stream from each disk, multiplex the set of streams into one stream, and send that resulting stream on to the computer. In the example of Figure 8-5, the one high-speed stream splits into four separate disk data streams at one-fourth the rate of the combined stream.

A RAID controller can also insert error correction codes. In an eight-disk RAID system, for example, you can add a ninth disk to hold nothing but error correction information. Any of the disks in a system built that way can fail without loss of data. When you replace the failed disk, most RAID controllers can reconstruct the contents of the disk from the surviving ones. Until that process is complete, however, your data is vulnerable to a second failure. Nor does RAID eliminate the need for backup. RAID cannot protect you, for example, from a catastrophic software (or user) error that destroys your file systems or deletes important files. You need removable backup media as well as reliable storage for irreplaceable files.

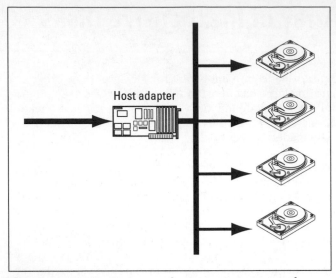

Figure 8-5: RAID arrays can give you vast amounts of storage and great reliability.

RAID levels

There are six different levels of RAID functionality. The simplest RAID system, RAID level 0, merely stripes the data onto multiple disks for better performance. There is no overhead for redundant data storage and no protection against failure. The highest level is RAID 5, which provides both striping for performance and redundancy for failure protection.

RAID level 0

RAID 0 was not part of the original RAID specification by Patterson *et al*, but instead was created by the industry to meet user needs. RAID level 0 spreads the data stream across multiple disks, as in Figure 8-6. You can get a similar effect to that of RAID 0 by having multiple disks and can use features in Windows 2000 or Windows XP to simulate RAID in the operating system.

Suppose your computer sends a sequence of data to a RAID 0 host adapter connected to two disks. The host adapter will interleave the data to the two drives, sending odd blocks to one drive and even blocks to the other. The block size is up to the host adapter and can be a byte, a sector, or some other size.

Because the data volume and rate to any specific disk is a fraction of the aggregate, you get better capacity and performance from RAID 0 than from a single conventional disk. There is no error correction or redundant data written to the array, however, so RAID 0 cannot survive a disk failure. You would use RAID 0 only in situations where you needed the capacity or performance gain, but not the enhanced data reliability. Be certain about the reliability issue, however — suppose you have a RAID 0 array of four 80GB drives that's full, and you lose one of the drives. You haven't lost 80GB of data; you've lost 320GB because your data was spread across all four drives and you have no way to reconstruct the files.

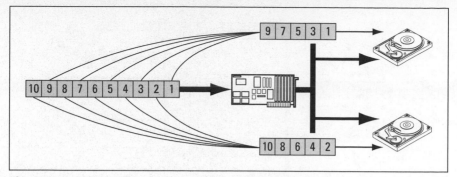

Figure 8-6: RAID 0 offers better performance than conventional disk setups, but does not enhance reliability.

The performance of RAID 0 is usually better for long reads and writes than short random requests because the rotation of the individual disks isn't synchronized. When the processor starts a read operation, for example, data can't start to arrive from the controller until all the disks rotate to the proper sector. The access time is therefore not the average, but the worst case position of all the disks in the array. A large cache memory on the RAID controller partially masks the effect.

You'll see in Chapter 25 how to set up a RAID 0 array in a desktop machine using two serial ATA drives and hardware built into the Intel D875PBZ motherboard. We've measured sequential read performance on that system in excess of 60MB per second on that hardware, and sequential writes at over 70MB per second.

RAID level 1

In the same way that RAID 0 focuses solely on capacity and performance with no concession to reliability, RAID 1 focuses on reliable data storage with no concession to capacity or performance. RAID 1, also called *disk mirroring*, uses disks in pairs with both disks of a pair storing the identical data. The redundant copy protects your data against hardware failures, but you're still vulnerable to user error deleting important files.

Figure 8-7 shows how RAID 1 works. Suppose your computer sends a sequence of data to the RAID 1 host adapter connected to two disks. The host adapter will write all the data to each of the two drives. The identical data is stored on both drives, so if one fails, the data is still available. The operation completes when both drives have written the data, so the write can take longer than for one disk alone because of delays for unsynchronized rotation and for I/O bus contention.

A smart host adapter can make RAID 1 faster for read operations than conventional systems because it can read data from either disk. If the operating system makes multiple read requests at the same time, the host adapter can have two reads in process at the same time, allowing the seek and rotational latency of the drives to overlap each other and delivering two operations worth of data after a single latency delay.

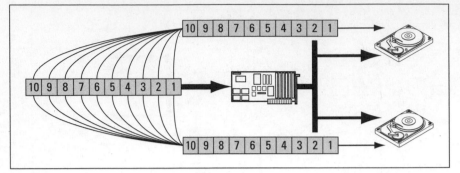

Figure 8-7: RAID 1 offers better reliability than RAID 0 or conventional disk setups, but does not increase performance.

RAID 1 is also supported by software in Windows 2000 and Windows XP, using a pair of disks as mirrors and doing all operations to both at the same time. The load on the processor, memory, and bus is higher, but otherwise the two approaches are very similar. Whether you implement mirroring in hardware or software, you pay twice for the disk capacity you need.

RAID level 2, level 3, and level 4

RAID 2 adds one or more disks to hold an error correction code with which lost data from a failed disk can be reconstructed. Figure 8-8 shows how the data flows in a RAID 2 system. When your computer sends a sequence of data to a RAID 2 host adapter connected to two data disks and an ECC disk, the host adapter interleaves the data to the two data drives. Odd blocks go to one drive, and even to the other. The host adapter computes the error correction code for the data written to the data drives and writes it to the ECC drive. RAID 5 is invariably used instead of RAID 2, however, because it offers lower overhead and better performance.

RAID 3 is the same as RAID 2, except that it uses a simpler code — parity instead of ECC. RAID 3 has the same small-transfer performance limitations of RAID 2, but less storage overhead.

RAID 4 is nearly the same as RAID 3, but instead of striping across disks at the byte level, it operates at the sector level. This makes RAID 4 like RAID 2 (Figure 8-8) except that it uses parity rather than ECC, and it interleaves sectors. RAID 4 therefore has good data reliability and storage efficiency, as do RAID 2 and 3, and retains fast writes for large data blocks. RAID 4 does not require synchronized spindles because it's easy to buffer sectors and write them out independently to all the drives. Multiple independent writes mean the I/O operations are processed in parallel, which in turn means that small writes can be faster. Unsynchronized rotation can slow reads for small data blocks.

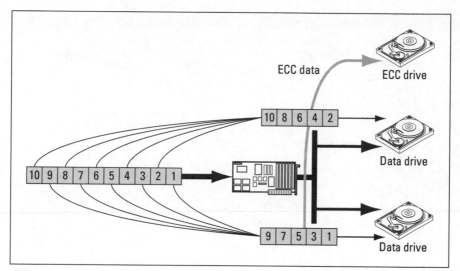

Figure 8-8: RAID 2 offers better reliability than RAID 0 or conventional disk setups, and has a smaller storage overhead compared to RAID 1.

RAID level 5

RAID 5 is the same as RAID 4, except that instead of dedicating a single disk to storing parity, the parity data stream is striped across all the disks along with the rest of the streams. Figure 8-9 shows how this works. Suppose your computer sends a sequence of data to a RAID 5 host adapter connected to four disks. The host adapter interleaves the data to the drives, ensuring that no one drive ever holds two blocks of a group protected by a parity block. The host adapter inserts the new parity information in the data stream that it sends to the disks, mixing the parity information in with the original data. As long as there is at least one more disk than there are original data streams, the loss of a disk can take out only one data stream, and so parity is enough to regenerate the lost data.

There are other RAID levels defined by specific companies, as well as combinations of levels. RAID 0/1, for example, is striping (as with RAID 0) that is mirrored on a duplicate set of disks (as with RAID 1). This combination gives you the speed of RAID 0 with the data reliability of RAID 1, but carries the high storage overhead of RAID 1, too.

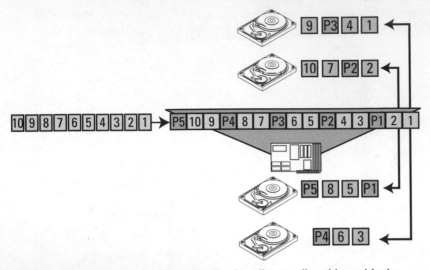

Figure 8-9: RAID 5 offers data reliability, handles small and large blocks, and does not require spindle synchronization.

Adding a Disk Drive

The key to upgrading your computer by adding disk drives is planning — thinking through the physical, electrical, performance, and software issues before you order parts and pick up your tools.

✦ **Physical** — The most basic decision is whether the drive will be internal or external to your computer. ATA drives must be internal. External USB drives are subject to getting banged around, but can be readily moved from one computer to another if they're all running Windows 2000 or Windows XP. You may be constrained in connections to your host adapter — ATA cables, for example, can be no more than 18 inches long (less for badly designed controllers that don't properly split the primary and secondary channels). We once built a machine in a full-size tower case with a motherboard whose IDE ports were in the middle of the motherboard. That positioning, combined with the 18-inch cable limit, meant that we couldn't put IDE drives in the upper bays of the case.

If the drive will be internal, think about both cooling and cabling. If you have the option, leave air space around the drive, and choose a drive bay where it will be in the air flow. For instance, some cases have drive bays low near the air inlet. Putting the drive there should give it the best cooling possible. If you're concerned about heat, consider sticking a CPU cooling fan on the drive. Be sure to mount the drive so there's solid metal contact between the drive bay and the drive so heat has a good path away from the drive. Figure 8-10 shows an internal drive installed in a 3.5-inch form factor mounting bracket, using the lower position on the mounting bracket to ensure good airflow over the top of the drive.

Figure 8-10: Position drives in mounting brackets so they'll get good air flow and heat conduction.

You can see in Figure 8-11 that the drive is positioned in the case just under the power supply, so the lower mounting position keeps the drive away from heat coming from there. We also positioned the drive as far into the bracket as possible to get the most metal-to-metal contact and improve the bracket's ability to conduct heat away from the drive and keep the disk assembly and electronics cool. Don't ever use a non-metallic mounting bracket on a disk drive because you'll lose the cooling from conducted heat through the bracket. Some cases work only with non-metallic brackets and therefore may have cooling problems before you even start assembling a system into them.

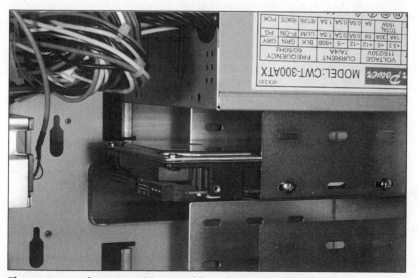

Figure 8-11: Choose positions within mounting brackets to get the best service access within the chassis.

✦ **Electrical** — You have to get power and the data cable to the drive. If you don't plan both the sequence in which drives sit on the cable and the routing of the power feed, you'll end up with a rat's nest that makes working on the computer difficult. Put the ATA master on the end of the cable. Each parallel IDE port you use must have a master and may have a slave. You can have a master on both ports and slave on none, on either, or on both (see Table 8-2).

Table 8-2
Parallel ATA Master/Slave Combination Requirements

	Primary	*Secondary*
Master	OK	OK
Slave	Requires Primary Master	Requires Secondary Master

✦ **Performance** — You have two (primary and secondary) parallel ATA channels on virtually all motherboards, letting you connect up to four drives. Newer motherboards provide serial ATA, but typically have ports only for two drives.

If you're using parallel ATA and have only two hard disks, make each one a master, putting one on each of the two IDE ports. If you have a hard disk and a CD-ROM, make the hard disk the master on the primary IDE port and the CD-ROM the master on the secondary port. If you have two hard disks and a CD-ROM, put both hard disks on the primary port, isolating the CD-ROM on the secondary port. The general strategy is to group faster devices together and away from slower ones. The idea behind splitting two hard drives (if that's all you're connecting) is that it gives the operating system the option to deal with the two independently.

Unless your motherboard has specific restrictions, you can mix parallel and serial ATA. The two run independently.

✦ **Software** — After you get the disk installed, you may need to tell the BIOS about it. You'll mostly want to use the automatic detection and configuration settings of the BIOS to set that up. After the drive is recognized by the BIOS, you partition and format the drive from within the operating system.

Top Disk Support Questions

Disks seem to generate more confusion than any other single part of a computer. That's probably because a lot of things come together on the disk drive: the BIOS, the operating system, the bus, the host adapter, other drives, the case, and the power supply. That leaves room for a lot of things to go wrong.

Q: How should I set up my IDE drive?

A: The settings the BIOS offers differs among systems, but typically you'll want to set the BIOS CMOS Hard Disk type to "Auto Configured" and IDE Translation Mode to "Auto Detected." If there's a choice, use "Large Block Addressing." After you do that, you should be able to boot and have the BIOS recognize the drive with the correct capacity. You'll then partition the disk using FDISK or something like PowerQuest's PartitionMagic if you're working in Windows 9X, or using the tools built into Windows 2000 and Windows XP. If you're installing a new drive, you should consider deleting any existing partitions and creating a new partition to make sure things start clean and properly coordinated between BIOS and drive. Remember that deleting partitions deletes all the data they contain beyond recovery by normal means.

Q: What can I do to make my IDE drive (from an old system) work with my new motherboard?

A: Many older PC BIOSes supported only the older cylinder-head-sector style addressing for IDE disk drives, instead of large block mode, even if the IDE drive itself was capable of supporting the more advanced mode. When a more advanced IDE drive is connected to a motherboard with a BIOS capable of supporting the more advanced mode, the drive will tell the system which translation modes it is capable of supporting. Unfortunately, the drive does not tell the BIOS which mode was being used when the drive was originally formatted, just what it's capable of. If a mismatch occurs between the old mode and what the newer BIOS picks, the disk drive may exhibit problems when used (including what looks like scrambled or missing data). There are two possible solutions:

1. Force the new system to use CHS Translation Mode. To do this, set up the BIOS Hard Disk type to "Auto Detected" and the IDE Translation Mode to "CHS." If your data is now present without corruption, you should be okay; otherwise, you'll need step 2.

2. Put the drive back with the old motherboard, back it up, connect it to the new motherboard, and reformat the disk drive to use a more advanced translation mode. All data on the hard drive will be lost (which is the point of the backup — be sure to verify the backup before you reformat).

Q: I installed a huge new ATA drive, but not all its capacity shows up, or I can't boot from it. Can't I use a large ATA drive with my motherboard?

A: Older motherboards may impose ATA hard drive size limitations at several capacity points. Connecting a drive larger than is supported to one of these systems may cause the drive not to be recognized by the BIOS or by your operating system's partitioning utility. If the hard drive is a master in a master/slave configuration, the system may freeze during boot. Many hard drive manufacturers supply a utility (such as Seagate Disk Wizard, Microhouse EZ-Drive, and Ontrack Disk Manager) that solves problems accessing the full capacity of the hard drive with Windows 9X. For systems running Windows 2000 or Windows XP, you'll probably need to either update the motherboard BIOS or see if the drive offers backwards compatibility jumper settings. Check the capacity you get using compatibility jumpers because the older system simply may not be able to see the entire disk.

Table 8-3 summarizes the approaches to fix problems with older systems trying to access large drives. Overall, you're much better off with Windows 2000 and Windows XP for very large drives..

Table 8-3
Fixing Large Drive Problems

Capacity More Than	95	98	ME	2000	XP
2GB	Update BIOS, use FAT32 disk partition. Third-party utilities may fix BIOS problems, as will third-party disk controllers.			Use NTFS or FAT32 disk partitions. PCs with BIOSes too old to handle 2GB disks do not meet minimum operating system requirements.	
8.4GB	Update BIOS to support INT13. Use FAT32 disk partition. Third-party utilities may fix BIOS problems, as will third-party disk controllers.			Use NTFS or FAT32 disk partitions. PCs with BIOSes too old to handle 8.4GB disks do not meet minimum operating system requirements.	
32GB	Disks 32GB or larger are not supported.	Update BIOS, use FAT32. Capacity jumper may help.		Use NTFS disk partitions. Fix hanging problems at startup using BIOS update and/or capacity limiting jumper on drive and/or third-party disk controller.	
68GB		Update BIOS, use FAT32. Capacity jumper may help. Patch to FDISK required.	Update BIOS, use FAT32. Capacity jumper may help.	Use NTFS disk partitions. Fix hanging problems at startup using BIOS update and/or capacity limiting jumper on drive and/or third-party disk controller.	
137GB		Disks 137GB and larger are not natively supported.		As above, Service Pack 3 required.	As above, Service Pack 1 required.

Q: How are drive letters assigned to new partitions or new drives?

A: The Windows and DOS operating systems assign drive letters (UNIX uses a completely different scheme to identify drives and the space on them). DOS assigns drive letters to all primary partitions and then to all logical drives in extended partitions. For example, suppose you have two drives set up as in Table 8-4. The first primary partition on the first physical drive is C; the first primary partition on the second physical drive is D. Next, the logical drives are labeled, covering first the logical drives on the first physical drive (E, F) and then the logical drives on the second physical drive (G, H). Your CD-ROM and any removable drives are assigned the next available drive letters after your hard drive partitions.

Windows 9x follows the DOS scheme for drive letters. Windows 2000 and Windows XP follow the DOS scheme by default, but in some cases let you use the Disk Administrator tool to change the letter assigned to specific drives.

For any of these operating systems, you can use only drive letters from A to Z

Table 8-4
The DOS Drive Letter Assignment Sequence
Isn't Always What You Want

Drive 1	Drive 2
Primary Partition (C:)	Primary Partition (D:)
Extended Partition	Extended Partition
Logical Drive 1 (E:)	Logical Drive 1 (G:)
Logical Drive 2 (F:)	Logical Drive 2 (H:)

Q: What will happen to my CD-ROM drive letter if I create a new partition or add a new drive?

A: If you consume the drive letter previously assigned to the CD-ROM drive, the CD-ROM gets assigned the next available drive letter after your hard drive partitions. You can prevent the CD-ROM drive letter from changing in the future by assigning it a higher drive letter to begin with (such as M or N), creating some unused letters between the last hard disk and the first CD-ROM.

Q: Can I install Windows 9x on the same disk as Windows 2000 or Windows XP?

A: You cannot install Windows 9x in the same folder (directory) that holds Windows 2000 or Windows XP, but you can install it to the same disk in a different partition or different folder. You'll have to install to a different partition if you have Windows 2000 or Windows XP in an NTFS partition, and if the NTFS partition is drive C, you'll have to convert it to FAT because the Windows 9x boot code doesn't understand NTFS. You'll also want to look into products such as PowerQuest's PartitionMagic to simplify choosing which operating system boots.

Summary

✦ Seek and access times, and sustained data transfer rate, are the most important determiners of disk performance in your system.

✦ RAID systems can give you greatly increased performance and reliability.

✦ Be sure to get enough disk space. Your requirements will always increase over time.

CD and DVD

Optical drives originated from the need for a high-capacity, removable medium for multimedia and software distribution. Inexpensive, high-capacity digital technologies for distributing music and video from the consumer electronics industry, including both CD and DVD, met the requirement well. Other optical formats, including magneto-optical drives, were popular for a while before writable CD and DVD technologies matured, but all of the others have essentially died out in the face of the overwhelming manufacturing volume pushing CD and DVD forward.

CDs provide a small, inexpensive, and rugged way to hold about 650MB of data; DVD extends the CD technology to provide far more capacity and greater data transfer rates. This chapter covers how CD-ROMs and DVDs work, how you can use CD-ROM and DVD drives in your computer system, and how you can make your own CD-ROMs. We'll look at the newest technology and discuss what you can expect from a quality CD-ROM or DVD drive. Chapter 17 covers how you can use writable DVD and video hardware to make your own DVDs.

◆ ◆ ◆ ◆

In This Chapter

Acquiring inexpensive, rugged, high-capacity storage

Understanding CD and DVD technology

◆ ◆ ◆ ◆

What Is a CD-ROM?

A CD-ROM most resembles the vinyl long-play records still dear to the hearts of audio fanatics. On a record, a single spiral in the vinyl winds from the outside to the inside, with the analog signal encoded in the deflections along the course of the groove. On a CD-ROM, a single spiral encased in plastic winds from the inside to the outside, with the digital data encoded by the presence or absence of tiny optical pits. A record stores sound as analog levels, which can degrade over time as the vinyl wears or becomes dirty. A CD-ROM stores its data as numbers, which never degrade unless the disk becomes unreadable.

Figure 9-1 shows what's inside CD media. In cross-section, a CD is a layer of reflective aluminum with lacquer on top and protective plastic underneath (recordable CDs use a similar structure, but use an organic dye instead of an aluminum layer). The zeroes and ones (transformed in a way that makes the recording more reliable) get turned into flats and pits on the surface of the reflective layer when the CD is mastered. The layers include:

✦ **Spiral data track** — The information on the CD-ROM is recorded in a continuous spiral starting at the inside edge of the recorded area and continuing to the outer edge of the disk.

✦ **Top surface** — The top of the CD-ROM is lacquer over the aluminum layer. The CD-ROM label is painted on top of the lacquer.

✦ **Reflective aluminum** — A reflective aluminum surface carries the flats and pits that physically encode the information. The flats and pits, by reflecting light differently, enable the CD-ROM drive to read back the information.

✦ **Plastic coating** — The back side of the disk is covered by a plastic coating that protects the aluminum layer.

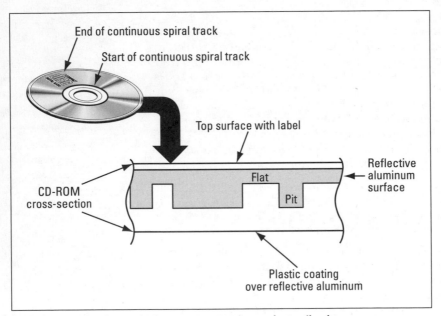

Figure 9-1: The data spiral on a CD-ROM is nearly 3 miles long.

The CD mastering process is similar to the vinyl record-making process. A mirror image of the disk, with all the pits and flats, is used to stamp out the plastic bottom of the disk with an accurate impression of the entire spiral. Aluminum is then deposited on the plastic and covered with lacquer, resulting in the finished disk. The accuracy required in the process is far greater than vinyl records needed: Adjacent turns of the spiral along the disk are only 1.6 micrometers apart, which means that there are nearly 16,000 of them every inch.

Coding Data onto a CD-ROM

The flats and pits on a CD-ROM do not directly correspond to the ones and zeroes that eventually make it into your computer. Instead, the data stream is coded in a particular way before recording, with the coding reversed when you read back the disk to recover the original data pattern. The conversion from your data to what's recorded changes every 8 bits of your data into 14 bits that get recorded, allowing the drive to compensate for limitations of the physical device. The following table shows how that transformation works for some of the 256 possible 8-bit values. For example, if a byte value of 3 needs to be recorded, the 8-bit value would be 00000011. After that byte gets remapped for recording, the result is 10001000100000.

Value	8-bit Representation	14-bit Representation
0	00000000	01001000100000
1	00000001	10000100000000
2	00000010	10010000100000
3	00000011	10001000100000
4	00000100	01000100000000

The pattern of pits and flats used on the CD to record the bits is interesting. A 1 is indicated by a change from a pit to a flat (or a flat to a pit). The length of the subsequent pit or flat (after the transition) indicates how many 0 bits follow the 1 bit before the next 1 bit occurs. If you look back at the table in this sidebar, you'll see that there is never a pattern in the 14-bit representation where two ones occur together, which is necessary since you can't put two transitions back-to-back. The actual 14-bit code is more restrictive yet; a 1 will always be followed by at least two 0s. This pattern limits the minimum size of the pits and flats and in turn allows designers to make decisions about the wavelength of the laser in the drive and about the lenses used with the laser.

When the 14-bit codes are read back from the CD, the drive converts back to the 8-bit code the computer expects to see and (after passing the data through some powerful error-correcting circuits) sends the data out onto the I/O bus.

Mastering a CD is straightforward, if not easy. You feed data to the laser head at a constant rate, turn the master disk at a constant rate, and sweep the laser head from the inside to the outside at a constant rate. The laser burns pits into the master as required. The end result is a precise, even spiral of pits and flats.

Reading a CD from beginning to end — without pauses or other interruptions — is straightforward, too. The read laser head sweeps the same way the record head did when making the master, allowing light to reflect back off the aluminum surface plated onto the CD, as in Figure 9-2. Light reflected from a flat on the CD bounces back cleanly, sending most of the light back to a photodetector in the drive. Light reflected from a pit on the CD is scattered by the shape of the pit, sending most of the light away from the photodetector. A sensor converts the change in intensity of the reflected laser beam as the beam sweeps from a pit to a flat into the pattern of 1s and 0s for the 14-bit representation.

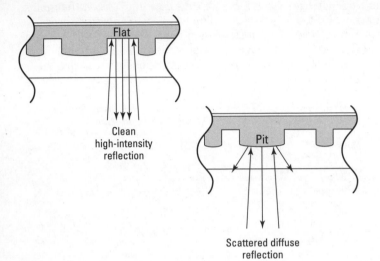

Figure 9-2: The presence and absence of reflected light, and the transition between them, indicate the pattern recorded on the CD to the drive.

As with magnetic disks, there's more room per revolution of the disk to pack in data as you go farther out from the center. In the same way that magnetic disks pack in more sectors at the outside, so do CDs pack in more pits and flats, and therefore more data.

The similarities between CD and magnetic disk don't stop there. If you look at the pattern

00000010001000000001001000010000001001000100000

you can't necessarily tell where one bit pattern stops and the next one starts. If, instead, we give you the same information, like this,

00000 01000100000000 10010000100000 01001000100000

you can tell that the sequence starts with the last part of a bit, followed by the bits for the sequence 420.

The information that gives you the bit boundaries, and that divides the information on a disk into sectors, is called *framing*. The framing information on a CD doesn't address the data as cylinder-head-sector (as on a magnetic disk) because the spiral arrangement of the data means that there aren't distinct cylinders and because there's only one head. The lack of those features makes sector placement on a CD a little more complicated than on a regular disk. The smallest unit above the byte is called a frame, containing 24 bytes. Frames are grouped into blocks, which contain 98 frames (2,353 bytes). A CD-ROM actually carries only 2,048 data bytes per frame — the remainder goes to added error correction, synchronization, and addressing bytes.

When your computer asks the CD-ROM to read a specific frame, the sequence of events is similar to that for a read from a magnetic disk. The head has to move to the right place and pick off the data. Because the data is arranged in a spiral, though, this is a difficult process. The controller in the CD-ROM uses the following sequence:

1. Position the head as close as possible to where the frame should be.

2. Wait for the CD to turn enough for pits and flats to spiral under the laser beam, and start tracking outwards along the spiral.

3. Wait for synchronization with a frame, and read the frame address.

4. Adjust position based on how far the frame the head found is ahead or behind the one you wanted.

Unlike CD-ROM drives, CD audio drives rarely change position to a specific place — they do it only when you say to go to a specific track, which is almost never on the computer time scale of billions of operations every second. In an application like that, a few tenths of a second longer to find the right place is far less important than making the drive reliable and inexpensive. Because computer CD-ROM drives were originally built from the CD audio technology, it was inevitable that the first generation drives were slow to seek from one place to another.

The sustained transfer rate off a first-generation CD-ROM drive was also driven by the capabilities of the CD audio equipment, which meant that the drive transfers about 1.2 megabits per second (153.6K per second). Video compression technology gets pretty lousy below about 1.5 megabits per second, which drove the industry to quickly develop the second, "double speed" generation of CD-ROMs. Since then, CD-ROM manufacturers boosted performance to 4, 8, 16, 24, 32, and now 48 times the basic audio CD rate by spinning the disk faster and building better drive mechanisms to hold or reduce the seek times. Table 9-1 shows what that means. Manufacturers have boosted the data transfer rates up to 7.2 megabytes per second from the 150 kilobytes per second of the original CD-ROM drives. The sustained transfer rates from CD-ROMs are now as high as some economy hard disk drives.

Table 9-1
Increases in CD-ROM Speed
Increase the Data Transfer Rate

Speed Multiplier	Data Transfer Rate (Per Second)
1	150K
2	300K
4	600K
6	900K
8	1.2MB
12	1.8MB
16	2.4MB
24	3.6MB
32	4.8MB
40	6.0MB
48	7.2MB

Although they're essentially a commodity item, CD-ROM drives do have differences besides transfer rate. Unless you're simply buying a cheap drive you can use to load software, look at the stated reliability of the drive. We've found all the optical drives — both CD and DVD — to be some of the least reliable components in computers, perhaps only exceeded in failure rate by fans and power supplies.

Even ignoring copy protection schemes that embed errors into sectors on a CD-ROM, you may encounter problems reading disks on some CD-ROM drives. The major component of the problem is vibration from slightly out of balance disks spun at high speeds, creating vibration in the laser that affects the signal read off the disk. The problem started to be reported with 8X or faster CD-ROM drives and has continued with faster units. The vibration problem is more severe even than issues of tolerance in the manufacture of the CD-ROMs. The vibration dampening built into the disk carrier and drive mechanism is crucial — better-designed drives isolate the laser and pickup from vibration, producing a cleaner and more reliable signal (all the more reason to buy from quality manufacturers).

Tip The importance of the speed rating of a CD-ROM drive is overhyped. If your current CD-ROM works reliably, you'll probably not benefit from a faster CD-ROM drive. Multimedia files don't require the fastest drives, and software loads are something you do once and forget. If your 8X or faster CD-ROM is working reliably, consider keeping it.

Keeping the Data Flowing at a Constant Rate

Older CD-ROM drives used the constant linear velocity (CLV) approach to reading the disk, in which the rotation rate varies based on the distance of the head from the center in a way that keeps the rate of travel along the data track constant. Because the length of one rotation's worth of the data spiral gets longer as the head moves from the inside to the outside of the disk, the distance traveled along the spiral per rotation gets longer. The size and spacing of the pits and flats remain constant, however, so more pits and flats occur per rotation towards the outside of the disk. If the rotation rate (in RPM) stayed constant, the increased data content towards the outside would mean that less data flowed at the inside of the disk and more at the outside. Slowing the rotation rate at the outside of the disk keeps the data rate constant.

Newer CD-ROM drive designs abandoned CLV for constant angular velocity (CAV), in which the rotation rate is independent of the head position. CAV is the same approach used in hard disk drives. CD-ROMs do still vary the rotation rate, however, to help adapt to the transfer rate required by the computer. The reason for the rate changes is that seeking to the correct block is time-consuming for a CD-ROM, and if the computer can't take data at full rate, the drive spinning at full rate will move past the point the computer is reading. When that happens, the drive has to seek back to the current read point — a slow operation. By slowing the rotation rate to match the computer, the drive avoids the seek and gives better performance. The drive avoids having to reposition the head backwards, saving tens of milliseconds.

Caution   Hooking a CD-ROM onto the same ATA port as a hard disk is going to reduce hard disk performance. If you can, keep the CD-ROM on the secondary port away from the hard disks.

Tip   CD-ROM drivers for ATA drives are built into Windows 9x, but if the drive is on the secondary port, you may have to set up the driver manually. You can do this with the Add New Hardware Wizard in the Control Panel. Windows 2000 and Windows XP should recognize drives on secondary ports automatically.

Bootable CD-ROM

Until early 1995, you had no way to boot your computer from the CD-ROM drive, which meant that if you built a new machine (or replaced the disk in an old one), you had to boot from a floppy, install drivers, and build up the disk contents from there.

The El Torito Bootable CD-ROM Format Specification — standardized in January of 1995 — changed that. (Legend has it that the name El Torito is from the El Torito Mexican restaurant where the specification was initially worked out.) Essentially, all systems now have BIOS support for El Torito, so if you have a bootable CD-ROM, you can load the drive, start the machine, and have it come up from the operating system on the CD-ROM. If you're building a machine up from an empty hard disk, the bootable CD-ROMs you get for Windows, FreeBSD, and Linux let you start the install without shuffling floppies or worrying about drivers. Bootable CD-ROMs are so successful and prevalent that many manufacturers are dropping floppy disk drives from their systems, relying on CD-ROM if an emergency boot is ever required.

What Are All Those CD-ROM Disk Formats, Anyhow?

The more you look into how computers are built, the more specifications you find. That's because manufacturers need precise definitions of what to expect to build products that work with each other. A large pile of standards exists just for CD-ROM alone. Here are some of the more important:

✦ **Red Book** — The Red Book defines the physical format of audio CDs. This is also called CD-Digital Audio, or CD-DA.

✦ **Yellow Book** — The Yellow Book defines the physical format for data CDs, so its purpose is similar to that of the Red Book. It's possible to mix audio and data on the same CD.

✦ **Green Book** — The Green Book defines the physical format for CD-Interactive, or CD-I, a format used in a game player from Philips. However, having a CD-I compatible drive doesn't mean you can do anything with a CD-I disk on your PC. In general, you can't without some added hardware and software in the computer.

✦ **Orange Book** — The Orange Book defines the physical format for recordable CDs. There are two kinds — magneto-optical and write-once. The CD-R is a write-once device. (Magneto-optical drives have remained expensive and are not widespread.)

✦ **CD-ROM/XA** — This stands for CD-ROM/eXtended Architecture and is a combination of Yellow Book and Green Book. CD-ROM/XA has generally superseded the Yellow Book.

✦ **CD Plus** — Also called CD Extra, this is a specific combination of audio and data on the CD.

✦ **ISO 9660** — Once called the High Sierra format, ISO 9660 defines the file and directory layouts on a CD. Extensions such as Joliet and Romeo have been defined to handle Windows 95 and NT long file names.

Some of the other standards you'll see referenced include single and multisession Kodak Photo CD and Video CD.

The only time you'll really need to worry about any CD standards is when new ones emerge because the product you're looking at may or may not support the newer standard. Otherwise, the drive and software manufacturers tend to support them all to avoid being at a competitive disadvantage.

Recordable CD-ROMs

Recordable CD-ROMs (CD-R) are the least expensive option for offline data storage. If you need archival copies of files — say, of work you've done and can't afford to lose, of critical audit data, or of original customer material — CD-R is for you. CD-R works on the same pit and flat principles as CD-ROM. The difference is that a CD-R disk uses a different material for the reflective surface that can be burned by a laser to form pits, and a CD-R drive includes a more powerful laser to burn the disk.

Tip Making your own bootable CD-ROMs lets you store both diagnostic software and an archive of data to load onto an empty computer. Creating a bootable archive CD-ROM means you can create and test a disaster recovery disk, ensuring that it has everything you need to reconstruct your operation.

It used to be that CD-R was very picky about delays while burning, with any interruption in the data flow to the drive likely to ruin the disk you were recording. The enormous increases in system speed since the advent of CD-R, combined with improved interfaces into the CD-R drives, eliminated that problem, making CD-R creation so nearly foolproof that CD-R is even suitable for writing out files stored on network drives.

Tip Not all CD-R media is rated for the fastest rates recorders can operate at. The faster the drive spins while burning, the less time the laser has on a pit. Drives can compensate by boosting the laser power, but you should be sure the blank disks you get are rated for the burn speed your drive is capable of. If the disks are rated for lower speeds, reduce the burn speed in your software.

CD-Rewritable (CD-RW) is a variant of CD-R in which you can erase the content of the disk and reuse the media. The CD-RW is a read/write optical disk, a removable-media device holding 660MB. Not all CD-ROMs can read CD-RW disks, however, and not all software writes CD-RW in a format compatible across many machines. The most reliable use of CD-RW is for file archiving on a single machine; go beyond that boundary and you'll risk compatibility problems.

DVD

With even small hard disks now in the tens of gigabytes, and with people filling those disks with great abandon, it's not surprising that interest developed in creating a higher-capacity version of CD-ROM. The same DVD format that replaced VHS videotapes provides that technology. (DVD used to stand for Digital Versatile Disk and some other variants, but the "official" name is now simply DVD.) Video drove the development of DVD — consider that the DVD of the movie *The Lord of the Rings — The Two Towers* has 7.29GB of files! Table 9-2 shows why the new format was required: You just can't fit a lot of high-quality video on a CD-ROM with MPEG 1 or MPEG 2 compression (MPEG 4 didn't exist at the time), and if you add a high-quality stereo sound track, the situation gets worse. MPEG 2 data streams can run at a variety of data rates, so in Table 9-2 we've included data for 4 and 10 megabits per second. MPEG 2 video at 4 megabits per second is about as low quality as you'd want to use, while 10 megabits per second is fast enough to give the full video quality MPEG 2 is capable of.

Table 9-2
Data Storable on a Conventional CD-ROM

Content	Mbps	Minutes per CD-ROM
CD-quality stereo	1.3781	62.36
Radio-quality mono	0.0861	997.73
Uncompressed video (CCIT-601 standard digital video is a little slower, at 167 megabits per second)	184.3200	0.47
MPEG 1 compressed video	1.5000	57.29
MPEG 2 compressed video	4.0000 10.0000	21.48 8.59

Both the consumer entertainment and the computer industry wanted a new, higher-capacity format. The consumer entertainment companies wanted to deliver over 2 hours of video disk-quality movie on a single, small disk. The computer companies wanted to do that too — for training videos and games — and also wanted to store greater volumes of computer data. The result was DVD.

Compared to CD-ROM, DVD is simply all-around better. DVD-ROM holds up to 25 times more data than CD-ROM (see Table 9-3), and over 4 times more on recordable DVD. It uses high-quality MPEG 2 video compression, resulting in near studio-quality pictures. It stores higher-quality sound with multiple channels. Its plastic disk is the same size as CD-ROM and should be as durable. DVD drives can read CD-ROMs, letting you use either format in a DVD-equipped computer.

Table 9-3
DVD Capacities Far Exceed CD-ROM

Sides	Layers	
	1	2
1	4.7GB	8.5GB
2	9.4GB	17GB

As always, manufacturers took a while after the initial product introductions to drive the cost of DVD drives down. DVD drives for computers initially shipped at between $500 and $1,000, but came down in cost as manufacturers designed for lower cost and achieved higher manufacturing volumes with later product generations. In 2003, we found drives priced as low as $27 on the Internet, with free shipping. Given pricing like that, we no longer build computers using CD-ROM drives — we build in DVDs.

DVD uses a combination of improvements to outperform CD-ROM:

✦ **Smaller pits and flats** — Figure 9-3 shows that the geometry of the pits and flats, as well as the spacing between turns of the spiral, is smaller on a DVD. The pits are less than one-half the length of those on a CD-ROM, and the spacing along the spiral allows twice as many turns.

✦ **Shorter wavelength laser** — The laser in a DVD uses a higher-frequency beam, resulting in a shorter wavelength that is better able to see the smaller pits and flats. The lens for the laser is also improved, creating a more tightly focused beam.

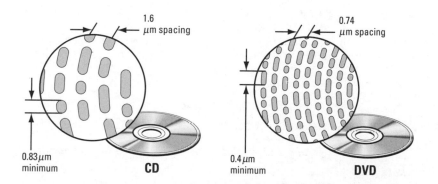

Figure 9-3: Compared to CD, DVD uses smaller pits and a more closely spaced track.

✦ **Two-layer format** — Figure 9-4 shows how a single-sided DVD disk can deliver two sides worth of content. The key is a partially reflective, partially transmitting layer at the bottom of the disk, and a laser that can focus on either the bottom or top data layer.

Although CD-ROM recording format standards define how files and file names (and audio tracks) are stored, no standards for how video and other specialized files are compressed and stored on CD-ROM exist. For this reason, you find CD-ROMs with QuickTime, Video for Windows, and MPEG video. If you don't happen to have the magic decoder software, you can't play the disk.

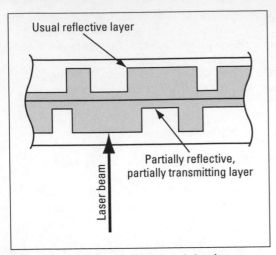

Figure 9-4: The partially transmitting layer near the bottom of a DVD allows the laser to read either of two surfaces.

DVD designers specified MPEG 2 video compression. MPEG 2 video uses data rates of between 4 and 10 megabits per second, much faster than MPEG 1. Table 9-4 shows that all sizes of DVD hold over 2 hours of video (plus the audio tracks) at 4 Mbps, and that two-sided DVDs hold over 2 hours at 10 Mbps.

Table 9-4
DVD Video Capacity in Hours versus MPEG 2 Data Rate

	Single-Sided Capacity		Double-Sided Capacity	
Data Rate (Mbps)	**4.7**	**8.4**	**9.4**	**17.0**
4	2.67 Hours	4.78 Hours	5.35 Hours	9.67 Hours
10	1.07 Hours	1.91 Hours	2.14 Hours	3.87 Hours

Recordable DVD

Although DVD designers had the wit to specify standard read-only disk and video formats, they failed to agree on one recordable format. Including formats supporting both write-once and rewrite operations, there are five distinct writable DVD formats. Each has its own characteristics (Table 9-5), and its own proponents. Some drives support only one set of formats (that is, DVD-R/RW, DVD+R/RW, or DVD-RAM); others support multiple ones. For example, the Sony DRU510a handles DVD-R/RW, DVD+R/RW, and CD-R/RW.

Table 9-5
DVD Format Comparison

Format	Write Speed	Random Write	Defect Management
DVD-R	2X 4X	No	No
DVD-RW	1X 2X	No	No
DVD+R	2.4X 4X	No	No
DVD+RW	2.4X 4X	Optional	Yes
DVD-RAM	2X	Yes	Yes

We've shown two write speeds in Table 9-5 for all but DVD-RAM, reflecting both the original speeds of the formats and the faster speeds of the newer media and drives. Older drives may have firmware upgrades available to write the faster media, but likely at the slower speeds shown in Table 9-5. Be sure to use blank media rated for the faster speed if you have a newer drive operating at high speed.

✦ **DVD-R** — There are actually two writeable DVD-R formats, both similar to the read-only DVD format — called *authoring* and *general use*. The laser frequencies to write media are different for the two, so different equipment is required for each.

✦ **DVD+R** — The writable DVD+R format is a variation of the DVD+RW format and is broadly similar to the DVD-R general use format.

✦ **DVD-RW** — Rewriteable DVD-RW media are available with a 4.7GB capacity and, like DVD-R, contain technology to prevent copying encrypted disks.

✦ **DVD+RW** — The rewriteable format related to DVD+R also holds 4.7GB and optionally supports defect management for better reliability.

✦ **DVD-RAM** — DVD-Random Access Memory is a rewriteable format designed specifically for data storage. DVD-RAM incorporates Defect Sector Management (DSM) to improve storage reliability. However, DVD-RAM media are incompatible with most DVD-ROM drives and set-top video players. You can get both 4.7GB and 9.4GB media.

In practice, there's not a lot of difference between the DVD+R/RW and DVD-R/RW formats — it seems mostly like the unfortunate result of large companies failing to cooperate in the consumer's best interest. Many companies now ship DVD writers able to handle both, making your life easier. The Sony DRU510a we've designed into the desktop machine you see how to build in Chapter 25 is an example of a multi-standard drive.

Blue Lasers — More Capacity on the Horizon

In the same way that a shorter wavelength red laser diode lets DVD use smaller pits and flats than CD-ROM, even shorter wavelength laser diodes allow even denser structures and increased capacity. The target for designers was a blue laser diode, with a wavelength as little as 60 percent that of the red diodes used in CD-ROMs. Designers expect a fourfold increase in capacity.

Unfortunately, blue laser diodes were terribly hard to make, delaying when they came to market. Most of the materials researchers tried required a lot of power to generate the shorter wavelength light. Only some of the power turns into light, though — the rest turns into heat, which causes the diodes to degrade. A material made from Gallium Nitride finally proved successful, leading to blue LEDs and lasers and opening up a wide range of applications. There's more detail in the book *The Blue Laser Diode: The Complete Story* by the inventor Shuji Nakamura, et al., (see `www.amazon.com/exec/obidos/ISBN=3540665056/barrypressA/ref=nosim`).

Top Support Questions

CD and DVD drives usually just work on newer systems running Windows 2000 and Windows XP. Windows 95 wasn't as well developed, so you can encounter problems if you're still running that operating system.

Q: I added an IDE CD-ROM (or DVD) to my Windows 95 system, and it's not recognized. What's wrong?

A: First, make sure your IDE controller itself is recognized by Windows 95 and isn't in compatibility mode. The drive connected to the controller can't be seen until that's true. If the controller is seen and the drive isn't, try detecting new hardware (Start ➪ Settings ➪ Control Panel ➪ Add New Hardware). If that doesn't work, try reinstalling Windows on top of itself. The reinstallation should preserve most of your settings, and the more comprehensive detection should finally see the drive. Your motherboard may also have what Intel calls a PIIX-4 IDE interface, which requires a patch for Windows 95 or an upgrade to Windows 98.

Q: How long will CD-ROM and DVD disks last?

A: Properly made disks will last for a very long time, but poorly made ones can have a very short lifetime. Key manufacturing issues include the purity of the materials making up the disk, proper control of tolerances, and the integrity of the seal at the edges of the disk. There's not much you can do to check the materials. Imation suggests looking at the data side of the disk (the side without the label) with a very bright light (the sun or an overhead projector) behind the disk. Be careful not to look directly at the light. If you see a large number of pinholes — bright points of light coming through the disk — or you see the label through the metal, the disk is doomed. Look at the label, too — it should be smooth and free of defects. If not, substances in the air and environment might attack the metal layer. Exposing disks to high temperature can accelerate aging and cause failure, too.

Q: My system pauses for a long time at boot after seeing my optical drive. Can I stop it from doing that?

A: Your motherboard BIOS may be looking for a bootable CD-ROM in the drive and taking a while to decide that there's no disk there. You can keep a disk in the drive or you can change the BIOS settings to disable booting from CD-ROM.

Q: My optical drive doesn't work. How can I find out what's wrong?

A: Optical drives normally spin up the disk when it's inserted, so you can find out if the drive is even minimally alive by inserting a disk, noting which way the label is turned before you close the drive. Wait a while and then eject the disk. If the label hasn't turned, it's likely the drive itself isn't working. If the label has moved, your problem could be operating system, BIOS, cabling, or the drive. You could run a set of diagnostics or simply try a different drive.

Summary

- ✦ If you want a DVD, or at least a CD-ROM, you're better off with a CD or DVD writer.

- ✦ Use a recordable drive to make archival copies of relatively large sets of files and to publish your finished work.

Removable Storage

Removable storage has a long history in personal computers, from early 8-inch, 160KB floppy disks, through a limited selection of high-capacity removable magnetic media, to the latest external disk drives and flash memory disks usable with virtually any recent vintage PC. You'll continue to see developments in removable storage driven largely by new technologies for digital cameras and other personal electronics.

Removable disks are also useful for backing up your system. Good backup practice requires that you back up to a removable medium (or to another computer located somewhere else), and the speed and convenient file access of removable disks make them very desirable for this job.

Cross-Reference This chapter covers magnetic and flash memory removable disks. You can find the discussion of optical removable storage in other chapters. Specifically, you can find CDs and DVDs discussed in Chapter 9, and more on DVDs in Chapter 17.

Floppy Disks and Competitors

Although they're finally dying out, floppy disk drives had one of the longest lifetimes for any technology in computing. Floppy drives were exotic, new technology in the late 1970s, but by now are barely still commodity items built in huge quantities. Floppy disk drives are no longer sold with all current-generation PCs, having fallen victim to what's now itself a commodity item, the CD-ROM, when the price of CD-ROM writers and blank media became as low as those for floppy drives and disks. At the end of the floppy's lifetime, the 3.5-inch, 1.44MB floppy disk drive was a universal standard, with 5.25-inch and the older 8-inch floppies only distant memories. Higher capacity floppy formats, including

In This Chapter

Understanding floppy disks

Connecting with Universal Serial Bus

Performing file transfer and backup

both a 2.88MB format, developed by Toshiba and used by IBM, and the 120MB LS-120 format, never sold in enough volume to matter.

Floppy drives were two-headed devices, recording information on both sides of a flexible oxide-coated Mylar surface and using one head on each side of the disk. Figure 10-1 shows the layout. The cross-section view shows the structure of a floppy disk drive with a disk inserted. The heads are in direct sliding contact with the disk (which is why computers turned off the drive motor when not accessing the disk — it avoided excessive wear). Small gaps in the heads confine the magnetic image to the current track. Separate gaps on each head assembly trailing the read/write head trim down the magnetic image, keeping adjacent tracks from interfering with each other.

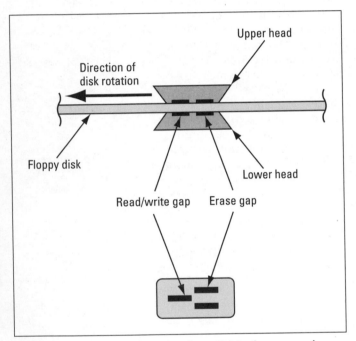

Figure 10-1: Floppy disk technology didn't change much for years.

One contender to replace the standard floppy drive was the LS-120 format, using devices that read both a 120MB disk and conventional 3.5-inch floppies. Table 10-1 compares the LS-120 with a conventional floppy, showing that the technology offered not only improved capacity, but also had nearly ten times the data transfer performance.

Technical benefits notwithstanding, the LS-120 drives and disks never had a large enough installed base to be useful for file transport, the main application for large floppy-like disks. The LS-120 format had a window of opportunity as digital photographs and compressed music files became common because floppy drives became too small to hold a useful amount of information. Although incapable of reading floppy disks, the Iomega Zip drive was more commonly used for carrying files around, and for a while seemed to be a strong candidate to replace the floppy disk. The first generation Zip drives stored 100MB on a single removable disk, while later versions stored 250MB. Even the Zip drive is becoming obsolete, however, eclipsed by the very low costs for CD-R drives and media.

Table 10-1
Comparison of LS-120 with Conventional Floppy Disks

Specification	LS-120	Conventional High-Density Floppy
Formatted Capacity	120MB	1.44MB
Maximum Sustained Transfer Rate	565 kilobytes per second	62 kilobytes per second
Average Seek Time	70 milliseconds	84 milliseconds
Track Density	2,490 tracks per inch	135 tracks per inch
Number of Tracks	1,736 on each of two sides	80 on each of two sides
Rotation Rate	720 RPM	300 RPM

Universal Serial Bus

It used to be that connecting almost anything to your computer was a pain because configuration and setup was difficult and because there just weren't enough total ports. Even years ago, it was reasonable to want to connect a modem or two and a mouse, along with a joystick and a printer or two. Today, you can add MP3 players, digital still and video cameras, personal digital assistants, home automation controllers, GPS receivers, scanners, game pads, video capture interfaces, and more to that list. If every one of those devices needed its own parallel or serial port, or a card added inside the PC, and if every one of them created its own set of compatibility and setup problems, you'd be likely to have thrown the lot out a window before making it all work.

Manufacturers aren't too keen on frustrated consumers because they stop buying, so a new technology to solve the problem was inevitable. The technologies contending for the role were the Universal Serial Bus (USB) and the IEEE 1394 (FireWire) standards, with USB achieving the dominant market position for nearly everything but video camcorders. USB operates at 1.5 or 12 megabits per second for version 1.1 (depending on the device), and up to 480 megabits per second for version 2.0. USB lets you connect microphones, speakers, cameras, modems, telephones, mice, joysticks, printers, scanners, GPS receivers, memories, and seemingly anything else to a simple, thin cable replacing the mess of cables at the back of your computer. Instead of finding a free bus slot, plugging in a new card, setting switches, and hoping everything still works, you just plug the new device into a free USB port on your computer or on a separate USB hub. You don't have to crack open the computer case at all.

Although the number of USB ports built into PCs is growing — we've seen as many as eight — you're likely to end up adding more either because you ran out of ports or because it's inconvenient to cable everything down to the ports on your desktop computer sitting on the floor. The USB specification supports *hubs*, devices that expand one port to many and allow you to cable in a tree-like fashion. Figure 10-2 shows how hubs expand the number of ports, including the capability to cascade hubs to expand the configuration further than one hub allows. You must not create loops in the tree, but otherwise you can plug anything into anything else that has an empty socket. In Figure 10-2, you could equally well plug the telephone into the monitor or the speaker into the keyboard. Some USB devices have hubs built into them, as also illustrated in the figure.

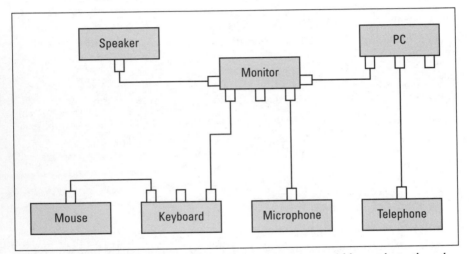

Figure 10-2: The USB cabling scheme requires that you avoid loops, but otherwise you can plug things in where it's convenient.

If you have enough USB devices that you need to expand your system with a hub, be sure to get a powered hub. Unpowered hubs expect to get device power from the computer or other source, but the computer itself is unlikely to be able to supply the necessary power for as many devices as you can use with a hub. Not enough power will cause erratic operation or failure. The powered hubs supply their own power and avoid that problem.

Operating system support for USB has been available in Windows since Windows 98 and Windows 2000 and is available for Linux as well. You may need to do some research (start at www.linux-usb.org) and configuration work, and you should be running a Linux kernel no older than version 2.5, but the capability exists, supports dynamic device detection, and supports a wide range of devices (see www.linux-usb.org/devices.html).

External USB Storage

Not only do recent versions of Windows include USB support, Windows 2000 and Windows XP include generic USB storage device drivers, which means you can plug any USB-connected storage device into a USB port on a PC running those operating systems and access its files. PC developers have been wonderfully inventive with the opportunity those drivers created, leading to the built-in ability to access a variety of devices:

✦ **Cameras** — Most digital cameras contain either a built-in memory, a socket for a memory card, or both. Socket formats typically are Compact Flash, MMC and its successor Secure Digital, and the Sony Memory Stick. These memories are most often built with flash memory, which is random access memory able to retain its contents after the power goes off. Disk drives are available in the Compact Flash format, with capacities of at least a gigabyte. You can access the pictures the camera stores on the memory through the Windows driver, although you may not have access to camera settings.

✦ **Memory keys** — Also called Flash Disks and a variety of other names, these devices are simply flash memory and a USB interface in a package you can stick in your pocket or on a key ring (see Figure 10-3). Capacities of a gigabyte and more are available, making them a great alternative to floppy disks and CD-R for carrying files around.

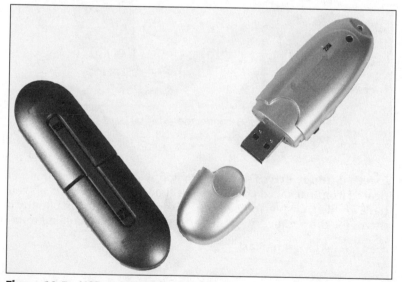

Figure 10-3: USB-connected memory keys
©2004 Barry Press & Marcia Press

✦ **External hard disks** — At 60 megabytes per second (480 Mbps / 8), USB 2.0 is fast enough that it's effective for connecting hard disks to your PC. Therefore, you can carry around a brick holding as much as 250 gigabytes (more as hard disks get larger), which is useful for very large files and as a removable backup device. You can't replace the media in an external hard disk, but the ability to disconnect it from the PC means failures and errors in the PC won't damage the data stored in the disconnected disk. The Seagate external drive in Figure 10-4 can connect via either USB 2.0 or IEEE 1394, and holds 160GB.

Figure 10-4: USB-connected external hard disk drive
©2004 Barry Press & Marcia Press

✦ **External floppy drives** — Although floppy drives have all but disappeared from packaged computers, at times a floppy disk is all you have for file transfer. You can get USB-connected external floppy disk drives for those times, with all the power necessary coming from the USB port.

Small Scale File Transfer and Backup

It used to be that everyone who did file transfers or backups did them to floppy disk because every PC had a floppy disk drive, the media were cheap, and good software existed to stream backup files out to disk. With the large files common today, and the large disks on PCs that easily store many large files, however, floppy disk backup is impractical — you'd be looking at nearly 43,000 floppy disks to back up a full 60GB hard drive. Removable media alternatives for backup today — ignoring the very high-capacity, high-speed Digital Linear Tape (DLT) drives because they're so very expensive — include CD-R/RW, DVD-R/RW, Zip disks, LS-120, and memory keys. Hard drives dedicated to backup are also a common choice because they're big, fast, and inexpensive.

For file transport, only CD-R offers the combination of nearly universally readable media and very low media cost. The varying CD-RW formats are often incompatible, and the other devices are not so common you can assume one's available on an unknown PC. USB ports to host memory keys are universal, but PCs running Windows 98 or Windows Me won't be able to read the drive without installing device drivers you might not have. We recommend memory keys when you know the receiving system has the necessary drivers, and CD-R otherwise.

Tip

You may be able to improve the performance you receive from a memory key under Windows 2000 or Windows XP. Try reformatting the key with the NTFS file system and enabling write caching on the device. You'll lose any chance at compatibility with Windows 9X systems and will have to be very careful to stop the device before you unplug it, but the performance gain could be dramatic. We recorded times to write hundreds of 1 to 2 megabyte files to the drive that were 37 percent less just by changing file system type.

However, although the NTFS option is easy to get to in Windows 2000, Microsoft didn't make formatting a memory key with NTFS under Windows XP straightforward. You'll first have to go into the Policies tab in the device properties and change the setting from optimized for quick removal to optimized for performance (turn on write caching while you're there). After that's done, you'll have to open a command window (the NTFS option isn't available with the graphical format dialog boxes) and use the `format` command. On a drive with letter f:, for example, you could use `format f: /fs:ntfs /c /x`, which not only formats the file system but also enables compression and closes any open files. After you've formatted the memory key with NTFS, any Windows 2000 or Windows XP system should recognize it properly.

File backup is a different story. CD-R is relatively slow and holds only 650 to 700MB per disk, so a multi-gigabyte backup will take a long time and require you to stay by the computer to feed disks. The net effect is that most people won't bother to take the time to do backups, which puts their data at risk. For that reason, we recommend a separate hard drive for backup. You can use a secondary drive directly installed into the PC if you must (and if you have the discipline not to use it for file storage), but we like using an external hard drive you can disconnect and put away for safekeeping when the backup is done.

Most systems can be configured in the BIOS to boot a specially formatted CD-R. In some systems, you can boot the system from either an external drive and or a memory key, too. Test boot your system from whatever external media you want to use for emergencies before you need the capability.

Backup with External Disk

Historically, individual backup media such as floppy disks, tapes, and CD-Rs were significantly smaller than the hard disks being backed up, so backup software had many tasks to manage, including the following:

✦ Identify the files to be backed up

✦ Determine what files would be backed up where

✦ Provide options to minimize the total number of backup media consumed

✦ Compress files as they are transferred to backup storage

✦ Index what versions of what files were stored on what backup disk or tape

✦ Provide mechanisms for restoring files from backup

The advent of huge, inexpensive hard disks, such as the Seagate external drive pictured in Figure 10-4, made highly simplified backups possible. In particular:

✦ **Determine what files would be backed up where** — Even the smaller, 160GB external drive is larger than most people's drives, and much larger than the actual data worth backing up, so only one backup medium is necessary. Every file backed up goes to that one place.

✦ **Provide options to minimize the total number of backup media consumed** — The historically useful variations of a full backup (backing up everything), differential backup (backing up everything since the last full backup), and incremental backup (backing up everything since the last backup of any sort) simply aren't relevant.

✦ **Compress files as they are transferred to backup storage** — The backup medium is a fully capable Windows hard disk, and can be compressed using features built into Windows. No action on the part of the backup software is necessary.

✦ **Index what versions of what files were stored on what backup disk or tape and provide mechanisms for restoring files from backup** — Because the disk is visible to Windows, users can simply browse files on the disk. Mechanisms are required for full system restores, but individual files can be retrieved using Windows Explorer.

All the backup software needs to know is the set of files to be backed up; it then ensures that an image of those files exists on the external disk every time it's run. For efficiency's sake, the software doesn't bother to rewrite files that haven't changed, but that's an implementation detail and not a defining part of the process.

The BounceBack Express software comes with the Seagate drive to perform backups. (If you're not running Windows, you can do much the same thing as the BounceBack software using the Unison File Synchronizer at `www.cis.upenn.edu/~bcpierce/unison`.) We reformatted the drive in Windows to use the NTFS file system and to be compressed and then set up the backup settings as in Figure 10-5. The "File Server" backup set runs overnight, every night, and copies the entire contents of our file server (where we keep *all* our data) to the external drive. You could do the same thing with your local files if you don't use a file server. The software runs the "Default Backup" backup set every time you push the backup button on the front of the drive. We've configured it to also back up the file server, but you could equally well configure it to back up the project you're currently working on.

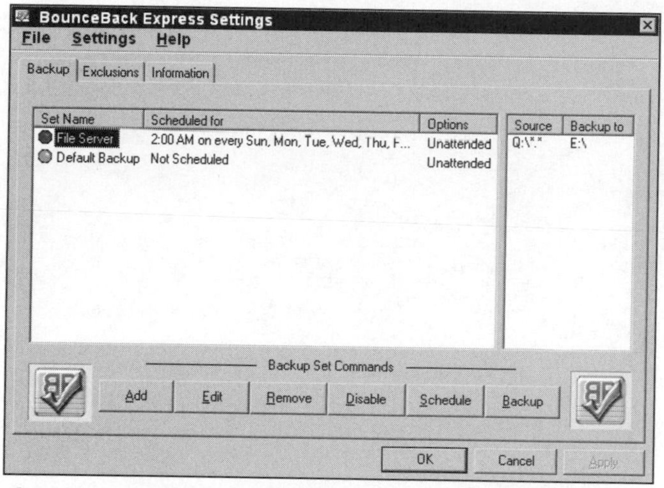

Figure 10-5: BounceBack Express Settings dialog box

That's literally all that's involved. You don't need to worry about what file is on what tape or CD — everything's on the external hard disk. If you *do* have a requirement to archive saved versions, there's an upgrade version of the software available that adds that and other features at `www.cmsproducts.com/seagate/upgrade`.

Summary

✦ Several removable disk technologies exist, each with its own combination of features.

✦ USB memory keys offer a great combination of capacity, portability, compatibility, and price.

✦ You need to consider CD-R in addition to removable disks when evaluating your removable storage requirements.

Networks and Communications

◆　　◆　　◆　　◆

In This Part

Chapter 11
Modems

Chapter 12
Wired and Wireless
Networking

Chapter 13
Hubs, Switches,
Routers, and Firewalls

Chapter 14
Configuring a
Windows Network

Chapter 15
Internet Services,
Antivirus, and
Anti-Spam

◆　　◆　　◆　　◆

Modems

There are many ways to connect to the Internet, but all of them require a modem to send your data in one form or another. Survey data collected in 2003 and provided by Cisco Systems says nearly 60 percent of U.S. households subscribe to Internet service, with 34 percent of those households having broadband service. Most broadband subscribers used cable TV Internet service, followed by DSL, with wireless at a distant third. Nearly 70 percent of the homes with local area networks also had broadband service.

These statistics are a significant change from estimates as recently as 2001, when U.S. broadband usage was a mere 11 percent, surpassed only by South Korea where a whopping 57 percent had broadband access. That change accounts for the differences between this chapter and the version in the previous edition of the *PC Upgrade and Repair Bible*, in which we focused almost to exclusion on dial-up analog modems and Integrated Services Digital Network (ISDN). We've drastically reduced the discussion of how analog modems work, eliminated the discussion of ISDN, and added material on broadband access technologies. (That said, take a look at ISDN if you can't get any other form of broadband access. It will give you 128 kilobits per second in both directions and is very widely available.)

The ways to access the Internet we cover include:

+ Dial-up
+ DSL
+ Cable TV
+ Wireless
+ Satellite

Wireless Internet access in this chapter is distinct from wireless LAN technology, which you'll read about in the next chapter.

In This Chapter

Exploring what a modem does

Understanding dial-up, DSL, cable, and wireless Internet access

Choosing Internet access

Choosing a modem

Signals and Very Long Wires

Modems are the underlying magic in computer communications and networks. What makes them interesting (and difficult to design) is that doing what a modem does — pushing tens of thousands to millions of bits per second across miles of distance despite really awful interference — can't be done the obvious way. The modem's job is to overcome the limitations of wires, space, and the rest of the communications systems.

The obvious approach to sending your data is to do what most of the signals in your computer do: use one voltage level for a one bit and another for a zero. On your motherboard, for example, a one is somewhere between 2 and 5 volts (depending on your processor), and a zero is nearly 0 volts. On your computer's motherboard, signals like that go up and down hundreds of millions of times per second, and (with careful design) it all works well. On a telephone line, cable TV network, or radio wave, factors computer designers can't eliminate intervene to make this approach impossible.

The first and most obvious difference between the wires on your computer's motherboard and an Internet connection is the length the signal must travel. Wires on your motherboard are measured in inches; Internet connections are measured in miles (well, kilometers, too). The difference in distance has different effects depending on how you transmit your signal:

✦ **Wired** — The wires used for telephone lines and cable TV networks have a property called *capacitance*, which is the ability to store electricity. A short wire has almost no capacitance, while a very long wire has significant amounts. Capacitance is a problem because you have to fill the wire up with electricity before the change will show up at the other end.

✦ **Wireless** — Radio signals weaken over distances, increasing the probability of errors in the reconstructed data stream. The faster the transmitted data rate, the more signal power required at the receiver.

The second characteristic that distinguishes the wires on your computer's motherboard from a telephone wire is noise. Both wired and wireless signals pick up noise from magnetic fields, sparks, lightning, and almost any other electrical activity. Computer designers are very careful about keeping wires away from each other to minimize noise, but neither telephone and cable TV wires, nor radio signals, have that luxury. Wires are often strung along the same poles as power lines for thousands of feet, guaranteeing they'll pick up noise. Antennas for wireless signals collect any noise from sources in their field of view. Both wired and wireless systems are out in the weather, too, subject to corroding connections, fields from lightning strikes, and other effects, making the circuit as bad as it can be.

To see the problem transmission limitations create, consider the familiar telephone line. Telephones are designed to send voices back and forth, not symphonic music, which means the frequency response of a telephone circuit is very limited. The lower frequency cutoff is about 150 Hz; the upper is less than 4 KHz. Figure 11-1 shows a typical telephone line frequency response. The response changes somewhat from call to call because you're likely to get a different connection through the switch each time, and the condition of each line depends on its physical characteristics.

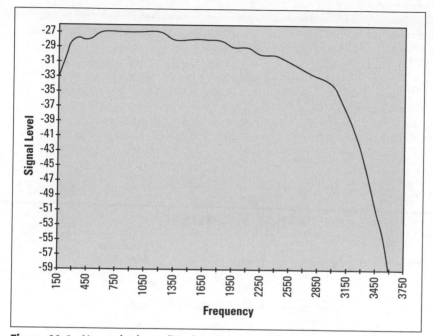

Figure 11-1: Your telephone line frequency response rolls off quickly as frequencies approach 4 KHz, which limits the achievable data rate.

What's important about the graph in Figure 11-1 is the frequency response of the telephone line rolling off badly at the higher end. The loss of high-frequency response reduces the data rate any communications channel can support because it restricts the bandwidth of the modulated waveform the receiving modem can hear. Bandwidth limitations restrict the maximum data rate a modem can achieve for a given transmission power.

Dial-up Analog Modems

The word *modem* is really an acronym, formed as a contraction of MOdulation and DEModulation. It's been used so commonly, though, that it's often no longer capitalized as most acronyms are — it's just a word now. The first thing that happens to your data as it goes out to the Internet is *modulation* — changing your data into a signal that can be shipped over long distances. (*Demodulation* is the job of undoing modulation — recovering your data from the incoming modulated signal.) The fundamental job of a modem is to convert the data stream into signals that can be transported within practical limits imposed by the transmission system (as in Figure 11-1 for telephone lines). The method the modem uses — its modulation technique — has to be standardized between the sending and receiving modems so that what's transmitted can be reconstructed at the other end.

Modem standards are typically set by the International Telecommunications Union-Telecommunications Standardization Sector (ITU-T, or more commonly ITU) or the Institute of Electrical and Electronic Engineers (IEEE), but in the past have been set by the Consultative Committee for International Telegraph and Telephone (CCITT) and the old Bell System.

More than enough different dial-up analog modem specifications exist to keep anyone confused; Table 11-1 summarizes many of them starting with one of the earliest dial-up modems, the Bell 103. The V.92 specification is dominant today, ISDN having failed to replace analog modems due to excessively high pricing and egregious mishandling by the telephone companies. Many of the specifications incorporate slower, fallback operation to handle poor line conditions.

Table 11-1
Modem Standards

Specification	Operation	Circuit	Maximum Rate (bps)
Bell 103	Full duplex	Two-wire switched	300
V.21	Full duplex	Two-wire switched	300
Bell 202	Half duplex	Two-wire switched	1,200
		Conditioned leased	1,800
Bell 201	Half duplex	Two-wire switched	2,400
V.26ter	Full duplex	Two-wire switched	2,400
Bell 212	Full duplex	Two-wire switched	1,200
V.22bis	Full duplex	Two-wire switched	2,400
V.27	Full duplex	Four-wire leased	4,800
	Half duplex	Two-wire switched	4,800
V.29 (includes Group 3 fax)	Full duplex	Four-wire leased	9,600
	Half duplex	Two-wire switched	9,600
V.32bis	Full duplex	Two-wire switched	14,400
V.FC (non-standard)	Full duplex	Two-wire switched	28,800
V.34	Full duplex	Two-wire switched	33,600
V.90	Full duplex	Two-wire switched	56,000 to subscriber; 33,300 return (subscriber limited to 53,000)
V.92	Full duplex	Two-wire switched	56,000 to subscriber; 48,000 return (subscriber limited to 53,000)

The 56 Kbps V.92 and V.90 modems are not problem free, largely because some telephone lines and switches can't support the technology. The modem industry estimates that perhaps 80 percent of telephone lines in North America can operate with the new technology. These modems fall back to V.34 operation when the lines can't support the faster standard. In addition to bad telephone lines, the issues with V.90 modems are these:

✦ **One analog hop** — The 56 Kbps modem technology is very sensitive to timing relationships, something that can be destroyed by multiple conversions between analog and digital transmission systems. Your telephone lines are analog; telephone company equipment changes the signal to digital at the telephone switch or other equipment. The signal must remain digital all the way to your Internet service provider (ISP); if not, the modems revert to slower 33.6 Kbps V.34 operation.

✦ **No digital conversions** — The digital voice transmission specifications in North America are different than those elsewhere in the world. The digital version of your 56 Kbps signal can't survive translation between different digital systems, which means you likely won't be able to make international calls at 56 Kbps.

✦ **Asymmetric data rate** — The upstream data rate (the rate out of your computer) is less than 56 Kbps; it's the rate *into* your computer that's 56 Kbps. Asymmetric operation works for Web access, but not if you're running a server or trying to upload files to another site.

✦ **Data rate limitation** — In the United States, the Federal Communications Commission has limited the signal power levels 56 Kbps modems can use to prevent signal crossover to adjacent lines in wiring bundles. The limited signal power restricts the modems to operation at 53 Kbps or slower.

How Many Characters Per Second?

Knowing that your modem transmits at 28,800 or 53,000 bits per second isn't as useful as it seems because nothing else in your computer involves single bits. A far more interesting number is how many characters per second your connection transmits; however, even though there are 8 bits in a character, you can't send the 3,600 or 6,625 characters per second that simple division of 28,800 or 53,000 bits per second would suggest. The reason you don't get that rate is that your modem sends more than just your data bits — it sends additional bits to indicate the start and stop of each character. These bits are, predictably, named the *start and stop bits*. Current-day personal computer modems all use one start and one stop bit. That means that every character requires sending 10 bits, so if your 53,000-bits-per-second modem (that's the most you get from a 56K modem) keeps the telephone line completely full, you'll send 5,300 characters per second.

The other connection on your modem is the one to your computer. It's called a *serial port* because, although it gets data from the computer 8 bits at a time, it transfers bits serially — one at a time. The serial port is a connector on the back of your computer if you're using an external modem, but it's buried in the circuits on the card if you're using an internal one.

The serial port on the back of your computer follows the Electronic Industries Alliance (EIA) specification RS-232C, providing a number of signals:

✦ **Send and receive data** — All the bits that actually go out the connector go on a single wire (plus a ground). There's another one for data from the modem back to the computer.

✦ **Control transmission** — Two wires control when your computer is allowed to send data to the modem: one to say the computer wants to send, and the other to reply that it's okay to do so.

✦ **Control reception** — Two more wires control when the modem can send data to the computer. The idea is the same as transmission control: one wire says the modem wants to transfer, and the other says it's okay to do so.

✦ **Monitor the connection** — One more wire lets the modem tell the computer when it has established a connection with a modem at the other end.

A few more signals are defined in the RS-232C specification, but they're rarely used.

You'll find two kinds of serial port connectors on the back of your computer. The one originally defined in the RS-232C standard has 25 pins in two rows. Because only nine of those pins are used (except in very rare circumstances), it's possible to reduce the 25-pin connector to a 9-pin one. IBM did this initially for the PC/AT, and most vendors followed this design because it saves space. (For instance, you can put a parallel printer port and a 9-pin serial port on one adapter card, but there isn't room for the parallel port connector and a 25-pin serial port in that space.) You can get adapters between the 25-pin and 9-pin connectors in case you need to connect equipment that uses different forms. The 9-pin version has been around for long enough that 25-pin serial ports are relatively rare now on PCs.

Tip   The chip in your PC implementing the serial port, called a 16550, can stack 16 characters in either direction before overruns or underruns occur. That cuts the processing load considerably, making serial communications far more efficient, but might cause erratic operation or other problems if you're connecting mice or other specialized devices to the port. If your mouse won't work, or if it works erratically, check the user's manual for the device to see if you need to shut off the first-in, first-out (FIFO) queue in the 16550, and for directions how to do that if it's necessary.

Fax: Extending the Modem

Because communication is so valuable in your computer, it's no surprise that facsimile transmission (fax) and other extensions to pure data transmission have migrated to your computer and its modem.

As the figure below shows, a standalone fax machine is really a very complex device, including a scanner, compressor, modem, and printer. The scanner converts the image into an array of pixels — a *bitmap*. The compressor uses a fax-specific algorithm (called Group 3 compression) to reduce the size of the data to be transmitted. The modem sends and receives the data stream. The decompressor reconstructs the bitmap from the compressed data stream, and the printer gives you the hard copy fax.

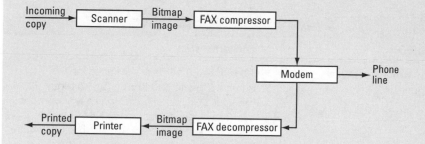

Most of the operations that a standalone fax machine performs can be duplicated by your computer. Working from the right side of the figure, your modem does the necessary data communications and fax compression. Your printer handles the problem of creating hard copy.

The only issue would seem to be the scanner, which isn't as common as the rest of the components. However, you might not always need a scanner. The scanner's job is to create the image you want to send, which in a standalone scanner comes from a paper copy of the fax. In your computer, the material you want to send is usually in the computer already, so printing it so you can scan it makes no sense. Instead, fax software sets itself up to look like a printer. Instead of creating paper, it sends the resulting image to the modem.

If you're connecting a dial-up modem directly to your computer, we recommend using an internal modem in a PCI slot. Such modems will be automatically detected by the computer and, if you bought from a capable manufacturer, will install the drivers painlessly. Our preference for dial-up service, however, is to use an external modem combined with a router, such as the 3Com OfficeConnect 56K LAN Modem. You avoid all issues of configuring your computer to talk to the modem — your PC just accesses a LAN that has an Internet gateway — and get a built-in firewall and multi-PC access in the same package. If your ISP supports it, and you have two telephone lines to spare, 3Com offers a dual-modem version that can give you connections at over 100 Kbps.

DSL

There are ways to send digital data down a copper telephone line besides analog dial-up modems. The most common broadband technology over telephone lines is called Digital Subscriber Line (DSL). Table 11-2 shows some of the variants of DSL you might have available in your area.

Table 11-2
Common DSL Technologies

Technology	Characteristics
ADSL (Asymmetric Digital Subscriber Line)	1.5 Mbps to 9 Mbps to the subscriber; from 16 Kbps to 640 Kbps return. A recent variant is DSL Lite or G.Lite, which is slower but easier to install. G.Lite runs at 1.544 Mbps to 6 Mbps to the subscriber and 128 Kbps to 384 Kbps return.
HDSL (High data rate Digital Subscriber Line; also High bit rate)	Symmetric operation at T1 or E1 speeds. Typically requires two or three subscriber lines.
RADSL (Rate Adaptive Digital Subscriber Line)	Data rates of 128 Kbps to 7.168 Mbps to the subscriber, and 30 Kbps to 1.088 Mbps return.
SDSL (Symmetric Digital Subscriber Line)	Symmetric T1 or E1 operating over a single telephone line.
VADSL (Very high-speed ADSL; also Veryhigh-rate, and others)	Subset of VDSL.
VDSL (Very High Data Rate Digital Subscriber Line)	12.9 to 52.8 Mbps over wire lengths from 4,500 feet to 1,000 feet, respectively.

Unlike cable TV, you can't just go to a store and buy a DSL modem — be sure to coordinate carefully with your telephone company and service provider.

Two-way DSL data transmissions share the telephone wires with your regular telephone service — you don't need a second telephone line, and callers won't get busy signals — letting you make telephone calls and send data at the same time. Conventional ADSL technology requires a device called a splitter to be installed where the telephone line enters the building so the ADSL signals can be separated from the telephone voice signal. If you look at the ADSL entry in Table 11-2, though, you'll see mention of another technology — G.Lite — that modifies ADSL to eliminate the need for a splitter. No splitter means no service call to the home or office, so installation costs are less. G.Lite is slower than

ADSL, but for many people the loss in speed won't be noticeable compared to the gain in speed when you replace a slow modem.

ADSL works by forcing very high frequencies down the telephone line, frequencies well above what you can hear and well above the frequencies shown as usable in Figure 11-1. Figure 11-2 shows how that works. Transmissions from you to your ISP use frequencies starting at 30 KHz and ending below the transmissions from your ISP, which themselves occupy the range from 138 KHz to 1.1 MHz. These frequencies are available because the 4 KHz limit in Figure 11-1 is really a result of limitations in the telephone switch, not limitations of the copper wires carrying your signals. The DSL equipment your telephone company runs splits off the high frequency signals before they reach the telephone switch.

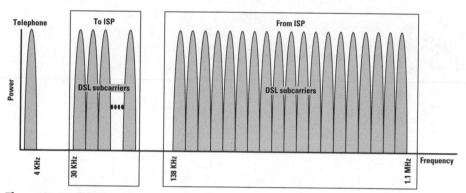

Figure 11-2: DSL spectrum occupancy

Telephone lines are noisy, however, and are more so at the higher frequencies used for DSL. Noise can interfere with data, causing errors or blocking transmission. Standards-based ADSL (what's shown in Figure 11-2) combats noise by dividing the available spectrum into *subcarriers*; it then shuts down transmissions in noisy subcarriers and diverts the corresponding data traffic to surviving subcarriers.

> **Caution**
>
> Most broadband Internet connections are always on as long as the power and your computer are on. Being always on means other computers on the Internet may be able to see your computer, even if you're not actively doing anything. You need to be aware of computer security if you're going to use broadband; see the discussion in Chapter 13.

Cable Television

Cable TV Internet service uses a combination of fiber optics and coaxial cable, which are capable of a far larger frequency range than the telephone company can use on their simpler twisted pair wires. Cable modems get only a small fraction of the total bandwidth on the cable — typically the equivalent of one TV channel — which limits the speed you get.

Cable modem service has become widely available, slowly growing to fulfill some of the inflated hype cable operators generated in the mid-1990s. If your cable TV network doesn't offer cable modem service, it's likely because your cable system operates only in one direction, bringing signals from the cable operator's facilities (the *headend*) to you, as shown in Figure 11-3. Until the cable operator upgrades the network for two-way traffic, the only cable service options are to provide no service or to provide service using your telephone line and a modem for the return path back to the headend. Most operators simply choose not to provide service.

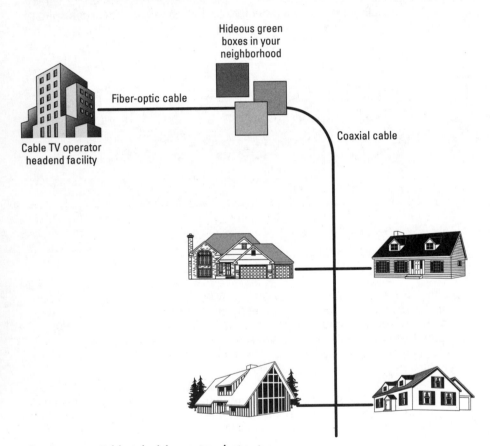

Figure 11-3: Cable television network structure

In a sense, cable television data networks look like wireless radio networks using a base station. The base station resides in the cable operator's headend; and transceivers (usually called cable modems) sit at each connected site. Radio frequency signals traverse the cable between either end.

Cable television networks have a wider spectrum available for signals than free space wireless systems because the cable confines the signals so that they don't radiate and interfere with other services. Most North American cable television systems start the frequencies they use for transmission from headend to user at 54 MHz, which is channel 2, and have an upper limit somewhere between 200 and 750 MHz. Each television channel occupies 6 MHz of this spectrum. (You can guess at the bandwidth of your system by taking the number of channels, multiplying by 6 MHz, and adding 54 MHz — see Table 11-3 for some examples.)

Table 11-3
The Number of Channels Your Cable System Can Carry Depends on the Upper Frequency Limit

Number of Channels	System Upper Limit (MHz)
13	132
34	258
70	474
116	750

Newer cable television systems — ones using fiber optics for the trunks out from the headend — have greater bandwidth and better performance than older, more restricted systems. Fiber-optic upgrades reduce the noise on the return path between you and the headend, too, helping make the most of the bandwidth you have from you to the Internet. Radio systems need a strong signal-to-noise ratio to operate reliably, but the return spectrum on a cable system (which starts at 5 MHz and extends to somewhere between 25 and 40 MHz depending on the system) is a difficult band to use. The first 10 MHz (5 to 15) are extremely noisy; the region from 15 MHz on up is merely noisy. The combination of limited bandwidth and noise restricts the available data rate, giving cable modem systems the same asymmetric data rate characteristics as DSL systems. In the forward direction from the headend to you, most modems use a single 6 MHz channel and transmit at 4 to 25 Mbps.

Cable modem technology has another unavoidable problem, diagrammed in Figure 11-3, which is that the cable, which runs from the ugly green boxes on the street to hundreds of homes, is shared among all those homes. The cable acts like a single LAN segment carrying TCP/IP broadcast and normal messages everywhere along the segment. Because broadcast messages are the foundation of Network Neighborhood browsing in Windows, people on cable television networks don't necessarily even need network sniffer tools to find other computers — they might be able to simply use the tools built into Windows and Linux. If you set up file sharing on your computers, your disks are potentially visible to everyone on the same segment. A firewall will protect your LAN; see Chapter 13 for how to set one up.

In many areas, you can go to a computer equipment store and buy a cable modem built by Linksys, Toshiba, or other companies. You can do that because of standards defined through the work of CableLabs and many cooperating companies, cooperation that created competition in the market and helped to lower the price you'll pay for a cable modem.

Fixed Wireless and Satellite

Advances in component technology have made high-speed microwave radio communications a strong competitor to wired technologies for Internet access. Systems using terrestrial line of sight or satellite relay links offer broadband access at prices competitive with cable or DSL, and without the requirement to be within a specific distance of a telephone switch or to rip up streets to install new fiber-optic cables.

Terrestrial line of sight wireless uses one of several approaches. The service once marketed by Sprint Broadband Direct, for example, adapted the CableLabs cable modem standards for radio use. Figure 11-4 shows how the Sprint service works — a site on a tower or mountain visible from a large part of a city communicates with adapted cable modems tied to antennas on subscribers' roofs. The two-way Internet traffic goes by wireless link to the tower site and then by fiber-optic relay to the Internet backbone. Download speeds (to your computer) can be as high as 8 megabits per second, but upload speeds are generally limited to 128 kilobits per second. Latencies can be 200 to 300 ms with little network activity, and around 3 percent packet loss is common, too, unless you're actively sending or receiving data. With the network loaded with traffic, such as when you're downloading a large file or playing on Microsoft's Xbox Live service (which has continuous traffic for voice communications), latency can go as low as 20 ms, and packet loss goes to near zero.

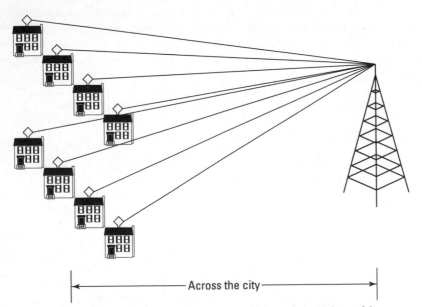

|←————————— Across the city —————————→|

Figure 11-4: Fixed wireless service using cable modems adapted for wireless

The Sprint service requires a clear line of sight from homes to the tower, free of trees, hills, buildings, and other obstructions.

Other services use the IEEE 802.11 wireless LAN standard for neighborhood-sized wireless zones, reducing line of sight problems, and use wired connections between those zones and the Internet. Figure 11-5 shows this architecture. One home in a neighborhood has the central site, and is connected to the Internet backbone through a wired connection that will be shared among all subscribers. Wireless LAN equipment meeting the IEEE 802.11 standard (see the next chapter) connects the subscribers to the central site and, hence, to the Internet. Latency and packet loss can be very low assuming a good wired connection to the central site, but are completely dependent on the specifics of the individual system.

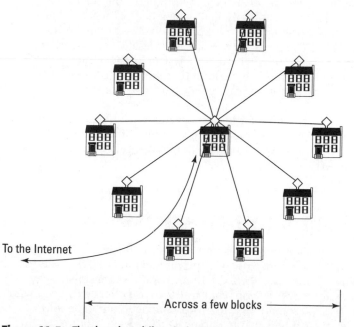

To the Internet

← Across a few blocks →

Figure 11-5: Fixed and mobile wireless service using IEEE 802.11 equipment

Wireless access doesn't have to be line of sight. DirecTV, for example, offers their Direcway Internet access service in the United States to anyone with a clear view of the southern sky, delivering an advertised download rate of 500 kilobits per second. The system architecture is very much like the line of sight system in Figure 11-4, except instead of communicating with a tower in your city, you communicate with a satellite over the equator. You'll still need line of sight to the satellite, but it's higher in the sky than a tower, eliminating many visibility problems.

The most severe problems with satellite Internet access are speed, availability, and latency:

✦ **Speed** — Satellite power is limited, which restricts the data rate you can receive with the relatively small antennas used by the satellite systems. That incoming data rate is shared among all users in a wide area, too, so if there are a lot of people active, you'll get less performance.

✦ **Availability** — Weather effects between you and the satellite reduce the signal power you receive, and attenuate your signal going back up to the satellite. Solar storms increase the interference. Severe weather and storms can cause you to lose the connection, making the Internet inaccessible unless you have a dial-up connection for contingency use.

✦ **Latency** — Radio waves travel at the speed of light, but it's 25,000 miles to the satellite and another 25,000 miles back down. It's actually the round trip to the Internet and back you care about, so the total distance is 100,000 miles. At the speed of light, that's over one half second travel time, all of which adds to the latency you see. That's an enormously long time; so long that you won't want to use satellite Internet access for Internet gaming or telephony.

All wireless access technologies have the same security problems as wired ones because they can make your computer accessible to other people connected to the network. Use a firewall to protect your computers (see Chapter 13 for how to set one up).

Choosing Your Internet Access

Broadband Internet access not only gives you a faster connection, it gives you a connection that's always on. Only dial-up modems impose the wait for a connection so many people are used to — broadband modems are always communicating, ready for anything you want to do. If you choose to keep your computer on all the time — something the power management capabilities, now in nearly all PCs, make a reasonable choice — there's no wait for when you want to find something on the Internet. Firewall security is essential if you keep your PC connected, but it's cheap and reasonably effective.

The two most commonly used broadband technologies are cable modems and DSL, but because broadband availability varies greatly by area, your choice may be driven more by what you can get than by competition. For example, although we live in a suburb of a large city, we happen to live in a broadband black hole where neither DSL nor cable modem service is available. The telephone company freely admits they have no current plans to upgrade the area, and the cable company has been promising Internet service is coming in 2 years for the last 10 years.

If you do have a choice between cable and DSL, then despite our misgivings over what passes for customer service with the cable companies, we recommend cable modems because they're significantly faster than DSL and the technology has proved to be reasonably reliable over time. If you can't get one of those two, try www.dslreports.com/search or more pointedly www.dslreports.com/prequal to find out what you can get in your area.

The benefits of broadband notwithstanding, you need to evaluate any communications technology on the basis of what it will do for you now and whether its cost is justified by those capabilities. Cable and DSL modem equipment costs may not be significantly different than the cost for dial-up modems, including external modems and routers, but the monthly fee is greater. Whether you're considering a 56 Kbps modem, cable, DSL, or some other technology, evaluate it in terms of the data rates you can get and how the combined setup meets your communications requirements. Don't get caught in the trap of waiting for tomorrow's communication technology.

Another factor to consider is whether or not your communications link is the choke point. In many cases, the limitation is the network or server and not your computer or your communications link. For example:

✦ **Server overload** — When a new version of a popular game goes on the Internet, or when the next disaster strikes, it creates an immediate, enormous demand on download servers or news servers. If the servers can't keep up with the demand, or if the communications link into the server can't keep up, there's nothing you can do at your end to make things better.

✦ **Network overload** — Even if the specific server you're working with has the performance and communications link necessary to give you what you want at a high rate, the network connections between you and that server may be overloaded to the point where you still see poor performance. For example, we've played multi-player games over the Internet at times when the response was as good as on a local machine and at times when the remote players couldn't move responsively at all. The computers and communications links at both ends were the same; all that changed was the performance of the intermediate network connections.

Even if the servers and network you're tied into can support you well, you can then decide if the improved performance is worth the cost. Table 11-4 shows how different connection speeds determine how long operations take for different kinds of data. Generally, tasks you do regularly that take more than a minute or so are annoying. The table shows that large sound and video files exceed that threshold, as do large software files. If you're transferring large files regularly, or if you use the Internet so frequently that the delay for modems to connect is a nuisance, you'll probably want to consider broadband.

Our experience, too, is that having computers always on and always connected to the Internet encourages children to use the computers and use the Internet. Our kids, for instance, have had computers available as readily as pencils since before they can remember and use one as often as the other. Parents absolutely have the responsibility to monitor what their kids are exposed to on the Internet, and there's no shortage of garbage and worse out there; however, there's also reason to think any successful approach to encouraging good computer and Internet skills is worth thinking about.

Table 11-4
Transmission Times for Various Connection Speeds

		Transmission Time at Data Rate (Seconds)							
Application	*Size(KB)*	*33.6*	*53.0*	*64*	*128*	*256*	*512*	*1,024*	*2,048*
Text and	2	0.6	0.4	0.3	0.2	0.1	0.0	0.0	0.0
E-Mail	100	30.5	19.3	16.0	8.0	4.0	2.0	1.0	0.5
Graphics	10	3.0	1.9	1.6	0.8	0.4	0.2	0.1	0.1
	200	61.0	38.6	32.0	16.0	8.0	4.0	2.0	1.0
Sound	10	3.0	1.9	1.6	0.8	0.4	0.2	0.1	0.1
	500	152.4	96.6	80.0	40.0	20.0	10.0	5.0	2.5
Video	10	3.0	1.9	1.6	0.8	0.4	0.2	0.1	0.1
	10MB	3,040	1,930	1,600	800.0	400.0	200.0	100.0	50.0
Software &	20	6.1	3.9	3.2	1.6	0.8	0.4	0.2	0.1
data files	20MB	6,090	3,860	3,200	1,600	800.0	400.0	200.0	100.0

Choosing a Modem

We should probably admit to some bias here — with the exception of computers with severe security requirements, we don't understand why anyone would have a computer that wasn't in some way connected to the Internet. You are bound to share work or personal interests with other people in the world, and an Internet connection is one of the easiest ways to find them. You need not be a computer fanatic to get your computer connected, and it need not be computers themselves you're interested in.

Choosing a dial-up modem

If you're running dial-up, the minimum modem you should install is a V.90 unit, although if you're buying a new modem you'll want to get one implementing the later V.92 standard. Modems meeting the V.90 and V.92 standards work for connections using the V.34 standard at rates up to 33.6 Kbps and will connect with all the major online services and Internet service providers. It's more likely you'll find a service with modems that don't support 56 Kbps on their end than one that a V.90 or V.92 modem can't connect to.

Even if you don't get the full 53 Kbps rate from a V.90 modem, you may nevertheless want one of the subtle benefits from V.90 — if you play games over the Internet, they will be more responsive with modems that have less transmission latency. Table 11-5 shows the performance we measured for several modem technologies. (Note, however, that a V.90 or V.92 modem connected to a V.34 modem will give you only V.34-class latency.)

Table 11-5
Modem Latency Comparison

Modem Equipment	Representative Ping (ms)
V.34 (analog)	180
V.90 and V.92 (digital)	120
Wireless	20 to 300
ADSL and Cable TV	12
Satellite	> 500

The "Ping" values in Table 11-5 are the time it took for a low-level message to leave our computer, go through the modems, reach the nearest Internet computer to us, and return. The round-trip times are higher inside games. For fast-action games, a difference in faster response time can be the difference between winning and losing. Table 11-1 shows that a V.90 modem connected digitally will have response times 60 ms faster than an analog connection and will deliver that faster response even if it's running no faster than 33.3 Kbps.

Tip   Even though your dial-up modem and those at your ISP are capable of 56 Kbps connections, you might not get connections at that rate because many telephone line problems make a consistent 56 Kbps connection difficult. Speeds of 33.6 Kbps or faster require perfect line conditions along the entire length of the connection. These modems are capable of pushing the limits of analog phone lines, commonly offering connect speeds of 21600, 24000, and even 26400 bps or higher. Variations in line quality are typically the cause of low connection rates, which is why you can sometimes get a bad connection, hang up and call again, and do better. If you rarely connect at rates above 19200 bps, check that your computer's serial port is set for 38.4 Kbps or higher, and try dialing another number (ideally, to another modem distant from the first to see if the problem is at your end or the other one).

Choosing an internal or external modem

There's not a lot of basis on which to choose between internal and external modems for desktop computers. If you're using broadband Internet access, an external modem is better because it simplifies sharing the modem among several computers, and simplifies putting a hardware firewall between the modem and your computers.

You have the option of internal or external if you're using dial-up, however, because dial-up is slow enough without sharing it among several computers and because (unlike broadband connections) dial-up modems disconnect from the Internet when you're not using them. Here are the factors that should influence your choice of an internal versus external dial-up modem:

✦ **Internal bus slots** — An internal modem requires a bus slot, while an external modem connects to a serial or USB port. If you get a USB modem, or if the serial port for your external modem is provided directly off your motherboard (as is often the case), the external modem won't consume a bus slot. There's no difference in the I/O port or interrupt usage unless you use USB — you have a serial port on a conventional modem whether you use an internal or external unit.

✦ **Status lights** — Some people find the status lights on the front of an external modem very useful. Among other things, they show you when data is being sent or received.

✦ **Cost** — Because an external modem has to include a case, power supply, connectors, and lights, it has components an internal modem need not have. That means it costs more.

✦ **Security** — As we discussed in the section on dial-up analog modems, equipment such as the 3Com OfficeConnect 56K LAN Modem combines an external modem with a firewall. With the constantly increasing number of worms, Trojans, and crackers prowling the Internet, that security can bring you important peace of mind.

Summary

✦ You should have an Internet connection, preferably broadband.

✦ A 56 Kbps modem meeting ITU-T recommendation V.90 or V.92 is the least you should have; we recommend cable TV, DSL, or wireless broadband.

✦ Good Internet security requires a firewall, something that's much easier with an external modem.

Wired and Wireless Networking

♦   ♦   ♦   ♦

In This Chapter

Considering network
characteristics

Examining Ethernet and
wireless technologies

Selecting networking
technologies

♦   ♦   ♦   ♦

Networking adds new technologies to the basics of personal computing, ones that let computers communicate with each other. You need both hardware and software to build your network; be prepared for the fact that networking software is more complex than the hardware.

A relatively small set of characteristics define networking hardware:

♦ **Medium** — A physical connection, a medium, carries signals from one computer to the next. That connection can be coaxial cable, twisted-pairs of wires, fiber-optic lines, infrared light, radio waves, or anything else that can carry digital information.

♦ **Point-to-point or shared media** — In a point-to-point topology, the connections in a wired computer network usually run between pairs of devices, whether they be computers or network elements. Wireless networks (and some older cable technologies) typically share the radio spectrum among several computers in a shared media configuration.

♦ **Baseband or modulated** — The signals between computers can be either baseband, meaning that digital information is directly impressed onto the transmission medium, or modulated, meaning that the information is impressed onto a carrier signal. Modulation adds complexity, but helps signals carry across difficult environments.

✦ **Full- or half-duplex** — Half-duplex connections permit transmission in only one direction at a time. Full-duplex connections support simultaneous transmissions in both directions.

✦ **Access methods** — If the media supports multiple computers on the same physical pathway, a mechanism exists so that the computers can tell when it's okay to transmit versus when the pathway is busy.

Network Characteristics

If you're going to network your computers together, you have to decide what technologies to use. You should base that decision on what the competing choices do well and what they do poorly. We start by looking at some of the most important characteristics in networks and then look at specific technologies and how they relate to those characteristics.

Point-to-point or shared media

Depending on the communications technology, you can hook one device at each end of a connection (typical of fiber optics) or many along the length (easy with copper or wireless).

Point-to-point connections can still look like shared media. For example, twisted-pair Ethernet connects ports on a *hub* to computers (or routers or other devices). There is one device on each end of the wire, and nothing in the middle. Because of the way the hub works, though, all the separate connections appear to be a single wire.

Point-to-point connections have the advantage that when a problem occurs with one computer's connection, the others generally stay operational. Shared media connections have the advantage that they don't require all the wiring to be collected at a central point. One connection can be strung from unit to unit and return only one cable to a more central place.

Baseband or modulated

The technology a modem uses to transmit data down a phone line is an example of modulated transmission. The digital information is impressed on a carrier signal, which in turn moves the information across the media. In the case of a modem, the carrier frequency is in the range of sounds you can hear. Here are some other possibilities:

✦ **Fiber optics** — The carrier is a light wave. The modulation is often variations in the intensity of the beam.

✦ **Infrared** — The carrier is a light wave, as with fiber optics, but the medium is open air. The modulation is commonly a variation in the intensity of the light wave.

✦ **Wireless** — The carrier is a radio wave. The modulation can be variations in amplitude, frequency, or phase.

✦ **Power lines** — You can send signals back over the power lines you plug your computer into. A low-frequency radio wave could be the carrier, likely using frequency or phase modulation.

✦ **Tin can and string** — As silly as it sounds, you could make this work at low data rates. You could let a standing vibration on the string be the "carrier," pulling more or less on the string to vary the frequency (which would be the modulation). The point isn't that this is realistic, but that what might not come to mind today might be the transmission technology of tomorrow.

Several of these media support baseband transmission, too, sending the signal over the medium without a carrier. For example, you can use fiber optics and infrared beams like Morse code, simply turning the signal completely on or off. Wireless connections work for baseband transmission too, sending pulses that vary the time between pulses to represent zeroes or ones.

No one scheme — baseband or modulated transmission — or even any specific form of modulation is best all the time. Some are less expensive to implement (copper), some are good for high rates and long distances (fiber optics), and some are very easy to deploy (infrared). It's typical, but not universal, to find baseband technologies in short-range applications and modulated technologies in longer range ones.

Full- or half-duplex

Connections can allow transmission one way at a time (half-duplex) or both ways simultaneously (full-duplex). With the exception of telephone lines, full-duplex operations generally require two independent half-duplex connections — one in each direction. (Telephone lines use a special transformer called a hybrid to prevent echoes and allow transmission both ways over two wires.)

Copper Ethernets either operate half-duplex (only one transmitter at a time) or use independent pairs of wires, one in each direction.

Access methods

A shared-access medium requires a way for the transmissions of one computer to be kept separate from those of the rest. There are four common ways of doing that:

✦ **Carrier sense multiple access with collision detection (CSMA/CD)** — As in Ethernet, a computer waits for silence on the wire. When it hears no other transmissions, the computer transmits its own data. When a collision occurs, each computer waits a random time and tries again.

✦ **Time Division Multiple Access (TDMA)** — Each computer sharing the medium can be assigned a time slot (in a rotation) according to a clock shared by all the computers. So long as a computer stays in its slot, it can transmit freely. Computers listen to all time slots except their own.

✦ **Frequency Division Multiple Access (FDMA)** — Broadband systems are frequently capable of supporting multiple transmission carriers on different frequencies. If the frequencies are separated far enough, filters can eliminate all but the one you're interested in.

✦ **Code-Division Multiple Access (CDMA)** — In the same way that pairs of people can talk separately in a crowded room, listening only to each other, computers can shut out other conversations on the same wire. They do this by coding their data at the transmitter in a way known only to the receiver, mixing it up with a high-speed series of random numbers. The receiver applies the same code again to extract the data. Receivers without the right code see only noise except for the signal they're supposed to see — the one for which they do have the right code.

Each of these access methods has its advantages and disadvantages. CSMA/CD requires only loose coordination between individual computers, and readily takes advantage of having fewer machines on the wire. It's more effective in baseband systems (such as Ethernet) than in broadband ones; however, it's vulnerable to one computer failing and taking out communications for all the computers on the same wire and tends to suffer when the traffic on the wire climbs to a significant percentage of the raw capacity.

TDMA is common in telephone networks, being used to combine circuits into a high-capacity connection. TDMA is also common in wireless systems because it allows many users on a channel at relatively low equipment cost. It guarantees a circuit a specified data rate, but limits flexibility in changing the rate. The time division structure has to be specified in advance, so there are likely to be upper limits to how much of the total channel capacity a given circuit can have. Synchronizing the timing among all the computers is critical, because a mistimed transmitter can step on someone else's interval, and a mistimed receiver can get the wrong data.

FDMA is common in wireless systems because it simplifies distinguishing one signal from the others. It's also used as a way to increase the data rate over fiber-optic links. The electronics supporting the link can't run as fast as the fiber is capable of transporting, so rather than try to force them to run faster (making them much more expensive), it's easier to send several optical carriers down the fiber at different frequencies. (This is called *wavelength division multiplexing* when applied to fiber optics.) Filters at the receiving end split out the beams and send each one to its own set of electronics.

Finally, CDMA is uniquely suited to noisy transmission channels. The properties that let it ignore other conversations also let it ignore noise, and give it a degree of privacy (we pointedly said privacy and not security) not inherent in the other technologies. The best CDMA implementations can carry as much or more traffic in a channel as other technologies; most CDMA systems carry somewhat less.

Network Technologies

After you have a medium running from one place to another, you need to put a network on top of it. There are many different approaches, the most common of which is Ethernet. Most of the other network technologies have been developed to address one or another limitation of Ethernet — speed, distance, or the need for a cable. Table 12-1 summarizes the key characteristics of the most common local network technologies — Ethernet and wireless.

Table 12-1 Characteristics of Common Network Technologies		
Characteristic	*Ethernet*	*Wireless*
Data rate	10 or 100 Mbps	1 to 54 Mbps
Maximum distance between stations	185 m (607 feet) for 10Base-2; up to 2.8 km (1.7 miles)	10s of feet to miles for optical fiber
Logical topology	Bus	Bus
Physical topology	Star, bus	Point-to-point or star
Media	Optical fiber, twisted-pair, coaxial cable	Radio
Access method	CSMA/CD	TDMA, FDMA, CDMA

In addition to networks having overall characteristics, every network implementation has a specific medium it uses to transmit signals. Collectively, we'll call the network medium its cable (or cable type), ignoring the fact that wireless transmissions don't have a physical cable.

Ethernet

Ethernet was among the earliest networks. The initial version of Ethernet used a thick coaxial cable about 0.4 inches in diameter. Later copper-based versions used a thinner coaxial cable, before the evolution to today's twisted copper pairs. For example, one of the oldest surviving variants of Ethernet, 10Base-2, uses flexible coaxial cable to carry the LAN signal, and makes connections with a twist-lock BNC connector. Limitations on the transmission characteristics of the 10Base-2 signal and cable cause restrictions on the way you use 10Base-2 to connect computers:

✦ **No external transceiver or AUI cable** — The 10Base-2 transceiver is built into the adapter card in your PC. A tee coaxial connector mounts on the back of the board, and the cable attaches to both sides of the tee. If one side of the tee has no cable attached, a terminator attaches directly to the tee. You must not use a segment of cable to space the tee away from the adapter card.

✦ **No spur directly connected segments** — No branches off the 10Base-2 cable are allowed — even to connect a computer to the associated tee connector. The cable must run to the tee connector directly on the adapter card.

✦ **Maximum transmission length** — The maximum segment length is 185 meters (607 feet). You can attach up to 30 computers to a segment. There are no special spacing requirements between computers except that the minimum spacing is 0.5 meters (1.6 feet).

If you open the coaxial cable at any point, the entire network segment goes down. You can remove a computer from a 10Base-2 segment, but you have to do it by removing the tee connector from the back of the computer. It's very common to use a short spur segment from the tee connector to the back of the computer, but it's a very bad idea. The spur causes signal reflections, degrading the signal on the network and causing errors. The error rate goes up as the load on the network goes up, and as the number of spurs (and their length) goes up.

Tip   If you have a 10Base-2 network, check the connectors, terminators, and especially the tees often. Cracked parts make your LAN unreliable or inoperative.

By far the dominant Ethernet cabling technology is twisted-pair — a bundle of four pairs of wires, each pair twisted together, and the entire set wrapped in an outside jacket. There are two variants of twisted-pair network wiring, 10Base-T (which runs at 10 Mbps), and 100Base-T (which runs at 100 Mbps). The two variants are commonly termed 10/100Base-T when it doesn't matter which one you're talking about.

10/100Base-T attaches only one computer to each wire segment, combining segments to form the network. Each segment contains two twisted-pairs of wire: one pair for transmitting and one for receiving. The wires have an RJ-45 modular connector (slightly larger than the usual RJ-11 connector on most telephones) at each end (Figure 12-1). One end connects to the computer, while the other connects to a device that joins all the separate segments together (Figure 12-2). That device is called a *hub* or a *switch*, depending on its internal characteristics. You can get hubs and switches to join from 4 to 24 (or more) segments together and can join hubs and switches together to create even larger networks. Ethernet switches increase twisted-pair network performance by letting many computers transmit at the same time, separating the traffic of each computer pair from the rest.

Twisted-pair connections can be up to 100 meters (328 feet) long. If you allow 10 meters (total) for connections within a wiring closet and from the wall to the computer, the in-wall wiring can be up to 90 meters. Both unshielded twisted-pair (UTP) and shielded twisted-pair (STP) are used, differing in that STP has shielding wrapped around the conductors to minimize noise and interference. Therefore, STP has better transmission characteristics than UTP, but twisted-pair wiring is almost universally done with UTP. Twisted-pair wiring provides separate wire pairs for transmitting and receiving. Twisted-pair can therefore operate in full-duplex, which means that it's possible for a computer to transmit and receive simultaneously.

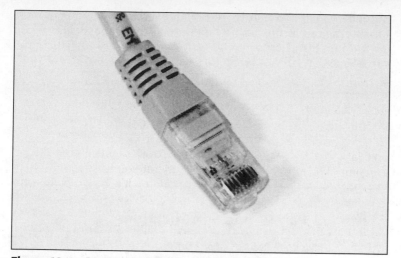

Figure 12-1: RJ-45 connector on Ethernet cable
©2004 Barry Press & Marcia Press

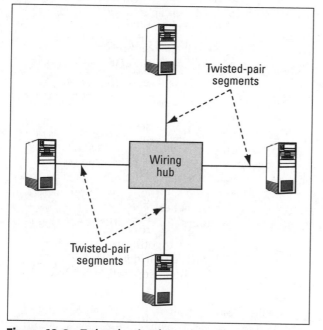

Figure 12-2: Twisted-pair Ethernet (10/100Base-T and gigabit Ethernet) attaches one computer per cable. If any one wire goes down, the rest of the computers are unaffected.

In addition to the division between shielded and unshielded wire, there are categories of twisted-pair wiring, differentiated by their capability to transport the network signal without distortions, called Category-3, -5, -5e, and -6. Category-3 is the usual voice-grade wiring that is commonly pre-wired in buildings.

Categories-5, 5e, and 6 use successively higher-quality cables and connectors. If you ever plan to upgrade from 10Base-T to 100Base-T, you want to start with Category-5, 5e, or 6. Your network runs no better than its worst wiring component. In other words, use Category-3 connectors with Category-6 wire and you have a Category-3 network.

Table 12-2 summarizes the twisted-pair wiring categories. You should avoid Category-3, but any of the other three are suitable for home, home office, and small networks. If you're building a large LAN, plan on using Category-5e or Category-6.

Table 12-2
Twisted-Pair Wiring Specifications

Specification	Frequency Rating	Application
Category-3		Basic, nonupgradeable twisted-pair networks
Category-5	100 MHz	Basic Fast Ethernet networks without full-duplex links, or (risky) gigabit Ethernet networks
Category-5e (Enhanced Category-5)	100 MHz	Fast Ethernet networks running full-duplex Gigabit Ethernet networks
Category-6	250 MHz	Gigabit Ethernet networks (solid)

Ethernet cables in the walls typically terminate at RJ-45 jacks, and you use *patch cords* to connect from the wall jacks to computers, hubs, switches, or other devices. Patch cords have RJ-45 plugs at both ends. If you have the tools to attach the modular connectors, you can make twisted-pair patch cables yourself. If not, you'll have to order them in the right length. Either way, if you make a cable that reverses the transmit and receive pairs between the connectors — a crossover cable — you can connect two computers directly, without a wiring hub.

Twisted-pair interfaces monitor the link status, and most provide a light to indicate that the link is up. You have to check the lights at both ends, though, because link status is based on the receive side only.

Ethernet is designed for shared media. Point-to-point wiring (such as twisted-pair) connects the wiring segments together electrically in most cases, creating a shared medium through the wiring hub. Similarly, Ethernet can be either half-duplex or full-duplex, depending on the physical medium and attached network devices. Ethernets use carrier sense with collision detection to support multiple access. When any given transmitter has something to send, it listens on the network to try to verify that no other device is currently transmitting. If the network appears idle, it starts to send. Because transmitters can be relatively far apart, however, it's possible for two transmitters to sense that the network is idle and both start to transmit at roughly the same time. Ethernet transceivers detect this occurrence and schedule a retransmission. The time for the retransmission is based on a random number to help the two colliding stations avoid further contention.

The shared medium amounts to a "cloud" that interconnects all nodes on the network equally. Addresses in each network message define both the source and the destination of the message.

Tip

Keep in mind that an unencrypted shared medium (such as Ethernet) is inherently insecure. On any one network segment, every packet arrives at every transceiver, and a transceiver programmed to listen to all addresses indiscriminately hears them all. This is useful for building network analyzers, but it means that, with the right software, the traffic from the executive suite to marketing is equally visible to anyone else connected to the network.

Another downside of Ethernet has been its limitation to 10 or 100 Mbps on a single segment. As fast as that seems, when you start to transfer huge files across the network (such as raw video recordings) or connect tens or hundreds of computers to a single segment, network performance accessing the file servers quickly becomes intolerable. Gigabit Ethernet solves that problem, offering full-duplex Ethernet operation on your existing unshielded twisted-pair wiring at 1,000 Mbps.

Table 12-3 shows the variants of Gigabit Ethernet:

Table 12-3
Gigabit Ethernet Variants

Designation	Media	Distance
1000Base-SX	Multimode optical fiber (850 nm)	500 m
1000Base-LX	Multimode and single mode optical fiber (1300 nm)	500 m to 2 km
1000Base-CX	Short-haul copper ("twinax" shielded twisted-pair)	25 m
1000Base-T	Long-haul copper over unshielded twisted-pair	25 to 100 m

The compatibility with existing wiring simplifies deployment, although distance limitations may be a factor. The first uses of gigabit Ethernet were to connect servers to networks and to interconnect switches as the network backbone. High-performance applications such as video editing are driving gigabit Ethernet out towards individual computers. The need for gigabit Ethernet isn't speculation. A high-performance server can, today, generate sustained network traffic in the 300 Mbps and up range, so a highly loaded backbone with several servers will benefit from the performance boost. You could see performance gains in the home or small office too — for example, a 10GB video file that takes about 20 minutes to transfer between computers over 100 Mbps Ethernet would take only a minute and a half over gigabit Ethernet.

Ethernet adapters are one of the products that we're picky about. Networks are difficult enough to set up and keep running reliably; you don't need extra excitement on that front. We've found adapters from 3Com, Linksys, and NET-GEAR dependable, as well as adapters built into the Intel motherboards, and have the scars to prove that less expensive isn't always better. We've thrown away a network card that was a solid piece of hardware, for example, because it had an admittedly buggy driver that the vendor never fixed.

We recommend using motherboards with built-in Ethernet adapters, such as that on the Intel D875PBZ motherboard (Figure 12-3). Otherwise, 10/100/1000Base-T adapters — stay with the top manufacturers — are a commodity you can buy based on price and availability. Either way, market price pressures have driven the adapters to be integrated into little more than a single chip.

Ethernet RJ-45 connector

USB 2.0 connectors

Figure 12-3: 10/100/1000Base-T Ethernet adapter built into the Intel D875PBZ motherboard

©2004 Barry Press & Marcia Press

Gigabit Ethernet is new enough that it's particularly important to use adapters (and other network components) from first-line manufacturers.

Wireless transmission

Wireless networks use radio or light waves to communicate between stations. The frequencies for radio-based networks vary based on national licensing. Systems in the United States often use bands designated by the Federal Communications Commission for "unlicensed" operation, meaning that, after the manufacturer has qualified the equipment, the operator doesn't need special training or licensing. Optical systems often use infrared frequencies (light waves just below the visible spectrum). Some of the key characteristics are:

✦ **Range** — Radio systems have ranges up to tens of miles. Infrared systems are typically limited to a few hundred feet.

✦ **Blockage** — Radio waves penetrate walls and floors with varying degrees of success. Light waves require a direct line of sight between the transmitter and receiver.

✦ **Data rate** — Radio systems don't always carry the usual 10 Mbps Ethernet rate, particularly at longer ranges. Radio data rates vary from 1 Mbps to hundreds of megabits per second, with the most common variants running between 1 and 54 Mbps. Short-range infrared systems tend to operate at speeds of 10 to 100 Kbps, although some operate as fast as 4 Mbps.

Wireless networks can operate with point-to-point topologies, like twisted-pair networks, or with shared access, like coaxial-cable networks.

Optical wireless and many radio wireless networks use a central node, called a *base station*, which corresponds to a wiring hub in a 10/100Base-T network. Transmissions between computers go through the base station and are retransmitted after reception if the destination is also on the wireless network. (Base stations are commonly attached to a wired network as well, giving the mobile units access to the wider network.) Networks organized with a base station generally transmit out of the base station on one frequency and receive on another; the computers reverse the frequency assignments. Radio networks without a base station let all units transmit on the same frequency.

In either scheme, wireless networks require a method for collision detection. The carrier sense/collision detection approach used in Ethernet doesn't work well on wireless networks because of the time delay between the start of the transmission and when the receiver notices the carrier. The relatively long latency while the receiver locks up on the signal creates too long a window in which a second transmitter might start operations and step on the transmissions of the first one. That's why many wireless networks use an access scheme that positively identifies the next station allowed to transmit.

Some radio networks use *spread spectrum* technology to isolate transmissions from one another. Spread spectrum is an inherently noise resistant transmission. There are two forms of spread spectrum: frequency hopping and direct sequence.

✦ A *frequency hopper* divides the overall allocated spectrum into many small bands, transmitting for only a brief moment in one before hopping to the next. The hops are made in a predetermined sequence. Frequency hoppers resist interference and jamming by either avoiding the noisy channels or dwelling in them for a very short a time.

✦ The second form of spread spectrum, *direct sequence*, enables all the transmitted signals to use the entire allocated band at once. The greater the ratio of the available channel bandwidth to the data rate, the more interference and jamming-resistant the signal will be.

The advantages that wireless networks have over wired ones are mobility and not having to run wires (not as silly as it sounds). In addition to being able to move around — useful if you're taking inventory in a warehouse, for example — a wireless connection can solve the problem of linking networks that have physical barriers between them. Point-to-point wireless links can solve the problem of how to cross roads and railways between building networks, or of how to cross parts of a town without the expense of a leased telephone line. Multidrop wireless networks can simplify linking stations on several floors of the same building when it's impractical to run wires between the networks. Wireless networks are generally more expensive than their wired equivalents, so you want to use them only where mobility or access is an issue.

IEEE specification 802.11 standardizes the most common wireless LAN technologies. There are three variants, IEEE 802.11b, 802.11a, and 802.11g.

✦ **IEEE 802.11b** — Also known as WiFi (for Wireless Fidelity), IEEE 802.11b networks run at rates from 1 to 11 Mbps over relatively short ranges. You can run a WiFi network in *ad hoc* mode, in which two computers talk directly among themselves, or in *infrastructure* mode, in which the computers talk through a central *wireless access point* (Figure 12-4). Access points are commonly packaged with routers to create a device that interfaces both the wireless network and a LAN together and to an external Internet connection. IEEE 802.11b networks operate at 2.4 GHz frequencies, a band shared by wireless telephones, Bluetooth networks, and a variety of other equipment. IEEE 802.11b network installations have grown explosively in recent years, and the equipment has become quite inexpensive.

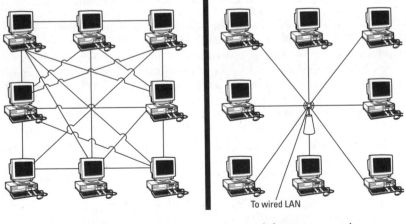

Ad hoc mode   Infrastructure mode

Figure 12-4: Wireless LAN modes

Sharing Frequencies with Spread Spectrum

There's an interesting operation computers do on numbers, called "exclusive or" or "XOR." The XOR operation is interesting because if you do it twice, you get back your original number. For instance, if we compute

```
11001010 XOR 11111111
```

we get 00110101. All the bits in the initial number have flipped. If we repeat the operation on the result and do

```
00110101 XOR 11111111
```

we get 11001010 again. Now, suppose we take two digital signals: one a real data stream and one a much faster stream of random numbers. If we XOR the two streams together, we pretty much get garbage out, but we can throw away the garbage and get back the data stream if we repeat the XOR using the exact same random number sequence.

In a nutshell, that's what direct sequence spread spectrum does. It combines your data with a fast random number stream in the modulator and extracts it back out from the random numbers in the demodulator. Of course, if you followed that as well as we did the first time someone waved the idea at us, you've got a blank look and you're thinking "So what?" (or worse) about now.

Here's why this is really good. The frequency spectrum a signal takes up is proportional to how fast the data goes. Double the data rate, and (everything else being the same) you double the spectrum. If you keep the power level the same, the power at any specific frequency is less because the total power is being divided over a greater range of frequencies. In the transmitter, having the modulator mix the data with the random numbers widens the spectrum of the transmitted result (because we use a fast random number stream).

Now, watch what happens in the receiver. You mix the random numbers back in with the received signal, and two things happen: First, the actual signal gets contracted back from its wideband spectrum to the narrower one needed for the actual (slower) data rate. Second, the random number mix spreads out any noise signals that the receiver happened to pick up. Unless they contain just the right random number sequence (which they don't), the mixing operation works just like spreading data in the transmitter. The power of the data signal gets collected back into a narrow range, and the power of the noise gets spread out into a wide range. Signal power goes up and noise power goes down.

The best part of this is that lots of us can talk in the channel at the same time. Your transmitter and receiver use a different random number sequence than ours. Because we use a different sequence, my receiver doesn't despread your transmission; it stays spread out, so it remains low power noise. We simply don't hear you.

✦ **IEEE 802.11a** — You won't get the full (raw) data rate from a wireless network, which means IEEE 802.11b wireless LANs (WLANs) are relatively slow. They're fast enough for surfing the Internet, but terrible for file transfers and other operations on a LAN. Engineers developed IEEE 802.11a in response, a WLAN specification running in the 5.6 GHz frequency band and operating at 54 Mbps. IEEE 802.11a equipment never dropped in price enough for the standard to be used widely because of the challenges its higher frequency band presented, and has now been eclipsed by the IEEE 802.11g standard.

✦ **IEEE 802.11g** — If you imagine (functionally) a hybrid with IEEE 802.11b frequencies (so it's cheaper) and IEEE 802.11a speed, you have the idea for IEEE 802.11g, which runs in the 2.4 GHz band at speeds up to 54 Mbps. Standardized equipment only first appeared in 2003, but it entered the market at the then-current prices for IEEE 802.11b gear (which immediately dropped in price).

IEEE 802.11g runs at full speed in pure IEEE 802.11g WLANs, or can throttle back somewhat to operate compatibly in IEEE 802.11b WLANs.

Unfortunately, the IEEE 802.11 designers were not experienced cryptologists, and they inadvertently produced a system that was by default easily penetrated and — even using what's called Wired Equivalent Privacy (WEP) — relatively insecure. It's been demonstrated that, with the right equipment and software, you can monitor WEP-encrypted WiFi traffic and recreate the encryption key. After you have the key, the network might as well have no security because you'll be able to use the network just as if you were authorized to use it. Worse yet (or better, depending on which side you're on), the more traffic on your network, the easier it is to penetrate, and you can penetrate a WEP network anonymously.

IEEE 802.11g equipment offers a WiFi Protected Access (WPA), a newer, stronger security technology. WPA is itself a subset of the yet more capable IEEE 802.1x security standard.

Even if your equipment doesn't support WPA or IEEE 802.1x, however, you *can* (at the price of some one-time aggravation) make a WiFi network more secure. Here's what you should do:

✦ **Disable broadcast SSID** — WiFi WLANs identify themselves with a *service set identifier (SSID)*, which names the network and works (loosely) like a password. Unfortunately, most wireless access points *transmit* their SSIDs by default, which is pretty much like standing in the street and shouting your bank card PIN. Unless you have equipment that requires the access point to broadcast the SSID, turn this feature off. If you do leave it on, change the SSID to something other than the default.

✦ **Turn on WEP, and use 128-bit keys** — You shouldn't rely on WEP to be absolutely secure, but the cracker next door isn't less likely to have the tools, systems, or know-how to break it. WEP is a lot better than nothing (unless you're using 64-bit keys, which are far weaker than 128-bit keys).

Access points and adapters typically let you set up the WEP key either by typing a passphrase or by entering a hexadecimal (base 16) value. We've had trouble making passphrases work across multiple vendors' equipment, so we recommend generating a hexadecimal value using a long passphrase and then using the hexadecimal value everywhere. Keep a copy of the key somewhere secure because you can't be sure you can regenerate it later.

✦ **Set MAC address restrictions** — Most access points let you list the physical (Media Access Control — MAC) address of equipment allowed to connect to your LAN. A typical MAC address looks something like 00-0C-38-55-F4-AD. You can use a MAC restriction list containing all your devices to ensure only authorized devices connect, although you can't limit who might be able to listen.

Figure 12-5 shows the Microsoft model MN-700 IEEE 802.11g base station, which incorporates a router, wireless access point, and a 10/100 Ethernet switch. You control it through a Web browser, and can set it to act either as a wireless router or a simple wireless access point. Having that choice is convenient because it lets you add the unit to your existing LAN if you already have a working router connected to the Internet.

Figure 12-5: Microsoft model MN-700 IEEE 802.11g base station
©2004 Barry Press & Marcia Press

Figure 12-6 shows the corresponding notebook adapter. Microsoft has another surprising product in its line, too — the Xbox wireless adapter. What makes the Xbox wireless adapter interesting from a PC point of view is what it will do for your wired LAN.

Figure 12-6: Microsoft model MN-720 IEEE 802.11g notebook adapter
©2004 Barry Press & Marcia Press

Suppose you have several rooms each with their own wired LANs that you'd like to connect together, but can't run Ethernets between them. A wireless access device connecting to a PC with USB is inexpensive, but connects only one PC unless you then route out through the PC to the LAN. That takes a little work (see the next chapter) and can prevent PCs on your other LANs from seeing the computers on the other side of the wirelessly connected PC.

You can do the job easily with the Xbox wireless adapter, and without any routing issues, because it acts like an access point that connects wired equipment — PCs, printers, Xboxes, and more — to a wireless LAN. This application isn't documented or supported by Microsoft, but here's what we did:

✦ **Set up the base station** — Connect the base station to one of your LANs, either as the Internet router or a wireless access point. Set up at least the security controls for WEP.

✦ **Configure the Xbox wireless adapter** — You need an Xbox for this because the configuration software comes as an Xbox game disk. Connect the adapter to the Xbox, run the software, configure security, and verify that the Xbox connects to the network (for example, check that it gets an IP address assigned through Dynamic Host Configuration Protocol (DHCP) — see Chapters 14 and 15).

✦ **Cable the Xbox wireless adapter to the LAN** — All that's left is to hook the adapter to the uplink port on your hub or switch (or to a normal port using a crossover cable). You have to disable the DHCP server on that LAN if you have one because you want the DHCP server on the other LAN instead. After you do, every computer on the wirelessly connected LAN should connect over to the other LAN, and (if you have a connection) out to the Internet.

Choosing Your Network Technologies

All local area network equipment decisions really boil down to how many computers you have, what your bandwidth requirements are, and whether you have mobile users. We recommend twisted-pair Ethernet — 10/100Base-T — for nearly all applications, and gigabit Ethernet when you need even more speed.

If you need to move around, or if wires are hard to run between computers, go with IEEE 802.11g. Be sure to secure your network as tightly as you can if you use a WLAN because most building walls won't block radio waves. You can't know who's listening in.

If you have a local area network and use an Internet (or other network) connection extensively enough to have a broadband connection, you want to tie that connection to your local area network. We show you how to do that in the next chapter.

Summary

✦ In most cases, you probably want twisted-pair wiring and 10/100 Mbps adapters.

✦ Wireless LANs are a great convenience, both for mobility and to eliminate the need for wiring.

✦ Wireless LANs, and any LAN connected to the Internet, require that you plan for your network security.

Hubs, Switches, Routers, and Firewalls

In This Chapter

Designing local area networks

Working with hubs, switches, and routers

Securing your network with packet filters and firewalls

After you've put network and communications equipment into your computer and set up your network cabling, it's time to connect it to a network. You've got two levels of networking to think about — how to build your local area network, and how to hook up into wide area networks. We look at local area network equipment and structures in this chapter.

Cross-Reference Chapter 11 covers connecting your LAN to the Internet.

Designing Small Local Area Networks

Network design involves a lot of different (and sometimes conflicting) considerations, including:

+ **Capacity** — The rate at which information can be sent over the network. You care not only about the rate between pairs of computers, but also about the aggregate rate among many pairs of computers.

+ **Security** — How vulnerable your data and systems are to accidental or malicious damage (or theft).

+ **Scalability** — Networks grow, and you'll want to be able to accommodate growth without having to rip all your equipment out and start over. You'll need to think about connecting more users, more sites, more storage, and more capacity.

Larger networks require you think about the latency and jitter across your network, and about both redundancy and uninterruptible power. You'll no doubt consider other factors specific to your situation, too, so rather than attempt to give you a step-by-step recipe for assembling a local area network — and inevitably fail to cover your actual situation — we'll start by describing a very simple network, touching on the most important concepts, and then move on to discuss more complex ones.

The simplest network is two computers connected back-to-back using Ethernet network interfaces and a crossover cable rather than a standard straight-through patch cable (see Chapter 12 for what those are). Figure 13-1 shows what that looks like.

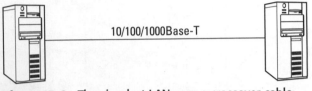
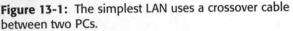

Figure 13-1: The simplest LAN uses a crossover cable between two PCs.

The performance you get from this simple LAN is better than almost any other network you can make because with full-duplex–capable network adapters, it runs at full speed both ways without any possibility of collisions. Using 100Base-T adapters, you see 100 Mbps both ways, or 200 Mbps total. That's a significant speed advantage. For example, suppose you start transmitting two large files, one from each of the machines in Figure 13-1 to the other. On a half-duplex network, either one computer or the other — but not both — can transmit. If both want to transmit (as is likely if both have large files to send), one has to wait. The net effect is that the total bits per second you can transmit over the network is substantially less than the raw rate of the cable — it's the raw rate less the time for a lot of things:

  ✦ Time spent waiting to see if it's okay to transmit

  ✦ Time spent waiting to retransmit after a collision

  ✦ Time lost because a transmission was garbled because of collision

  ✦ Time lost retransmitting data that didn't get to the destination

  ✦ Time spent waiting for the destination to reply that it received the transmission

The wasted time goes up as you attach more computers to the network because it is likely that more than one computer will want to transmit at any one time. The wasted time also goes up as the length of the cable (and therefore the end-to-end signal propagation time) increases because it is more likely that two computers at either end of the cable may start to transmit within the time window required for propagation along the length of the cable.

Full- and half-duplex operation matters because it's likely you want to have more than two computers on your network. When that day comes, you need a hub or a switch to join all the network segments, as in Figure 13-2. You have to replace the crossover cable when you add the hub or switch because the topology in Figure 13-2 is designed for straight-through patch cables.

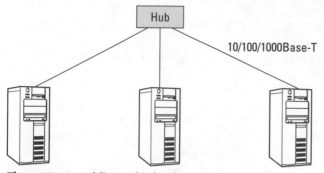

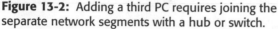

Figure 13-2: Adding a third PC requires joining the separate network segments with a hub or switch.

Whether you choose a hub or a switch to join the segments determines whether your network runs half- or full-duplex, and so has a major effect on your network speed. Both a hub and a switch connect all the connected network segments electrically, but if you use a hub, you only get half-duplex operation. You need a switch to run full-duplex.

Ethernet Switches

The reason a hub forces half-duplex operation is that, internally, it connects all the segments together all the time. That permanent connection forces the independent physical network segments to look like one larger logical segment on which only one computer can transmit at a time. An *Ethernet switch* changes that, implementing the idea that connections between physical segments need exist only when there's network traffic between those segments. Instead of a single connection joining all segments, you use what's called a *switching fabric* (see Figure 13-3). The switching fabric is capable of connecting any one interface to any other without involving the rest and can create many such connections at once.

The Ethernet switch's capability to create independent pairwise connections on demand makes each computer-to-computer transmission look like the full-duplex direct connection in Figure 13-1. Network packets entering the switch can go between ports A and D, for example, at the same time other packets go between B and E or between any other pairing of the remaining ports. Because of that, although a fully occupied, eight-port hub connecting 100Base-T segments can transfer no more than 100 megabits per second over the entire LAN, a similar Ethernet switch can readily transfer up to 400 megabits per second because it can support four paths independently, and if the full-duplex connections are busy in both directions, it could transfer up to 800 megabits per second.

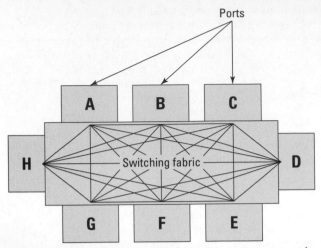

Figure 13-3: An Ethernet switch partitions your network into separate segments.

Expanding Your Network

Although you can get hubs and switches with tens of ports, you might find — say, for a LAN gaming party — that you need more ports than just one can provide. The normal ports on a hub or switch are made to connect to PCs, but you can link hubs and switches together one of two ways. You can either use the *uplink* port many hubs and switches provide, connecting an uplink port on one to a normal port on another, or you can use a crossover cable to connect two normal ports. (If you're using crossover cables, we recommend getting them in yellow, and buying patch cables in any color but yellow. That way, you can keep straight what cable does what.)

Figure 13-4 characterizes how you might connect a lot of computers together. High-traffic computers everyone needs to access might connect directly to the core switch. Other computers or printers might connect directly, or might connect through smaller attached hubs and switches. A tree architecture, as in Figure 13-4, is best, and in any event, you want to avoid long strings of hubs. Any path through a hub is half-duplex; paths exclusively through switches are full-duplex if the network interfaces in the PCs support full-duplex.

If you have a mix of faster and slower Ethernet technology, the general strategy is to use the fastest parts in the core of the network where the traffic is greatest (surrounding the central switch), and the slower ones out at the edges (connected to the outer hubs and switches). Edge clusters with high traffic loads are candidates for the faster technology if you have enough units. If your network gets large enough, or your traffic is great enough (such as if you're slinging around raw video files that are tens of gigabytes long), even 100Base-T can seem slow — you might selectively inject some gigabit Ethernet if that happens.

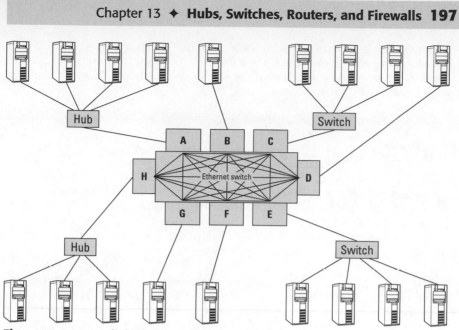

Figure 13-4: Cascaded Ethernet switches and hubs

As you add computers to your network, you probably want to use at least one of them as a *server*, a computer used to provide network resources. The network in Figure 13-2 with a file and print server might look something like the one in Figure 13-5. The computers where you work are called *client computers* (using the computer industry's common client/server terminology).

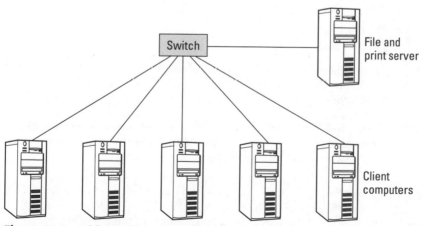

Figure 13-5: Adding a file and print server

The advantage of setting up a server — even on a home network — is that it keeps the resources you use available no matter what's happening on any other client PC. Your brother can be crashing his PC hourly, and no matter what other PC you're using, you need not care what he's doing, because your e-mail files and the printer are accessible through the server. So long as no one sits down at the server and starts using it directly as a PC, it should stay stable and reliable. Better yet, you can load the server up with huge disks and use that storage from any PC on your network.

Routers

There comes a point when it's neither practical nor desirable to keep connecting networks together with Ethernet hubs or switches. You don't want to connect to a network that is not under your control without some safeguards, and the connections from LANs to the Internet are rarely direct Ethernet feeds. Instead, you want a way to link your network to other ones, exchanging messages when needed but otherwise remaining isolated.

Networks solve these problems using a set of conceptual *layers*, each serving a different function. Figure 13-6 shows three layers from a larger structure called the Open Systems Interconnect (OSI) Reference Model. The layers shown in Figure 13-6 are the bottom three of seven layers in the full OSI model:

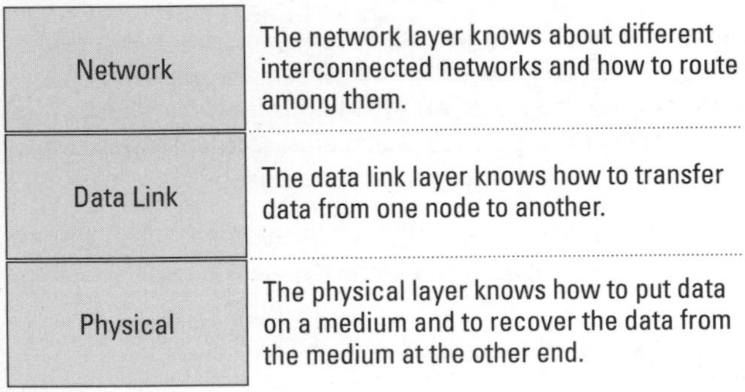

Network	The network layer knows about different interconnected networks and how to route among them.
Data Link	The data link layer knows how to transfer data from one node to another.
Physical	The physical layer knows how to put data on a medium and to recover the data from the medium at the other end.

Figure 13-6: The OSI Reference Model structures network systems design.

✦ **Network layer** — The network layer tracks interconnected networks and routes packets among them. The network layer operates independently from the media technology layers below it.

✦ **Data link layer** — The data link layer identifies stations on the medium and provides low-level control for transmissions between stations. In an Ethernet network, the data link layer defines unique identifiers for each station, defines the way in which stations find out each other's addresses, and defines the mechanisms for handling collisions.

✦ **Physical layer** — The transmission media — LANs most commonly use twisted-pair cables and the electrical drivers for those cables — form the physical layer. The physical layer converts data to signals on the network cable and recovers signals from the network back to data.

Figure 13-7 shows how two computers connected back-to-back (as in Figure 13-1) communicate using the OSI Reference Model. A protocol stack implements the network layers on each computer. Each layer in the stack interoperates as a peer with the same layer on the other computer, so the network layer on Computer A in Figure 13-7 communicates peer-to-peer with the network layer on Computer B. The two network layers don't connect directly, though — they have to send messages back and forth through the data link layer. A lower level peer relationship exists between the data link layers, which in turn communicate with each other by sending messages back and forth using the physical layer. It's the physical layers that are actually connected, so they have a real connection and do communicate directly. These three layers of the model are just that, however, a model. Real networks correspond roughly to the model, but have differences and make compromises so the overall system runs efficiently and economically.

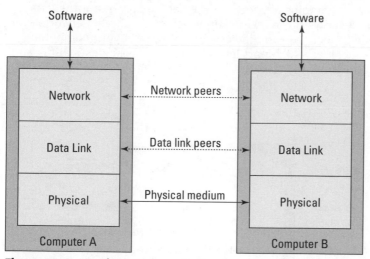

Figure 13-7: Peer layer communication in a network

The key characteristic distinguishing the network layer from the data link layer is that the network layer is independent of the underlying media characteristics. Devices operating at the data link layer, such as Ethernet switches, exploit the physical characteristics of Ethernet (and the similarities among the many versions of Ethernet) to do their work. Devices operating at the network layer, called *routers,* transfer network data from one port to the next with no knowledge of the underlying media connected to the interfaces.

Because networks operate at both media-dependent and media-independent levels, it follows that your computer has both physical and logical (that is, network) addresses.

✦ The **physical address** on an Ethernet (also called a *MAC address,* for Media Access Control) is a unique number wired into your Ethernet card by its manufacturer — the physical address for one of our computers, for example, is 00-20-AF-F8-29-B4.

✦ The **network address** is completely independent of the physical address — if you change Ethernet cards, for instance, you change the computer's physical address but not the network address. Network addresses for the Internet Protocol (IP) consist (today) of four numbers each from 0 to 255, such as 206.142.111.239. Future versions of IP will add more numbers to those addresses, but the change isn't likely for several years.

If you have more than one network interface (a network card and a modem connected to the Internet, for example), you will have more than one network address. For example, 206.164.111.239 might be a network address temporarily assigned to your computer by your Internet service provider (and therefore assigned to your modem port), while you might use 192.168.0.1 for your local area network.

To connect two different networks without merging them physically, you need a device — a *router* — that joins networks at the network layer, not the data link layer. Figure 13-8 shows these relationships. Routers contain network-layer software that connects as a peer to the network software in your computer, receives messages, decides which port leads to the message's destination, and sends the message down to the data link layer in the right protocol stack.

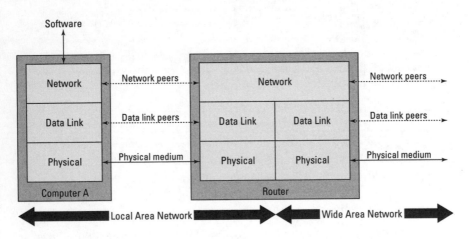

Figure 13-8: The network layer joins otherwise incompatible networks.

Suppose software on your computer needs to send a message to a computer on the Internet. Your software passes the message to the IP network layer on your computer, which figures out which of the data links on your computer leads to the Internet. The message gets handed off to the data link layer for that interface, passed to the physical layer, and sent down the wire. The physical layer in the router picks up the message and percolates it up through the data link layer to the network layer in the router. That software in turn figures out that the next data link to receive the message is the one leading to the Internet, and sends it down the protocol stack and on its way.

The magic is that the IP network layer in the router allows the data link and physical layers to need peer relationships only with compatible hardware and software at the other end of a connection. The data link layer and physical hardware in your computer — an Ethernet card — don't know and don't care that the ultimate connection is out to the Internet, or that that connection is through a modem and not the Ethernet. Similarly, the modem data link layer and hardware don't know and don't care what your local area network looks like. The network layer in the router is the only software that has any tie to both links. This is weapons-grade magic because it means that, no matter what kind of network you want to attach to your local area network, the right router (meaning one with the right data link and physical interfaces) can do the job without any change in your local network.

Transmission Control Protocol

Most of the time, you hear IP, the Internet routing layer, mentioned as part of TCP/IP, which stands for Transmission Control Protocol/Internet Protocol. The reason for that is that very little software actually talks to IP directly because IP itself leaves a lot of network-induced problems unsolved. Protocols above IP, such as TCP, solve those problems.

The first problem IP has that you need to solve comes from IP's function, which is to route information from here to there and back. IP doesn't guarantee that your messages will actually arrive at the destination, doesn't guarantee that they'll arrive in the order you sent, and doesn't give you any indication of whether the network has the capacity to transmit as much data as you want. Every one of these problems stems from the nature of the underlying network:

✦ **Unreliable delivery** — Neither IP nor the Internet itself guarantees that the data you send will get anywhere. Your Internet connection could get dropped, the modem could garble the data, a communications link could be full to capacity, the computer at the other end could mishandle the message, or a thousand other things could go wrong. Any one of them can cause your message to get lost.

✦ **Out-of-order delivery** — IP and the Internet don't make any promises about the order in which messages get delivered. Because it takes a lot of messages across the Internet to do anything useful, they can arrive in a sequence very different from the one in which they were transmitted. Most programs send messages and replies in a tightly defined sequence, so out-of-order delivery would be very confusing. It would be like getting the check in a restaurant before you've even seen the menu.

✦ **Capacity limits** — Getting your message sent through your modem provides no assurance that it's actually going anywhere. For instance, suppose your message arrives at a router, but its destination circuit is already full of traffic. Your message can get dumped if the router doesn't have enough memory to hold the incoming messages until they can get a turn on the output circuit.

Every one of these problems is solvable, and most of the time programs communicating on the Internet want them to be solved. It's not efficient to require every program that communicates over the Internet to include code to solve the problems independently — that would mean many, many different implementations, would increase software costs, and would make interoperability among programs unlikely. Instead, a protocol layer on top of IP — namely, TCP — provides these services to programs. A program hands data off to TCP for transmission, and having done so can assume that the data will make it to the other end intact and in order. If TCP can't do that, it explicitly notifies the program. If there are no error notifications, the program can assume TCP did its job.

The implementation of how TCP does what it does requires that programmers handle a mind-numbing set of details, but the ideas behind TCP are pretty straightforward:

✦ **Put sequence numbers in messages** — Every message TCP sends out onto the network gets a sequence number. By looking at the sequence numbers of messages as they come in, the TCP receiver can tell whether it has the next message yet, or whether it has to wait for the network to deliver some out-of-order messages.

✦ **Tell the sender when messages arrive** — The TCP receiver sends a message (an acknowledgment) back to the sender when messages arrive correctly and in sequence, telling the sender the sequence number of the highest correctly received message.

✦ **Retransmit failed messages** — The TCP sender keeps a timer for every message it sends. If the receiver doesn't acknowledge the message within a certain interval of time, the sender retransmits the message. This process keeps up until TCP has tried a specified number of retransmissions, after which it reports an uncorrectable failure to your program.

✦ **Retransmit garbled messages** — Even if your message gets to its destination, it might have been corrupted in transmission. TCP uses error detection codes it wraps around your message to know when this has happened. When the TCP receiver detects a garbled message, it explicitly sends a message back to the sender requesting retransmission.

Only the garbled (or lost) messages are sent again. If other messages in the sequence after the bad one arrive properly (even if that happens before the bad one finally gets there), they don't need retransmission.

✦ **Limit the number of outstanding messages** — The TCP sender limits the number of messages it sends before receiving an acknowledgment, which has the effect of limiting the average data rate you need on the connection between you and the destination. More than one message can be outstanding, however, so in most cases the sender doesn't have to wait out the round-trip delay for an acknowledgment to arrive. Sending multiple messages in advance of acknowledgment greatly increases the amount of data you can get through the connection.

Don't assume that when someone refers to TCP/IP (including in this book) that the reference is exclusively to TCP and IP — it's common usage to call the *complete set of Internet protocols* TCP/IP.

User Datagram Protocol

The reliable transport services of TCP come at a price. In particular, the need to wait for acknowledgment messages limits the data rate you can put into the communications channel. This limitation (along with all the other work TCP does) creates an additional processing load at both ends of the channel.

Some applications, including Internet phone and videoconferencing, and many multi-player Internet games, can't afford the overhead TCP imposes. The volume of data those applications send and their need for uninterrupted data flow make the waits TCP can impose for message acknowledgments unworkable.

Take Internet videoconferencing, perhaps using Microsoft's NetMeeting, as an example. If your data does get damaged in transit, the worst that's likely to happen is that you'll see a glitch in the video or hear noise in the audio. Slowing the data transmission — one consequence of what TCP does to provide reliable delivery — reduces the frame rate and creates gaps in the sound. Because your eyes and ears handle noise better than gaps, you're better off with more data, even if it contains a few errors.

The situation is about the same for multi-player games across the Internet. The rapid, timely flow of data between computers is more important than getting every bit right — the programs mostly send updates to the same data over and over, so even if you drop a message, it won't matter.

The Internet protocols solve this problem by replacing TCP with the User Datagram Protocol (UDP), which does none of the corrective things TCP does. UDP does not provide in-order delivery, acknowledgments, retransmissions, or flow control. It's relatively basic, but in exchange for that simplicity UDP gets more data sent for a given link capacity and imposes less workload on the processor.

Domain Name Service

A usable network needs to do a few more things than move messages around. One of the most important is providing a way to translate the computer names people deal with (for example, `www.theonion.com`) to the numbers computers want to see (such as `66.216.104.235`). The Internet function that does this for you is called the *Domain Name Service*. Computers providing that service are called *domain name servers*. Both phrases are abbreviated DNS.

Internet domains are a hierarchical structure based on the words you find separated by dots in computer names. The last word in the computer name (for example, `com`) is the least specific part of the domain name, called the top-level domain name. Common top-level domains include `.com`, `.org`, and `.net`, plus ones for each country; there's a reasonably comprehensive list at `www.norid.no/domenenavnbaser/domreg.html`.

The word immediately to the left of the root is the domain name (for example, *idsoftware* in `www.idsoftware.com`). Domain names are chosen by their owners (for example, id Software). There are really no controls on who can register a name, but a given name can be registered by only one person or organization (so it's unique on the Internet). The lack of controls has spawned some interesting disputes after someone unrelated to a company registered the name the company would most likely want (for example, disputes followed registration of `mtv.com` and `gateway.com` because the companies you instinctively think of weren't who registered the names).

Finally, the rest of the words in the computer name are subdomains, with the leftmost word being the computer itself. In the name `www.idsoftware.com`, `www` is the computer name. Similarly, in the name `clyde.isp.net`, `clyde` is the computer name. The complete name less the computer name (`isp.net`) is commonly called the *domain name*, but in fact all the subsets (`isp.net` and `net` in this case) are domain names, too.

Network Security and Firewalls

The analogy between the Internet and the real world is remarkably complete — there are many good people in both, and enough losers to make both the Internet and the real world places to be careful. As in the real world, though, attacks and threats on the Internet don't just occur randomly — they happen in predictable ways. The seven layer OSI model, of which you saw the lower three layers in Figure 13-6, gives you a good framework with which to analyze Internet security. Figure 13-9 shows the complete seven layer model, and describes the sort of attacks you can anticipate at each layer of the model. Most of the attacks you'll hear about in the media occur at the application layer, going after Web servers, browsers, and the information they have access to, but application layer attacks on unprotected or vulnerable services are common, as are data link layer attacks on unprotected wireless networks.

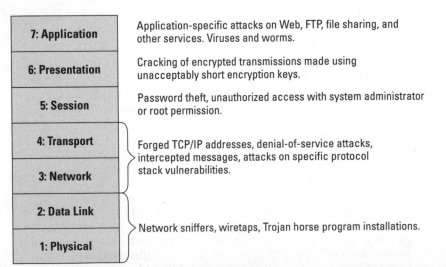

7: Application	Application-specific attacks on Web, FTP, file sharing, and other services. Viruses and worms.
6: Presentation	Cracking of encrypted transmissions made using unacceptably short encryption keys.
5: Session	Password theft, unauthorized access with system administrator or root permission.
4: Transport	Forged TCP/IP addresses, denial-of-service attacks, intercepted messages, attacks on specific protocol stack vulnerabilities.
3: Network	
2: Data Link	Network sniffers, wiretaps, Trojan horse program installations.
1: Physical	

Figure 13-9: Security vulnerabilities against the seven layer model

Using only specific defenses against the many specific threats isn't terribly worthwhile because, like the sturdy but useless Maginot Line, the defense fails the first time an unanticipated threat shows up. You can, however, use an understanding of attacks in terms of how they operate against the seven layer model to deploy defenses against entire classes of threats at once. Two main approaches are the most useful:

✦ **Packet filters** — You can examine traffic at the network layer, looking at the source and destination addresses. The filter can disallow traffic to or from specific addresses and ports and can disallow traffic with suspect address patterns.

✦ **Firewalls** — You can also examine traffic as high as the application layer, checking the internal content of specific application messages. Traffic that fails those tests can be rejected.

Hardware packet filters are simple, inexpensive, and can block many incoming attacks. Hardware firewalls are more expensive; most home and small office networks can use a combination of hardware packet filters and software firewalls.

Packet filters

Internet messages use an IP address to locate the specific machine, and a port number to identify the program that will handle the message. The combined address/port information is available in nearly every TCP/IP message and is available for both the sender and receiver of the message. Packet filters look at the TCP/IP addresses, and possibly the port numbers, although not the internal content of messages.

Packet filters generally operate using a top-to-bottom list of rules. For example, a somewhat secure rule set might be the sequence, in order:

1. Permit all outgoing traffic.
2. Deny new incoming connections.
3. Accept everything else.

This rule set improves your LAN's security because it rejects unsolicited connection attempts from the Internet to your computers. It explicitly protects against unauthorized access to shared drives and files because it blocks incoming traffic using TCP. A filter using this rule set breaks the normal protocol between FTP clients and servers because normal FTP operation includes a connection from the server into the client, but you can fix that by reconfiguring your FTP client to specify passive (or *PASV*) mode. Essentially all FTP software today supports PASV mode.

You'd use this packet filter in a router connecting your computer to the Internet, as shown in Figure 13-10. By placing the filter between the LAN and the Internet, you're guaranteed all Internet traffic goes through the filter. If your packet filter software is capable enough to examine the subnet of the source address based on which physical port delivers the message to the router, you can set up rules to avoid spoofed TCP/IP addresses (see the text in

Figure 13-10). *Spoofing* makes messages from the Internet appear to have originated on your LAN; the spoofing filter prevents this by rejecting messages coming on a port with impossible source addresses. The anti-spoofing filter is an important part of protecting machines on your network on which you've installed filters to limit particular services to machines on your subnet.

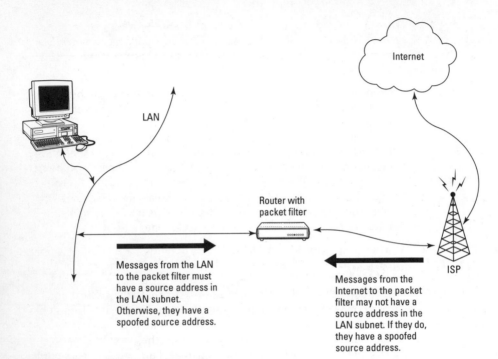

Figure 13-10: Packet filter deployment

Network Address Translation

The inexpensive hardware routers now available, such as the Microsoft wireless IEEE 802.11g base station discussed in Chapter 12, improve your LAN security by rejecting incoming packets that aren't responses to requests from your PC, but do it with a very different approach called *Network Address Translation (NAT)*.

The original impetus for the development of NAT was the problem of sharing a single Internet IP address among several PCs. NAT maps normal network messages on your LAN, using individual IP addresses and standard port numbers on all your PCs, to a single IP address and a large number of otherwise unrelated port numbers for transport out on the Internet. Your Internet IP address will be assigned by your ISP; your LAN addresses will likely use one of the three ranges of private IP addresses in Table 13-1 (more on private addresses in the next chapter).

Table 13-1
Private TCP/IP Network Addresses

Subnet Address	First Node Address	Last Node Address
10.0.0.0	10.0.0.1	10.255.255.254
172.16.0.0	172.16.0.1	172.31.255.254
192.168.0.0	192.168.0.1	192.168.255.254

A pure NAT implementation rejects all unsolicited incoming messages because it doesn't know which PC is the intended destination. That's the same effect as the rule set mentioned earlier, but with the added benefit that you need only one live Internet address. That saves you money if your Internet access charges more for additional IP addresses. However, at times, you want to accept incoming traffic, such as to access video from the home surveillance system on your PC.

 Chapter 23 shows you how to set up the surveillance, and the sidebar "Cable/DSL Router Security and TrackerCam" shows you how to forward selected incoming messages from the Internet to one specific PC.

Standalone firewalls

Packet filters and NAT reject incoming attacks, so they protect you from worms and keep people from connecting to your shared disk drives, but don't protect you from messages you choose to receive, such as e-mail and Web pages. Firewalls examine more information than a packet filter, so they can exercise a finer degree of control over what moves between your LAN and the Internet and have the potential to identify e-mail viruses and other threats before they reach their target application. Figure 13-11 shows an abbreviated sketch of the TCP/IP packet headers, illustrating the difference between packet filters and firewalls by highlighting what parts of a TCP/IP packet is examined by each. The firewall has all the information available to the packet filter, but also examines the source and destination port numbers and the content of the packet data.

That additional information gives a firewall far more power than the simpler packet filter because the additional information gives the firewall the capability to look all the way up the protocol stack to the application layers. Using that information, a firewall can, in addition to controlling access to and from specific host addresses, do the following:

✦ Allow or disallow specific application services such as FTP or Web pages

✦ Allow or disallow access to services based on the content of the information being transferred (such as scanning for viruses and Trojans)

Combinations of these functions are possible too, such as only allowing incoming FTP access from the Internet to a specific designated server.

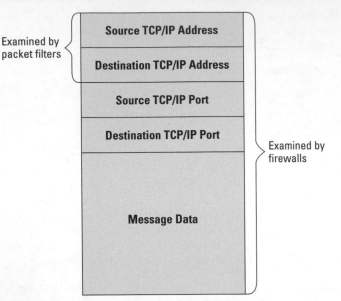

Figure 13-11: Packet filter and firewall information sources

The capability to screen traffic based on message content makes it possible to create filters for objectionable content, such as sites inappropriate for minors (although it's very hard to define rules for that filtering, which is why there are companies whose business is to sell lists of sites you might want to filter for various reasons, along with filter software to use based on those lists). Content screening also makes possible defenses against specific attacks by looking for telltale signatures in the incoming attacking packets. When the firewall detects those signatures, it discards the packets and logs the events.

The most direct implementation of a firewall uses the same architecture shown in Figure 13-10, but sites a firewall between the LAN and the ISP rather than a packet filter. This is the most secure application of a single firewall because it protects all the computers behind the firewall.

A problem exists with the Figure 13-10 architecture, however, because it provides no good place to locate publicly accessible servers. You don't want servers out on the Internet in front of the firewall, where they're unprotected, but you don't want them behind the firewall either because you have to create holes in the firewall protection to permit access to the servers. A variant of Figure 13-10, shown in Figure 13-12, is a good answer to this problem. The firewall router in the figure has three ports, rather than the two on the earlier packet filter. The third port connects to another LAN typically called the demilitarized zone (DMZ). The idea is that the computers in the DMZ are less secure than those back on the secure LAN, but in return those computers are accessible from the Internet. You put Web and FTP servers in the DMZ, keeping all other computers back on the secure LAN. The rules in the firewall prevent incoming traffic to the secure LAN, allowing only outgoing connections. The DMZ LAN is intentionally less secure, but you should still restrict what can be done there. You should use anti-spoofing filters, limit the allowable ports to those used by the servers on the LAN, and disallow access from known attacking sites.

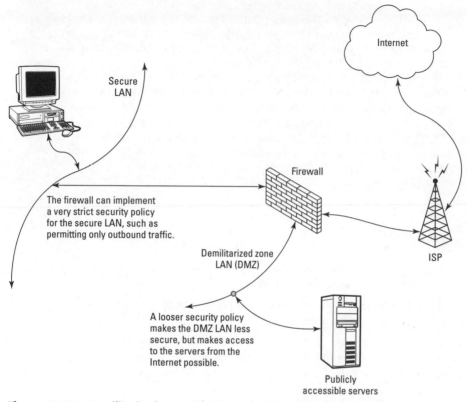

Figure 13-12: Demilitarized zone (DMZ) used with a firewall

We can't recommend a hardware router running NAT highly enough as the first line of defense between your LAN and the Internet. Commercial Cable/DSL routers with Ethernet interfaces are regularly advertised on sale for $30 or less, and if you have both an old retired PC and some ability with Linux, the Linux Router Project (LRP) has software you can use to convert that old machine (see `lrp.steinkuehler.net/DiskImages/Dachstein.htm`) into a first-class router.

On-computer firewalls

Don't think you're defenseless without a hardware router or firewall between your LAN and the Internet. Even if you use a product like Windows' Internet Connection Sharing to let one of your computers tie a modem to your LAN, you can still improve your network security.

Start by analyzing the threats:

✦ The PC hosting the modem, ICS, and the network interface card (NIC) is vulnerable to attacks at all levels shown in Figure 13-9.

✦ The LAN itself is reasonably protected from attack by the NAT layer. The LAN uses private addresses not routable on the Internet itself. Threats from servers back to client software are possible, as is access to content you might choose to block in some circumstances.

The biggest threat is to the PC directly connected to the Internet; the answer is either to install a packet filter or firewall product directly on that computer, or to have your ISP install packet filter or firewall protection for your access. The latter isn't widely available from ISPs; a more readily available solution is a PC-hosted solution such as Zone Labs' ZoneAlarm. Combine that with antivirus, anti-spam, and anti-adware software, and you'll be reasonably well protected. Don't forget to check for and apply security patches to your software as they are issued.

Summary

✦ Consider individual and aggregate network capacity requirements in designing local area networks.

✦ Network performance is not uniform — it varies across physical regions of your network.

✦ As your requirements go up, you gain capacity by subdividing your shared media segments into independent ones.

✦ Hardware routers and firewalls can give your network better security at low cost.

Configuring a Windows Network

✦   ✦   ✦   ✦

In This Chapter

Examining networking protocols and plumbing

Understanding IP, DNS, and the networking alphabet soup

Configuring file and printer sharing

✦   ✦   ✦   ✦

Many people believe networks are simply incomprehensible. Networks are more complicated than individual standalone PCs because you have to deal with the interactions as well as the PCs themselves, but networks are organized in a definite, hierarchical way. If you work your way through that hierarchy, you'll understand there's a consistency to them that makes working with networks straightforward.

Network Protocols

Computers talk to one another only in very structured ways. A computer has to identify itself and carry on a "conversation" with another computer to cause that remote computer to do some work. Because computers lack the flexibility of people, those conversations consist of precisely formatted messages sent between the computers following a strict, rigid pattern called a *protocol*. The jobs protocols carry out on your network are typically some of these:

✦ Exchange and forward messages

✦ Ensure messages are received correctly, and in the proper order

✦ Identify other computers able to communicate

✦ Interpret from human-readable computer names to numeric addresses and back

✦ Provide services to other computers and access services on those computers

✦ Examine credentials of users attempting to use network resources

✦ Provide secure message transmission using encryption

The universal way people describe network layers is the Open Systems Interconnection (OSI) reference model. Figure 14-1 shows the layers in the OSI model, from the hardware functions at Layer 1 to the application functions at Layer 7. The annotations at the right of the figure name elements occurring at each layer, including network interface cards that implement Layer 1 and the TCP protocol that implements Layer 4.

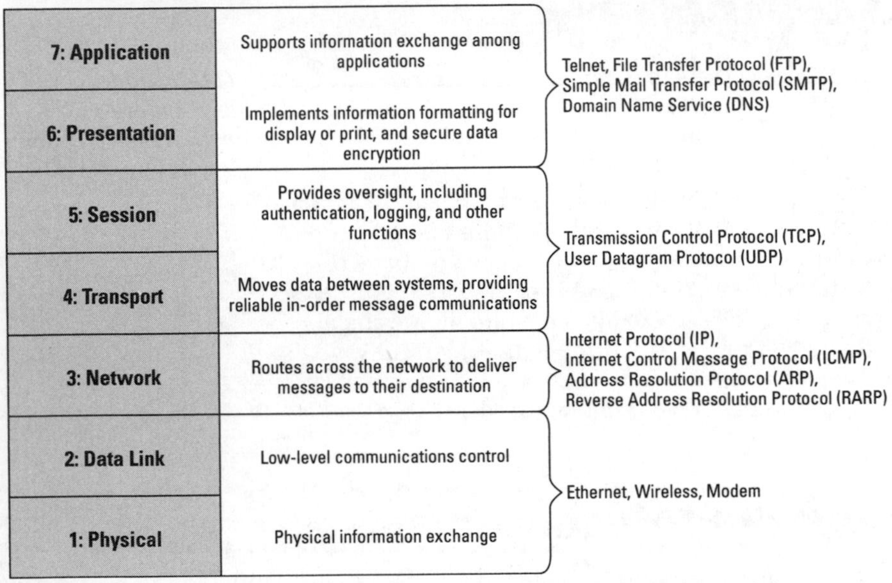

7: Application	Supports information exchange among applications	Telnet, File Transfer Protocol (FTP), Simple Mail Transfer Protocol (SMTP), Domain Name Service (DNS)
6: Presentation	Implements information formatting for display or print, and secure data encryption	
5: Session	Provides oversight, including authentication, logging, and other functions	Transmission Control Protocol (TCP), User Datagram Protocol (UDP)
4: Transport	Moves data between systems, providing reliable in-order message communications	
3: Network	Routes across the network to deliver messages to their destination	Internet Protocol (IP), Internet Control Message Protocol (ICMP), Address Resolution Protocol (ARP), Reverse Address Resolution Protocol (RARP)
2: Data Link	Low-level communications control	Ethernet, Wireless, Modem
1: Physical	Physical information exchange	

Figure 14-1: The Open Systems Interconnection (OSI) reference model

The TCP/IP protocol suite, the backbone of the Internet, evolved from a project to connect multiple networks together into a larger, survivable whole. The predecessor of the Internet, what was called the ARPANET, used 50 Kbps telephone lines for the network backbone and evolved to the multigigabit-per-second fiber-optic backbone of the Internet today. Changes and extensions to TCP/IP are managed by a volunteer organization called the Internet Engineering Task Force (IETF). Anyone can propose changes or extensions to TCP/IP, but nothing will happen unless the IETF agrees.

Inside the Network Pipes

We've said on many occasions that nearly everything involving a lot of money — such as medicine, rocket engines, and networks — is ultimately plumbing. Network plumbing makes the applications you use work, implementing the transport between your computer and servers across the network.

Media and network addresses

You don't need a map or street address to get to work or home because you know physically where you're going. However, a cross-country vacation drive to Butchart Gardens (www.butchartgardens.com) requires finding the address and looking it up on a map. You use the city to decide what highways to travel, and use the street address to home in on the garden entrance. On the second day, you know how to get there from your hotel using the physical location you learned once you reached the gardens the first time.

Networks follow the same model. The *Media Access Control (MAC) address* of a computer on a LAN is the equivalent of physical knowledge of where you're going, and is wired into the network interface card. The *network address* (most often an IP protocol address) is the equivalent of a building's mailing address. MAC addresses are scattered randomly on networks, much like street addresses in the real world; logical addresses follow a pattern determined by network administrators and are stored in *routing tables* which are themselves like street maps for your network. An upgrade is slowly rolling out across the Internet to increase the number of logical TCP/IP network addresses, but the current version of TCP/IP (called IPv4) will hold sway for many years to come. IPv4 represents network addresses as a sequence of four decimal numbers, each called an *octet* and ranging from 0 to 255. You write octets with a dot between them, such as 19.38.40.206.

A TCP/IP message to a computer not part of your LAN goes to the computer defined as the *default route*. That computer (or router) has the responsibility to forward the message on a communications link leading to the destination, using routing tables to identify the correct link. Default routing usually sends messages from your LAN through a computer or router connected to your Internet service provider (ISP). A chain of routers, starting at your ISP, cooperates to deliver the message on the LAN hosting the destination computer.

A standard TCP/IP utility called traceroute (tracert under Windows) shows you how a message routes from one computer to another. You can run tracert in a Windows DOS window. Alternatively, graphical traceroute programs are available over the Web, with versions available for your PC, too:

1. Assuming you have a computer hooked to the Internet, open a Web browser and go to the address http://visualroute.visualware.com, which is a public service maintained by the company that developed the excellent VisualRoute traceroute program. You'll have to register by giving them an electronic mail address to use this server; if you don't want to do that, find another server at www.traceroute.org.

2. Enter the destination TCP/IP address (216.234.247.68 in the earlier example).

3. Press Enter and wait for the results. The following listing shows the results we received (we've omitted some columns and text from the actual results to fit in one column):

```
================================================================
=== VisualRoute (R) 7.3a+ report on 18-Sep-03 7:36:09 PM ===
================================================================
Report for 216.234.247.68 [www.ilovebacon.com]
Analysis: '216.234.247.68' was found in 10 hops (TTL=247).
----------------------------------------------------------------
| Hop | IP Address    | Node Name                              | ms |
----------------------------------------------------------------
| 0   | 161.58.180.113 | win10115.iad.dn.net                   |    |
| 1   | 161.58.176.129 | -                                     | 0  |
| 2   | 161.58.156.140 | -                                     | 0  |
| 3   | 129.250.26.206 | ae0-3.r02.stngva01.us.da.verio.net    | 0  |
| 4   | 129.250.5.34   | p16-0-1-1.r21.dllstx01.us.bb.verio.net | 31 |
| 5   | 129.250.28.164 | ge-1-0-0.a10.dllstx01.us.ra.verio.net | 31 |
| 6   | 129.250.31.44  | ge-1-1.a00.dllstx04.us.ra.verio.net   | 31 |
| 7   | 157.238.228.38 | -                                     | 31 |
| 8   | 12.96.160.233  | ge-0-1-0.ibr4.dllstx2.theplanet.com   | 31 |
| 9   | 12.96.160.39   | core2-v2.dllstx1.theplanet.com        | 31 |
| 10  | 216.234.247.68 | www.ilovebacon.com                    | 32 |
----------------------------------------------------------------
```

4. Many of the intermediate routers were part of verio.net, an Internet backbone provider. The times listed on each line are the duration of a round trip from the originating computer to the listed point and back. Those times varied from 0 to 32 milliseconds. Relatively large jumps in times suggest transport over longer distances, or through congested routers. The consistency of the times from lines 0 to 3 and lines 4 to 10 suggest the time difference between lines 3 and 4 is due to a transport delay.

The protocol software in the operating system delivers arriving messages to the software implementing the service requested by the sender. *Port numbers* in messages tell the protocol software which message receiver on the machine gets the message. A complete Internet address includes the port number and the TCP/IP address. Most Web servers listen on port 80, for example, so connecting to the Wiley Web server on the computer www.wiley.com requires the complete address 208.215.179.146:80. Your client software provides default port numbers, which you can override.

Overall, network addresses have three levels:

✦ **Logical addresses** route messages traveling to the destination across wide area networks.

✦ **Physical addresses** route messages on local area network physical segments and, therefore, onto the destination computer.

✦ **Port numbers** dispatch the message to the right software.

Domain Name Service and Address Resolution Protocol

People don't remember strings of arbitrary numbers well. You're likely to have to work to care about the Internet address `66.135.192.87`, but you probably know about `www.ebay.com`. Worse yet is that changes eBay makes in their infrastructure could alter the numeric address of the computer, invalidating the numeric address you finally memorized.

No one explicitly cares about MAC addresses. Wide area networks (WANs) require logical network addresses, and the ways systems use MAC addresses are all invisible. Indeed, even logical addresses are somewhat submerged because people use names that the network converts behind the scenes to the logical addresses.

Two TCP/IP protocols do the name/address conversions:

✦ **Domain Name Service (DNS)** — DNS converts between computer names and logical addresses. Your computer queries a domain name server, also called a DNS, and receives back the address. DNS translates from names to numbers or numbers to names, depending on the request.

✦ **Address Resolution Protocol (ARP)** — ARP translates logical to physical addresses. There's no ARP server; the collection of computers on the LAN cooperate through the protocol to provide resolution services.

Computer names are organized hierarchically on the Internet. The root is unnamed; immediately underneath are the top-level domains such as `.com`, `.org`, `.net`, `.jp` (Japan), `.uk` (United Kingdom), and `.au` (Australia). The authorized set of top-level domains is maintained online by the Internet Assigned Numbers Authority (IANA) at `www.iana.org/cctld/cctld-whois.htm`.

People and organizations can register domain names (such as `wiley.com`) under each top-level domain. The owners of specific names have the ability to use the names directly (you can send mail to addresses at `wiley.com`, for example), or to further subdivide the domain with a finer-grained structure (`www.wiley.com` is the Wiley Web server within `wiley.com`).

Master domain name servers maintain the domain name search tree, with subordinate computers branching below the master servers to handle lower levels.

Dynamic Host Configuration Protocol (DHCP)

Except for the fact that you have to assign a unique network address to every computer and tell each computer its Internet gateway address to provide a default route, TCP/IP is quite simple to use. Software implementing the Dynamic Host Configuration Protocol (DHCP) can make the address and gateway assignment process automatic for standalone or connected networks, making TCP/IP the right protocol choice for all LANs.

DHCP works in an incremental fashion to give a computer its address and gateway:

1. **Find a DHCP server.** The computer requesting an address assignment starts with no address and no information about the LAN, so its first task is to find a server. The computer does that with a broadcast message, which is a message sent to any computer physically able to receive it.

2. **Ask for an address.** Asking for an address is implicit in the broadcast message looking for a server, but is a required function of the protocol.

3. **Receive an address from the server.** Servers receiving the broadcast request message send back a message directly to the client with the allocated TCP/IP address. The server replies using the MAC address contained in the broadcast request because the destination machine receiving the reply doesn't have its address yet.

4. **Accept and install the assigned address.** The PC looking for an address might receive assignments from several servers, so it sends messages to one of the servers saying it accepted the address and tells the rejected servers they can make the address available again. The PC sets up its assigned address and joins the network.

DHCP does a few more things behind the scenes:

✦ **Netmask** — TCP/IP addresses segment into both a network number and the host number identifying the specific computer in the network. A value called the *netmask* lets TCP/IP break the overall address apart. A typical netmask value is 255.255.255.0, which identifies the upper three octets of the IP address as identifying the *subnet* and the lower octet as identifying the computer itself. If you applied a netmask of 255.255.255.0 to the address 216.234.247.68, the subnet would be 216.234.247.0, and the computer-specific identification (or node number) would be 68. Because DHCP delivers the netmask along with the address, the partitioning of the overall address into network and node subaddresses is dynamic and can be set to reflect the number of computers on the LAN.

✦ **Default gateway** — Typical computers on a LAN won't know the details of their default route to send messages to other subnets. DHCP provides the default gateway address when it sends the address assigned to the requesting computer.

✦ **Name server address** — A computer requesting automatic TCP/IP address assignment also isn't likely to know the address of a local domain name server, so DHCP responses include the DNS address too. After it knows the DNS address, a PC can look up numeric addresses for any name.

✦ **Address lease expiration** — Computers get moved around and connected to or disconnected from networks. They crash, too; all these actions present the opportunity for TCP/IP addresses to fall out of use. A DHCP server has a limited range of TCP/IP addresses it's permitted to hand out, so the protocol includes a timer that, when it expires, causes the assigned address to become invalid and become available for reassignment. In DHCP terms, assigning an address to a client is called leasing the address to the client; when the timer runs out, the lease is said to have expired. At that time the client is required to request a new TCP/IP address from the server. There's a provision in the protocol to request the same TCP/IP address as the client had before, so it's possible for renewed leases to be invisible to computers communicating with the DHCP client over a lease renewal.

If you don't use DHCP, you can set TCP/IP addresses, netmasks, default gateways, and DNS addresses manually on each PC. Regardless of how you assign addresses, though, you have to decide what addresses to use. You have three options:

✦ **Use assigned addresses** — If your LAN is connected to the Internet, you'll be assigned a block of TCP/IP addresses by your Internet service provider (ISP). You can configure those addresses into your PCs along with the ISP's DNS address and the address of the router the PCs use to access the Internet.

✦ **Use arbitrary addresses** — Standalone networks you will never connect to the Internet can use any TCP/IP addresses whatsoever. Should you change your mind and go to connect to the Internet at some later time, though, you'll have to change the TCP/IP address of every computer on your LAN. That's easy if you've used DHCP, and really tedious if you configured all the addresses manually.

✦ **Use private addresses** — The Internet Assigned Numbers Authority (IANA) reserves three blocks in the TCP/IP address space for private networks. You can use addresses from any of the three blocks, which themselves differ in how many hosts they permit within a subnet. No address in any of these blocks is directly routable across the Internet. The IANA-reserved blocks are shown in Table 14-1. Legitimate TCP/IP addresses formed from the subnet address in the second row would be 172.16.0.1, 172.16.0.2, and so on up to 172.31.255.254.

Table 14-1
Private TCP/IP Network Addresses

Subnet Address	First Node Address	Last Node Address	Number of Usable Addresses
10.0.0.0	10.0.0.1	10.255.255.254	16,777,214
172.16.0.0	172.16.0.1	172.31.255.254	1,048,574
192.168.0.0	192.168.0.1	192.168.255.254	65,534

The *first node address* in Table 14-1 is reserved as part of the formal subnet address, while the *last node address* is reserved as the broadcast address for the subnet. Because those two addresses are reserved in every address block, a block of 16 node addresses (for example) has only 14 usable addresses. The Number of Usable Addresses column at the right of Table 14-1 shows the maximum number of addresses less two, so it's the maximum number of computers and other devices you could connect to one subnet in the block. You're not likely to fill any of the blocks.

Routers commonly implement a technology called Network Address Translation (NAT) that enables you to route from computers using these addresses to the Internet. The individual computers can initiate transactions out to the Internet through the NAT function, but computers on the Internet can't see your computers unless you make special provisions in the router. That invisibility provides additional security to your computers. See Chapter 13 for how to set up routers and NAT and how to set up TCP/IP on your PC.

Configuring TCP/IP

Windows 2000 and Windows XP provide a network properties dialog box you use to install software components and configure settings for your LAN. You can access the dialog box through Network and Dial-up Connections in the Control Panel. Double-click on that icon, click the right mouse button on the LAN connection icon in the resulting Windows Explorer display, and launch Properties for the connection. Figure 14-2 shows the dialog box.

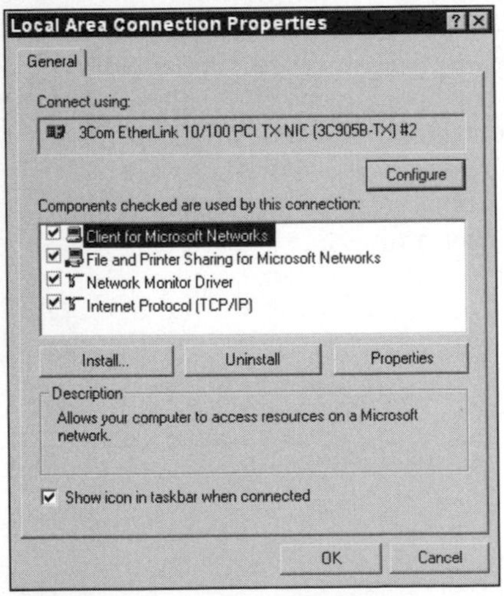

Figure 14-2: Windows 2000 and Windows XP network connection properties

Choose Internet Protocol (TCP/IP) in the list of components and then click on Properties to bring up the dialog box in Figure 14-3. If you're running a DHCP server on your LAN (such as from a router connected to the Internet, as in Chapter 13), the automatic settings shown for both the IP address and the DNS server address are what you want. If you're entering either the IP address or the DNS address manually, select the appropriate option and type in the corresponding numeric values (no names are allowed here). You'll need the subnet mask and default gateway address along with the IP address.

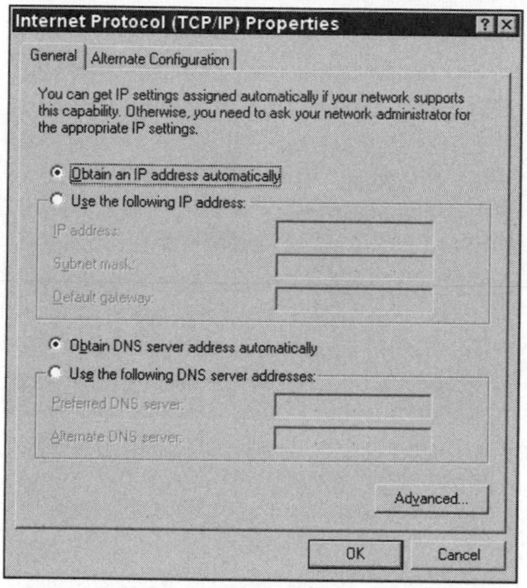

Figure 14-3: Use the TCP/IP Properties dialog box to set up network addressing.

The easiest approach, by far, is to run DHCP in a router. For manual addressing, if you have a standalone LAN or your router provides Network Address Translation between the LAN and the Internet, you can use the addresses from Table 14-1. If your LAN is directly routable to the Internet, with no NAT function, you'll need to use addresses provided by your Internet service provider.

You configure TCP/IP for Windows 98 in much the same way as we described for Windows 2000 and Windows XP. You get to the Properties dialog box through the Network applet in the Control Panel, leading to a dialog box much like that in Figure 14-2. TCP/IP properties are organized differently in the Properties dialog box for the protocol, but the information is essentially the same.

Configuring File Sharing

Getting useful work done requires that you install software operating at Layers 5 through 7 — applications providing services on the network. Microsoft calls some of the applications you'll learn about in this section *clients*, reflecting the fact that they are clients to servers on other computers. The clients, and the associated servers, fall in the category of what we're generically calling applications.

You'll want to add both clients and servers on computers on your LAN. You might choose to designate specific computers as *file servers*, as shown in Figure 14-4, and at the same time you might use some of your computers to provide shared access to your printers. File servers — at least, ones you'd put on a LAN for home or small business — are simply PCs with a lot of disks attached. File servers let you put large volumes of disk storage in a single place rather than on many computers spread across the network. File servers simplify looking for files, too, because if you put all your data files on a single server, then the files you're looking for are in specific places. When you make all the computers on your LAN capable of file sharing, it's harder to know where to look for shared files.

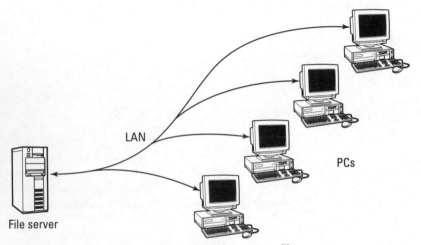

Figure 14-4: File servers support shared access to files.

Making it a file server is one of the best things you can do with an old, spare computer. Fill it with a lot of disk space and make it the place where you put *all* the data files you work on. You want a file server to be a computer you put in a corner and don't use directly because computers people leave alone rather than use to run programs are less likely to crash. When *your* PC crashes, though, the file server keeps on humming, storing the last file you saved with a minimum of fuss and ensuring it's still available even if your computer is thoroughly broken.

Windows 2000 and Windows XP

The items shown in the list in Figure 14-2 include the components you need to let other computers share files and printers on your PC and to access files and printers on other PCs. The key items in the component list in the middle of the dialog box are Client for Microsoft Networks and File and Printer Sharing for Microsoft Networks. They should be installed by default, but if not, use the Install button to add them. Client for Microsoft Networks is a client, while File and Printer Sharing for Microsoft Networks is a service.

The two components have these functions:

✦ **Client for Microsoft Networks** — The Microsoft network client software enables you to find computers on your network and access shared files and printers on them.

✦ **File and Printer Sharing for Microsoft Networks** — The file and printer sharing software is the server component corresponding to the Microsoft Networks client, responding to requests from the client for access to resources on the server computer.

After you have both running, share a disk or folder by opening Windows Explorer and right-clicking the drive or folder you want to share. If you're running Windows 2000 or Windows XP Professional, left-clicking Properties displays the dialog box shown on the left in Figure 14-5. Clicking the Share this folder control enables the lower controls in the dialog box, but might give a share name such as E$. Use the New Share button to create a share with the right name and then click the Permissions button to bring up the dialog box on the right side of Figure 14-5. Verify that the names listed in the dialog box have the right access permissions, but be careful not to be too broad with permissions unless your PCs are behind a firewall.

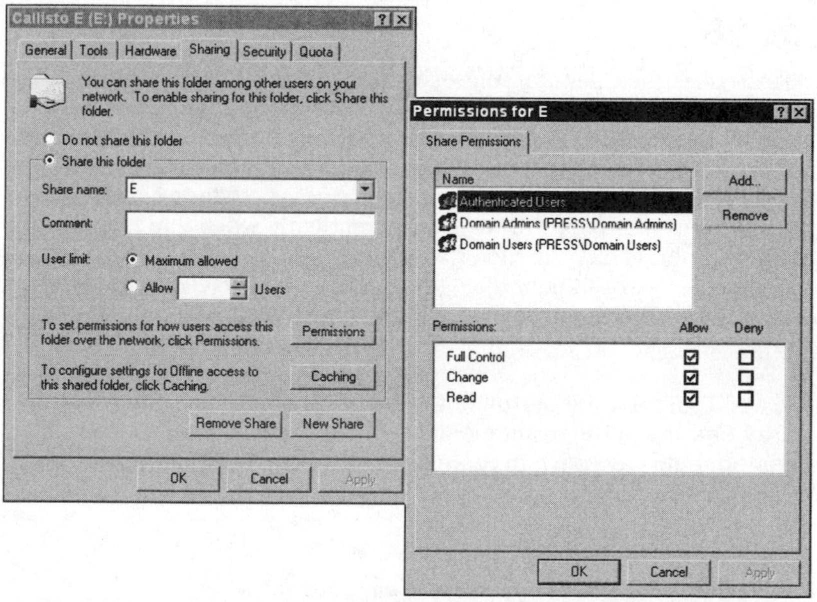

Figure 14-5: Enable Windows 2000 and Windows XP Professional file sharing and set permissions with these dialog boxes.

Microsoft wrote Windows XP Home assuming home users can't figure out the dialog boxes in Figure 14-5, giving you instead the dialog box in Figure 14-6. Check the "Share this folder on the network" control to enable read access to the drive or folder; check "Allow network users to change my files" to enable read/write access.

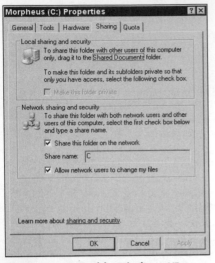

Figure 14-6: Enable Windows XP Home file sharing and set permissions with this dialog box.

Windows 98

Windows 98 also uses the Client for Microsoft Networks and File and Printer Sharing for Microsoft Networks components. Installing and configuring those components on Windows 98 is similar to the process for Windows 2000 and Windows XP, but not identical. Start the Network control panel applet (Start ➪ Settings ➪ Control Panel ➪ Network) to begin the process. Windows will have installed the Client for Microsoft Networks automatically when you added the network adapter; if not, click Add, then Client, and then Add. That sequence brings up the Select Network Client dialog box, where you'll select Microsoft, then Client for Microsoft Networks. Click OK and you'll return to the Network applet.

Click the File and Print Sharing button in the Network applet and then select file and/or print sharing in the resulting dialog box to direct Windows to add the server components. You have to reboot after you click OK all the way out of the sequence of dialog boxes.

Configuring Printer Sharing

The same server software we just described in the preceding section for file sharing implements printer sharing, too. You share a printer in much the same way as a drive or folder — right-click the printer in the Printers section of the Control Panel and then select Sharing. Under Windows 2000 and Windows XP, you'll see a dialog box such as in Figure 14-7. Select Share this printer, type in a share name, and click OK. The printer will be visible to all computers on your LAN.

Windows 98 provides a similar dialog box you set up in much the same way.

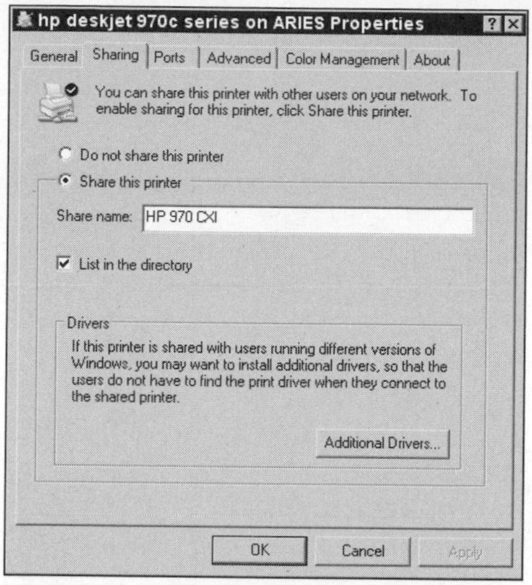

Figure 14-7: Enable Windows 2000 and Windows XP printer sharing and set permissions with these dialog boxes.

Summary

✦ Networks operate through layered, well-defined, highly structured conversations called protocols.

✦ Protocols are implemented by software components you install into the operating system and by applications embodying higher level protocols.

✦ Setting up your network software involves making sure you have the necessary protocols installed and configured.

✦ Old computers often make good file and print servers when they're no longer fast enough for direct use.

Internet Services, Antivirus, and Anti-Spam

In This Chapter

Examining Internet applications and protocols

Protecting against viruses, worms, and Trojans

Curbing spam

The protocols you learned about in Chapter 13 that make the Internet work — IP, DNS, and their friends — don't themselves do work you care about directly. All they do is transport messages from one place to another. Programs that do work over the Internet that you care about use protocols, too, but more importantly use those protocols to access services on remote computers. You'll learn about Internet protocols and services in this chapter, as well as about the attacks directed at your PC across the Internet and what you can do in defense.

Internet Services

Using an Internet service is very much like making a telephone call. You start the program (pick up the phone), choose which remote computer will handle your request (dial the number), and wait for it to do your work (your friend picks up the phone). A program on the remote computer responds to your request for service (answers the phone in our analogy). That program sits in the *server* computer you connect to, waiting for a message from your *client* computer to arrive.

Ping

The simplest client/server pair forms a service called ping, which lets you find out whether another computer is reachable on the Internet and, if so, how long the round trip to that computer and back takes in milliseconds. The ping server software is really built into the IP protocol software handling the server computer's network traffic — it's not a separate program. A typical invocation of `ping` (from a Windows DOS window) looks like this:

```
Pinging wiley.com [208.215.179.146] with 32 bytes of data:

Reply from 208.215.179.146: bytes=32 time=206ms TTL=244
Reply from 208.215.179.146: bytes=32 time=225ms TTL=244
Reply from 208.215.179.146: bytes=32 time=190ms TTL=244
Reply from 208.215.179.146: bytes=32 time=223ms TTL=244
```

This output shows several things:

✦ **Decoding names to network addresses** — A domain name server (DNS) resolves machine names to numeric addresses. A single machine can have many names, all of which resolve to the same Internet address. In the example just given, the name `wiley.com` resolves to the Internet address `208.215.179.146`, but if you tried it, so would `www.wiley.com`.

✦ **Round-trip response time** — The parts of the replies that say things like `time=206ms` show you how long it took from the time the client machine sent out the `ping` message until a reply came back (1 ms is 1 millisecond, or one thousandth of a second). The variability in the times you see reflects that networks don't always respond identically. Differing amounts of traffic on the communication lines or differing loads on the server are common causes.

You'll see very different response times depending on the access equipment you use. For example, we've measured typical `ping` responses from a nearby server of 120 ms with a V.90 modem, from 20 to 300 ms with a wireless broadband router and modem, and under 10 ms with Asymmetric Digital Subscriber Line (ADSL).

✦ **Routing hop count** — The part of the replies that says `TTL=244` tells you about the route the message took from here to there. The acronym *TTL* stands for *Time to Live*, which is a measure of how many reroutings from one point to another the packet has to go before IP declares it undeliverable. The number following TTL (called the *hop count*) is a number that usually starts at 255 and counts down by one every time the message gets rerouted through an intermediary computer.

`ping` is one of your most important tools in troubleshooting Internet problems. It shows you whether the Domain Name Server is working, whether the computer you're trying to talk to is reachable, and how long it takes to get there. It does this at a very low level — only the most basic Internet functions have to be up and running.

World Wide Web

The Internet service you're most likely to use (with the possible exception of electronic mail) is the World Wide Web. Your computer runs client software called a Web browser that talks to Web server software on the remote server computer. Your messages are transported across the Internet using the *Hypertext Transfer Protocol (HTTP)*.

The combination of a Web browser, HTTP, and a Web server is more complex than many other protocols because in combination they do much more than move information from one place to another. Additional functions the combination supports include the following:

✦ **Page formatting** — Messages sent from the Web server to your Web browser are coded in the *Hypertext Markup Language (HTML)*, which defines an embedded structure and a set of codes that tell the Web browser what the image it displays on your screen should look like.

✦ **Hypertext links** — Links from one page in your Web browser to another are identified by special codes in the message from the Web server. When you click on a link, the Web browser sends a request to the right Web server (possibly one you've not communicated with previously) to send it the page data.

✦ **Image, movie, and sound links** — Web pages can contain images as well as text, using codes that specify from where to retrieve the image.

✦ **Forms** — Web pages can contain forms that let you fill in information and send it out to the Web server. The source code of the Web page specifies how forms are defined for display on your screen, how that information gets to the Web server, and what processing software on the server will do.

Even a single Web page may draw information from more than one Web server. The Web uses a standard specification for addressing servers and information on those servers. A standard Web address is called a *uniform resource locator (URL)*. URLs (such as `www.aros.net/~press/utilities/utilities.htm`) have three parts:

✦ **Protocol** — The protocol used to access the referenced information need not be HTTP. It is in the example in the preceding paragraph, but can equally be other protocols such as FTP (for example, `ftp://ftp.aros.net/pub/users/press/bput95s.zip`). The first part of the URL defines what protocol to use and is separated from the rest of the URL by the `://` characters.

Note   Recent versions of both Microsoft Internet Explorer and Netscape Navigator let you omit the `http://` element from a URL, supplying it for you. If your URL requires another protocol, you have to provide it.

✦ **Server** — The second part of the URL is the name of the server computer holding the information or services you want. This is `www.aros.net` and `ftp.aros.net` in the two preceding examples. The computer name might be suffixed with a port number to tell TCP how to find the daemon on the server. The default port for HTTP is 80, so `www.aros.net` is equivalent in a URL to `www.aros.net:80`. The server computer name is the only part of a URL you have to supply with current Web browsers.

✦ **File or service location** — A forward slash separates the server computer name from the rest of the URL. Both the forward slash and anything after it are optional, depending on what's being addressed. In an HTTP URL, the file or service location points to a file on the server that is either sent back to you by the server or run as a program on the server. In the latter case, the program creates output dynamically and returns it to you.

File transfer

It's common to want to retrieve files onto your computer from another, or to send files from your computer to another. The *File Transfer Protocol (FTP)* is the Internet standard protocol to do that, although Windows has its own internal file transfer protocols, and Web browsers can use either FTP or HTTP for the purpose. As with other Internet application protocols, FTP operates between a client and a server. The FTP client is the program that initiates the FTP connection; the FTP server is the program that receives the connection. You can send files either way across an FTP connection, regardless of which of the two computers is the client and which is the server.

Because it is specific to the problem of transferring files from one computer to another, the primitive operations in FTP reflect the things you need to do:

✦ **Authenticate access** — This being an imperfect world, it's often necessary to impose restrictions on who is allowed to connect to the FTP server. FTP implements a username and password authentication scheme and refuses the connection without a valid login. It's common on many FTP servers to allow the username "anonymous" to log in with any password whatsoever; it's convention is to use your e-mail address for the password. Files kept in an anonymous login area are available to anyone with Internet access — this is the basis on which much of the software downloaded across the Internet is accessed.

✦ **Navigate the remote file system** — In the same way that you need mechanisms such as the DOS Change Directory (CD) command or the Windows Explorer to move around as you use your computer, you need the capability to find files on the remote computer. FTP defines commands and responses between client and server that report the current directory (folder in Windows terms), change to a different directory, and list the contents of the current directory.

✦ **Set the file type** — Some operating systems, such as Linux (but not Windows), distinguish between pure text files and files that contain other information and alter the characters at the end of each line in a text file when sending and receiving. Altering line markers in files is a problem when you send a binary file (such as a program) because every time a Linux computer sees an end-of-line character in the binary file, it converts it to a pair of characters (carriage return and line feed). That transformation is okay for text, but it completely corrupts programs, word processor files, spreadsheets, sound files, photographs, and most everything else. FTP lets you control whether files are transferred as text or binary, giving the remote system the information it needs to do its job properly.

✦ **Send or receive files** — This is, of course, the point of the protocol. FTP can transmit files from the client or server and can send one or many files at the same time.

Early versions of the FTP client — starting over 30 years ago — on a number of different computer systems provided a command-line interface. The same FTP client interface is standard in Linux and still available in Windows — try opening a DOS window on a PC connected to the Internet and typing FTP. (Type quit to exit FTP.) The command-line interface is much less convenient than the graphical Windows interface provided by clients such as WS_FTP, but it's there. The commands you can enter into the command-line version are very directly related to the primitive operations in the FTP protocol (such as open a connection to a server, enter username and password, change directory, set the file type, send or receive files, and close the connection). The responses from the server appear directly onscreen, interleaved with your commands.

Electronic mail

The Internet protocol for exchanging electronic mail is the *Simple Mail Transfer Protocol (SMTP)*. As far as we know, there's no Complex Mail Transfer Protocol, but SMTP is quite complex enough. (It's an Internet tradition to prefix Simple to the name of protocols, displaying a cavalier disregard for the truth of the resulting phrase. One of the most complex Internet protocols is called the Simple Network Management Protocol.)

SMTP itself allows you to exchange text mail messages with users on computers connected to the Internet. Addresses you can mail to are typically like max@acme.com — there's the username, an at sign, and the name of the user's mail server computer.

Because electronic mail can be sent to you at any time, it's best to have it held at a computer that's always on the Net (such as one at your Internet service provider). After electronic mail for you reaches your mail server computer, it's common for you to retrieve it to your own computer using the Post Office Protocol (POP3 — there have been several versions).

SMTP includes primitive operations for the things involved with sending mail:

✦ **Validate recipient address** — The server verifies that the addressee on the message exists.

✦ **Deliver to a user's mailbox** — One computer connects to another and exchanges mail between the two.

✦ **Read receipt** — You can request receipts when the recipient opens the message you sent.

Some SMTP mail servers support forwarding — you can receive mail on one system and (transparently to the sender) forward it to a completely different address on another system. For example, a message sent to `max@acme.com` could be relayed by the acme.com mail server to `sam@whizbang.ca`. Though the idea is useful, many servers implement forwarding without authenticating the sender, giving spammers the opening they need. We talk about spam and what you can do about it later in this chapter.

The worst thing about raw SMTP is that it accepts only text messages, not binary files. People commonly want to mail arbitrary files, however, and send text that includes fonts, colors, and other formatting. Three approaches to handling this requirement are common: UUE, MIME, and HTML:

✦ **User-user encoding (UUE)** — It's possible to recast the binary data stream you want to send differently. For example, you could take every 6 bits (creating numbers in the range from 0 to 63) and remap the resulting numbers onto the printable characters. This expands the data stream, producing 8 bits from every 6, but it results in a new data stream that contains nothing but text characters acceptable to SMTP. This was the original way of sending binary data through SMTP on the Internet — encode the data, mail the text, and decode at the other end. Current-generation electronic mail client programs, such as Windows Messaging, which is included with Windows, support this transformation automatically.

✦ **Multipurpose Internet Mail Extensions (MIME)** — Internet software like Web browsers actively know what sort of data is stored in different kinds of files — that EXE files are executables, ZIP files are compressed archives, WAV files are sound clips, and so on. The MIME coding standard for electronic mail allows the properties of files to be sent along with the files themselves. Technically, MIME uses the same approach UUE does, expanding a smaller number of bits to a larger number that transforms strictly to printable characters.

✦ **Hypertext Markup Language (HTML)** — You won't send binary files this way, but many electronic mail clients let you compose messages as Web pages, and therefore let you format text and include pictures.

Not all Internet mail clients know how to automatically decode messages sent using UUE, MIME, or HTML text. If you have one of those, the tip-off will be a bunch of gibberish in the text.

Some Internet mail systems limit the maximum size of a mail message you can send. We've seen limits as low as 1MB; you'll undoubtedly encounter others. This isn't much of a problem for small text messages, but it's easy to create messages containing coded binary files that are that large. The effects you'll see if you exceed the maximum size limit are unpredictable — the most benign thing we've seen is for the mail server to send back a message saying it won't deliver the mail. We've had messages silently disappear without notice, had the mail server crash at one end or the other, and had our mail client crash. Just keep in mind the most important rule of the Internet:

The Internet is not perfectly reliable.

That doesn't mean the Internet's not useful, and it doesn't mean you can't depend on it. It means you have to assume that things will go wrong. It means you have to have planned how you will detect when things fail and what to do about it. In the case of large messages, for example, you could send a short text-only message in advance stating the other message is coming, so that if the recipient doesn't get the large message, they're likely to let you know.

Telnet

In the same way that you can connect a terminal program to your modem, you can connect the equivalent program to the Internet and log in to remote computers (or at least the ones you have an account on). Many *Internet service providers (ISPs)* provide remote computer access to Linux or other UNIX servers on that basis. The client program that lets you connect to a remote computer is Telnet. If we log in to our Internet service provider, for example, here's a typical example of what we get in the Telnet window:

```
login: xxxxx
Password:
Last login: Wed Jul  2 18:18:12 2003 from xxxxx
Copyright (c) 1980, 1983, 1986, 1988, 1990, 1991, 1993, 1994
        The Regents of the University of California.  All rights
reserved.

FreeBSD 4.8-RC (SHELL) #36: Tue Mar  4 01:48:32 MST 2003
-----------------------------------------------------------------
        Welcome to ArosNet.

        All access may be logged for auditing and security purposes.
        See /etc/rotd for more information.

******** IRC Bots and other unattended processes are not allowed on
        this machine.

-----------------------------------------------------------------


For the user-friendly menu, type 'menu'.

>>
```

Our ISP runs the FreeBSD version of UNIX (see www.freebsd.org), but this output is typical of what you get logging in to most UNIX computers. Telnet provides a completely character-oriented terminal — the line at the bottom is a command prompt to a UNIX command shell, which is analogous to COM-MAND.COM in Windows 9X or CMD.EXE in Windows 2000 or Windows XP. UNIX has commands comparable to ones in Windows, some of which are shown in Table 15-1.

It's also possible to connect to UNIX computers through a graphical interface called X Window, using what's called an XTerm. Telnet doesn't do that — you need more complex software. Telnet ships with Windows — simply run **telnet** from Start ➪ Run — but Windows does not include an XTerm.

Table 15-1
Comparable UNIX and Windows Commands

Windows Command	UNIX Command
`dir`	`ls`
`attrib`	`chmod`
`cd` and `chdir`	`cd`
`cls`	`clear`
`copy`	`cp`
`del` and `rmdir`	`rm`
`md` and `mkdir`	`mkdir`
`more`	`more`
`move`	`mv`

Newsgroups

The *Network News Transfer Protocol (NNTP)* is the mechanism underneath a worldwide Internet bulletin board covering nearly any subject you can think of — the Usenet newsgroups. For example, if you're a Quake player, you'll find no fewer than five relevant newsgroups:

```
alt.games.quake
rec.games.computer.quake.announce
rec.games.computer.quake.misc
rec.games.computer.quake.playing
rec.games.computer.quake.servers
```

If you're interested in barbequed food, you might look at the following:

```
alt.food.barbeque
```

Both moderated and unmoderated newsgroups exist. The protocol arranges to distribute postings worldwide; in many ways the newsgroups are the broadest, fastest medium yet devised for spreading information. (Newsgroups spread viruses in file attachments, too. You should have your machine protected by good antivirus software, and never open attachments you're unsure of.)

You can access the general Internet newsgroups in two ways. If you want to use a program local to your PC, you'll need a newsreader client. Microsoft's Outlook Express functions as a newsreader and is included with Windows. UNIX systems include a variety of readers. You'll also need access to a news server — see your Internet service provider for that.

Alternatively, you can search, read, and post to the newsgroups through the Internet search engines. Using Google, for instance, go to `www.google.com/grphp`. You can search many groups directly from that page, or you can use the links on the bottom of the page to find specific newsgroups. Newsreader clients are typically faster and more efficient for reading traffic in a specific newsgroup, so when you find a newsgroup and topic that's interesting through a search engine, you can then fire up your newsreader and go look in depth.

Either way, you need to know two characteristics of newsgroups:

✦ **Content** — The same widespread, often-uncensored characteristics of newsgroups that make them valuable also make them a conduit for information that might be unacceptable or offensive to some people. You might want to supervise minors' access to the newsgroups.

✦ **Significance and accuracy** — Don't expect all the messages in a newsgroup to be polite, accurate, or even interesting. In most newsgroups, the bulk of the messages (and people) are none of those. Reading all the traffic in even a small number of active newsgroups can take hours, and you might not find what you're looking for when you're finished.

Time

One of the annoyances of life is that clocks are usually somewhat wrong. A consequence of that fact is that the clock in your computer is probably wrong. Worse, some motherboards are simply incapable of keeping time accurately. For example, a computer we had for years gained more than a minute a day if we let it. It wasn't worth pulling out the motherboard and sending it back to the manufacturer to repair it, and Internet software such as we describe here kept the clock on track until we finally retired the old warhorse.

Very accurate clocks do exist, and some servers on the Internet are slaved to them. An Internet protocol, the *Network Time Protocol (NTP)*, lets your computer get the current time from one of those servers, as do a number of other forms of time servers.

Windows XP includes a built-in network time client (see the Internet time tab in the Date and Time control panel applet), as does Linux (use the `rdate` command). If you're running earlier versions of Windows, a very convenient program — Socket Watch (see `www.locutuscodeware.com/swatch.htm`) — automates the process of keeping your computer clock accurate. You can configure Socket Watch to start when you boot Windows, and it simply waits for you to connect to the Internet. When you do, Socket Watch reaches out to the time server you specify and updates your clock. Simple, and no effort on your part. You can expect the clock in your computer to remain accurate to within several seconds or less assuming you connect to the Internet periodically.

Instant messaging

As useful as electronic mail is, it's not interactive. You can carry on "conversations" in extended time, but it's not the same as spontaneous conversation. Nor is the telephone always the answer; it's expensive to carry on extended group discussions at multiple sites using long-distance conference calls.

In the same way that Citizen's Band radio allowed people access to low-cost party lines, computer chat has grown to provide the same capability. There are several Internet versions of chat, including both *Internet Relay Chat (IRC)* and several proprietary messaging communities.

Internet Relay Chat

Internet Relay Chat works like this. You connect to an IRC server using IRC client software, such as mIRC (www.mirc.com). When you connect, you choose one or more channels you want to "talk" in. You can search for channels with names containing a string you specify, but it's somewhat hit-or-miss whether you'll find the one you want. The last time we looked, the IRC server on our Internet service provider handled over 17,200 channels. Newsgroups covering your interests are sometimes a way to find out about IRC channels, as are sites such as www.irchelp.org/irchelp/chanlist. Closed, private IRC channels exist, but IRC is mostly an open, public system with many people on a channel at once. It's like a public meeting.

Proprietary messaging

Several companies, including AOL with ICQ and AOL Instant Messenger, Microsoft with MSN Messenger, and Yahoo! with Yahoo! Messenger, offer more private instant messaging services, ones that make it convenient to carry on conversations with people you know. Although traffic goes through servers, instant messaging appears to you to be between the client on your PC and the one on the other person's machine. You can have multiple conversations at once, each in its own window.

Viruses and Worms and Trojans, Oh My!

The Internet, a creation of people, is a perfect mirror for the real world of people. A seemingly infinite number of people are online, ranging from altruists with the best motives (www.toysfortots.org) to child pornographers destined for their own special part of hell.

Somewhere between the two are those who would corrupt or break into your computers, attacking your PC for their own amusement or other ends. Their attacks take several forms:

✦ **Viruses** — Much like their biological namesakes, computer viruses infect parts of your computer, damage what they will, and spread through those infections.

✦ **Worms** — Worms are similar to viruses, but operate in a more stand-alone manner, taking action on their own to spread to other computers.

✦ **Trojans** — Trojans, like their Trojan horse namesake, are attackers wrapped in something benign. Trojans typically open up a compromised computer to later attack from outside.

✦ **Cracks** — In addition to attacks through programs sent to your computer in the hope you'll run them, you'll be subject to direct attack by people looking for specific vulnerabilities in your software that let them take control of your PC.

The rise of the Internet, and the corresponding decline in the exchange of floppies, has made the Internet the most common vector for attacks on your computers. All these types of attacks will come at you when connected to the Internet.

Viruses

Viruses can infect your computer several ways, the most popular of which are through infected removable disks (such as floppies), programs, and documents.

A virus can infect any removable, bootable disk, even if there are no files on the disk. The infection lies in what's called the *Master Boot Record (MBR)*, the part of the disk used to start your computer well before the operating system begins running. Reformatting the disk does not necessarily remove the infection, and merely inserting a floppy in an infected machine can spread the infection to the floppy. Antivirus software helps protect your PC from disks you insert while the PC is running, but if you leave an infected floppy in your PC and accidentally boot it when you turn on the computer, the virus can spread before your antivirus software even loads.

The best way to protect against booting an infected floppy disk is to change your BIOS settings so your PC won't boot a floppy in the first place. Figure 15-1 shows the boot sequence controls for a typical BIOS. Your BIOS is likely to be different, so you'll have to hunt around to find the controls (be careful not to change anything inadvertently). In the BIOS shown, you'd move the highlighted Diskette Drive line down to below the Internal HDD line by pressing d (other BIOS setups will likely be different, so read the screen for instructions). Alternatively, you could press the spacebar to disable the device from the boot sequence altogether. This change is completely risk-free because if you ever do have to boot from a floppy intentionally, you can just redo the BIOS settings.

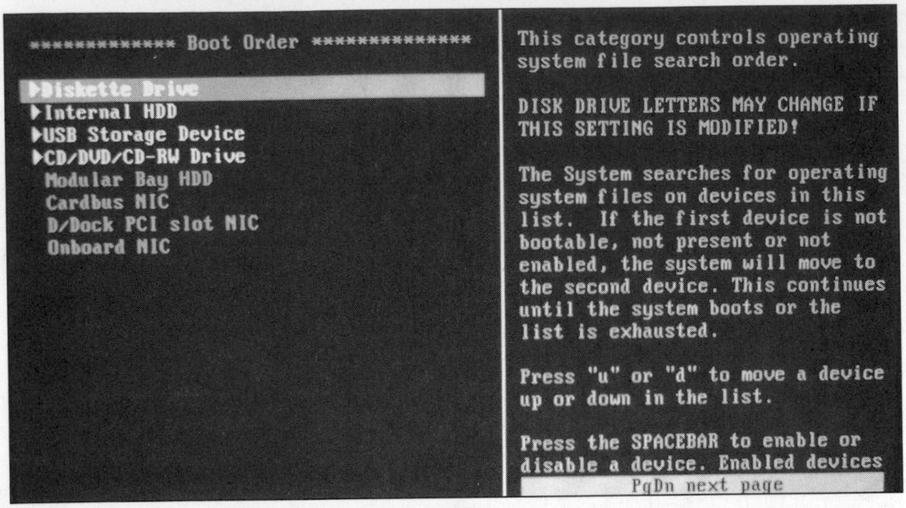

```
************** Boot Order ***************      This category controls operating
                                              system file search order.
▶Diskette Drive
 ▶Internal HDD                                DISK DRIVE LETTERS MAY CHANGE IF
 ▶USB Storage Device                          THIS SETTING IS MODIFIED!
 ▶CD/DVD/CD-RW Drive
  Modular Bay HDD                             The System searches for operating
  Cardbus NIC                                 system files on devices in this
  D/Dock PCI slot NIC                         list. If the first device is not
  Onboard NIC                                 bootable, not present or not
                                              enabled, the system will move to
                                              the second device. This continues
                                              until the system boots or the
                                              list is exhausted.

                                              Press "u" or "d" to move a device
                                              up or down in the list.

                                              Press the SPACEBAR to enable or
                                              disable a device. Enabled devices
                                                    PgDn next page
```

Figure 15-1: BIOS boot sequence controls

©2004 Barry Press & Marcia Press

The most common path for viruses onto your computer, however, is the Internet. Virtually any file someone sends you — attached to electronic mail, in a chat room, or as a Web site download — could be infected. If you never download files and never open attachments to electronic mail, you're relatively safe, but that approach gives up some of the most useful functions of the Internet. Instead, we recommend you understand and follow these guidelines:

✦ **Don't open unexpected electronic mail file attachments** — A very popular approach for spreading viruses is to exploit the combination of Windows' support for long file names with embedded blanks and some applications' limitations on how long displayed file names can be. For example, a program limiting file name display might show a file name as `cute puppy.jpg` while the real file name is `cute puppy.jpg.exe`. That latter file name is an executable program, so instead of bringing up a photo like Figure 15-2, you'll run a program that infects your computer with whatever malicious garbage the virus writer chose, something like deleting all your files or worse.

✦ **Run antivirus software** — The section "Antivirus and anti-adware software," later in this chapter, discusses software you can use to help recognize viruses trying to infect your computer and block them. Use that software, and keep it up-to-date.

✦ **Block macro viruses in Microsoft Office and other applications** — Viruses need not be executable programs; indeed, over half the different viruses cataloged by antivirus software developers reside in application data files, exploiting the programming languages built into the applications. Figure 15-3 shows the dialog box to use in Microsoft Word, with the security level set to reject any macros not from sources you know and trust. Be careful whom you trust, too, because both friends and experts make mistakes.

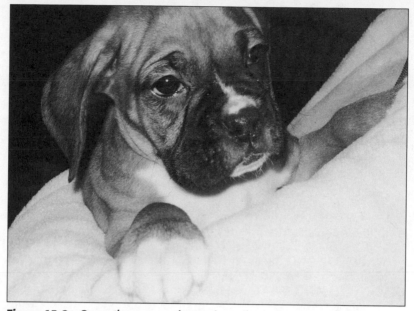

Figure 15-2: Open the wrong electronic mail attachment, and this isn't what you'll see.
©2004 Barry Press & Marcia Press

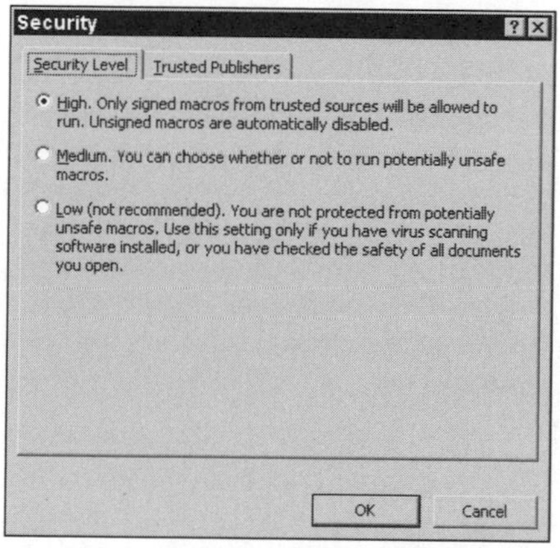

Figure 15-3: Set application macro
security to reject unknown macro sources.

Although Microsoft Office is the most common target for macro viruses, check every program you use for macro settings and restrict what macros can do without permission if you can.

Worms

Worms differ from viruses and Trojans in how they propagate. Although all three favor the Internet for attacks, viruses propagate on contact, worms actively seek to burrow into PCs, and Trojans seek to mimic something innocuous. Perhaps the most common worm attack is to seek out vulnerabilities in applications and the operating system, holes in the software that let the worm execute on the victim machine. We recommend the following to defend against worms:

✦ **Actively check for and apply security patches** — Every operating system has flaws an attacker can use. Whether you run Microsoft Windows, Linux, or some other operating system, check the operating system manufacturer's Web site periodically for security patches applicable to your system. Microsoft implements a patch service at `windowsupdate.microsoft.com`. You'll usually want all the critical updates and security updates they post; taking the recommended updates and driver updates is entirely optional. Windows 2000 and Windows XP offer an automatic update service that will notify you when there are updates available. Figure 15-4 shows the dialog box you use in Windows XP, which is part of the System control panel applet. Windows 2000 has a separate Automatic Updates control panel applet that looks much the same.

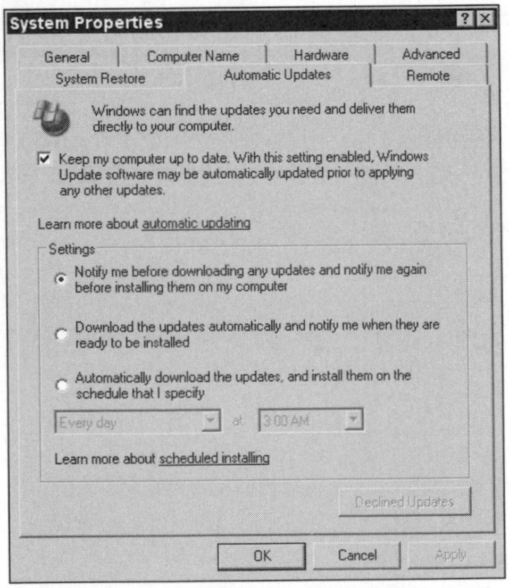

Figure 15-4: Automatic Windows updates notify you when updates are available.

We're generally conservative about loading software onto our computers, be it from Microsoft or anyone else, but the Windows security updates and critical updates are definitely ones to keep on top of.

Both Microsoft and the maintainers of the FreeBSD operating system maintain mailing lists to distribute security notices. Signing up for the security mailing list for operating systems you use could give you a few days head start on patching critical vulnerabilities before the more mainstream patch sites have the update, and before the attacks begin.

✦ **Run hardware and software firewalls** — There's no good reason for a computer on the Internet to contact your computer without permission, so you should run a firewall to block inbound connection attempts. We prefer hardware firewalls for that job. The best protection against worms and Trojans also limits the programs that can connect to the Internet outbound from your PC; we prefer ZoneAlarm for that protection. Both hardware and software firewalls are covered in Chapter 13. If you have one, don't forget to secure your wireless LAN, too.

✦ **Check if your system is vulnerable** — It's not enough to install patches and firewalls — you have to test them to know if you've done the setup properly. The Gibson Research Corporation Web site (`www.grc.com`) includes a test for open ports leading to incoming vulnerabilities (see the ShieldsUP! tool) and for outgoing connections (see LeakTest), but there's no comprehensive test for all the patches you'll install.

✦ **Set up Windows Explorer to always show file extensions** — By default, Windows Explorer eliminates the file extension for known file types from its display, so the example we used above of `cute puppy.jpg.exe` would display in Windows Explorer as `cute puppy.jpg`. If you turn off the setting to hide file extensions, as in Figure 15-5, you'll always see the real story (unless your columns are too narrow, in which case you'll still see an ellipsis).

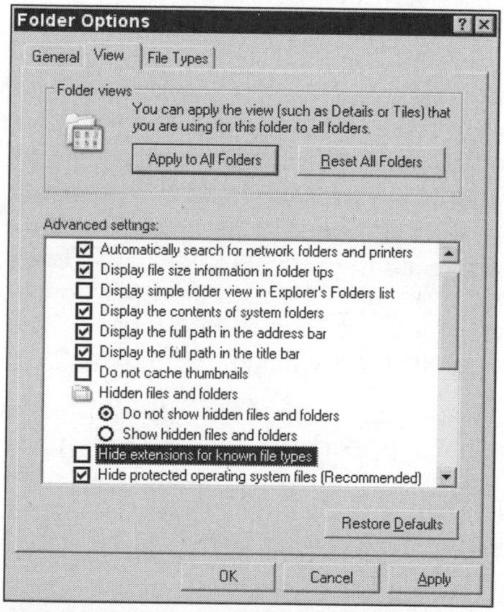

Figure 15-5: Clear the highlighted Windows Explorer setting to force file extension display.

Once you've done that, be careful starting files with the extensions COM, EXE, BAT, SCR, VBS, PIF, or CMD. They're all executable under some version of Windows. Don't believe a program is safe just because you recognize its icon.

Trojans

Trojans are programs that masquerade as other benign or desirable software, but have unadvertised effects. One non-destructive example is the bundling of the Gator advertising software in a variety of file-sharing applications. Those programs typically state that you're agreeing to the advertising Trojan in their license agreement, so it's conceivable what they do is legal. Far more insidious are the Trojans that let people remotely spy on and control your PC. Three of the most common are called Back Orifice, SubSeven, and NetBus; let them on your PC, and the remote attacker might as well be sitting at your shoulder watching the screen, typing on the keyboard, and moving the mouse. Trojans can arrive in electronic mail or be distributed in newsgroups and other file download sources. Here's how to reduce your vulnerability:

✦ **Run hardware and software firewalls** — This is the same approach we've suggested before, and by the time you've finished reading this book, you'll see it many more times. Even if you don't have a spare, unused PC (which could make the total cost zero), you can set up solid hardware and software firewall protection for between $20 and $100, completely blocking inbound attacks from the Internet with a low probability of penetration from the outside.

✦ **Use security options in your Web browser** — Web browsers offer settings to control what Web sites are allowed to do, settings you can use to restrict downloads and other behavior. Internet Explorer categorizes Web sites into one of four zones, with the *restricted* zone being a list of sites for which you want to enforce tighter security. It's effective to populate the restricted zone yourself, but unreliable in a security sense because it's difficult to identify all the sites you want restricted before you encounter them. You can preload the list from IE-SPYAD, available at www.staff.uiuc.edu/~ehowes/resource.htm. Be sure to read the readme file that comes with IE-SPYAD to find out how you can edit the list to remove sites you don't want to restrict and enable restrictions on sites that aren't activated by default.

✦ **Lock down application security** — Make sure your applications are themselves as secure as possible. For example, patches for Outlook on the Microsoft Web site block executable attachments in electronic mail, and settings you can make in Outlook cause HTML formatted messages to open as if they're in Internet Explorer's restricted zone (see the Security Zones part of Figure 15-6).

✦ **Run antivirus and anti-adware software** — Even though a hardware firewall blocks most incoming attacks, and a good software firewall detects and blocks outgoing connection attempts should a Trojan find its way onto your PC, you still want to try to block the Trojan before it can activate. The antivirus and anti-adware software discussed later in this chapter help provide that protection.

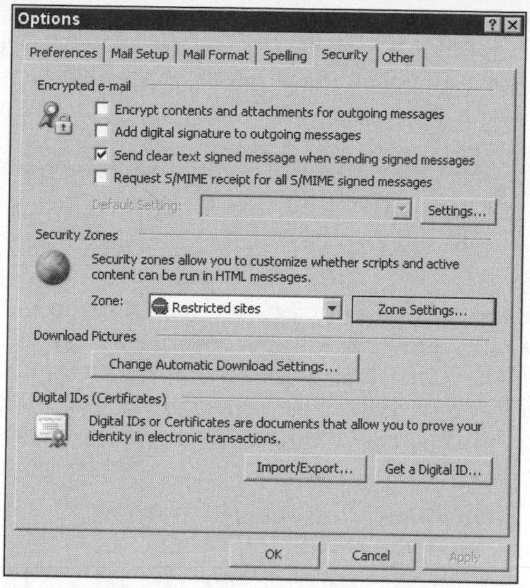

Figure 15-6: Use these Outlook settings to force HTML electronic mail into the restricted zone.

Cracks

Although many Internet attacks on your computers will be by virus, worm, and Trojan programs based on others' work and launched by people with little or no skill of their own, some people have skills sufficient to directly attack your computer — an activity generally called cracking — using specialized tools to analyze and penetrate your network. Attacks of this sort start by gathering information, from your Web site if you have one, from newsgroup postings you've made (remember, the newsgroups are searchable using Google and other search engines), and by scanning your network using `ping` and related tools that scan for open ports much like the tests at Gibson Research. We're not recommending you become an Internet hermit, sharing no information or postings on the Net, but there are specific steps you can take to reduce your vulnerability.

✦ **Consider what you publish** — Before you're done, look a second time at electronic mail you send, Web pages you publish, and newsgroup messages you post, reviewing them for what information you're revealing to a potential attacker. Think about both attacks on your computers and the potential for identity theft when you review. Posting that you're running Windows 98 Second Edition on your PC is bad enough because it helps a cracker know what attacks to direct at your PC; posting the make and model of your hardware firewall is just stupid — consider, for example, that a Google search for *NETGEAR vulnerability* returns over 20,000 hits, while a search for *Linksys vulnerability* returns over 12,000. Firewalls don't advertise their make and model number to the Internet, so by giving out that information you just make the cracker's job easier.

✦ **Use a hardware firewall and close all open ports** — Not only should you use a hardware firewall to protect your network from the Internet, you want to make sure you configure it to block all incoming ports so crackers can't reach the computers on your network. Don't forget to make sure the firewall's management tools are accessible only from your LAN, denying the cracker the ability to reprogram its configuration. Do not rely on passwords for that purpose because there are some very sophisticated password guessing and attack programs available.

✦ **Don't run unnecessary services on your PC** — Layered defenses help protect you if your outer defenses — your firewalls — are breached. Your inner defense layer is how you configure your PCs themselves. Don't run programs you don't need, such as Web, FTP, or Telnet servers, because they increase the number of points available for attack.

✦ **Apply operating system and application security patches regularly** — As we described in the section on worms, get in the habit of checking for and applying security patches for your software regularly. Security patches fix vulnerabilities in your software, reducing the footprint a cracker has to attack.

✦ **Back up your data and software** — In the end, protecting your computers from attack is an arms race, not a sure thing. If you have backups of all your data and programs, backups that you remove from the computers when they're complete, then no attack can destroy everything.

Antivirus and anti-adware software

We think that nearly every computer should be connected to the Internet, but we also think that every PC connected to the Internet should be protected by up-to-date antivirus and anti-adware software. Firewalls help protect you from attacks others initiate; antivirus and anti-adware software help protect you from attacks piggybacking on electronic mail, in Web sites, and on disks you bring in.

At a minimum, antivirus software scans files you read from disk, scanning program files every time a program launches, and (perhaps) data files every time a program accesses them. Some antivirus software scans your e-mail as it arrives, too. We used to recommend a specific antivirus product, but after severe, unresolved problems with that manufacturer and several others, we no longer think any of them are particularly better than the rest. You can choose software from Frisk Software International, F-Secure, Kaspersky Labs, McAfee, Symantec, Trend Micro, and others; Freebyte maintains a list of free antivirus software (see `www.freebyte.com/antivirus`).

Antivirus software works by scanning files, looking for patterns characteristic of known viruses. Antivirus data files define the patterns of the software, so you have to update the data files regularly to make sure you have the latest patterns. (There's a technique called *heuristic scanning* that looks for likely virus indicators, but as delivered in current products it's prone to both false positives and to missing actual viruses.) You can configure most antivirus products to update themselves regularly; we have ours set to update weekly.

Even if you do everything right, you'll find the virus writers still conspire to cause you grief, and you shouldn't be upset when that happens. For example, Figure 15-7 is typical of a lot of electronic mail we received while the Sobig.F virus was circulating on the Internet during the summer of 2003. The message is from a site in Denmark, reporting to us that we've apparently sent them a message infected with that virus.

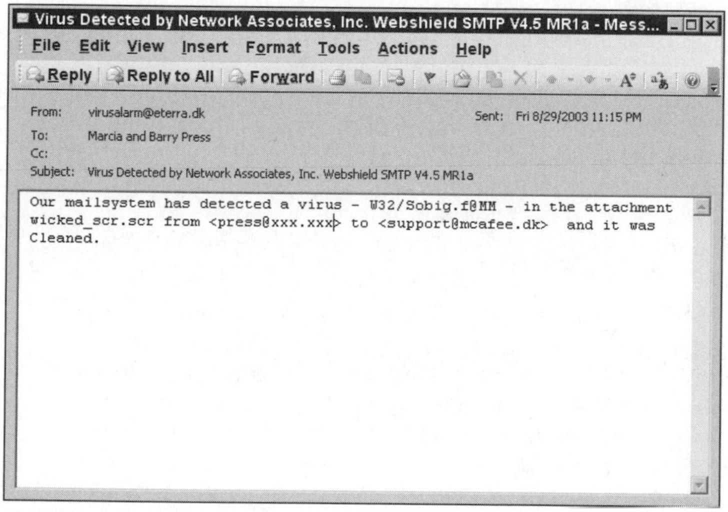

Figure 15-7: You'll be affected by viruses even when you do everything right.

Unfortunately, we never sent a message to eterra.dk, much less one infected with Sobig.F. The virus scanner there detected the virus, which is good for the protected site, and then sent us a completely useless electronic mail message. Analyses of the virus on the Internet (for example, www.f-secure.com/ v-descs/sobig_f.shtml) report that the virus forges the sender's address using addresses found on the infected PC. It's worse than merely ironic that the virus scanner that sent us this e-mail is too stupid to know the virus forged the sender's address because the volume of electronic mail clogging the Internet from this one virus was made worse by these useless messages.

The importance of installing and updating antivirus software notwithstanding, a lot of virus hoaxes exist, too. You can find catalogs of them on the Internet (see www.datafellows.fi/news/hoax.htm and www.vmyths.com). In general, keep in mind that any electronic mail that urges you to forward it to all your friends is itself a hoax.

For political reasons more than technical ones, antivirus software typically doesn't have the ability to scan for and reject adware, which includes files called *cookies* that can help track your Web usage, software that displays advertising, or programs that report information from your computer back to a server. There's a market for tools to help defeat those threats, however, leading to both anti-adware programs and Web sites offering information and advice. We recommend a combination of several approaches:

✦ **Run Ad-aware** — Lavasoft (www.lavasoft.de) makes available its Ad-aware tool in both free and paid versions. The free version scans your PC on command; the paid version adds a component that stays resident while your PC runs, blocking adware in real time.

✦ **Block suspect sites** — Much of the adware on the Internet comes from Web sites, either through opening windows hidden on your desktop, you clicking yes on warnings about downloaded software, or other means. The rest comes bundled in with software you intentionally install. You can suppress much of the malign operations of known adware sites by installing IE-SPYAD (www.staff.uiuc.edu/~ehowes/resource.htm). Other forms of adware come in as add-ons specifically programmed for Microsoft Internet Explorer; you can block many of them with SpywareBlaster (www.javacoolsoftware.com/spywareblaster.html).

Even if you don't want to load the wholesale site restrictions these tools provide, you can still build your own list in the Internet Explorer restricted zone. Any time a site tries to install software — watch for warning pop-ups, and read them all carefully — you can add it to the list. We generally exclude all addresses at the site, so, for example, after Gator tried to install its code on our PCs, we added *.gator.com to our restricted sites list.

✦ **Read the newsgroups and reviews before installing software** — Search the newsgroups and any reviews on download sites (for example, www.download.com) for information about adware bundled in with programs. For example, if you went to the description page for WeatherCast (download.com.com/3000-2054-10179240.html), you'd find out it comes bundled with a load of adware from WhenU. Had you found the program by searching the site for *weather forecast* and then merely clicked the Download link based on its relatively large number of downloads, you'd have missed the warning.

✦ **Be careful where you click** — Web sites have the unfortunate habit of popping up intentionally confusing windows on your screen, and it's sometimes difficult to know how to close them without activating them. For example, despite having taught her what to look for, our 12 year old was caught by a deceptive window and accidentally installed some adware called Memory Blaster. Read what you see onscreen carefully, and don't click on windows blindly. We also recommend installing the Google toolbar (toolbar.google.com) and activating its pop-up window blocker.

Ad-aware is good at removing adware. If you do end up infected with a worm or virus, however, strong measures may be required. We'll discuss what to do in Chapter 24.

Dealing with Spam

Spam, or more formally *unsolicited commercial e-mail*, is electronic mail dumped in your inbox you didn't ask for and that, generally, comes from a source you don't know. Spam is the electronic equivalent of the junk mail that fills your post box, only it costs the sender far less, clogs the Internet and your inbox, and is quite often something you'd really rather not see. A sampling of the spam we've received in one of our inboxes includes offers for automobile warranties, debt reduction, adult videos involving barnyard animals, mortgage refinancing, get rich quick schemes, photos of singles we can date, adult videos without the barnyard animals but with cheerleaders, male and female organ enlargement, health insurance, pheromones guaranteed to attract others, mail-order Russian brides, low-cost travel, eBay training, Viagra, free money, more adult photos and videos, improved Web site traffic, billions of addresses to send spam to, the fountain of youth, secret information on anyone, millions of dollars to be exported from Nigeria, anti-spam tools, antivirus tools, university diplomas, and worse.

Just so there's no misunderstanding, it's all a fraud. Only idiots conduct major financial transactions with someone offering no mutual references and who can't spell well enough to graduate from sixth grade. We're married and not really good candidates for dating singles. eBay is too simple to need training to use, we're partial to the organs we have and want to keep them, and people falling for the Nigerian spam (see www.snopes.com/inboxer/scams/nigeria.htm and www.secretservice.gov/alert419.shtml) demonstrate the triumph of human greed in the face of all common sense. Spammers selling anti-spam tools have even more *chutzpah* than we can believe.

As of August 2003, 50 to 60 percent of the electronic mail on the Internet was spam (depending on whose statistics you read). One of the best-known organizations fighting spam is The Coalition Against Unsolicited Commercial Email (CAUCE). On their Web site (www.cauce.org) you'll find information about spam, about legislation targeting spammers, and more.

Spam has proven almost impossible to stop despite many determined efforts, both because it's an escalating arms race between the spammers and the anti-spammers and because of an unfortunate legacy from the early non-commercial days of the Internet. When the Internet began, its users were typically either government or companies and universities doing research for the government. A culture of openness and sharing grew in that environment, including sharing of resources to relay traffic among the many computers at the time not directly connected to the Internet. Prime among those relay functions was the sendmail program, which for years was distributed with settings that by default allowed anyone at all to relay electronic mail through a sendmail server. After a pair of lawyers invented spam (overlawyered.com/archives/02/mar3.html), though, all those open relay servers were just what the spammers needed, and far too many of them are still in operation all over the world.

An open relay server is spam heaven because of how electronic mail works. A spammer sends a message to an open relay, attaching a long list of blind carbon copy (BCC) addresses. The transmission to the relay is one message, requiring almost no network bandwidth. The relay then dutifully sends copies of the message to every addressee, using up processing and network bandwidth on the relay server. Those servers are often on high capacity network connections, so the load may not even be noticed by lazy systems administrators. Spammers harvest electronic mail addresses off Web pages and newsgroups, buy and sell lists of addresses, and launch their traffic off any servers they can exploit.

The open relays are slowly closing in response to anti-spam fighters, and spam filters are constantly improving, so spammers are constantly upping their game. Some of the current spammer tricks include:

✦ **Infect PCs to use as spam relays** — Suspicion is building that some of the more recent Internet viruses, worms, and Trojans are not designed to damage the target computers, but instead to exploit their Internet connections by serving as spam relays. As the number of open relays goes down, building armies of infected relays is a way to build back the bandwidth needed to shovel out all the messages.

✦ **Disguise plain text with alternate encoding** — Spam filters, including ones you can set up in your electronic mail reader, commonly look for key words in the message content to identify spam. (Chances are good, for example, that any electronic mail the average person gets mentioning Viagra is spam.) Many electronic mail readers support an alternative text encoding using 6 bits per character instead of 8 that makes the text impossible to read directly, and defeats the rules in many readers.

✦ **Break up HTML text with comments to obfuscate the content, and don't include plain text along with the HTML** — Spam is rapidly moving to all-HTML messages. HTML encoding lets spammers break up key words (Viagra) with comments (Via<!—comment—>gra) to defeat keyword scanners, and lets them send the message only in obfuscated form with no plain text equivalent. Misspellings are common too against keyword scanners (V1agra).

✦ **Eliminate all plain text in favor of graphics in HTML messages** — As anti-spam scanners became smarter about extracting obfuscated text from messages, spammers retaliated by eliminating the text altogether, replacing the text with images of text downloaded through HTML links.

✦ **Include text stating you've signed up for the spam e-mail** — Their messages are frauds anyhow, so you shouldn't be surprised that spammers have precisely no compunctions about lying. One of the most common lies is text such as "You are receiving this e-mail because you have either signed up to receive messages from us or a third party. If you would like not to receive further e-mails from us, please follow the instructions at the bottom of this mailing." There are two lies there, one that you signed up, and the other that you won't receive further e-mails. You'll get a lot more because by following those instructions, you're confirming you have a live electronic mail address and that you read spam.

Bad as it seems, not all is lost. Over time, you can radically reduce the volume of spam you receive using these techniques:

✦ **Use spam blocking tools** — If you can, filter your electronic mail for spam before it even reaches your mail reader. Our ISP offers SpamAssassin (www.spamassassin.org), a wonderful anti-spam tool. Not only does SpamAssassin use sophisticated spam detection approaches that are constantly updated, but also it can wrap identi-fied spam in another message explaining why SpamAssassin classed the message as spam. If you still want to open the message, it's there, but if you want to scrap it unread (and therefore bypass the tracking links spammers put in many HTML messages), you can. SpamAssassin also flags the subject line with ***** *Spam* *****, so you can also build rules in your mail reader to automatically divert incoming spam to a folder for later disposal.

If your ISP won't offer spam filtering, consider getting another ISP. If that's not practical, consider third-party filtering services such as those offered by SpamCop (mail.spamcop.net/individuals.php). You can keep using your existing e-mail address if you want with SpamCop's service, which costs $30 per year. Other anti-spam tools are listed at Tucows (www.tucows.com/spam95_default.html).

✦ **Don't put your personal electronic mail address anywhere on the Web, newsgroups, or chat rooms** — Spammers run programs to scrape electronic mail addresses off the Internet, searching Web pages, newsgroups, chat rooms, and anywhere else addresses might be recorded. Don't give out your private address freely that way.

✦ **Use disposable e-mail addresses for filling out forms** — There are times when you have little choice but to give out an electronic mail address to do business over the Internet. For situations like that, you can create "disposable" addresses that forward to your real address with limits you set. Spam Gourmet (www.spamgourmet.com) is a good disposable address service, and is free. You can create any number of addresses, and can limit how many messages can be sent through the address before it starts rejecting everything.

Another way to create disposable addresses is to sign up for an account at Hotmail, Yahoo!, or other free electronic mail hosting serv-ices. Be sure you don't let yourself be listed in their member profiles, which the spammers scrape regularly. If you prefer using services other than those two, there's a free e-mail address directory you can use to find alternatives (emailaddresses.com/free_email.htm).

✦ **Never use "Remove Me" or "Unsubscribe" links or reply to spam** — Doing so just confirms yours is a live address and will attract even more spam.

✦ **Use rules in your electronic mail reader and don't preview spam** — Most electronic mail readers offer rules to handle incoming mail. A very simple rule is one that moves all mail where you're not in the To or CC fields into a spam folder. Most people don't use BCC, so the chances are any incoming mail where you're not explicitly named is spam.

Summary

✦ Application programs give you access to Internet services using specific Internet protocols.

✦ You must be prepared before you're attacked by viruses, worms, or Trojans. All you can do after the fact is damage control.

✦ Preparation includes firewalls, antivirus and anti-adware software, and backups.

✦ You can reduce the volume of spam you receive with a combination of good practices and anti-spam software. Your ISP should be able to help.

Multimedia and Peripherals

◆　　◆　　◆　　◆

In This Part

Chapter 16
Sound Cards,
Speakers,
Microphones,
and MP3 Players

Chapter 17
Digital Cameras, Video
Capture, and DVDs

Chapter 18
Keyboards and
Game Controllers

Chapter 19
Mice, Trackballs,
and Tablets

Chapter 20
Printers, Scanners,
and All-in-One Units

◆　　◆　　◆　　◆

Sound Cards, Speakers, Microphones, and MP3 Players

In This Chapter

Exploring analog and digital sound

Examining Musical Instrument Digital Interface (MIDI) and waveform audio

Choosing speakers

Using microphones

This chapter looks at what sound is and how computers create and reproduce sounds. Overall, your PC represents sounds as a sequence of numbers that represent the amplitude of the sound wave at points in time. The numbers are sampled at regular, precise intervals, and by playing them back at the same rate, your computer can reconstruct the waveform. Figure 16-1 shows a sound waveform; if the sampling is done fast enough and well enough, you can't tell if the waveform is the original or a reconstruction from its digital representation.

What Is Sound?

Sound is vibration — alternating greater and lesser air pressure — traveling through the air that is received at your ears and heard by your brain. Many people can hear sounds as low as 16 to 20 Hz (although you can feel lower frequency sounds than that if they're strong enough). Some people can hear sounds as high in frequency as 20 KHz.

How you perceive sound depends critically on the shape of the waveform. Figure 16-2 illustrates both some simple waveform shapes and (to the left of the basic waveform images) decomposition of those waveform shapes into frequency components. The top left waveform in Figure 16-2 is a *sine* wave, a smoothly varying signal of a single frequency. The frequency analysis at the top right verifies this — there's one frequency peak in the graph. A sound system that reproduces that one frequency can accurately reproduce the sine wave. The lower left waveform in Figure 16-2 is called a *triangle* or *sawtooth* wave. The lowest, or fundamental, frequency of the sawtooth wave in the figure is the same as that of the sine wave, but the frequency analysis at the bottom right of the figure shows many frequencies have to be added together to reproduce the specific shape of the sawtooth wave. If a sound system rolls off the high frequencies, the wave shape distorts. If the sound system cuts off all the frequencies above the fundamental frequency, the waveform becomes a sine wave like the one in the top left box of Figure 16-2, and on playback sounds quite different than the original sound.

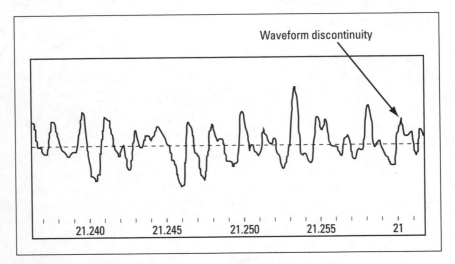

Figure 16-1: A sound waveform is a varying amplitude signal.

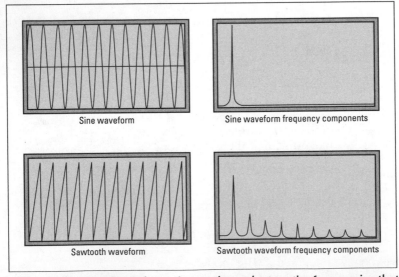

Figure 16-2: Waveforms have shapes dependent on the frequencies that make up the waveforms.

The need for high frequency sound components to form complex signals is why sound systems sound better when they support extended frequency responses. The added frequencies enable sound systems to better reconstruct the complex waveforms that make up the sounds you listen to.

The shape of the amplitude of a note is most of what distinguishes the sound one instrument makes from another. (*Timbre*, which is the tone quality, is the other key characteristic that distinguishes instruments.) Figure 16-3 shows the leading part of a note, called its *attack*, followed by the *decay*, the *sustain*, and the *release*. An acoustic guitar, for example, has a sharp attack, quick decay, and medium length sustain. A flute or clarinet has a slow attack, slow decay, and long sustain.

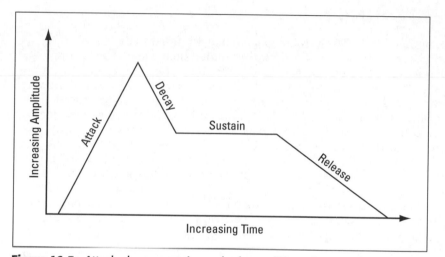

Figure 16-3: Attack, decay, sustain, and release differentiate one instrument sound from another.

Old, slow PCs lacked the computational power, hardware, and software to digitally sample and replay sounds, so they created musical instrument sounds by manipulating attack, decay, sustain, and release with what was called a frequency modulation (FM) synthesizer. Figure 16-4 shows how this works. One or more *waveform generators*, providing the raw pitch and timbre, couple into *envelope shapers* that provide the attack/decay/sustain/release amplitude profile. All the separate signals then get combined in the *summer*, forming a single instrument. That single instrument is called a voice. If you need to play multiple instruments at one time (multiple voices), you need more than one of the complete channels in Figure 16-4. Each distinct instrument in an FM synthesizer uses a collection of generators, shapers, and a summer to create the output voice. FM synthesizers typically have 4 to 32 voices.

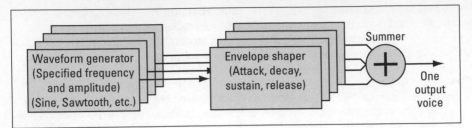

Figure 16-4: FM synthesis uses relatively simple hardware to create passable music effects.

Analog Audio

Faster, more capable PC hardware, beginning with the Creative Labs SoundBlaster cards, works directly with sampled digital sound. Figure 16-5 shows how sound generation is implemented in most computers. Software running on a processor receives a request to make a sound, retrieves the necessary data, and sends commands to the sound card. A small processor on the sound card receives the command and data, and coordinates the operation of specialized chips (including digital-to-analog converters similar to those in your video card) to create sound waveforms. Those waveforms then pass through filters (to eliminate noise and other effects) and amplifiers (to boost the signal strength) and then show up at the output jacks on the card. You connect those jacks to your computer speakers or stereo system, which adds more amplification, lets you control the bass and treble, and hands off to your speakers. The speakers translate the electrical signal into a corresponding sound pressure wave, which is what you hear.

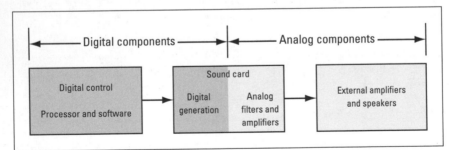

Figure 16-5: Generating sound in your computer combines digital and analog components.

Some sound systems alter this scheme to use the *Universal Serial Bus (USB)*, sending the digital version of the sound to the speakers and therefore moving all the sound card functions out to the speakers. Those systems don't need separate sound playback hardware in the PC itself.

The analog components in a sound card, external amplifier, and speaker operate much the same way as a traditional stereo sound system. Because of this similarity, the specifications for computer sound system analog components are similar to those for stereos. Here are some of the more important characteristics:

✦ **Output power** — This is a measure of how strongly the amplifier can drive an output device, such as a speaker. Power is measured into a load, which in the case of a speaker is typically rated at 4 ohms (the measure of resistance). Just as with stereo equipment, the output power has more to do with how things sound than how loud you can crank it up. Signals with sharp attacks (drums, gunshots, explosions) need a lot of power to move the speaker quickly even at moderate volume, so larger output power specifications are better.

✦ **Frequency response** — This is the measure of the range of frequencies the components are capable of handling. Not all the sounds you'll put through the card actually use the full range, though, and no amount of quality in the sound system can compensate for bad sound recordings missing the high or low frequencies in the first place. A broader range of frequencies is better.

✦ **Total harmonic distortion** — Frequencies that are multiples of a base frequency are called *harmonics*. The sounds you hear are full of harmonics because, as shown in Figure 16-2, harmonics are part of the higher frequency components that give each signal its distinctive shape. Amplifiers create harmonics that aren't part of the original signal through an effect called *harmonic distortion*. The transistor amplifiers you find in modern stereos and in sound cards produce odd harmonics, which can be objectionable to listen to. The sum of all the harmonic distortion your amplifier produces is called its *total harmonic distortion*, or *THD*. Smaller THD numbers are better.

Keep in mind that when you're talking about computer sound cards, you're not talking about connoisseur-grade stereo. You're talking about a card you'll use for presentations, accents in the user interface (the beeps, blurps, and other noises Windows makes when it wants your attention), background music, and games. You won't get the same quality as in an exquisite stereo, and you probably don't need that level of quality unless you're a professional musician creating music with your computer.

Waveform Audio

So far in this chapter, you've seen two ways to create sound from your computer — playing back a sampled audio waveform and synthesizing waveforms from a sequence of timbre/attack/decay/sustain/release commands. These two ways are both used in your computer. Sampled waveforms are in *wave files* (which have the extension .WAV), while command sequences comprise MIDI files (which have the extension .MID). This section covers waveform audio; the later section, "Musical Instrument Digital Interface," covers MIDI. Waveform audio, including its compressed version, such as MPEG Layer 3 (MP3), is overwhelmingly the most common form.

Most sounds begin as live audio sounds in the real world. The fundamental process for creating digital waveform audio from those sounds is shown in Figure 16-6, in which the audio source gets conditioned, filtered, and sampled by an analog-to-digital (A/D) converter. A sampling clock strictly times the action of the converter so that measurements are taken at fixed intervals. The sampling clock has to run at twice the frequency of the highest frequency component of the input signal to be able to reconstruct the signal faithfully, so to sample music with a maximum frequency response of 22 KHz, the clock has to run at 44 KHz.

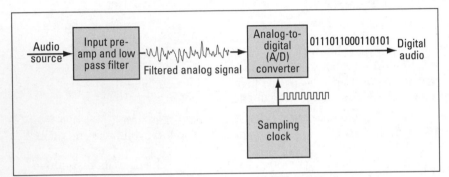

Figure 16-6: Digital audio sampling measures the amplitude of the input signal at fixed intervals.

Many people believe that because the frequencies you can hear are limited, sampling rates as high as 44.1 KHz, which are required to sample the 22 KHz frequencies at the upper limit of CD reproduction, are excessive. It's true that telephones reproduce signals no higher than 4 KHz. The lowest A on a piano is 27.5 Hz, while the highest A is 3.25 KHz. A sound system limited to 4 KHz (a telephone, for instance) sounds nowhere near as good as one that can extend up to 20 KHz, though, because of the harmonics needed to reproduce the sound of instruments accurately, to reproduce the specific wave shapes instruments generate instead of a smooth sine wave. The added frequency range in better sound systems reproduces higher frequencies precisely so that the system faithfully delivers the recorded signal.

Each element in Figure 16-6 has a specific function:

✦ The **input pre-amp** conditions the signal to the amplitude the A/D converter wants to see, isolating it from the characteristics of the audio source.

✦ The **low-pass filter** removes frequencies over one half of the sampling clock rate, ensuring that the digital samples will be ones that accurately reconstruct the input signal.

✦ The **A/D converter** measures the amplitude of the input audio signal each time it is clocked. Each measurement produces a number corresponding to the measurement. Stereo cards have two input pre-amps, two low-pass filters, and two A/D converters.

✦ The **sampling clock** triggers the A/D converter at regular intervals. The faster the clock runs, the faster the A/D converter samples and the higher the maximum frequency you can digitize.

Every time the A/D converter samples the waveform, it outputs the sampled data to your processor, which typically writes it to a file. If you're recording stereo, there are two converters, each outputting at that rate. The high sample rates are why wave sound files can get so large — Table 16-1 shows how extreme the volume of data can get. Recording raw, uncompressed stereo sound at 44 KHz (equivalent to what's on an audio CD) takes over a gigabyte for an hour's worth of material.

Table 16-1
The Relationship Between Sampling Rate, Data Rate, Frequency, and Disk Space Used for Uncompressed Waveform Audio

Sampling Rate (KHz)	Stereo Maximum Frequency (KHz)	16-Bit Data Rate (Kbps)	Recorded Seconds per MB	Recorded MB per Hour	Quality
8.00	4.00	256.00	32.00	113	Telephone
11.03	5.51	352.96	23.22	155	
22.05	11.03	705.60	11.61	310	
44.10	22.05	1,411.20	5.80	620	CD

A 74-minute CD holds around 660MB. CDs that extend the recordable surface radius can extend that to 700MB and 80 minutes. Compression can be used in waveform audio files, so the sizes predicted by Table 16-1 are upper bounds for audio recorded as MP3 files and accurate for files recorded as audio playable in a CD player.

Waveform audio hardware

Your PC implements wave audio input and output hardware on a card that fits in your computer, in chips on the motherboard itself, or in external hardware connected to a USB port. No matter where the hardware lies, Figure 16-7 shows the wave audio components involved. There are two parallel channels everywhere for stereo, although they share a common sampling clock and bus interface. The low pass filter on the output side, before the amplifier, removes frequencies higher than one half the sample rate (similar to those on the input side), ensuring that you get a clean signal out of the digital-to-analog converters.

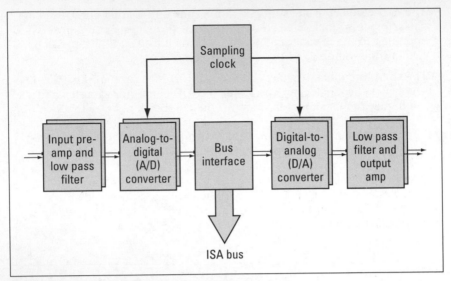

Figure 16-7: Waveform audio components

The input and output sections of the sound hardware are independent of each other, letting you run them at the same time in what's called *full-duplex* operation. Full-duplex is important for videoconferencing, voice-enabled gaming, and Internet telephony applications because it lets you both speak and be spoken to at the same time. Much of the fun in multi-player games is the conversation among players — multi-player games don't work anywhere near as well in private.

The hardware's technical characteristics define the performance of the wave audio section of your sound hardware:

✦ **Sampling rate** — This is the clock rate at which the converters can operate. A good typical sound card can sample at rates in the range of 5 KHz to 44.1 KHz.

✦ **Bus interface** — If not built into the motherboard or connected externally to the computer, your sound hardware will be built onto a PCI bus sound card. Sound cards once had to be compatible with the SoundBlaster hardware interface, including I/O addresses, interrupt level, and direct memory access channels, but those requirements have become unimportant as sound-enabled DOS programs and games vanished in favor of newer ones using the Windows sound interfaces.

Sound cards typically provide bass and treble controls, mixers, input selects, and volume controls. Software in Windows allows you to set these controls onscreen.

The Turtle Beach Santa Cruz sound card (see Figure 16-8) is representative of a PCI board you'd add to a PC to improve on the sound hardware built into the motherboard. The Santa Cruz hardware supports six-speaker surround sound; digital sound outputs; EAX, A3D, and DirectSound positional audio (and others); and full-duplex operation.

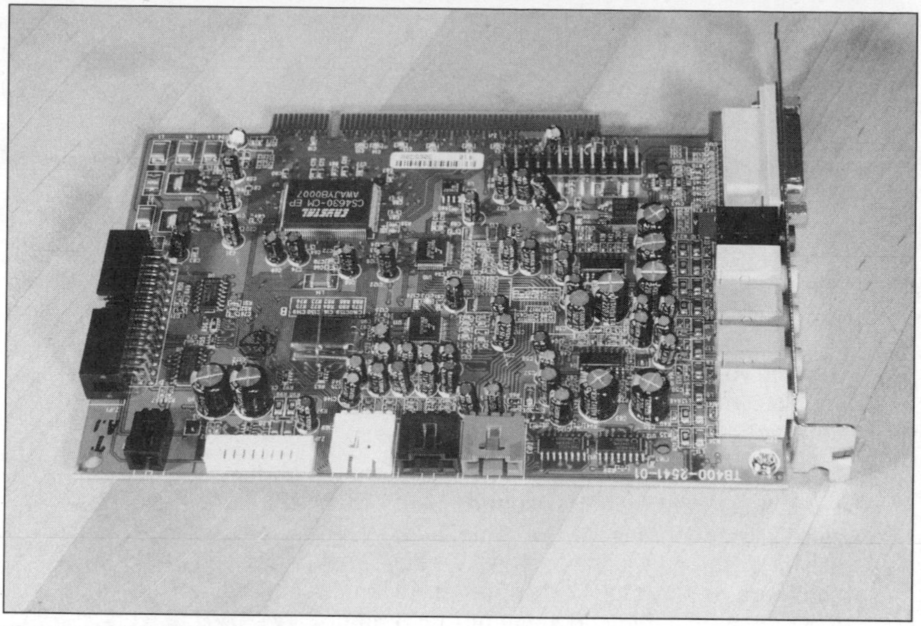

Figure 16-8: The Turtle Beach Santa Cruz sound card
©2004 Barry Press & Marcia Press

The hardware acceleration on the card is particularly interesting in that it can adapt its processing power for the tasks being performed, be they MP3 decoding, 3D audio for games, or MIDI.

Audio compression

Because raw, uncompressed sampled digital audio takes so much space to record, compressing the data for storage on disk is important for storing large volumes of audio, such as you'd want to do if you'd rather play back music from a large library on your PC than have to change CDs to find the songs you want. Compression also enables sharing recordings you've made with others across the Internet, since it's not terribly practical to send tens of megabytes per recording down a telephone line.

Lossless compression — techniques that can reproduce the digitized data stream from its compressed version without changing so much as a single bit — can't squeeze the information enough to be useful. Practical approaches use *lossy* compression, meaning there's some loss of quality in the reconstructed waveform when compared to the original digital source.

Many lossy audio compression technologies exist. Each uses different approaches to making audio files smaller, but you can think of them all in terms of how good they sound for a given degree of compression. Any specific compressed data rate, 128 kilobits per second, for example, establishes a compression ratio (about 11:1 for the 128 Kbps example) relative to the raw CD audio rate of 1,411.20 kilobits per second. For the chosen rate, different technologies offer better or worse sound quality; for a given sound quality, different technologies require a higher or lower data rate and, therefore, offer better or worse compression.

The most popular audio compression technologies include:

✦ **Moving Picture Experts Group Layer 3 (MP3)** — MP3 and the newer MP3PRO format are without question the most common, most popular PC audio compression format because many free players and compressors are available, because the format is not proprietary to any one company, and because it does not impose digital rights management restrictions. MP3 players include not only software for your PC, but also DVD equipment for your home stereo and portable devices you can carry around with you. The MP3PRO format isn't as well known or supported, but offers better sound quality for a given data rate.

✦ **Ogg Vorbis** — Ogg Vorbis is a free, unpatented audio compression technology offering better sound quality than MP3 for a given data rate (or smaller files for the same quality). You can compare the two at www.xiph.org/ogg/vorbis/listen.html. A limited amount of hardware to play Ogg Vorbis files exists, including Digital Network's Rio Karma portable and some of KiSS Technology's DVD players.

✦ **Windows Media Audio** — WMA is a Microsoft-developed compression technology also with better sound quality than the older MP3 format. Microsoft has submitted their Windows Media Series 9 compression to the Society of Motion Picture Television Engineers, but how that plays out remains to be seen. The Microsoft technology also includes provisions for digital rights management, which may restrict what you can do with some sound files more tightly than demanded by copyright law.

✦ **Real Audio** — RA is an older compression format proprietary to Real Networks and offering performance inferior to MP3 and its successors. Real Networks at one time bundled spyware with their software, so you might want to avoid them anyhow.

The popularity of sharing music files over the Internet, and the claimed monumental impacts to the music publishing business, have made copyrights and copy protection (euphemistically called *Digital Rights Management*, or *DRM*) front-page news. The developers and promoters of DRM technology are far more interested in restricting what you can do than preserving what rights you have under the law, however, so we suggest this approach:

✦ **Comply with copyrights** — What you can do with copyrighted material is set by law and, in some cases, by license agreements. Ethically, if you're going to have the material, you should comply with those. In our case, for example, we don't download or upload music files on the Internet; all the thousands of MP3 files we have are ones we made and keep to ourselves.

✦ **Refuse to accept DRM** — DRM technology provides mechanisms to control what can be done with protected information. Unfortunately, implementing DRM implies decisions about who exercises that control — probably not you — and how much of your privacy you give up so the information can be controlled. You don't have to buy products that include Digital Rights Management. That could well mean you don't buy the latest CDs if they're copy protected, but the history of copy-protected software says that if enough people reject DRM, it won't survive.

In the long run, DRM technology will start to show up not just in files or media, but as mechanisms embedded into your PC itself. What that implies, and what control over your PC you will lose, remains to be seen. The marketing spin has been that DRM is better for the consumer; you owe it to yourself to research the subject (start at www.eff.org/Infra/trusted_computing/20031001_tc.php) and make your own informed decision.

Who Controls Your PC?

Don't make the mistake of thinking digital rights management is some abstract notion you don't have to worry about. We state several times in this book that we intensely dislike Microsoft's Windows Product Activation (WPA). WPA is a form of digital rights management, is a liability to you, and has no value to anyone but Microsoft. Consider this sequence of events:

1. We upgraded a Dell machine that had been running for about a year to Windows XP Professional from Windows XP Home. At the end of the install, Windows said activation was required before we could log on.

2. We did the activation over the Internet, and the process completed normally. When we went to log on, however, Windows again said we had to activate. A second Internet activation failed, but telephone activation succeeded.

3. Attempting to log on after the second dialog again produced the dialog box stating activation was required.

4. We spent about 6 hours on the phone with Microsoft tech support trying different things, with no success. Every attempt to activate produced a dialog box saying Windows is already activated and activation isn't necessary, but every attempt to log on said logon could not proceed without activation.

Ultimately, after being disconnected from tech support and refusing to yet again wait for nearly an hour on hold, we gave up, reformatted the drive, and installed Windows XP Professional onto the empty disk. We had backups of all the useful data on the system, but should any of the other vendors of activation-locked software on the system have refused to re-activate, we'd have lost that software.

Continued

Continued

One of Microsoft's responses to us during this episode was to say that ours was an exceptional situation, whatever the cause. Our view is that perspective ignores users and suggests it's permissible for there to be more than zero WPA failures. Six hours on the phone, lost data, and possibly lost software says to us that the customer's data, software, and system are secondary concerns to Microsoft's profits. That's particularly evident when you add in the fact that Microsoft's largest customers receive software not locked with product activation, just the customers without enough leverage to fight it off.

This episode illustrates that smaller customer's PCs and data integrity are all potential victims of MS's anti-piracy campaign. Microsoft has stronger digital rights management technology in development, technology called Palladium that isolates third-party software from anything you do to your PC's hardware or software. It won't protect *you* from those third-party applications, though, so there's nothing to prevent, say, the RIAA (which has considered attacking the PCs of consumers suspected of file trading) from creating an application *you can't remove* that summarily deletes any MP3 file found on your system, regardless of its source. U.S. Senator Orrin Hatch said of destroying file traders PCs during a hearing: "If that's the only way, then I'm all for destroying their machines."

If you're unwilling to tolerate Microsoft's point of view, that some losses due to product activation are acceptable and that third parties can be given uncontrolled rights on your PCs, you should evaluate alternatives to Windows and Microsoft Office. Your options include Linux and OpenOffice, alternatives that have been written by people in some cases strongly opposed to the denial of your legitimate rights in the name of commerce.

Musical Instrument Digital Interface

The wider range of sounds possible with wave audio allowed sound cards such as the Creative Labs SoundBlaster and its later competitors to replace older synthesized audio designs. The newer cards didn't eliminate synthesizers, though — they're alive and well in PC sound cards supporting the *Musical Instrument Digital Interface* (*MIDI*, pronounced *mih-dee*), which is a standardized way of telling a synthesizer what you want it to do. Although it can't create all the sounds that wave audio can, MIDI has the key advantage that it takes far less data to represent things with MIDI than with wave audio. A typical MIDI sequence may consume only 10KB per minute and, for things MIDI does well, can sound as good as wave audio.

The most valuable application of MIDI is in recording, editing, and playing music. A MIDI file is a sequence of commands — mostly notes — that you send to a synthesizer. Because the file contains commands, not the music itself, you can edit it, speed it up, slow it down, change the pitch and key of the music, and change the instruments playing. A MIDI file plays against a set of instruments. Each instrument being played is assigned a channel number; a MIDI file contains interleaved messages for each instrument ("play this note this loud until I tell you to stop"), along with systemwide messages to set tempo and other variables.

Two of the key measures for MIDI synthesizers are *polyphony* (the number of notes the synthesizer can play at once) and *timbres* (the number of different sounds or instruments it can play at once). The hardware on sound cards can be limited in the degree of polyphony and timbres available, but with the advent of the incredibly fast processors now available, software synthesizers can support 200 voices or more at once.

CD Audio and Line Interfaces

Most sound cards offer two other capabilities besides waveform audio and MIDI — they can accept analog audio signals from your CD-ROM or DVD drive, letting you play audio tracks through your computer's speakers, and they can both accept and output "line" audio signals (the sort that you get at the tape in and tape out jacks on your stereo preamplifier). A device called a *mixer* goes in front of the waveform audio input electronics on your sound card to implement these capabilities, as shown in Figure 16-9. Each of the individual sources routes to the mixer, which contains volume controls for each channel plus a master volume control on the output channel. The mixer itself is controlled by the processor in your computer, from which it receives messages to set the volume for each channel and the master control. The processor can also mute any or all of the channels, so you can suppress noise that may occur on channels you're not using.

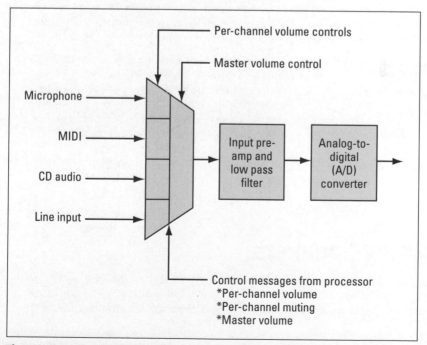

Figure 16-9: A sound card mixer controls volume and muting.

The mixer gives you more than volume control on multiple inputs; it lets you do more with your sound card. For example:

✦ **Recording sound outputs** — You can record the MIDI output from your sound card or music from an audio CD in your CD-ROM drive.

✦ **Combining sounds** — Suppose you want to build up multiple tracks in a sound file. You can record the first track, then play it back and simultaneously record additional sound on top of it. Or, suppose you want to record a voice and sound track to go with a presentation. You can do that by pulling in CD audio or MIDI for the music and adding the voiceover from the microphone input.

USB Audio

Computers using USB — a digital connection — between the computer and the speakers don't require a sound card because most of the functions of the sound card are moved to the speakers in a USB setup. Here's what happens:

✦ **Wave audio** — Digital audio streams from WAV files or from effects embedded directly into programs require neither a sound card nor synthesizer software if you're using USB speakers. The digital stream goes from the processor out the USB port to the speakers, where it gets converted to analog audio and played.

✦ **MIDI audio** — All PC processors since the 200 MHz Intel Pentium MMX processor have been capable of doing the MIDI synthesis operation in software, which is all you need to support MIDI on a USB speaker-based system. MIDI commands go into the synthesizer software, which in turn outputs wave audio to the speakers.

✦ **CD-ROM or DVD audio** — Some very old CD-ROM drives are incapable of digitally transferring the data on an audio CD to your PC. If you have one of those drives, you'll have to have a sound card to input the analog audio signal and play audio CDs. (Of course, if you really don't have a sound card, it's less expensive to replace the CD-ROM drive with a new one than it is to add a sound card.)

The sound card manufacturers recognized the threat to their products from USB speakers and responded by adding new technology such as 3D sound effects to their cards.

Choosing Speakers

Choosing speakers for your computer is as easy — and as difficult — as choosing speakers for your home or car stereo. The speakers that come packaged with computer systems are generally abysmal, not worth using even with the cheapest transistor radio. If sound quality matters to you, you'll want better speakers than come with most computers.

If you have an auxiliary or tape input on your stereo, you can find out what a good set of speakers can do for you by wiring your sound card over to your stereo. Use your stereo pre-amplifier and amplifier to power the speakers, not your sound card, because the sound card doesn't have enough power to drive the speakers properly. You'll need a male mini phone connector on the computer end, and male RCA phono jacks on the stereo end. If you get a cable set up for stereo, you'll hear both channels through the stereo. Be careful to make sure the stereo volume control is all the way down when you power things up, just in case the output level from your sound card is higher than your stereo expects.

What you're going to hear when you do this experiment is that there's more, tighter bass; clearer, cleaner treble; and overall much more appealing sound. This will be true for playing audio CDs, for multimedia titles and presentations, and for games. The difference will be even more dramatic if you have a sound card able to exploit multiple surround sound speakers through your audio system. Live with the difference for a while, and then reconnect your old computer speakers. If you're appalled by the difference, you're in the market for new computer speakers. It's important to evaluate speakers both ways — how much better the new ones sound and how much worse the old ones sound after you've spent some time with the new ones. You hear differences one way that you don't with the other, so you need to do both to get a complete evaluation.

The kind of speakers you want depends somewhat on what you do. Action games sound better with strong bass and do a far better job of localizing sounds with speakers both behind and in front of you. You might want a more full-range speaker for music, but can do well with a good budget speaker for the voice tracks in a self-paced training presentation.

There are important differences between computer speakers and stereo speakers you need to think about:

- ✦ **Magnetic shielding** — Most speakers depend on strong electromagnetic fields to provide a reference for the moving cone that actually generates sound. Strong magnets help create better sound, but can lead to problems with distorted images or colors on your monitor. Good computer speakers are shielded to compensate for that sensitivity of monitors.

- ✦ **Power amplifiers** — Every sound system needs a power amplifier strong enough to drive the speakers. There's one built into your stereo, but not into your sound card. (More precisely, the one in your sound card is usually too weak to do the whole job.) You need amplified speakers to couple into your computer and provide good sound. If you use speakers designed for a stereo, you'll need a separate amplifier between the computer and the speakers.

Be careful about amplifier power ratings because they're not all the same. The ratings to look for are *Root Mean Square (RMS)* power, which is the average power to a single speaker, and Total power, which is the RMS power times the number of speakers. Ignore Peak power ratings because they don't relate much to the sound you'll get from an amplifier.

✦ **3D sound** — You need a capable sound card and additional speakers to hear surround sound from your PC.

Surround sound requires additional speakers and connections to those speakers from your computer. Few motherboard sound systems provide the multi-channel outputs, but many sound cards do. The speaker configurations used with surround sound are the same as used with home theaters and other surround sound systems. Surround sound speaker layouts have names like 4.1, 5.1, 6.1, or 7.1, meaning there are 4 to 7 separate audio channels, each with their own speaker, plus one subwoofer channel for very low bass. Figure 16-10 shows a typical 5.1 setup. The subwoofer position is largely a matter of convenience because the very low bass is not sensitive to placement.

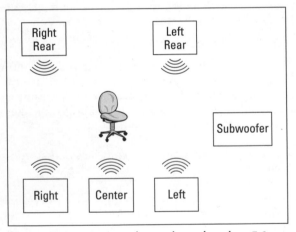

Figure 16-10: Surround sound speakers in a 5.1 configuration

The Acoustic Authority A3780 computer speakers are high-quality, general-purpose desktop units. They're analog speakers, not USB, but the combination of a hefty power amplifier, massive subwoofer, and huge magnets in the mid-range drivers give them a great sound. They have a 2.1 configuration — a subwoofer and two higher frequency satellite speakers — with a wired remote to control power, volume, and bass (see Figure 16-11).

Figure 16-11: The Acoustic Authority A3780 speakers offer good sound at a moderate price.

Photo courtesy Cyber Acoustics, LLC

MP3 Players

MP3 compression lets you store audio tracks in a relatively small space. MP3 files compressed at 128 Kbps require less than a megabyte per minute, so one of the commonly-available 256MB flash memory cards can store well over 4 hours of music. Nor do MP3-encoded files require much processing to decompress — a relatively slow processor (so it requires little power) is enough. Those two characteristics — small file size and battery-power-compatible decompression — make portable MP3 players possible. In a box smaller than your hand you can store many hours of music and the electronics necessary to play it back on headphones. Use a tiny hard disk instead of flash memory and you expand the internal storage to gigabytes, approaching enough music to play all day without repetition.

Figure 16-12 shows the flow of music from different sources to your MP3 player. You compress music from CD, the Internet, or recordings you've made to MP3 format using software such as Musicmatch. (Some CDs include varieties of copy protection, taking away your right to make legitimate copies for your own use, and likely no longer conform to the CD technical standards. Philips, the co-inventor of the CD format, has threatened to sue companies calling non-standard disks CDs, but has not followed through.) You then copy the MP3 files out to the MP3 player.

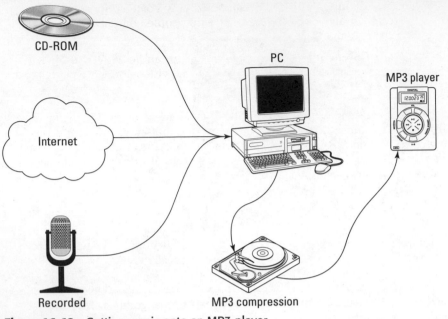

Figure 16-12: Getting music onto an MP3 player

If your MP3 player supports the common Windows USB storage interface, the player looks like a disk drive to Windows, and therefore, what software you use to download to the player is a matter of personal preference. If your player uses a non-standard proprietary interface, as do some cameras that include an MP3 player function, you could be forced to use the manufacturer's software. Being forced to use specific software might in turn impose digital rights management and restrict what you can do with your property, legal rights notwithstanding.

Other compressed file formats compete with MP3, but may or may not be supported on your player. Ogg Vorbis is an open source competitor, while Windows Media Audio, RealPlayer, and others commonly use proprietary formats to offer increased compression in exchange for accepting digital rights management. MP3PRO is a higher compression extension to MP3, but not widely supported.

Working with Microphones

Unless you're doing high-quality professional sound recording, your application for a microphone is likely to be one of these:

✦ **Voice annotation** — You can record sound files and attach them within documents in many applications, including Microsoft Word and Excel.

✦ **Voice recognition** — Software listening to your microphone can match what you say to a vocabulary, giving your computer some ability to react to what you say.

✦ **Internet phone** — You can create a two-way voice connection across the Internet, allowing conversation with people connected to the Net and using compatible software.

✦ **Videoconferencing** — Much the same as for audio with an Internet phone, you can create a two-way voice and video connection across the Internet.

You can choose the microphone you use to make these applications easier, although for the most part you're looking for one that stays out of the way and delivers clear sound. You can get microphones built into webcams (such as the Logitech QuickCam Pro 4000), ones that sit on your desk, and ones combined with headphones in a headset.

Voice annotation

Windows includes a simple application called Sound Recorder that lets you record from a microphone (or any other source on your sound card); a variety of third-party applications, of which we're partial to GoldWave (www.goldwave.com), offer that capability with far more control and features. Using any of these programs and a microphone connected to your sound card, you can record your comments and embed them into a document.

You can also simply record into a file, making your laptop a portable voice recorder with very large capacity.

Reaching for a microphone every time you create an annotation is awkward. That problem, combined with the problem of ambient noise in an office, makes the headsets telephone operators use (ones that combine a headphone with a small microphone) very desirable.

Speech recognition

Speech recognition is terribly difficult for computers to do well despite the best efforts of brilliant researchers over many decades. Speech recognition is a software-intensive process that tries to make choices to classify what the computer recorded. *Phonemes* — the first classification applied in many recognition systems — are the basic sound units in spoken language, covering voicing, articulation, accent, and others. A recognition system simplifies the speech recognition problem by turning raw sound into phonemes, reducing the volume of data and the number of choices higher layers in the processor have to examine. As the recognition process continues, it abstracts basic structures to more complex ones — words, phrases, and understood concepts.

A microphone suited for speech recognition is essential for accurate results. A speech recognition microphone will isolate sounds from the speaker, keeping out background noise and the voices of other speakers. A directional microphone, one on a headset, or even a throat microphone are candidates to consider.

After training, PC software can recognize speech in real time with accuracy of about 90 percent or better. You'll have to decide if that's good enough, keeping in mind that 90 percent accuracy means on average one word out of every 10 will be wrong and need to be corrected. You'll also find that dictation is very different than writing — not everyone thinks in ways that lead to coherent dictation.

Whether speech recognition software is useful for you depends on what you expect. We can both type between 50 and 100 words per minute, so there's no direct speed gain from dictation, and the time it takes to go back and correct recognition errors makes recognition take longer than typing would have to begin with. Some friends of ours, however, are hunt-and-peck two-finger typists so slow it's painful to watch and will do anything to avoid typing. They're good candidates for speech recognition.

Voice over IP and Internet phones

As recently as early 2000 when the third edition of this book was published, broadband Internet connections were still relatively rare, and Internet telephony was most often a clumsy lash-up using programs like Microsoft NetMeeting. The problem at the time was not only the availability of appropriate software, but also that running real telephones over a computer network is hard — telephones need a continuous, uninterrupted stream of data to give you continuous speech. If the transmission pauses even slightly, say due to congestion in the network somewhere along the way, there's a gap in the sound as the supply of wave audio data runs dry. Moreover, you need to send 64 Kbps of data each way to maintain a telephone connection, and you can't do that through a conventional modem. You either need to compress the data down to rates of 20 to 53 Kbps or less, or you need a broadband connection.

It's Hard to Do Recognition Well

We once tested some voice recognition software being developed by a major software manufacturer for integration into other products. The software did word recognition using menu commands in individual Windows applications along with some built-in phrases as the range of what it would recognize.

The end result for us during testing was that the software wasn't accurate enough to be useful, correctly identifying only 50 to 80 percent of the words we spoke. This isn't good enough to replace keyboards, mice, and other input forms because the effort to deal with the errors is much greater than the value of the words it gets right. (Other recognition software is much more accurate than this.)

The episode that really tells us how hard recognition can be occurred with that software. One of the commands it was always supposed to recognize was "Close window," which was supposed to do the obvious thing — close the active window. We spent about half an hour training the software to know voice and speech patterns, and then tried to see if the computer would recognize the phrase. After about 10 times with no results, and completely exasperated by then, we said "Close the @#$% window."

Of course, that worked.

The situation is completely different today.

The first change since 2000 was the development of the *Voice over Internet Protocol (VoIP)*, which gives you the ability to run real-time voice data streams over the Internet without constant pauses and hiccups. Equipment is available to support VoIP, including gear that plugs into your broadband-connected LAN on one side and your analog telephone equipment on the other. The Cisco ATA 186, for example, supports two voice ports, each with its own independent telephone number, connecting the unit to your LAN through its 10/100Base-T Ethernet port.

The second change is the emergence of telephone companies offering the equivalent of conventional *Plain Old Telephone Service (POTS)* using VoIP. One of the best known is Vonage (start reading at `www.vonage.com/learn_tour.php`), which offers a package of domestic U.S. local and long distance calls, and calls to Canada for a flat-rate price. (You pay for your broadband connection separately.) The service includes the usual POTS feature set, including Caller ID, Call Waiting, and voicemail. Because the service works over your broadband network, it travels alongside your regular network traffic without tying up a telephone line. The service works no matter where you plug into an Internet broadband connection — if you carry the equipment with you, you have your local phone service at hand anywhere in the world you can get broadband. Better yet, you can install the equipment behind your firewall (see Chapter 13), with only minor configuration required to forward UDP ports 5060 and 5061 to the Cisco ATA Vonage uses.

Picking a Sound System

The issues you need to think through regarding sound cards, speakers, and microphones center around what kinds of sounds you expect to handle, how much you care about the quality of sound reproduction you get, and how many people you want to hear what you're doing.

✦ **Kinds of sounds** — The simple beeps and honks that punctuate the user interface in Windows are simply attention-getters. They quickly become part of the background — sounds you notice more by their absence. Any combination of sound card and speaker that works reliably will do. Although adequate sound hardware is almost universal, games and presentations work much better with good speakers instead of the paper-cup-sized ones sold as a package with many computers.

The kinds of sounds you'll play are different based on the applications you run. Games stress impulsive sounds (good bass and high end), while for presentations you'd want to have speakers that deliver clear, understandable speech (which requires good mid-range with good power handling). Never buy speakers whose performance matters to you without hearing them first, preferably driven by the sound card you expect to use.

✦ **Sound quality** — Beyond the minimum threshold that keeps sound from being annoying, the sound quality you want really depends on how closely you're going to listen to it. Background noise has the minimum requirement. Presentations, telephony, and videoconferencing require good intelligibility, but not necessarily good fidelity. Casual music requires good fidelity. Critical listening to music requires you abandon the computer and move to your high-quality stereo — sound boards aren't as good as a quality stereo.

Multimedia information, such as training sequences, falls into the same category as presentations — it needs to be intelligible to everyone listening.

✦ **Privacy and groups** — You don't want to impose your sounds on others in close office environments. It gets irritating quickly. However, you definitely want everyone to hear if you're doing presentations.

Remember that — except for laptops — sound is relatively easy to upgrade. Sound cards are relatively inexpensive, and simply plug in. Speakers can be unplugged and swapped out, as can microphones. Business users may want to consider headsets plugged into the sound cards rather than speakers. Small, lightweight headsets can be plugged into telephones and computers, switching between the two to answer the phone.

Top Support Questions

Troubleshooting sound problems is a little different than most other troubleshooting because the usual troubleshooting approach of stripping the PC down to bare essentials often doesn't apply. The following questions and answers help highlight what can go wrong and suggest the approaches you can use to diagnose and repair the problem.

Q: I only hear sound out of one speaker. What's happening and what can I do?

A: You can troubleshoot this by isolating the problem to the sound card/ computer, cable, or speakers. You can test your speakers on an alternate source, such as a Walkman, portable stereo, or other audio source. If the test works (and you used the same cable), the problem is probably in the computer or sound card setup. If the test fails, try a different cable. If that works, the cable is the problem; otherwise, you might have a problem with the speakers. Check the cabling between speakers and make sure the balance control is set properly. If your speakers have independent power sources, make sure both are working (don't forget that batteries fail).

Q: Why does the volume control on my speakers not work?

A: Your speakers require either an external power supply or batteries to power the amplifier, which is what implements the volume control. Make sure that you have fresh batteries or the appropriate power supply and that the power switch is turned on.

Q: Why does the red light on my speakers not turn on when I turn on the power switch?

A: Verify that you have fresh batteries or that you're using a power supply for the speakers and that it's powered on. If the speakers plug in, make sure there's power at the wall outlet.

Q: Can I use any speakers with any subwoofer?

A: Not necessarily, because some speaker/subwoofer combinations have non-standard connections. What you can do, though, is to cable the speakers as if there are two independent sets of speakers (the speakers themselves and the subwoofer). You do that by connecting a "Y" adapter to your sound card. Plug the tail of the Y into the computer and speakers into the branches. (Alternatively, some subwoofers work when plugged into the line-out jack on the sound card, eliminating the need to split the speaker-out jack connection.)

Q: I need to set up my computer for videoconferencing, but the noise is too distracting to my office mates. What can I do?

A: The best answer is the same solution as for noisy speakerphones — get a headset. You can get headsets that plug into your sound card speaker and microphone jacks directly, giving you good sound quality, keeping background noise out of your conversation, and keeping peace in your office.

Q: There's a microphone jack on the front of my speakers. Do I have to use it?

A: No. The microphone jack is strictly for convenience, as is the headphone jack you might have on your speakers. A headphone jack on your speakers usually mutes the speaker itself when you plug in the headphones, so if you have both microphone and headphone jacks, you can conveniently choose whether you'll use the speakers or a more quiet headset/microphone combination.

Q: I haven't used my microphone in a while, and it's stopped working. I checked all the connections, and they're okay. What happened?

A: Some microphones have small batteries inside that can drain over time. If you have one of these, you may need to take the microphone apart and replace the battery.

Summary

✦ Computers produce sound using wave audio, FM synthesis, and MIDI synthesis.

✦ Wave audio can reproduce any sound. FM and MIDI synthesis mostly reproduce music.

✦ Computer speakers have important differences relative to conventional stereo speakers, including shielding and built-in amplifiers.

Digital Cameras, Video Capture, and DVDs

◆   ◆   ◆   ◆

In This Chapter

Charge-coupled devices and digital still cameras

Image resolution and memory

Video capture data rates, decimation, frame rates, and compression

◆   ◆   ◆   ◆

In the same way that sound cards let you capture audio, you can get cards and other devices that let you capture still images and video. The volume of data you create that way can be immense and used to require compromises to fit within the limits of what a personal computer can do. PCs are now so powerful that the limits of what they can do with images and video are virtually gone — even the major studios and special effects houses now use farms of PCs to do much of the behind-the-scenes work.

The improvements in digital still cameras have been particularly dramatic. When we wrote the first edition of this book in early 1996, we used a 35 mm Canon film camera for all the pictures we took because the available digital cameras couldn't produce publication-quality images. For over 5 years now, we've used digital cameras exclusively for all the photographs we've taken. The picture quality is good enough that we no longer bother with film.

Still Image Photography

Let's start with a simple problem — taking a photograph and getting it into your computer. For a long time, your only option was to literally take a photograph, have the film processed, and scan the picture. That process has the disadvantage that it's slow. Unless you use something like a Polaroid instant camera that develops the print while you wait, you have to go somewhere to get the processing done. Even then, you have to go to where your computer and scanner are before you have the digital result.

There's another way. Building electronic sensors into a still camera — substituting the sensor for the film — creates a camera that records the electronic image directly. You can see the image in the viewfinder or download it to a computer for viewing, printing, and further processing. Figure 17-1 shows what's in a digital camera. The biggest difference between an electronic camera and a film camera is that, rather than focusing light through a shutter on a strip of film, the electronic camera focuses the image on a *charge-coupled device (CCD)* or *Complementary Metal-Oxide Semiconductor (CMOS)* array. The body of the camera is filled with electronics and batteries, and an LCD display (like in a laptop computer) serves as the primary or secondary viewfinder. No shutter exists because the image sensor is constantly capturing images.

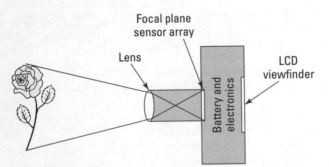

Figure 17-1: A digital still camera substitutes an electronic sensor for film, recording the picture directly in memory.

Since you use no film, the camera has to do something else with your picture when you push the button. What it does is store it in memory.

Image resolution and memory

The amount of memory an image requires depends on its horizontal and vertical resolution, in pixels, and on the size of each pixel (which in turn determines the number of possible colors for each pixel). Using 24-bit pixels (over 16 million colors), an image of 300×200 pixels requires less than 180K of memory. An uncompressed image of 1,600×1,200 pixels (still in 24-bit color) requires nearly 5½MB. Uncompressed images from the Kodak DX4530 we used for this book — at 2,580×1,932 resolution in 24-bit color — consume 14.3MB. Compressed images range from 500K to several megabytes. Professional digital cameras, at resolutions as high as 4,536×3,024 pixels, require even more memory.

Figure 17-2 shows how good a picture from a digital camera can be (there's a color version at the back of the book). Except for conversion to black and white, what you see here is exactly as we received the file and has not been retouched for publication. If you look carefully, you'll see a level of resolution, sharpness, and tonal gradation competitive with that of film cameras.

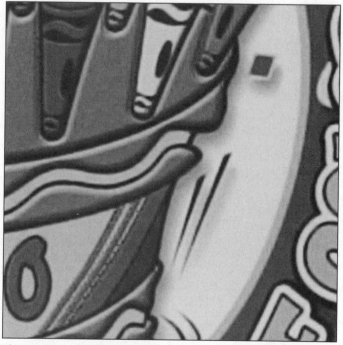

Figure 17-2: Photo from a Canon EOS 1D professional digital camera

Photo by Jansen Gunderson

Similarly, Figure 17-3 is the same photo taken with the Kodak DX4530, and is also reproduced in color at the back of the book.

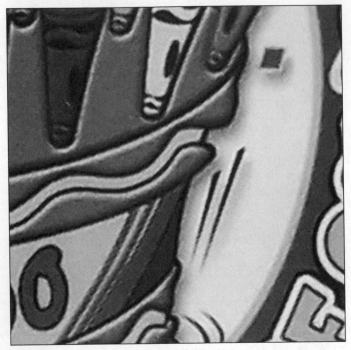

Figure 17-3: Photo from a Kodak DX4530
Photo by Jansen Gunderson

The number of pixels in the image, and therefore the amount of memory an image occupies, is a critical issue for digital cameras. Consider what happens when you want to print your photograph on your 1,200 dpi (dots per inch) color printer, filling the entire page with the picture. Suppose we try to print a low-resolution, 320×240 image onto a page. If the printable area on the page is 10×7.5 inches, then along the 320-pixel dimension we have about 30 pixels per inch — 1/400th of what the printer can do. Figure 17-4 shows different views of a digital photograph we took to illustrate what can happen. The image on the left in the figure is the complete photo, with good resolution — it's 2,580×1,932 pixels, and would print at nearly 550 dpi if reproduced full width on this page. We took a small section of the image — including part of the dog's right eye — and blew it up on the right side of the figure to show the effects of pixel replication. The image on the left is small but sharp, while the image on the right is larger and unacceptably pixelated. This is the same effect that happens when you blow up an image too far trying to make it fit on a printed page. No matter how high the printer resolution, it can't make up for lack of detail in the source image.

The low-quality results you get from excessive pixel replication mean that — depending on how far you're going to enlarge your photo — you may not be satisfied with the results from a low-resolution digital camera. Mid-range digital cameras (such as the Kodak DX4530 we used for this edition) have resolutions approaching what you can get with 35 mm film, though, so if you're careful to compose your photo so you fill the viewfinder and don't have to crop, you'll get excellent results.

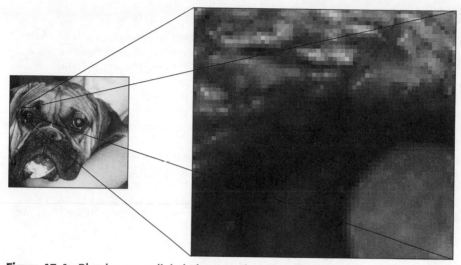

Figure 17-4: Blowing up a digital photograph replicates the pixels.
©2004 Barry Press & Marcia Press

Medium- and high-resolution digital photos come at a price, however, which is that they require more memory to store in the camera. Flash memory in your camera stores the photos you take, similar to film in a conventional camera. Uncompressed images on the Kodak DX4530 require 14.3MB, so if the camera contains 32MB of memory, you can store only two images. A camera like that would be useless, but there are two ways to solve the problem:

✦ **Image compression** — The same lossy image compression technology used as the basis for MPEG video compression (see Chapter 6) is applied in *JPEG (Joint Photographic Experts Group)* compression for still frame pictures. JPEG compression reduces the 14.3MB images to between 500K and 4MB, letting you store 8 to 64 photos in 32MB of memory. Higher compression levels would let you store even more photos, but you lose image quality at higher compression levels. Many cameras give you the option to trade off fewer pictures in memory for better quality, and some give you the option to reject lossy compression altogether, using lossless compression or no compression instead.

✦ **More storage** — This is the "bigger hammer" idea. Flash memory has gotten relatively large, and relatively inexpensive. After adding a 256MB Secure Digital card into the Kodak DX4530, for example, the camera reports it can store over 160 photos.

There are, sadly, far too many memory formats used in cameras. Different cameras have used floppy disks, CD-R, DVD-R, flash memory and hard drives in

CompactFlash format, Multimedia Card (MMC) and Secure Digital (SD) flash memory, and the Sony memory stick. The proliferation of formats tends to keep you from using old memory with new cameras.

A darkroom on your desk

You have to transfer the pictures from your camera to your computer before you can do much with them. Nearly every camera you can buy today uses a USB interface between PC and camera. Either Windows generic software or software specific to your camera controls the process, pulling images from the camera and storing them as files on your disk. Once you have files in a standard format, any image processing program can crop, recolor, and otherwise reprocess the pictures for you, and can send the results to your printer.

Let's do some calculations to analyze what resolution you want in a digital camera. Guidelines from Kodak suggest you'll want from 150 to 175 pixels per inch in your prints; using 150 pixels per inch, Table 17-1 shows the minimum number of pixels you'll want in your camera for a variety of print sizes. Table 17-2 repeats the calculation using the assumption you'd want a higher 300 pixels per inch resolution.

Table 17-1
Recommended Low-End Camera Resolution Specifications

Print Image		Camera Image		Total Pixels
Height	Width	Height	Width	(Millions)
4	6	600.00	900.00	0.51
5	7	750.00	1,050.00	0.75
8	10	1,200.00	1,500.00	1.72
11	14	1,650.00	2,100.00	3.30
16	20	2,400.00	3,000.00	6.87

Table 17-2
Recommended Improved Camera Resolution Specifications

Print Image		Camera Image		Total Pixels
Height	Width	Height	Width	(Millions)
4	6	1,200.00	1,800.00	2.06
5	7	1,500.00	2,100.00	3.00
8	10	2,400.00	3,000.00	6.87
11	14	3,300.00	4,200.00	13.22
16	20	4,800.00	6,000.00	27.47

There's another conclusion you can draw from Table 17-1. Knowing that computer monitors typically deliver 90 dots per inch or more (corresponding to 0.28 mm pitch or finer), it's apparent that even the least expensive digital camera should have enough resolution for pictures destined for Web pages.

Ultimately, digital cameras are still cameras, so the issues that are important for film cameras are equally important for digital ones. You still care about the focal length, resolution, contrast, and speed of the lens. You still have to have enough light to form a picture, so the effective "film speed" matters. You still have to use a flash in low-light situations, so the synchronization and control of the flash unit (and the time it takes to recharge) are important. You have to worry about parallax between the lens and the viewfinder and may want features like macro focus and a self-timer. These are cameras; only the "film" is different.

Choosing a digital camera

There's more to choosing a digital camera than getting the greatest number of pixels you can afford. You can get over 5 megapixels in a reasonably priced camera, enough to do an 8×10 print with good quality if you fill the frame. Getting a photo you'd want to print that size, however, requires you look at some other factors:

✦ **Auxiliary lenses** — Some cameras offer detachable lenses, or add-on lenses you can slide over the standard lens. You can add telephoto or wide-angle capabilities to your camera with auxiliary lenses, letting you fill the frame for shots you'd otherwise miss. Check how the lenses fit on the camera because some of them block the viewfinder and leave you no choice but to frame the picture with the LCD panel.

✦ **Battery system** — The power drain from a camera is relatively fixed, so the battery system in your camera determines how long you can shoot before you have to recharge or change batteries. Cameras that let you replace batteries with standard types let you keep shooting when there's no time to recharge.

✦ **Charging** — Cameras with fast rechargers get you back in action quicker if you can't carry spare batteries. The worst combination is a proprietary battery with a slow recharger because there's nothing you can do but wait when you run out of power. Watch for rechargers that don't handle 120 to 240 V if you travel internationally, or you could be stuck unable to recharge at all unless you can buy a power converter.

✦ **Color rendition** — Cameras render color with varying accuracy. The camera is only the first step in the color rendering chain, which includes your monitor and printer too, but bad color rendition by the camera makes everything else just that much harder.

✦ **Cycle rate** — Many digital cameras can capture a freeze-frame sequence of images in rapid succession. Some capture more frames than others, and some capture at faster or slower rates. Few let you control the frame rate.

I'll Eat Onion Rings with that Battery, Please

A lot of electronics are packed into digital cameras, all of which want to eat power from the batteries about as fast as you would chow down a carton of onion rings. Because the batteries have to fit in the camera (and the camera in your hand), there's a limit to how much power the electronics can use. Too much power drain, and the batteries have a very short life — you'll go through them like fast food.

It's a testament to the ingenuity of camera designers (and to improvements in battery technology over the past several years) that their products can run as long as they do on a handful of small batteries. The rate of improvement in battery technology has slowed, though, so it's going to be a major challenge to continue to make significant improvements in how many pictures you get from a set of batteries (or from one charging). We use only high-energy lithium photo batteries or rechargeable nickel metal-hydride (NiMH) batteries in digital cameras.

✦ **Delay** — Digital cameras impose a delay between when you push the shutter button and when they actually shoot the picture. Much of that delay is the time required for automatic focus operations, and some cameras enable you to prefocus by pushing the shutter button part way down. Too long a delay, and you'll miss the action shot you're trying for.

✦ **Dynamic range** — The sensor in your camera has limits to how bright or how dim the extremes in your photo can be before they wash out or fade out, respectively. Dynamic range refers to the difference between the brightest and dimmest areas, and the larger the possible dynamic range, the more shots you can take with good detail.

✦ **Exposure accuracy** — The automatic exposure metering in your camera can operate from a single spot, multiple spots, an average of the entire frame, or other measures. The metering the camera uses needs to match how you use the camera — for close-ups, for distant shots, or in other ways.

✦ **Feel** — Different people expect cameras to fit differently in their hands, and expect the camera controls to fall to hand in different places. Buying a camera before you've held it is asking to be disappointed.

✦ **Flash** — Nearly all digital cameras include a built-in flash, but some lack the ability to choose flash modes. You'll want at least fill flash, which fills in shadows, and automatic modes.

✦ **Focus** — How the camera focuses determines what you can shoot and how well. Close-up shots will be out of focus if the camera chooses the wrong parts of the photo as the focus point.

✦ **Memory** — How much memory comes with the camera determines if you'll need to add more. The type of add-in memory the camera requires determines if modules you already own will work, or if you'll have to buy new ones. You don't need a separate reader if the camera uses USB to download images to your PC. No matter what memory you use, it's going to keep your pictures stored in the camera when the camera is turned off.

✦ **Software** — Cameras often include image-processing software in the package. Some is good; some is junk. See if you can download and try out the software before you finalize your choice. If not, look for online or printed reviews.

✦ **Zoom** — It's pointless to buy a digital camera without optical zoom because you won't reliably be able to fill the frame with the image you want, which means you won't get pictures as sharp and high-resolution as you should. Cameras typically offer both optical and digital zoom; you want optical zoom for as much of the total zoom as possible to be sure you're using the entire image sensor.

Of these factors, most important are dynamic range, zoom, color rendition, and the battery system. It remains to be seen if the recent crop of printer docks, which are small color inkjet printers packaged with a camera dock, are useful. We don't suggest printing without having first enhanced the photos with your PC, so it's unclear if there's any value to combining the printer with the camera dock.

Keep an eye out for the low battery indicator while you're using a digital camera. We didn't see it once and had the camera shut down while it was compressing a shot to flash memory. The memory was corrupted and had to be reformatted, which caused us to lose all the shots it held.

Tip
Keeping track of hundreds of photos can be hard, and you won't be able to see them all onscreen at once. If you're running Windows XP, navigate in Windows Explorer to the folder with the photos you'd like to index and right click in the folder. Choose to customize the folder, and set it up for photos (use the one for fewer pictures). Turn off folder view if it's on, and then print the pictures from the task choices in the left pane. You'll be able to choose how many thumbnails print per page.

Video

If there's any one thing you might want to do with your computer that has the potential to overwhelm what even today's fast, high-capacity computers can do, it's capturing and editing digital video. The problem with digital video is that there's so much of it — naively recording broadcast-quality video transfers over 23MB per second onto disk. Here's where that calculation comes from. A full video frame occurs 30 times per second, and contains (approximately) 512 pixels by 512 lines, for $30 \times 512 \times 512 = 7.8$ million pixels per second. If we record 3 bytes per pixel (24-bit color), that's about 23MB per second, or 79GB per hour. Practical video capture devices, such as the Pinnacle Systems Studio Deluxe PCI video capture card, reduce that requirement down to about 13.5GB per hour, but you'll still need a lot of disk space to capture a significant amount of high-quality video.

You can capture lesser quality video, of the quality you'd use for videoconferencing over a broadband Internet connection, from an inexpensive webcam. The Microsoft NetMeeting software works between any two Windows PCs, giving you a full audio and video connection. Videoconferencing never worked well over modems because they were too slow to give useful frame sizes and frame rates, but broadband Internet connections at 256 Kbps and up work quite well.

Video capture and editing

High-quality video capture and editing requires more and better hardware than the simple webcams you'll use for videoconferencing. You need a quality video source, a well-engineered video capture card, a fast disk subsystem, and a processor fast enough to keep it all running, but with today's hardware, none of that's out of the ordinary.

If you have an IEEE 1394 or USB camcorder, you can dump video files directly from the camera to disk. If you want to record live video, you'll need a TV tuner card (see Chapter 6). If you have composite video signals (that is, separate video, left audio, and right audio channels), you can use either internal or external hardware for your PC to capture the signals, digitize them, and store them to disk. For internal hardware, we like the Pinnacle Systems Studio Deluxe. If you'd rather not open your PC, and you have a USB 2.0 port, you can use the Pinnacle Systems PCTV Deluxe, which includes the functions in Figure 17-5. Software supplied with the PCTV Deluxe enables you to make your PC into a personal video recorder — like a VCR, only better — and enables you to directly capture MPEG-2 compressed video from the tuner or from composite video sources. The video quality is good, and if you also have Pinnacle Systems Studio 8 (which will capture from the PCTV Deluxe), the combination is quite capable.

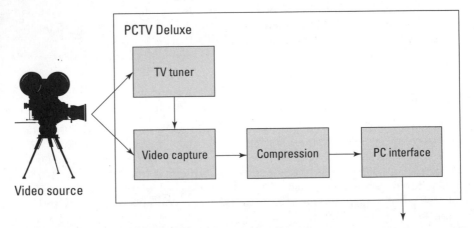

Figure 17-5: PCTV Deluxe hardware functions

The combination of quality video capture hardware, video editing software such as Studio 8 or Adobe Premiere, and a fast computer is more powerful than you might expect. You can digitize from composite or S-video sources, record clips to disk, then combine and edit clips to create a complete sequence. When you're done, you can output to a file for use on computers, or to video for re-recording back to disk.

Although most any recent vintage PC is good enough for video editing, don't make the mistake of using an underpowered computer for rendering compressed video files.

✦ **Processor** — Compressing about an hour and a half of uncompressed video onto a DVD with Pinnacle Systems Studio 8 takes about 10 hours on a 933 MHz Pentium III, but only about 5 hours on a 2.53 GHz Pentium 4. The 3.2 GHz Pentium 4 we used in Chapter 25 should take less than 4 hours. Any of those processors are fast enough for editing, but the compression speed difference is overwhelming unless you plan to always let the run take overnight.

✦ **Operating system** — The Windows NT File System (NTFS) used with Windows NT/2000/XP has the ability to handle very large disks and the huge files you'll create with digital video, and is more reliable than the FAT and FAT32 file systems used with Windows 9X. Windows 2000 and Windows XP have better graphics support (DirectX) than Windows NT, making them the choice for video editing.

✦ **Memory** — The same problem that makes a fast processor worthwhile — slinging around large quantities of data — makes it useful to have a lot of memory for disk cache and program operations. We consider 256MB a minimum for Windows 2000 and Windows XP; bumping that figure to 512MB gives the software room to work, caching video sequences and selected still images in memory. Ideally, you'd have 1GB or more of memory.

✦ **Hard disk** — At 13.5GB per hour, you'll fill a 160GB disk in less than 12 hours. You'll need to store multiple copies of your work, too, because you'll have both the raw capture files and your finished output. We suggest at least a 60GB drive if you're doing video editing, and much more if you're serious about it. The machine you'll see how to build in Chapter 25 has 320GB of disk, which means you can collect video for quite some time before getting around to editing and compressing.

If you're recording with the PCTV Deluxe, however, you'll need far less disk space because the unit will do DVD quality MPEG-2 compression in real time. Recording at 6 Mbps (0.75 Mbps) translates to 2.7GB per hour, which isn't likely to stress any current-generation disk.

✦ **Video adapter and monitor** — You'll want good DirectX support in your video card and an AGP interface to ensure all the features of your video editing and mastering software work well. DirectX is particularly important so you can see the video in real time as you record, and for smooth playback as you edit.

How high-resolution the display on which you edit depends on your software. Pinnacle Systems Studio 8 doesn't support windows bigger than 1,024×768, but Adobe Premiere will use all the screen space you have available, letting you show multiple control panes side-by-side.

✦ **Network** — If you're going to be moving large video files from one machine to another on a LAN, you might want to consider gigabit Ethernet for at least the machines involved in video. It takes over 20 minutes to move a 13.5GB file across an otherwise idle 100Base-T network, but only 2.5 minutes on gigabit Ethernet.

Digital video cameras may connect through a USB or IEEE 1394 (FireWire) port. Your PC will have a USB port already, but you may have to add the IEEE 1394 (FireWire) port. You'll want a USB 2.0 port (with no USB 1.1 devices connected) running at high speed to have enough bandwidth for high-quality video.

Making DVDs from video

Composing and editing video is somewhat different than handling digital still images. We've used Pinnacle Systems Studio 8 as the basis for the following example, but other video editing software does similar things. Here's what you'll do:

✦ **Plan, set up, and shoot** — You'll do this if you're making your own movies, and what you do is straightforward — you figure out what the end content is going to be, set up the different scenes you need, and shoot. All the usual ideas (for example, storyboards, rehearsal, and lighting) apply.

✦ **Capture the raw video and audio** — You need to get the video into your computer. You can record new footage directly into your computer with a USB or IEEE 1394 camera, record directly using a conventional analog video camera and a video acquisition card, or record onto tape that you then play back into the video acquisition card. If you're using your PC to make DVDs, you'll record live video through the video capture card.

If you're making a movie from new footage, you're better off putting each separate scene into a different file — you end up with smaller files (which are easier to handle) and have more flexibility to cut and splice scenes. You can dub external audio — music, narration, or other content — into your project; if you're doing that, you'll want to record the raw audio as wave audio files.

Tip   We recommend making archive backups of all your clips for a given sequence once you've recorded them so that they're not lost if you happen to make a mistake while editing. You can store the files elsewhere on disk or can back up to your usual backup system.

✦ **Start a new project and import raw clips** — Figure 17-6 shows a screen shot from Pinnacle Systems Studio 8 in the middle of an editing session. There are three parts to the window: the segment edit pane, the clip preview pane, and the timeline. The segment edit pane lets you work within a given video segment, including trimming the segment at either end. The clip preview lets you play a segment or several segments. The timeline lets you access all the clips you've loaded into your project.

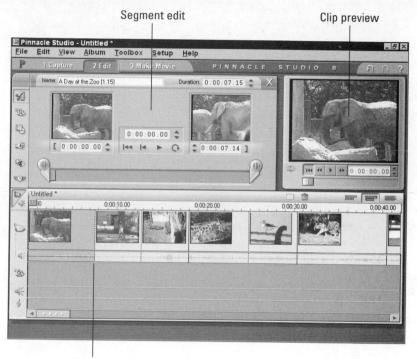

Figure 17-6: You want a high-resolution display card and large monitor for digital video editing.

✦ **Edit the composite output** — Once you've loaded your video clips, use the timeline and segment editing window in Figure 17-6 to remove extra scenes and, if you want, reorder the remaining scenes.

Making a DVD compatible with a DVD player gives you the opportunity to add menus to your disk. Figure 17-7 shows the basic operation in Studio 8 — you add menu segments to the timeline, and then link chapters in the menu to specific segments in your assembled timeline. Menus can link to other menus, or to video segments. The thumbnail image displayed for a menu button can be static or motion video.

Once you've edited your video segments and organized them with any menus you want (the video will just play if there's no menu), use the Make Movie tab in Studio 8 to burn the video to your DVD writer. You'll want to adjust the settings for disk output to make a DVD and to use automatic quality selection, which increases the compression level if necessary to fit all your content onto the disk.

Chapter thumbnail

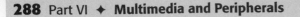

Menu segment   Linked chapter segment

Figure 17-7: DVD menu linked to a chapter

You'll likely also want to make cover inserts for your DVDs; many DVD authoring packages provide utilities for that purpose. You may want to grab still images from the video for use on the covers, something Studio 8 does easily.

Summary

✦ Digital still cameras let you get at your images faster, and without a scanner, but might not provide the resolution you need. The LCD viewfinders on some models might be difficult to use outdoors in sunlight.

✦ If you're willing to pay what high-end digital still cameras cost, and you're a good photographer, you can get professional-quality photographs with a digital camera.

✦ Data rates for raw, full-screen television video are easily within the capability of most computers, although you'll want to ensure you use a fast enough interface (such as PCI or USB 2.0) and a good quality video acquisition device. Make sure you have a lot of disk storage.

Keyboards and Game Controllers

✦ ✦ ✦ ✦

In This Chapter

Looking inside
a keyboard

Considering keyboard
layouts

Dealing with repetitive
stress

Choosing game pads,
joysticks, and wheels

✦ ✦ ✦ ✦

Y ou control computers with input devices, peripherals that signal your actions to the computer. The
common thread among all input devices — keyboards,
mice, trackballs, joysticks, tablets, and other more specialized devices — is that you use different gestures or
actions to carry out the different tasks you do and that
no one device is the best one for all of them. Just as you
don't (or shouldn't!) use a screwdriver and hammer as
your only tools, you won't want to use just a keyboard
and mouse as your only input devices.

Keyboards

Keyboards are an integral part of computers. Most of
the input you give your computer comes through the
keyboard. Despite being simple devices in concept,
good keyboards are relatively complex to build.

Switches and tactile feedback

The basic component inside a keyboard is a switch,
over 100 of them in each keyboard. Under every keycap
is a switch that signals your computer in two ways: once
when you push the key and again when you release it.

Keyboard switches are subject to a wide range of force,
so their design is not as straightforward as you might
think. One of the most severe problems is that people
really hammer their keyboards at times, yet expect
them to survive for years. Figure 18-1 shows two keyboard switch designs. The one on the left in the figure
has an obvious design flaw: letting the force directly
close the contacts. This design exposes the electrical
parts to physical damage under hard impact, eventually

resulting in unreliable operation. Better designs (such as the one on the right in the figure) direct the force only to mechanical parts, allowing the switch designer to control what happens to the contacts. No matter how hard you pound on a keyboard using the right-hand switch design, the force on the contacts is only that of the springs that support them. The base plate, not the contacts, absorbs the key impact force.

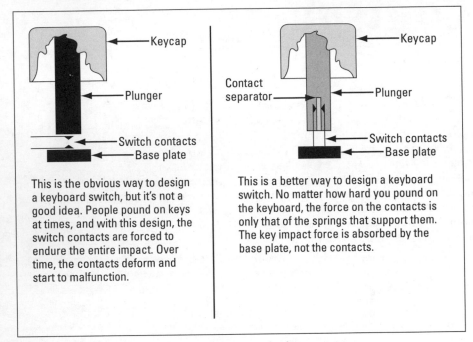

This is the obvious way to design a keyboard switch, but it's not a good idea. People pound on keys at times, and with this design, the switch contacts are forced to endure the entire impact. Over time, the contacts deform and start to malfunction.

This is a better way to design a keyboard switch. No matter how hard you pound on the keyboard, the force on the contacts is only that of the springs that support them. The key impact force is absorbed by the base plate, not the contacts.

Figure 18-1: Good keyboard switches protect the key contacts.

Keyboard switches need more than reliable contacts. People drop in paper clips and food; spill coffee, wine, soda, and other sticky stuff; and generally abuse the electronics terribly. The first line of defense in a good keyboard is a shield (see Figure 18-2) to keep debris and liquids out of the mechanism. The figure shows not only how a shield can cover the circuit board that mounts the switches, but also how it can come up under the keycap to protect against liquid spills. The debris and liquid shield completely covers the circuit board holding the switches and extends up under the keycaps. Anything falling into the keyboard gets caught by the shield and is kept out of the switches and electronics.

Tip

If you do spill, the resulting stickiness can make a keyboard unusable. You can shut down the computer, disconnect the keyboard, and then wash it out with clean water. (Yes, you can shower with your keyboard.) Let it dry *completely*, then try it out. If you're lucky, everything will work as before.

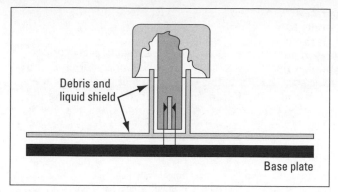

Figure 18-2: A good keyboard uses a shield to keep out dirt and debris.

Caution   Don't ever disconnect or reconnect a PS2 keyboard with the power on (USB is designed to make that okay, however). It's not dangerous to you, but it could be lethal to your computer. We once fixed a computer that had been the victim of half a dozen disconnect/reconnect cycles in reasonably close succession. The owner reported the machine had been operational until the keyboard became erratic after being unplugged. After several cycles it had started showing keyboard errors on boot, then more severe boot errors, and then went completely dead. Our testing showed the motherboard was completely inoperative. Because it was an older machine, the parts necessary to restore operation included a motherboard, processor, and memory.

People are often picky about the feel of their keyboards. Some like a distinct click and tactile feedback, while others like soft resistance and a quiet keyboard. Springs and cams in the switches determine what the keyboard feels like and are not something you can adjust. Try out any keyboard you're interested in before you buy it to make sure it is one you're willing to live with.

Keyboard Controllers and Key Matrices

Your keyboard has a simple interface into the computer: Each key press and key release results in a transmission from the keyboard that sends a code stating what happened. The switches themselves can't do that. They can only open or close a single connection.

The figure in this sidebar shows how a small microprocessor in the keyboard (called the *keyboard controller*) translates switch closings into the codes your computer expects to see. Every key switch uniquely connects a pair of wires that are part of a horizontal/vertical grid. The keyboard controller finds out which switches are pushed down (closed) by looking at pairs of scan lines. It starts on

Continued

Continued

the top horizontal scan line, and looks at each vertical scan line. Every connection is noted. The controller then moves to the second horizontal line, and again checks every vertical scan. It repeats this process until it has looked at all combinations of horizontal and vertical scan lines. The code representing the most recently pressed key gets reported to the computer when the key is pushed.

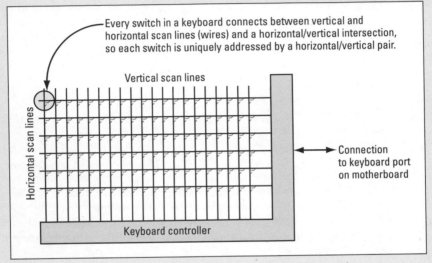

The keyboard controller polls the scan lines looking for key pushes.

The keyboard controller has another critical job, which is to eliminate bounce from the key switch contacts coming together or opening up. The key contacts are springs, and like any other springs, bounce a little when they strike or move away from another surface. This bouncing looks like multiple connections and disconnections at the speeds computers run, but it occurs in far less time than you could actually move the key. The controller exploits that timing to decide if a contact opening or closing is something you did or a bounce — if it happens a few milliseconds after the last one, it's a bounce; otherwise, it's you.

The keyboard controller's other job is to turn on the light-emitting diodes (LEDs) on the keyboard — the ones for Num Lock, Caps Lock, and Scroll Lock — in response to messages sent by the computer.

There are other ways to build keyboards than with switches. One way is to include conductive membranes separated by an insulator with holes in it. Membrane keyboards are used to withstand corrosive atmospheres and avoid generating sparks, but they are less common in conventional systems.

Keyboard layouts

Most keyboards use the standard QWERTY (or Sholes) key layout, meaning that the alphabetic keys are arranged in the following pattern:

QWERT   YUIOP

ASDFG   HJKL

ZXCVB   NM

The QWERTY keyboard layout was devised by Christopher Sholes early in the development of manual typewriters, with the objective of moving common pairs of keys away from each other to reduce jamming in those early mechanical keyboards. It's commonly reported that Sholes intended the QWERTY layout design to slow typists down to prevent jamming, but some studies indicate that QWERTY is at least as fast as other designs.

The most common alternative keyboard layout is the Dvorak keyboard, designed by University of Washington professor August Dvorak and William Dealey in 1936. The Dvorak layout uses the following pattern:

PY   FGCRL

AOEUI   DHTNS

QJKX   BMWVZ

The idea behind Dvorak's keyboard is that it's more efficient to put the most-used letters on the home row (the one where your fingers rest when you're not typing), to set up the key patterns so that your strongest fingers do most of the work, and to divide the letters so that the workload is balanced between your left and right hands. Dvorak International reports that in QWERTY, 31 percent of typing is done on the home row, compared to 70 percent for Dvorak. The Dvorak layout has 35 percent more right-hand reaches, 63 percent more same-row reaches, 45 percent more alternate-hand reaches, and 37 percent less finger travel. Other studies seem to show a smaller difference. Dvorak International further notes that Sholes himself devised another layout after mechanisms improved, but it never caught on.

Ergonomics and repetitive stress

If you type at all quickly, you can easily perform thousands of repetitive motions in a single hour of typing. Many sources, including the United States National Institute of Occupational Safety and Health, state that such work can contribute to repetitive strain injury. Most authorities recommend the following preventative measures:

✦ **Placing equipment** — It's crucial that your equipment is designed and arranged so that you can maintain good posture, with all parts of your body in the proper position.

✦ **Taking breaks** — Periodically changing what you are doing to something other than working at your computer is important. Short, relatively frequent breaks are worthwhile, particularly if you can stretch a little at the time. The point isn't that you have to stop working; rather, it's to recommend that you do other things besides work at your computer from time to time in order to give your body a restful change of position.

✦ **Knowing what to look for** — If you do develop a problem, you're much better off dealing with it before it becomes severe. Specific symptoms may arise in a number of ways, including tingling in the fingers; fatigue, numbness, and aching in the wrist and hand; and eventually severe pain in the wrist and hand. In a larger sense, though, if working at your computer leaves you sore and uncomfortable, you need to attend to the discomfort before it becomes serious.

Not all experts agree that typing causes repetitive strain injury. However, a large majority of authorities assert long-term or frequent use of a keyboard can cause problems. This is a medical issue, so if you experience pain or unusual discomfort from typing at a computer, you should consult a medical authority for information, diagnosis, and treatment.

Prevention is your best response to repetitive stress injury. Avoid the problem in the first place. Setting up your workplace so you maintain good posture is your first step. Here's what to do:

✦ **Table and chair height** — The relative height of your keyboard and chair should be adjusted so that, with your hands on the keyboard, your arms and legs are horizontal, and your back vertical.

✦ **Wrist angle** — The table and seat height should combine so that your hands rest on the keyboard with your wrists straight, not angled either up or down. If the keyboard is too high, you'll have to bend your hands down; if too low, you'll have to bend them up. Both positions are bad.

The newer split keyboard design lets you keep your wrists straight by angling the rows of keys so that you don't have to cant your hands outward to line up with straight rows of keys. Many of these units also have a support that will raise the front of the keyboard to eliminate any requirement to angle your hands upward. Whether you use a support like that depends on your workstation. Your goal is to keep your wrists comfortably straight.

✦ **Elbow angle** — You can adjust either the table or chair height to get your arms parallel to the floor. Whichever you do, your position needs to be relaxed and comfortable. At the same time, you're better off sitting straight with good back support, and with your feet flat on the floor.

The Logitech Cordless Comfort Duo (see Figure 18-3) is a representative keyboard and mouse combination providing a split keyboard, wireless connections to eliminate cables and untether you from the computer itself, and specialized keys you can dedicate to common functions such as reading e-mail or opening a Web browser. A small receiver plugs into the USB or PS2 keyboard and mouse connectors at the back of your computer. Batteries power the keyboard and mouse, with an expected lifetime of about three months.

Figure 18-3: The Logitech Cordless Comfort Duo includes a split keyboard design and wireless connections to eliminate cable constraints.
Photo courtesy of Logitech

If you do choose a wireless keyboard or mouse, however, be sure to consider the possibility of interference from other nearby devices. Some manufacturers have failed to design their products to operate in an environment where multiple units are in close proximity, leading to both problems where either the peripherals don't work or inputs from one set of devices are received on other, unintended computers.

There's no consensus on the best furniture and equipment, or on the value of split keyboards, wrist rests, and other products, but there's a lot of information available on this topic on the Internet. Search using keywords like *repetitive stress keyboard*, or go directly to sites focusing on the problem. One excellent starting point is "The Typing Injury FAQ" (Frequently Asked Questions) by Dan Wallach at www.tifaq.com. This site addresses a wide range of issues and provides pointers to many other resources on the Internet.

Another key step in preventing a repetitive stress problem is to give yourself the opportunity to recover. Many sources suggest you break up your typing with frequent rest breaks, taking at least a one-minute break every 20 minutes or 5 to 15 minutes every hour. You can have your computer remind you to take breaks using software such as WorkPace (Niche Software, Ltd., at www.workpace.com), which combines education on exercises and stretching with monitoring and reminders to take breaks.

Impaired access

Beyond the facilities built directly into Windows, a large variety of products and accessories are designed to facilitate ease of input from your fingers to your computer (for example, see the links at www.emr.org/linksA.html). In addition to alternative keyboard physical layouts, software is available that is intended to simplify or accelerate your rate of typing. Few of these have achieved widespread acceptance, perhaps because it's difficult to tailor them for the wide range of things any one person may do with a computer. Even an accessory as generic as the macro recorder — a program that could turn a keystroke into an entire sequence of key and mouse operations — was so unused that Microsoft removed it from Windows starting with Windows 95.

One important issue regarding computer keyboards is making them usable by people with impaired mobility. Typing on the usual grid of closely spaced keys is difficult without reasonably precise accuracy, and more difficult yet for people who need to use a typing stick. The close proximity of the keycaps and the ease with which you can hit the wrong key (or multiple keys) increase the error rate, requiring yet more keystrokes to correct. It can be difficult to reach the keys with your hands, and impossible with a mouth stick. Maltron (www.maltron.com) makes a keyboard for these users with the key layout optimized for distance, not two-handed typing. Using conventional keycaps — not larger or smaller ones — the span of the keys from left to right on the keyboard is a mere nine inches.

Game Controllers

Devices specialized for the motions you need to make playing video games, collectively called game controllers, are a big business because what you need to do to control a game often requires different gestures than you make surfing the Web or writing a report, and because in many games a split-second faster response is the difference between winning and losing. The controller giving you the best advantage is a matter of both personal preference and the type of game you're playing:

✦ **First and third person shooters** — Shooters are games where you attack enemies from the player's point of view (first person) or a point of view over the player's shoulder (third person), typified by games such as *Quake*, *Halo*, *Half-Life*, and *Unreal Tournament*. The best players consistently use a keyboard and mouse for shooters, using the mouse to shoot and look around the environment, and the keyboard to move and control other game functions. Other controllers have reached the market, but none have achieved close to the dominance of the keyboard/mouse combination.

✦ **Flight simulators** — Flight simulators let players take control of airplanes and spacecraft, so joysticks — controls similar to what actual pilots use — are often preferred.

✦ **Driving simulators** — Automotive racing games benefit from steering wheels, which sometimes include foot pedals for accelerating and braking. Wheels work for watercraft and motorcycles, too, although if you spend much time in arcades, you've seen actual motorcycle replicas built to let players lean into curves.

✦ **Other** — Game consoles typically have a game pad with small joysticks and many buttons and have shown these controllers to be useful with virtually all game types.

Joysticks

It used to be that joysticks were connected to your PC with an analog interface (see Figure 18-4) tied to some specialized circuitry usually found on the sound card. The handle on an analog joystick was pivoted at the bottom, rotating on the shafts of a pair of variable resistors. When you moved the handle, the shafts rotated and changed the value of the resistors. The computer measured this resistance change periodically and calculated the corresponding left/right and forward/backward positions.

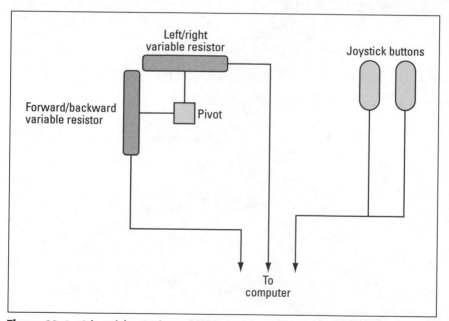

Figure 18-4: A joystick attaches variable resistors to a pivot, letting the computer measure the angle of deflection in two directions.

The problem with this approach, which was used in nearly every joystick made, was that getting an accurate, repeatable measurement took a relatively long time, and during that interval the processor couldn't do anything else, including updating the screen, playing sound, or calculating. Ultimately, the smoothness of movement suffered in highly interactive software.

Joystick technology has evolved a lot in the last few years. Digital joysticks, typically connected to a USB port, replaced the variable resistors in analog joysticks with digital optical position encoders, allowing your computer to simply be told the stick position. Digital joysticks are quick and accurate, leading to smoother game play and better responsiveness. Force feedback joysticks exploited the fact that the digital interface can send information from the computer as well as to it, adding motors that are commanded by the computer to push against your hand through the stick. The Logitech Freedom 2.4 Cordless Joystick (see Figure 18-5) is representative, using a wireless connection between the joystick and a small receiver connected to a USB port. The digital interface makes a lot more switches, buttons, and sliders available, too, putting more functions in reach without resorting to the keyboard. The wireless link is particularly nice for getting a little distance away from your big-screen TV, or for avoiding sweeping things off your desk when you put too much body English on a move.

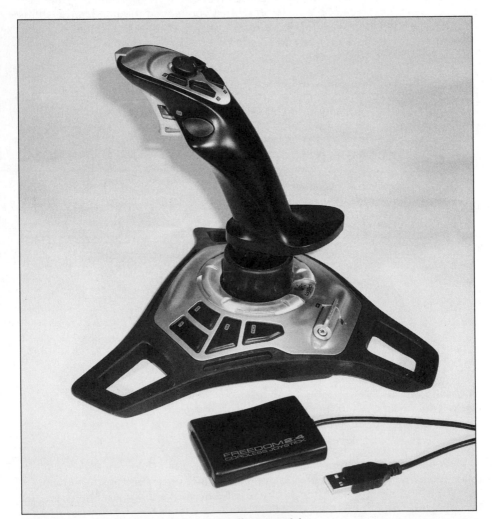

Figure 18-5: Logitech Freedom 2.4 Cordless Joystick

©2004 Barry Press & Marcia Press

Game pads

Dedicated game consoles, such as the Sony PlayStation or Sega Dreamcast, use a specialized controller, called a game pad, for input. Game pads typically have a directional button capable of sensing input in one of eight directions, a pair of joysticks, and a generous complement of buttons. Individual games assign specific functions to most or all of the inputs.

Even though the controls on a game pad don't mimic controls you commonly use, as does a racing wheel, they've become ingrained in the user interface of many role-playing and fighting games and seem most natural to players accustomed to that interface. The Logitech Cordless RumblePad (see Figure 18-6) provides that standard interface, combining it with a wireless link and USB connection for the receiver. The end result is that ports of console games to the PC, along with PC titles themselves, can deliver the same enjoyable experience as on a dedicated console.

Figure 18-6: The Logitech Cordless RumblePad duplicates the familiar game console interface on PCs.

Photo courtesy of Logitech

Wheels

Games bring perhaps the most unique environments to PCs, so it's predictable that games would lead to the development of specialized controllers. Two of the most popular game-specific controllers are steering wheels (and pedals) for driving games and game pads for fighting and other games imported from dedicated game consoles such as the Sony PlayStation 2 or Microsoft Xbox.

Figure 18-7 shows the Logitech Formula Force GP wheel. You mount the wheel to the top of a table, in front of your monitor, and put the pedals on the floor. The wheel connects to a USB port and controls your race car the way you'd expect — turn left to go left, turn right to go right. Press the right pedal to accelerate, the left to brake. Force feedback from the game through the wheel gives you a feel for the road.

Figure 18-7: The Logitech Formula Force GP wheel combines force feedback with the motions you expect for driving.
Photo courtesy of Logitech

Summary

✦ Look for both solid construction and a feel you like in a keyboard.

✦ Good posture and straight wrists are important to minimize repetitive stress. Get qualified medical help early for repetitive stress problems.

✦ Keyboards designed for the motion-impaired can improve the ability to use and communicate through the computer.

✦ Joysticks, game pads, and wheels can enhance gaming on the PC beyond the usual PC mouse-and-keyboard interface.

Mice, Trackballs, and Tablets

✦   ✦   ✦   ✦

In This Chapter

Examining mice and
how they work

Working with trackballs
and tablets

✦   ✦   ✦   ✦

Initially, a well-equipped personal computer had a display, keyboard, and printer. The display gave you 25 by 80 characters, so moving the cursor from character to character by pushing keys was reasonable. Life was simple enough that you didn't need a pointing device.

Life changed to put a lot more on the screen, however, and to put it onscreen using high-resolution graphics. It's impractical to point at things on a graphics screen by moving a pointer with the keyboard, so new technology was required. Pioneering work by Doug Englebart at Stanford Research Institute in 1963 created what we now call the mouse (along with the On-Line System and some incredibly innovative ideas), and enabled the pointing motions we all use in the graphical Windows (and UNIX X Window) interface. Development by Microsoft, Logitech, and other companies made the mouse the most common pointing device on personal computers, and as essential as a keyboard. Competitive devices such as trackballs and touch-sensitive pads have flourished, but are nowhere as prevalent as mice.

Cross-Reference This chapter specifically addresses pointing devices. For information on keyboards or other types of input devices, look in Chapter 18.

With the exception of the importance of rock-solid drivers, the most important thing to keep in mind about input devices is that there is an enormous number of them, each suited to some things more than others. This means that you can use a single one for everything, or you can have specialized controllers each suited for a specific task. A mouse is the most common input device, and applicable to nearly everything you do with your computer. A lot of people choose trackballs

Your Word Processor Is a 30-Year-Old Idea

For all of the power and features in the best word processors we have today, many of the features they implement are decades old. In addition to inventing (and patenting) the mouse, Doug Englebart created something called the On-Line System (NLS) while at Stanford Research Institute, publicly demonstrating it in 1968. The primitive terminals of the day couldn't support the interactions Englebart designed for NLS, so he invented a completely new terminal. In addition to the mouse, his terminal included a redesigned keyboard and a five-paddle device that you played chords on to type letters (think of a five-key, one-handed piano). Using the mouse with one hand and playing chords with the other, an experienced user could control the system and edit text surprisingly quickly. The combination of mouse and chords allowed operation without continually moving from keyboard to mouse and back, a problem we haven't eliminated in today's systems.

Unlike today's PC software that, until Windows 9x (and X Window under UNIX), rarely used the second mouse button, Englebart's mouse had three buttons that were all used by NLS, as were all the combinations of mouse buttons. His software allowed a seemingly infinite set of views into your documents, foreshadowing the relatively simplistic outline views in today's word processors. Running on a Digital Equipment Corporation mainframe (a PDP-10), NLS included spell checkers, text styles, group collaboration, and much more. In fact, it included so many features that — like many of today's word processors — it required some intensive training and practice to use competently.

Like many other people, we have word processors that we like and ones that we detest. NLS was one of the ones we really liked. NLS never made the transition from the Digital Equipment Corporation mainframes Englebart used to PCs, though, so only its concepts remain alive.

instead of mice, so you'll want to check that alternative for a general-purpose pointing device. If you're doing artistic or drawing work, you're probably familiar with tablets and will definitely want to consider one. It's simply faster and easier to draw with one.

Mice

Mice contain two kinds of input electronics. One part of the mouse detects movement and reports it, while the other part detects button activity and reports that. Switches (the buttons) are no problem; the trick is to convert movement into electrical signals the computer can understand. The most reliable mice now use optical sensors, but for decades nearly all PC mice used a mechanical ball. Figure 19-1 shows how a mechanical mouse works — the ball turns rollers inside the body of the mouse, which themselves turn digitizers to separate out and separately measure the left/right and forward/backward motion.

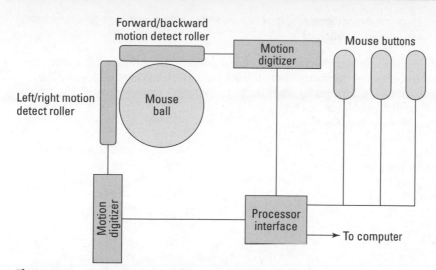

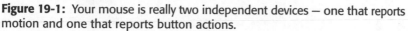

Figure 19-1: Your mouse is really two independent devices — one that reports motion and one that reports button actions.

Mechanical mice tend to ingest all matter of junk from your desktop, so they require periodic cleaning, and cleaning the internal rollers can be difficult. Mechanical mice are prone to picking up dirt and debris off your desk, and both gum and particulates from smoke from the air. When this happens, the garbage from your desk often gets wound around the rollers and stops them from rolling. That leads to "bumps" in the mouse movement or to situations where the mouse simply stops moving in one direction. If that happens to you, you'll need to clean the insides of the mouse. There's usually a panel that rotates and lifts off the bottom of the mouse, allowing you to remove the ball. Once you do, you can gently rotate the rollers and remove the dirt and lint. Don't use oil or grease in the mouse — it'll just attract more dirt.

Optical mice replace all the moving parts in the motion sensing assembly with a small image sensor — a camera — and enough processing to figure out which way the mouse has moved from one picture to the next (see Figure 19-2).

Optical mice use motion detection algorithms, not unlike the motion compensation algorithms used in MPEG 2 video compression, to see motion in an image as you move the mouse across your desktop.

Be the mouse optical or mechanical, the motion reports it sends your computer don't contain absolute position information because the mouse has no idea where it is on your desk. Instead, the mouse reports that it's moved a specified distance, measured in units called mickeys. One mickey is the least movement that the roller and digitizer can detect. In the first Microsoft mice, one mickey was about one one-hundredth of an inch. The newer ones improved this resolution down to about one two-hundredth, and later to one four-hundredth of an inch. Every time the mouse sends a message to the computer, it reports the number of mickeys it has moved since the last message. Mickeys are reported independently for each direction, and are used by your computer to update the mouse cursor position onscreen.

Mouse buttons are simply reported to the processor as being up or down. Mice had from one to three buttons, in part because Windows internally had provisions for left, middle, and right buttons, but now can include at least five buttons, thumbwheels, and more.

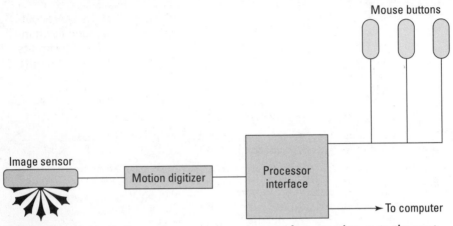

Figure 19-2: An optical mouse measures movement from one image to the next.

Mouse cursors

A key part of your mouse isn't hardware at all — it's the cursor the computer draws on the screen to show you where you're pointing. There's no direct connection between your mouse and the cursor position. Instead, Windows uses the movement reports from the mouse to update the horizontal and vertical position where it thinks the cursor should appear, erases the old drawing of the cursor, and draws the cursor again at the new position.

The mouse cursor also gets erased and redrawn by Windows every time a program draws on the screen near the mouse. (You can see this effect by starting a video clip — an AVI, MPG, or MOV file — in Windows and then moving the mouse cursor over the video playback window. Unless your video card has special hardware for handling cursors, you'll see the cursor flicker on and off or possibly disappear entirely until the video stops.)

Microsoft Intellimouse

We consider the Microsoft mice, in any of their serial, PS/2, or USB versions, the standard of comparison for all other mice, primarily because of the stability of the Microsoft mouse drivers and the durability of the units (see Figure 19-3). We've also found the Logitech mice to be as well made. We're fanatic about driver quality. Creating drivers is some of the most difficult programming people do, and many companies have demonstrated their inability to get them

Feeding Your Mouse

A serial port on a PC conforms to the Electronic Industries Association RS-232C standard, which defines both the electrical properties of signals at the port and the way in which those signals are used. The RS-232C port of your PC uses voltages to indicate logical states: a one bit is signaled by −3 V to −15 V on a pin, while a zero is signaled by +3 V to +15 V. Plus and minus 12 V are typical.

None of the pins in an RS-232C port were intended to deliver power. When Microsoft developed the serial mouse, though, they noticed that the typical output line in an RS-232C port could supply a little bit of power — around five hundredths of a watt. By using very low power electronics (and very little electronics at all), they could keep power consumption below that limit and run the mouse completely off the port.

That observation, and the engineering behind it, was a big part of making mice a part of every computer. Eliminating the mouse card that had to go inside the computer reduced cost and, perhaps more importantly, simplified installation. No screws to remove, no slots to find, no conflicts to solve. Plug it in and go.

Since then, electronics have become smaller, doing more in the same space and requiring less power. You can get cordless mice and keyboards today that use radio to communicate with your computer rather than the wire you're used to. By combining wireless links with gyroscopes or tilt sensors, companies have built "air mice" — mice that you simply hold in your hand wherever you happen to be. An air mouse is, for some people, a key element of a workable computer-based presentation system. (For others, an air mouse can be completely confusing. Rehearse with one before doing a live presentation.)

right. When you can, it's the safe alternative to buy a product that's completely compatible with the Microsoft mouse and uses the Microsoft driver. If you can't do that, make sure of the quality of the drivers from the manufacturer you choose. We very much doubt you'll be happy about saving a few dollars after you discover that the source of your crashes has been a buggy driver.

The Microsoft mouse had always been a two-button unit until 1996, when Microsoft announced the Intellimouse — a new design that added the wheel you see between the two buttons in Figure 19-3. The wheel combines with changes introduced with Windows 98 and Windows 2000 to simplify scrolling and zooming in documents, reducing the number of times you have to move your hand from mouse to keyboard.

The interface you choose for your mouse depends on your system and the other equipment you expect to use. The Universal Serial Bus is now commonplace, augmenting the more traditional choices you have:

✦ **Serial ports** — Serial port mice are almost extinct, replaced first by PS2 mice and now by USB mice.

✦ **PS/2 mouse port** — This is essentially a serial port, but at a different I/O address and with a different IRQ. The interface is a dedicated port that doesn't consume a serial port and is pre-configured for mouse support. If you have a PS/2 port on your motherboard, it's a better choice than using a serial port because you don't use up a port you could use for some other purpose.

✦ **USB mouse** — Like the PS/2 mouse port, a USB mouse port leaves the serial port free for other uses. If you use a USB mouse, make sure the BIOS in your computer offers *Legacy USB Support*, which means that it can make the USB mouse look like a conventional serial mouse for operation with the BIOS itself. You may have to explicitly enable the Legacy USB Support feature. Hard-core gamers have another reason, beyond convenience, to move to USB mice — fast reaction game response. Your computer gets updates from a USB mouse nearly twice as often as from a PS/2 mouse, leading to smoother, more responsive play at expert levels.

Figure 19-3: The Microsoft Wireless Intellimouse Explorer combines a comfortable shape with rugged construction and quality drivers.
©2004 Barry Press & Marcia Press

Trackballs

One of the most common alternatives to a mouse is a trackball, which is basically a mechanical mouse turned upside down (although optical trackballs exist that use optical sensors to detect rotation of the ball). You rotate the ball directly while the body stays put. Figure 19-4 is a typical trackball, the Logitech Cordless Optical TrackMan.

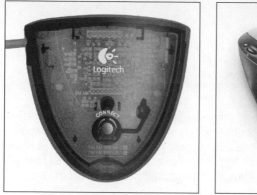

Figure 19-4: Logitech Cordless Optical TrackMan
Photo courtesy of Logitech

Trackballs solve three problems inherent to mice:

✦ **Space** — Only the ball moves in a trackball, not the body. By comparison, mice take space to operate (and even then, you'll end up picking up the mouse and moving it back on the desk when you run out of room). In some situations — a computer built into a rack of equipment, or most of the airline seats you'll find — you don't have that kind of space.

✦ **Staying put** — You can attach a trackball securely to a computer or shelf so it stays in one place. By comparison, a mouse won't stay where you left it if it's being bounced around. Airline seats are like that, but so are boats, cars, and most any other moving platform.

✦ **Fine control** — The buttons on a trackball aren't physically coupled to the ball like they are by the body of a mouse. People tend to move a mouse a pixel or two when they push one of the buttons. If you're doing drawings or other very fine work, that motion can destroy the precision you need. You won't have that problem with a trackball.

Unfortunately, trackballs have problems of their own, most prominent of which is that your hand is always moving relative to the buttons, and you may have to stretch quite a bit to reach the button you want. If you need to hold the button down while you rotate the ball, this can turn into the computer equivalent of patting your stomach while you rub your head. This problem has lead more than a few trackball manufacturers to add buttons to their products that latch down when pushed, telling the computer they're down until you push them again and making it easier to drag the mouse cursor while a button appears to be down. Movements like that are essential for the drag-and-drop functions built into Windows and Linux. Some people never get comfortable with a trackball, finding the movements awkward, while others are fanatic about them.

Tablets

Yet another pointing device is the tablet, a flat surface on which you can write, draw, and trace. Tablets come in a range of sizes, from card-sized through units several feet on a side. You can get ones with a corded or cordless stylus, and ones with buttons and other controls.

The real advantage of a tablet is that it lets you use the drawing motions you're used to — the fine arc around the heel of your palm and the stroke with your elbow and shoulder. These motions are completely impossible with a trackball or joystick, and unnatural and ineffective with a mouse. A tablet is the closest computer approximation to a sketchpad, and so is commonly found in the hands of artists.

While mice typically have resolutions of 400 points per inch or less, most tablets have a resolution of at least 1,000 lines per inch. A 5-inch wide tablet provides at least 5,000 lines of resolution, and for some tablets gives you as many as 12,700 lines. This is far beyond PC monitor display screen capabilities, and similar to the resolution of a printer for the entire page.

Not all software handles tablets equally well, so you'll want to check and see whether the tablet has drivers for the software you plan to use. You should check what functions the software and driver support. Many tablets come bundled with drawing software. If you choose one of those, check to see whether the software does the things you need.

Some of the companies that make tablets (such as Wacom) also build their digitizers into transparent surfaces you can use as a touch screen. When the user touches the screen, it sends a set of coordinates to the computer that your program can correlate to areas of the screen.

Wacom has long been the best known manufacturer of graphics tablets. The company has a range of products depending on what you do with a tablet. Figure 19-5 is their Graphire3 tablet (www.wacom.com/graphire/index.cfm) that combines a USB interface, high resolution, a pressure sensitive battery-free pen with eraser tool, and a cordless mouse. Buttons on the barrel of the stylus let you select objects in your software or choose special drawing functions. Wacom's stylus has an "eraser" on the top, letting you use the pad even more like you would a pencil and paper. The eraser has the same pressure-sensitive capability as the tip, so you can use it for shading, feathering, and other artistic effects.

Wacom also offers the Cintiq series tablets that combine a color LCD display and tablet. It's expensive even if you include the price of an LCD monitor, but for some artistic work, the ability to draw on a digital image is worth the cost.

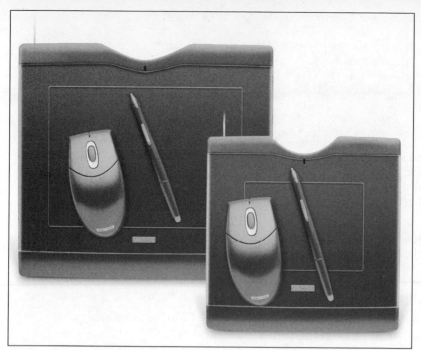

Figure 19-5: Wacom Graphire3 tablet
Photo courtesy Wacom Technology Corporation

Top Support Questions

Most of the problems you see with pointing devices are a result of underlying problems with serial ports or driver software. Using dedicated PS/2 mouse ports or USB connections and staying with the drivers that come with your operating system (rather than those from third parties) can help eliminate most of these problems.

Mouse

Q: My serial mouse isn't detected by Plug and Play. Why?

A: Check if you're using an adapter to connect a 9-pin serial mouse connector to a 25-pin serial port. If so, it's possible that some lines in the 9-pin connector required by Plug and Play aren't being bridged to the 25-pin connector. Try using a 9-pin port, a different connector that you know bridges all 9 signals, or a manual installation of your mouse via Add New Hardware.

Q: My mouse doesn't respond to double-clicks. Why?

A: If you can, try another mouse. If that works, the original mouse is probably defective. If the second mouse doesn't work either, check the speed setting for double-clicks. If it's set too high, it may be looking for the second click faster than you can push the button. Slow down the double-click setting and see what happens.

Q: My mouse jumps across the screen, or moves in bursts. Why?

A: Check if your mouse is connected to a serial port using the 16550 chip. If so, verify that the 16550 hardware functions are disabled for that port — that the chip is functioning as an older 8250 chip. Your BIOS may label the setting you need as turning on and off the FIFO (first-in, first-out) hardware buffer.

Q: My mouse stops going in one direction sometimes. If I move it away and then back, it continues past the sticking point. Why?

A: You probably have dirt in the mouse (on the rollers) or on the mouse ball. Remove the ball and check carefully for dirt, cleaning out any you find.

Tablet

Q: In my system with a tablet and mouse, the mouse has gone berserk, moving erratically and leaping across the screen. What's wrong?

A: If you have a tablet installed, check that the stylus hasn't accidentally come near the surface of the tablet, creating unintentional mouse motion inputs to your system.

Summary

✦ Mice and trackballs are devices that translate movement into inputs to your computer.

✦ Pointing devices adapt different movements to computer input, making specialized control easier.

✦ Drivers and software are critical to getting value from any input device you choose.

Printers, Scanners, and All-in-One Units

CHAPTER 20

In This Chapter

Ink jet and laser printing

Understanding page description languages

Using printer drivers and control software

Examining scanners

Choosing combined print, fax, and copy units

The once promised paperless society hasn't yet happened, despite radio, television, and computers. You'll ultimately need to get some part of what you do with your computer onto paper. That means you'll need a printer.

Printers: Getting the Ink (Only) Where It Belongs

Computer printers for personal computers started out as adapted typewriters. Instead of being driven by a keyboard (although some had them), they received instructions from the computer. Operation notwithstanding, they remained typewriters inside.

The point of a printer isn't to be a typewriter, of course; it's to get ink on paper in just the right amount and in just the right place. The same technology that created the microprocessors that drive your computer created smaller microprocessors that could be built into printers. When that happened, designers discovered that they could abandon the typewriter-based approach and build printers based on the job that needed to be done. When they started looking at how to do high-quality graphics along with text, they noticed that copiers and monitors (that is, raster-based devices) were a better starting point. The result was the laser and ink jet printers you have today.

Ink jet printers

Ink jet printers are really high-tech versions of the older dot-matrix printers, which used small pins to impact a ribbon and make character images from a rectangular matrix of dots. An ink jet printer cartridge squirts a matrix of dots a row at a time, using an ink reservoir, some circuitry, and tiny nozzles down at the bottom of the cartridge (see the side view in Figure 20-1):

✦ **Ink reservoir** — The reservoir has to ensure a continuous, uninterrupted supply of ink to the drivers and nozzles. It has to prevent sloshing and foaming as the head moves. The ink composition is very important — it has to flow smoothly out of the reservoir, not clog the tiny holes in the impulse drivers and nozzles, have enough surface tension to avoid smearing as it is ejected from the nozzle, dry soon enough to maintain the image, and avoid wicking out on the paper fibers (which would make the image fuzzy).

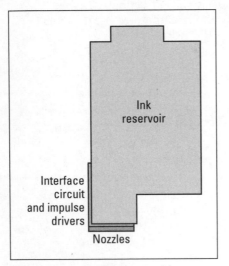

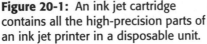

Figure 20-1: An ink jet cartridge contains all the high-precision parts of an ink jet printer in a disposable unit.

✦ **Interface circuit and impulse drivers** — The printer electronics command the driver behind each nozzle independently, so in a high-resolution printer, you find a lot of separate circuits. Each is terminated at a connecting point on the side of the cartridge that lines up with a corresponding pin on the print head. The interface circuit (a flexible printed circuit) routes these signals down to the impulse drivers and nozzles at the bottom of the cartridge.

When activated, the impulse drivers force a small drop of ink through the nozzle (one below each driver) and onto the paper that's in contact with the head. Impulse drivers work in two ways. Some companies use a small piezoelectric crystal (one that expands when hit with an electrical impulse); others use a small ball of vapor produced by heating a pocket of ink. Figure 20-2 shows the effect of the driver — forcing a small, precisely measured drop of ink down through the nozzle and onto the paper.

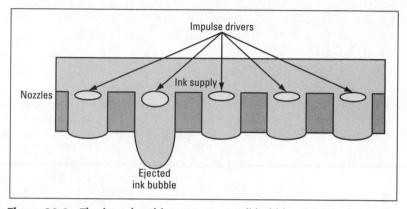

Figure 20-2: The impulse drivers create small bubbles, forcing drops of ink out from the nozzles.

The operation of the drivers and nozzles is shown by comparing the leftmost nozzle in Figure 20-2 with the one next to it. In the leftmost nozzle, the driver isn't activated, so the surface tension of the ink keeps it confined to the nozzle. In the next nozzle, the driver has activated, ejecting the ink out of the nozzle and onto the paper.

✦ **Nozzles** — The nozzles establish the precise position of the dots relative to one another and form the physical interface between the print cartridge and the paper.

The print head positions the cartridge laterally along the paper. The nozzle spacing positions the dots the printer puts on the paper perpendicularly to the head movement, while the printer electronics time the signals sent to the cartridge with the head motion to position the dots laterally. The net result is that ink jet printers — the modern version of the old dot matrix technology — can today achieve a resolution of 2,400×1,200 dots per inch, a resolution competitive with laser printers.

It's relatively straightforward to create a color ink jet printer — you simply have three or four heads (using the CMY or CMYK color model; see the "Scanners" section later in this chapter for information on color models) and carefully track the relative position of the heads among one another. Color ink jet printers often use one or two cartridges to do this, with cyan, magenta, and yellow in one and (optionally) black in the other. Some color ink jets use four separate cartridges, one per color.

When there are multiple cartridges, a calibration process is required to make sure they are physically lined up. Typically, the printer will output a set of test patterns, requiring you to select the specific pattern that has the best alignment.

You can recycle ink jet cartridges. Details for Canon cartridges are on the Web at www.ereturn.usa.canon.com. Recycling details for Hewlett Packard cartridges are at www.hp.com/hpinfo/globalcitizenship/environment/recycle/index.html and government.hp.com/products_planetpartner.asp.

Laser printers

Laser printers use fine, dry ink particles (called toner) to create an image on paper. This is the same process used in copiers. The key laser printer components are shown in Figure 20-3. The process starts at the point between the charging roller and the photoconductor drum. The charging roller imposes an electrical charge on the drum, which causes it to repel the toner particles. The drum rotates under the laser (which sweeps back and forth in lines), and everywhere the laser illuminates the drum, the charge dissipates. Those points attract toner from the toner roller — the laser effectively draws black and gray areas on the drum. The drum continues to turn, bringing the patterned toner image into contact with the paper. The transfer roller attracts the toner to the paper, where it sticks. The combination of the fuser roller and the backup roller heat the toner, bonding it to the paper and making a permanent image.

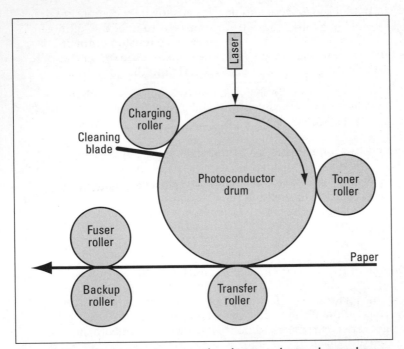

Figure 20-3: The laser writes onto the photoconductor drum where the image should be dark, allowing the drum to pick up black toner particles.

The laser is under the control of the raster processor in the printer, which has the responsibility of turning the codes sent from your computer into a bitmap of the image to appear on the page.

The same arithmetic — counting pixels — that causes your video card to need a lot of memory causes your printer to need memory as well. The raster processor generally can't keep up with the photoconductor drum as it rotates, and the drum can't stop in the middle of a page (because the image would end up distorted). That means that the entire image has to be in memory when the drum starts to rotate to print the page. If we assume quarter-inch margins and multiply out the number of pixels on a page at 600 dots per inch (a typical laser printer resolution), we find that we have nearly 32 million dots on an 8.5×11-inch page. If each pixel takes one bit in memory, we need nearly 4MB to hold the entire page (more if we're storing fonts as well).

Printers that enhance the apparent resolution of the image by controlling the darkness of each dot may require even more memory — if the printer can store four levels of intensity per dot, it needs nearly 8MB. Many printers are starting to compress the raster image in memory, decompressing it on the fly as the laser scans the page. Using lossless compression, this technique can reduce memory requirements by a factor of 1.5 or 2 to 1 or more.

You can get laser toner in different colors besides black (even for a black-and-white printer). Color laser printers use four sets of toner to create the image, typically making four passes around the photoconductor drum (one for each color) before imprinting the image on the paper. Because the image has to be rasterized separately for each color, the printer's memory requirements go up drastically. It's not unusual to require 32MB in a color laser printer (which, along with the more complex mechanism and lower sales volume, is why they're expensive).

Page description languages

Now that you have the means to put images where you want them on paper, you need a way for your computer to tell the printer what to do. Think back to how typewriters worked to get an idea of what you need to do with your printer:

✦ **Characters** — For the most part, what you did with a typewriter was print characters. The typewriter automatically moved from one character to the next, spacing them apart so the resulting text looked right.

✦ **Positioning** — You defined where you wanted the characters on the page by moving the paper around in the typewriter. You could scroll the paper up and down and move the print head back and forth.

✦ **Margins** — You set margins with stops on the body of the typewriter that limited the travel of the carriage. By coordinating the stops with how you registered the paper in the carriage, you established the margins where you wanted them on both the left and right sides of the paper.

✦ **Font** — Daisy wheel and golf ball typewriters let you change the font you typed by changing the print element. You had to reach into the typewriter, remove the old one, and put in the new one.

Early personal computer printers did basically these same four things based on codes sent from the computer. Characters were sent as is, while the other functions were indicated by special codes. The codes for printers from different manufacturers were incompatible with each other, and each program had a different set of printer drivers with those codes embedded. Worse, only printers with tractor feeds (mechanisms that engaged the holes in tear-off strips at the edge of the paper) could reliably move the paper backward as well as forward, so most printers required that programs send commands in order from top to bottom of the page.

As software became more capable — word processors, presentation graphics, and page layout programs in particular — the mess surrounding printer control sequences became impractical. WordPerfect had a different set of drivers than Microsoft Word, both of which had different drivers than other programs. If you bought a new printer, you had to get new drivers from each of your software vendors. If a vendor hadn't developed the driver yet, or chose not to, you had a problem. The software vendors had a problem, as well, because each of them had to invest a lot of money in creating and maintaining their printer driver libraries.

Windows eliminated this problem because it provided a printer-independent interface between software and the printers. That interface communicates through a printer-specific driver, which translates drawing commands into what's called a *page description language*. Two page description languages dominate the industry: PostScript (developed by Adobe) and PCL (developed by Hewlett-Packard). PostScript was originally developed for use with the Macintosh computers, but has migrated to PC systems. The two have roughly equivalent capabilities — you'd typically only explicitly choose one versus the other if compatibility at the page description language level were important for communicating with an outside service bureau.

The printer drivers also support monitoring to let you see what printers are doing. You can expect good printer monitoring software to help you do things like:

✦ **Status and resource monitoring** — You should be able to find out if the printer is jammed or offline; if it needs paper, toner, or other supplies; and what job it's currently working on.

✦ **Configuration** — Your printer management software should identify all the options attached to the printer and how each is configured. You should be able to remotely change the configuration, download fonts, and enable or disable options.

You'll want to be able to control how your applications print, no matter if the printer is local or remote. You should be able to control any aspect of the printer, including at least the following:

✦ **Print density** — You can control the overall darkness of the print. If you do a whole lot of large drafts before printing a final copy, turning down the print density can reduce your costs and boost print speed. You can reset to best quality when you're ready for the final copy.

✦ **Color or grayscale** — Color printers usually let you specify that the print should be grayscale only, turning off the color inks and reducing costs.

✦ **Duplex** — Some printers offer the option to print on both sides of the paper, either by feeding the paper in twice or directly using a more involved paper feed path. Either way, you should be able to turn the duplex print on and off to fit your immediate needs and you should be able to specify whether you flip the page over on the long edge (like a book) or the short edge (like a tablet).

✦ **Graphics resolution** — Printers can't always reproduce as many colors or grayscale tones as are in your images. In that case, the printer simulates the shade by a process called *halftoning*, which involves using a grid of mixed colors of dots that, viewed from a distance, blend to simulate the color you want. The resolution of the halftoning process is often controllable from the device driver and can be set to relatively low resolution to conserve memory or speed print times. In high-resolution printers, the halftone patterning should be unnoticeable when the driver does fine-grained processing.

Some printers offer more basic resolution control, allowing you to use less than the maximum resolution on the printer, which you might want to use if you're after a quick print and don't care what the graphics look like.

✦ **Paper size** — Most printers can accommodate a range of paper sizes, from envelopes through legal and European sizes. You should be able to specify the paper you've loaded to the driver; even better is if the printer can automatically tell your computer what paper is loaded. You should also be able to specify which way the print is oriented on the page (portrait is with the long way vertical, while landscape is with the long way horizontal). For printers with unprintable areas (due to the paper feed mechanism, for example), you should be able to control the size of this area.

✦ **Paper source** — If your printer has several paper trays, or has a manual feeder in addition to the paper tray, you should be able to specify from where you want paper to feed.

✦ **Other options** — You should be able to control all the other features and specifications of your printer, such as informing Windows how much memory is installed or if an optional paper tray is installed.

Choosing a printer

The basic issues in picking a printer are how much you print, whether you need color, what print quality you need, and what price range you're in. Ignoring specialized applications like phototypesetting, high-volume label printing, or form printers, the most likely choice is a color ink jet printer. If you do light faxing, but don't want to tie up a PC as a fax machine, consider an all-in-one multifunction unit (see the section "All-in-One Units: Combining Printing, Fax, and Copying," later in this chapter). If your printing load is more than light duty, consider a black-and-white or color laser printer.

Printers come with a variety of interfaces, including serial ports (that's right — another thing to connect to those two solitary ports), parallel ports, USB, and network. Most printers used to connect to a parallel port, but USB connections are now both nearly universal and far easier to work with. Network interfaces are commonly 10/100Base-T.

With resolutions up to 1,200×1,200 dpi, the HP Deskjet 5850 color ink jet printer (see Figure 20-4) is a high-resolution printer. It prints from 1 to 21 pages per minute depending on mode and includes a duplex unit for printing on both sides of the paper. USB, Ethernet, and IEEE 802.11b interfaces are standard.

Figure 20-4: HP Deskjet 5850
©2004 Barry Press & Marcia Press

The HP LaserJet 1012 black-and-white laser printer (see Figure 20-5) is a low-cost printer offering 600×600 resolution with intensity control, what HP calls Resolution Enhancement Technology, to produce the equivalent of 1,200×1,200 dots per inch. It can print at up to 15 pages per minute if your computer can keep up and connects through a USB port.

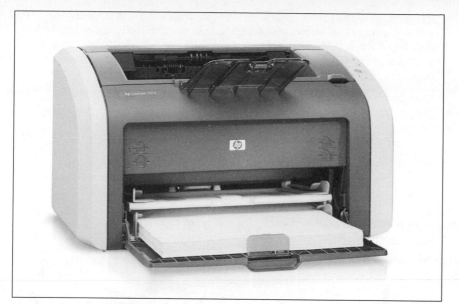

Figure 20-5: HP LaserJet 1012
Courtesy, Hewlett-Packard Development Company, LP

Scanners

Scanners do a specific, direct thing — they convert a printed image into an image in your computer. The image comes in as a bitmap — a rectangular array of pixels — from the scanner itself, so it doesn't matter if you're scanning pictures, text, or a combination of the two. The HP Scanjet 3970 (see Figure 20-6) is a typical one-pass color flatbed scanner with a high-speed USB 2.0 interface offering 48-bit color and 2,400×2,400 dpi optical resolution. The scanner is only $20 more than HP's Scanjet 3670, but offers double the optical resolution.

The essential characteristics of a scanner that define what kind of work you do with it are these:

✦ **Mechanism** — Scanners pass your image by a sensor. The mechanism that creates that movement can be one of several types, affecting the precision of the results you get and the price you'll pay for the scanner.

✦ **Number and accuracy of colors** — A scanner resolves colors into separate intensities for red, green, and blue. The number of bits for each color channel determines the number of colors the scanner can resolve, while the color calibration quality determines how accurately the scanner renders images.

✦ **Resolution** — As with a digital camera, a scanner turns your image into a bitmap. The number of pixels per inch in the bitmap — the resolution of the scanner — determines the quality of what you'll see on your screen or printer, and affects the accuracy of converting scanned text into characters.

✦ **Interface** — Scanners come with a variety of electronic interfaces, ranging from serial and parallel ports to USB. The interface you use determines how fast the image can get into your computer, and whether or not you have a suitable port on your computer.

✦ **Software** — More so than many other devices, scanners require application software to really be useful, to let you acquire, edit, crop, publish, and convert images to text.

The next sections take a look at each one of these characteristics.

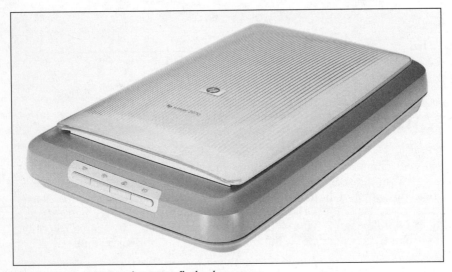

Figure 20-6: HP Scanjet 3970 flatbed scanner
Courtesy, Hewlett-Packard Development Company, LP

Mechanisms

Most digital still cameras use a rectangular sensor array so that they can capture the entire picture at one time. Scanners are different — they use a line sensor in conjunction with a mechanism that sequentially moves the sensor relative to the paper to capture the entire image. Scanners used to use a variety of mechanisms to move the sensor, but essentially all of them now hold the paper stationary on the scanner and move the sensor (inside the scanner) past the paper, which is what's called a flatbed scanner. As long as the sensor mount and drive mechanism are designed well, this approach results in precise, accurate scans. The ability to close a door over the document retains a closed light environment during the scan, allowing the device to control exposure to what the sensor needs.

If you're feeding stacks of paper into the scanner to scan successive pages, you'll want to consider a document feeder. These are most often accessories for flatbed scanners, usually holding 10 to 50 pages and supporting automatic scanning once you start the operation. (High-end production scanners can hold far more than this, and can scan far faster than the rates of the units discussed in this chapter.)

Number and accuracy of colors

Scanners report intensity for each of the red, green, and blue color channels. Even inexpensive, low-end scanners now use 16 bits per pixel per color, so a color scanner reports 48 bits per pixel (16 bits per color for each of three colors). That means the color scanner can resolve to one of over 280 trillion colors. A color scanner can give you better scans of black-and-white copy, too, because it can be used to drop out colors. Suppose, for example, that you have copy that's become discolored. If you can set up your scanner to scan with only one color, then choosing a color that drops out the discoloration helps to clean up the image even before you attack it with image processing software.

However, the number of colors a scanner resolves is independent of its color accuracy. Matching colors from scanner to screen to printer is notoriously difficult. The first time you scan a color image, you're likely to be in for a nasty shock — the piece of paper in your hand isn't likely to look at all like what you get onscreen, and neither one is likely to look like what comes out of your color printer. About that time you're going to understand exactly what that odd phrase "color matching" is all about.

From a hardware perspective, it's not at all surprising that you get differing results — in fact, it's nothing short of a miracle if you get matching colors without doing anything to make that happen. All your devices have independent calibrations, use different color technologies, and in some cases even represent colors using systems different from the red-green-blue system we've talked about (see the sidebar "RGB, CMY, and Some Other Alphabet Soup"). Most products don't include options supporting color matching, largely because there's been no industry standard for how to do this. Windows 95 introduced Image Color Matching (ICM), but even now there's been little improvement in coordination among products.

Resolution

We sometimes think that scanners are a lot like used cars because there's a very peculiar sort of specification that's become common for them, and you have to be careful that you know what you're getting. Specifically, scanner manufacturers report one or both of two different resolutions:

✦ **Raw, or optical, resolution** — This is the actual resolution produced by the scanner sensor, in dots per inch. As with monitors and printers, scanners have both vertical and horizontal resolution, and the two numbers don't have to be the same.

RGB, CMY, and Some Other Alphabet Soup

It's not practical for scanners, monitors, printers, or other devices to directly sample every possible color — there are just too many of them. Even your eyes don't (the red-green-blue, or RGB, color model is patterned after the response of your eyes to color). Instead, all these devices use combinations of a few colors, just as children do with finger paints.

So the question really is, why is there more than one color model?

The most obvious reason is that two sorts of color mixing exist — transmitted light and reflected light. These basic mixing approaches are called additive and subtractive mixing, respectively. See-through filters and color monitors use additive mixing, which corresponds well to the RGB model. When a color monitor has to create yellow, it turns on both the blue and green pixels. The light from both combines to form yellow.

Now, imagine a red filter with a light shining on it. If you're on the opposite side of the filter, you'll see red light transmitted through the filter. This is the same thing that filters in a color LCD screen do. If you stand on the other side of the filter, though, you'll see not the transmitted light, but the reflected light. The green and blue light that doesn't get transmitted through the filter gets reflected, and that's what you see. Those colors combine to form yellow, so if you look at light reflected off a red filter, you'll see yellow. This doesn't work if you put white paper behind the filter, since the red then reflects back through the filter and becomes visible.

This effect — that a red filter reflects yellow light — happens because the reflected light from the filter uses a subtractive mixing color model. Subtractive mixing is also what happens with images printed on paper. The primary colors for a subtractive model aren't red, green, and blue; they're cyan, magenta, and yellow (CMY). It's hard to get good, saturated colors with only cyan, magenta, and yellow, so printers use a fourth color — black — forming the CMYK color model. CMYK creates better colors, but not ones as good as spot color models (such as the Pantone Matching System) that mix more than four colors.

Video has yet other color models because some camera technologies work better with color sets other than RGB and because different video compression technologies work better in some color models than others.

✦ **Interpolated resolution** — This is the specification that may or may not give you what you paid for. Many scanners process the scanned image, doing the work either in the scanner or in your computer to compute more pixels than you actually read off the scanner. They do it by assuming that the change between one pixel and the next is linear.

Figures 20-7 and 20-8 show the problem interpolation can cause. In Figure 20-7, the actual image changes smoothly, and so calculating the interpolated pixels based on the linear assumption works well — the added pixels correspond well to what's in the image.

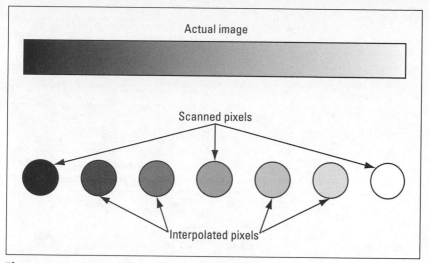

Figure 20-7: Interpolation of smooth intensity or color changes

In Figure 20-8, however, the assumption is a poor one because the real image has sharp edges the interpolator doesn't know about. Because the interpolator's assumption is bad, the "increased resolution" from the scanner does you no good because the calculated data is bogus. Your scanned image doesn't faithfully reproduce the actual image at the enhanced resolution. At the minimum, you'll want to be sure to find out the raw resolution of the scanners you're looking at. If you can't find out, find another scanner.

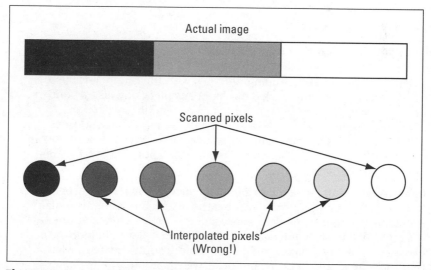

Figure 20-8: Interpolation of sharp edges

Interfaces

Scanners typically interface into your computer through a serial port, parallel port, or USB port (see Table 20-1). Most scanners now use USB, which is fast, reliable, and convenient.

Table 20-1
Typical Speeds of Scanner Interfaces

Interface	Typical Interface Speed	Minimum Transfer Time for 25MB Scan (Seconds)
Serial	115,200 Kbps	1,422.22
Parallel	2 Mbps	81.92
USB 1.1 (low speed)	1.5 Mbps	109.23
USB 1.1 (full speed)	12 Mbps	13.65
USB 2.0 (high speed)	480 Mbps	0.34

Page scan times in the 15- to 30-second range are common, with the time being primarily determined by the rate the sensor traverses the image. For a 25MB image, you'll want a full speed USB 1.1 or high speed USB 2.0 interface because anything else is going to be ridiculously slow. We prefer USB scanners because they are easier to set up and less prone to configuration problems than ones using serial or parallel ports. For most people, USB is the ideal scanner interface.

Software

You need two kinds of software to use a scanner:

✦ **Driver** — A device driver communicates with the scanner, issuing commands and reading back data. Most scanners now use a control interface called TWAIN, which serves as a standard way for any image-processing program to acquire data from an image source. TWAIN decouples specific knowledge of how to drive the scanner out of the image-processing software, making the application programs device independent.

✦ **Image processing** — Beyond the device driver, you need a program to (at least) initiate the scan, receive the image, and store it to disk. Programs like that come with every scanner we've seen, and are now built into Windows. If you want to do anything other than look at (and possibly print) the image, you'll need a more sophisticated program that can adjust colors, crop, and otherwise manipulate the image.

In addition, you may want software that can convert scanned text images to text. That conversion process, called *optical character recognition (OCR)*, matches pieces of the image with guidelines for what each character looks like, and outputs a "typed" document. The good OCR programs (such as those from Caere) are not only accurate, they can help you deal with pages that have combinations of text and graphics, can accommodate text wrapped in columns throughout the page, and can output the page in your word processor's format with the necessary control codes included to make the text look like what you scanned.

All-in-One Units: Combining Printing, Fax, and Copying

In a way, scanners, printers, fax machines, and copiers are all different ways to shuffle the same set of components. If you have an imaging device, a modem, and a printer, you can do all four functions.

If you buy all four devices separately, you've duplicated hardware and cost — you've bought three scanners and three printers. You can attach a scanner, modem, and printer separately to your computer and use software to get all four functions. This works, and is a good solution for many situations. But it requires you to be involved in copy and fax functions, for the most part, involvement that can interrupt what you're doing.

Instead of doing a lot of busy work, you have the option of choosing a combination piece of hardware, one that includes all these components. We'll call these products all-in-one machines for lack of a better term. (Some companies call them multifunction devices, for example — the terminology isn't much better, is it?) All-in-one machines are basically fax machines (which is the most complex function) that you can access as components from your computer when you need to, and can leave running independently as a fax and copier.

The advantage of an all-in-one machine is that you can leave it running unattended for fax and copier applications, even if your computer is turned off. Incoming faxes don't interrupt what you're doing with your computer (but are accessible from the computer for printing, OCR, and retransmission). You won't want to do heavy-duty copying with one, but it's sufficient for small jobs. Memory in the device buffers between faxes and printing, so no matter what goes on, you don't have to wait to get control back at your computer, and a print job won't cause you to lose an incoming fax.

The biggest problem with all-in-one machines is resolution and performance — neither the scanner nor the printer offers the image quality or speed you can get in more expensive separate units. If you can live with that limitation, though, one of these can save you money. If you send and receive faxes often, you might want to consider a standalone fax machine (instead of an all-in-one machine) along with one or more fax modems. The printer in an all-in-one machine may be too slow to really be of value other than, perhaps, as a color supplement to a network laser printer. The scanners in all-in-one machines are too low-resolution for publication work — they're good enough for OCR and presentations, but not for quality publication. The addition of one or two fax modems into the configuration allows you to do computer-based fax transmission and reception when you really need to do that, while the standalone fax machine allows you to be independent of the computers for all fax services.

Laser-printer-based all-in-one machines are available too, such as the Canon MultiPASS 730 and the HP LaserJet 3300mfp. You'll get better print and scan quality from the laser units in return for a slightly higher price and monochrome-only operation.

Summary

✦ Nearly all printing requirements can be met with ink jet or laser printers, which are most of the units sold.

✦ Printer drivers and software are at least as important as the printer itself.

✦ Interpolated scanner resolution isn't the same as raw optical resolution — don't get fooled by inflated specifications.

✦ In some situations, an all-in-one machine can save you several hundred dollars in duplicated equipment.

Integration

◆   ◆   ◆   ◆

In This Part

Chapter 21
Cases, Cooling,
and Power

Chapter 22
Laptops and
Handheld Computers

Chapter 23
You're Going to Put
That Where?

Chapter 24
Diagnosis and Repair

Chapter 25
Building an Extreme
Machine

◆   ◆   ◆   ◆

Cases, Cooling, and Power

✦   ✦   ✦   ✦

In This Chapter

Understanding the
mechanical structure
of a PC

Choosing a case type

Managing heat and
airflow

Protecting your data
with uninterruptible
power supplies

✦   ✦   ✦   ✦

The case and the power supply for a computer —
as basic as they might seem — are crucial parts
of the system. The case and power supply might not
be as flashy a topic as some of the others we cover,
but they're vitally important. Poor choices of case and
power supply can shorten the life of other components,
make a system unreliable, and make upgrades expensive
or impossible. Good choices can improve the usability of
the system, simplify maintenance, and make the system
easier to live with.

Cases, Fans, and Cooling

Your computer case has to do a surprising number of
things:

- ✦ Provide mechanical support and protection
  for the components

- ✦ Shield the computer (and your TV) from
  electromagnetic interference (EMI)

- ✦ Display and control basic system functions
  such as power on and reset

- ✦ Give you access to components for maintenance and repair

- ✦ Keep everything cool

- ✦ Sustain noise levels low enough to tolerate

The case houses the power supply, motherboard,
adapter cards, disk drives, and internal cables. The
mechanical relationships among the case, motherboard,
and cards are shown in Figure 21-1. The critical features
are that the case and mounts support the motherboard

in enough points to prevent flexing, that the motherboard be properly grounded, and that the adapter cards be properly supported and aligned with the connectors on the motherboard.

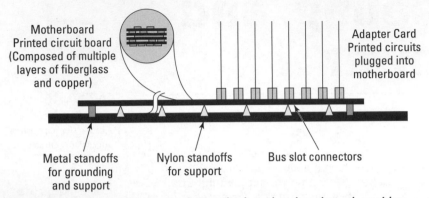

Motherboard Printed circuit board (Composed of multiple layers of fiberglass and copper)

Adapter Card Printed circuits plugged into motherboard

Metal standoffs for grounding and support

Nylon standoffs for support

Bus slot connectors

Figure 21-1: The case supports the motherboard and cards, and provides grounding and shielding for the motherboard.

✦ **Printed circuit board** — The motherboard and adapter cards are each composed of a sandwich of layers of fiberglass epoxy and copper conductors. Leads on some components are soldered directly to pads on the outer surface. Holes drilled through the board allow other components and connectors to be soldered. Microscopic cracks from flexing the board can break the conductors or soldered joints, causing a failure. That's why it's important that the case support the motherboard and why you have to be careful how you push or pull on printed circuit cards.

✦ **Metal and nylon standoffs** — At least two metal standoffs (see Figure 21-2) support the motherboard and provide grounding between the motherboard and the case. The case ground helps quiet noise in the system, making signal transmission more reliable.

Caution It's important to have enough standoffs that all parts of the motherboard are well supported because positive support for the motherboard (particularly around the connectors for the adapter cards and the keyboard) is crucial. Flexing the motherboard or wrenching an adapter connector can create nearly invisible cracks in the printed wiring or the soldered connections that cause the system to operate erratically or to fail altogether. The forces on the connectors when you insert a card are in the tens of pounds, which can easily destroy an improperly supported board.

✦ **Connectors** — Bus slot connectors for the adapter cards are soldered to the motherboard. Each connector contains many small metal fingers that wipe along matching metal pads on the card. Keeping the cards vertical — lined up perpendicular to the motherboard — when you insert and remove them is important to keep the contacts secure and to prevent stressing the connector's attachment to the motherboard.

Standoffs

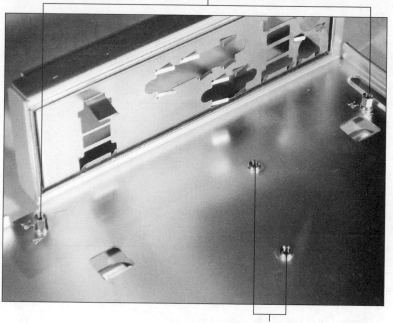

Threaded holes

Figure 21-2: Motherboard standoffs
©2004 Barry Press & Marcia Press

Tip

The connectors have to line up mechanically with the cutouts on the back of the case. The easy way to mount a motherboard so the connectors line up with the chassis is to put all the mounting screws into the motherboard loosely, then put in one or two adapter cards. Screw the adapter cards firmly to the case, which will set the motherboard into the correct alignment, then tighten the motherboard screws.

Drives come in 5.25-inch and 3.5-inch sizes (the numbers originally described the size of the media floppy drives of that size used). The 5.25-inch drives are 5.875 inches wide by 1.625 inches high, while the 3.5-inch drives are 4 inches wide by 1 inch high. The case usually provides spaces (called *bays*) for drives of both 5.25-inch and 3.5-inch sizes. Hard and floppy drives fit the 3.5-inch bays, while most other drives use the 5.25-inch size.

Figure 21-3 highlights the parts of a computer case. Your computer case will provide some bays that open to the front of the computer — called external bays — and others — internal bays — that are accessible only from the inside of the case. The external bays are most often for 5.25-inch drives (providing a 6-inch wide opening), holding CD-ROMs, DVDs, removable disks, tapes, and any other devices that use removable media. External 3.25-inch bays (a 4-inch wide opening) are for floppy drives and other smaller devices. You can use external bays for hard disks, too — just put a cover plate over the hole in the case — but you cannot convert an internal bay into an external one without cutting metal or plastic. Internal bays are most often for hard disks.

Power supply

Processor (under fan)   5.25-inch external drive bays

I/O   Memory   DVD writer

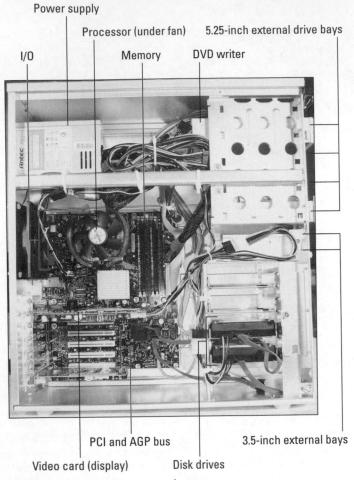

PCI and AGP bus   3.5-inch external bays

Video card (display)   Disk drives

Figure 21-3: Computer case elements

Desktop PC cases come in a range of sizes, from small ones with limited expansion capability to floor-standing monsters able to hold multiple systems. It's important to think through the expansion you might want to do before you buy a new case or new complete system because it's going to require drastic measures if you want to exceed the space or cooling available in the case. The size of the case also affects how hard the system is to work inside because small cases are almost always cramped and hard to work with and tend to force haphazard cable layouts that themselves complicate access and service. Large cases are much easier to work with, have more expansion capability, and have better airflow to aid cooling, but aren't as easy to fit into your office, home, or home theater.

Airflow and heat buildup

Airflow cools nearly every desktop computer sold today and is created by fans in the case itself and in the power supply. How much air pressure the fans create and how much air resistance the components and the shape of the case create determines how effective the cooling will be. Very small cases with limited airflow may be incapable of cooling faster processors, video cards, and disks that generate a lot of heat.

We measured the power consumption and temperature rise in three different systems to see how effective their fans and cases were at removing heat. Table 21-1 shows the results of those measurements. System A was a full-size tower, System B a mini-tower, and System C a full-size tower with auxiliary fans to improve airflow. System D is the PC you'll see how to build in Chapter 25. Degrees per watt (the right-hand column in the table) is the measure of how well a case cools the electronics inside, measuring how much the exhaust air temperature of the case will climb over the inlet temperature per watt of power dissipated inside the case.

Table 21-1
Cooling Performance Comparison (In Degrees Centigrade)

System	Inlet	Exhaust	Rise	Average Power Consumption (W)	Degrees per Watt
A	20.0	33.1	13.1	96.0	0.1366
B	21.9	30.7	8.8	46.8	0.1887
C	20.0	21.9	1.9	68.4	0.0276
D	18.6	30.8	12.2	149.4	0.0818

Systems A and D consume the most power and therefore generate the most heat. The airflow from the power supply fans is the only cooling Systems A and B have, while Systems C and D both have an auxiliary exhaust fan in addition to the power supply fan; System D controls the fan speeds based on measured temperatures. The temperature rise from the System C or D inlet to exhaust is less per watt than in Systems A and B because the cases are larger, with fewer restrictions on airflow, and because the auxiliary fan helps move more air.

Cooling

All PC processors should have cooling fans on the chip. A processor cooling fan assembly includes both a heat sink and a fan, as shown in Figure 21-4. The processor cooling fan gets power from either the motherboard or from a tap on a disk drive power connector. Heat created by the operation of the chip flows from the chip to the surrounding chip package. The *heat sink* (a finned structure clipped into close contact with the chip package) conducts heat from the chip package, removing heat from the chip and keeping it cooler. Cool air driven past the heat sink by the fan takes heat off the heat sink into the surrounding air. The fins on the heat sink increase the contact between the air and the heat sink, improving the rate of heat transfer. If the fan stops, however, little or no air moves, and the rate of heat transfer slows greatly. The chip will get hotter until its maximum ratings are exceeded. At that point it will fail, possibly permanently.

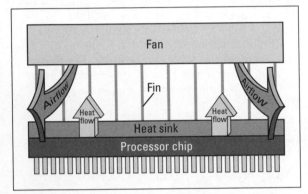

Figure 21-4: The fan drives air past the fins on the heat sink, cooling the fins and heating the air.

Checking Your Processor Fan Installation

Here's how to find out if your processor cooling fan is working right, and if it's mounted on the chip properly. (Be careful about discharging static electricity; see Chapter 1 for the right techniques.)

1. Turn off the computer, open it up, and unplug the processor fan.

2. Power up the machine and keep a finger on the fan's heat sink. If the chip and heat sink are in good contact, the heat sink will get very hot.

3. Quickly shut down the machine, reconnect the fan power, and start up again. Let the chip temperature stabilize by waiting a few minutes, and check the heat sink temperature with your finger again; you'll see that it's a lot cooler.

Don't leave the power on with the fan unplugged for more than a minute or so, or you'll cook the chip. Also, this test may not work with every motherboard, because some boards detect low RPMs from the processor fan and refuse to boot in that case.

Figure 21-5 is a close-up of the processor cooling heat sink and fan we used in the high performance PC you can see how to build in Chapter 25. It's rated to cool even the 3.2 GHz Pentium 4 processor, and does so without creating a lot of fan noise because of the large copper heat sink. The overall assembly exceeds Intel specifications for maximum heat sink weight, however, so you'll have to take precautions if you intend to ship the computer after assembly.

Figure 21-5: Processor cooling heat sink and fan
©2004 Barry Press & Marcia Press

If you look at the specifications for commercial-grade chips, you'll find that they are commonly rated for a "free-air temperature" of up to 70 degrees Celsius (158 degrees Fahrenheit), far above the exhaust air temperatures in Table 21-1. The limited airflow created by weak fans in most computers lets heat pockets build up in the case, causing the air temperature in the vicinity of the pocket to go well over the maximum ambient rating.

Figure 21-6 shows one way heat pockets come about. A stack of disk drives and other peripherals is common in most computers. Each drive includes both a drive mechanism and a board of electronics, both of which generate heat that gets trapped in the pockets between drives and boards. Stacking drives one on top of another tends to block the airflow, forcing most of the cooling air to flow around the sources of heat. This allows heat pockets to develop in the stack, as shown in the exploded view of the floppy drive and CD-ROM drive on the right of Figure 21-6. If the air temperature in the pockets exceeds maximum ratings, the drives will fail.

The example in Figure 21-6 happens all the time. You can solve the problem by making sure the case you use has a metal cage surrounding the drives that conducts heat away (plastic ones can't do that) and by making sure the sides of the drives have solid, metal-to-metal contact with the cage. If you mount 3.5-inch drives in 5.25-inch bays, make sure the spacer brackets you use are metal and themselves provide a good heat conduction path.

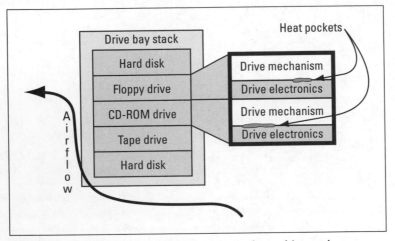

Figure 21-6: Trapped air in the case can overheat chips and cause failures.

Pockets of trapped heat can happen in a group of adapter cards plugged into the motherboard, too. Each card generates heat — graphics cards in particular — and the tight spaces between cards can impede good airflow. Figure 21-7 shows the normal airflow pattern in a tower or mini-tower case — the airflow runs from inlets on the front, past the motherboard and cards, and out through the power supply and vents in the back. A little air comes in from openings at the front of the drive bays and is drawn to the back, but not much unless you explicitly use a drive fan with front inlets. The horizontal positioning of the adapter cards can trap heat too, so the relative position of cards is worth some thought — you should leave gaps between cards to keep hot cards away from each other if possible, and order cards to prevent having two hot cards in adjacent slots.

Open space helps avoid blocked airflow. Bigger fans or more fans move more air through the case, lowering the internal case temperature, which helps to overcome blockages and heat pockets. Badly placed cables can block airflow.

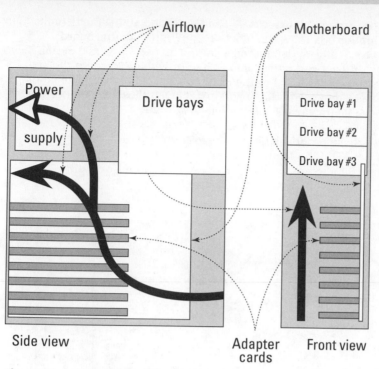

Figure 21-7: Tower case airflow

The ATX form factor

The IBM PC/AT established a motherboard form factor that survived for over a decade. As component technology and system designs evolved, though, problems with that design became more onerous. Four of the more significant problems were as follows:

✦ **Processor positioning** — The processor on an AT motherboard typically sits under the space reserved for some of the adapter cards. Processor cooling fans would intrude into the space for the cards, preventing full-length cards from being used in those slots.

✦ **Lack of low voltage power** — The chips used when the AT motherboard was designed all used 5 V power, and the AT power supplies were specified for that interface. The small line widths now in processors and other chips require 3.3 V, 2.0 V, or less, because they can't withstand the higher voltages without conversion.

✦ **High voltage switching within the computer case** — The PC/AT was a desktop unit that positioned the power switch inside the power supply, but on the side of the case at the back. That's inconvenient for tower cases, which led designers to move the high voltage power switch to the front of the case. The presence of high voltage within the case can be a hazard.

✦ **I/O port cabling requirements** — The PC/AT had no I/O ports built onto the motherboard. As the functions built onto motherboards expanded to include serial, parallel, sound, mouse, Universal Serial Bus (USB), and network ports, cables had to be built to route the signals from the motherboard to the front or back of the case. The labor involved has led to the building and installing of those cables becoming a noticeable fraction of the system cost.

The need to solve these problems in the AT motherboard form factor led to the definition of the ATX form factor incompatible with the older AT layout. The most apparent characteristic of an ATX case is the input/output (I/O) panel at the top of the motherboard (see Figure 21-8).

Figure 21-8: The ATX form factor simplifies internal cabling and improves component layout.
©2004 Barry Press & Marcia Press

The ATX form factor improved PC designs in several ways:

✦ **Processor positioning** — The processor in an ATX case is behind the I/O panel, out of line from the adapter cards. That repositioning provides clearance for fans above the processors. The memory sockets have been relocated near the processor to simplify motherboard design.

✦ **Lack of 3.3 V power** — Initially, the power connector on an ATX motherboard included 3.3 V along with the usual ±5 V and ±12 V supplies. As processor power requirements increased, the interface expanded to include an auxiliary 3.3 V connector to provide additional power. Current generation processors require more current than can reasonably be sourced directly from the power supply — the 3.2 GHz Pentium 4 Processor Extreme Edition can consume 71.5 A at 1.475 to 1.55 volts — and therefore use the modified ATX12V power supply specification, which adds a third motherboard connector supplying 12 V to be stepped down on the motherboard.

✦ **High voltage switching within the computer case** — The power supply in an ATX system is more like an instant-on television than older computer designs. The power connector to an ATX motherboard also includes a low-voltage signal that gets routed to a power on/off button on the front of the case. That signal tells the power supply to turn the main supply lines on or off. As long as power is connected, though, the motherboard receives a limited 5 V supply to keep standby functions running.

Caution Standby power makes it even more important to disconnect an ATX supply from wall power whenever you're working inside the case.

✦ **I/O port cabling requirements** — The I/O port connectors are built onto the ATX motherboard, terminating in a panel at the back. A standard layout for the panel exists, ensuring cutouts in the case will be in the right place.

Demand has lead to designs for smaller desktop PCs. The NLX form factor, available in the late 1990s, made small boxes possible, but never caught on. Later designs from Shuttle and Soltek have been well received, but used motherboards and cases built to a proprietary form factor. The Intel BTX specification includes a profile for a relatively small PC, but it's as yet unclear if it will supplant ATX and microATX.

Choosing a case

Although laptops and very small form factors leave few choices but proprietary designs, keep in mind that, despite all the competition in the PC industry, needlessly proprietary designs remain a favorite tactic of companies hoping to lock you in for expensive upgrades once you've bought their product.

 Tip Lots of companies use this tactic — a who's who of the PC industry is full of the guilty. You can rely on paying more if you get caught by one of these, and on being at the mercy of the manufacturer when they decide to stop supporting that model. You may not find out about proprietary models until it's too late, unless you ask about compliance with industry-standard form factors, interfaces, and software standards before you buy. Be sure to ask not only about memory and disk, but also about the motherboard and power supply.

You've been warned.

If you buy a complete computer from a manufacturer, your choices in cases are likely to be whether you want a tower, mini-tower, or desktop, or want it in blue. You might have an option for auxiliary fans available. If you integrate your own machine, you're in the market for a case and have a wide range of options. Things that make for a great case include:

✦ **Gobs of room inside** — We're far more interested in a machine that's easy to work on, reliable, and upgradable than in its being tiny. Your needs may well favor small size, but you'll pay the price in compromises. Having 10 external drive bays fits our definition of upgradability, for example, but having just one does not.

✦ **Airflow to keep the electronics very cool** — We like having lots of fans. Motherboards finally have working technology to control fan speed, meaning you don't have to choose between cooling and noise.

✦ **Attention to detail** — For example, you should look for heavy sheet metal that provides good support, simple case opening mechanisms that give you access to everything inside, and a lack of sharp edges that could cut you and internal cables.

Cases have evolved considerably from the plain beige or black boxes you're used to. We show you how to build a very quiet, very high performance PC in Chapter 25, but if your tastes run more to the visually extreme, the products are available to open windows to the inside of your PC, paint or carve designs into the case, and light it to show off your work.

Power Supplies

The power supply converts power coming into your computer from the wall outlet to the forms usable by the electronics in the system. It changes incoming alternating current (AC) at 120 or 240 volts to direct current (DC) at 3.3, ±5 and ±12 V. A good power supply does more than power conversion — it cleans up the spikes, surges, and sags in the utility power. Motors, copiers, appliances, and other electrical devices create noise in the power at your wall outlet, as do lightning strikes and other effects farther away. If that noise gets through the power supply into the electronics in the computer, it causes trouble ranging from erratic operation to complete shutdown. A high-quality power supply will be more resistant to these problems, giving you more reliable operation from your computer.

You need to know four electrical terms to understand and compare power supplies — voltage, current, power, and frequency.

✦ **Voltage** is the force pushing electricity through the wire. It's like the water pressure in your garden hose: More voltage is like more water pressure. Voltage is measured in volts (abbreviated V). In North America, common wall-outlet power is at 120 V. European power is commonly 240 V.

✦ **Current** is the amount of electricity flowing through the wire and is like the flow of water through a hose. Current is measured in amperes (or amps, abbreviated A).

✦ **Power** is the product of voltage and current (voltage times current), and is measured in watts (abbreviated W). If your computer draws 3 amps at 120 V, it uses 360 W.

✦ **Frequency** is the rate at which the power alternates between positive and negative voltages. Frequency is measured in Hertz (abbreviated Hz); a Hertz is one cycle per second. North American power arrives at 60 Hz; European power is mostly 50 Hz.

Selecting good power supplies

A good power supply is easy to describe but very hard to design. It must be reliable, and must deliver clean, stable power. The circuits in your computer are terribly sensitive to variations in supply voltage, so the power supply has to keep the voltage stable, filtering out the ripples in the incoming AC power and compensating for load variations from the computer circuits. Good power supplies have a wide tolerance for both fast input power variations and for ones over several seconds. By specification, ATX12V supplies must keep all voltages but the –12 V supply within 5 percent of nominal, and must keep the –12 V supply within 10 percent. Some high-quality supplies can maintain their outputs within 1 percent.

Tip

You do have a choice in how much power the supply can give the computer. Computers with faster processors, more memory, and more drives draw more power than smaller ones. You want to leave margin for adding new hardware in the future, too, want to run the power supply at about 50 percent total load, and have to be careful not to exceed the maximum rating on any individual output (including the standby power outputs). In addition to extending power supply life (by letting it run cooler), running below maximum capacity helps extend the power supply's hold-up time during short AC power dropouts. We commonly use power supplies of about 400 W capacity for high-performance desktop computers, such as the 380 W unit we use in Chapter 25. There's no loss in using a larger supply because the computer draws only what it needs — the power supply rating is the maximum, not a constant figure.

Uninterruptible power supplies

The best power supply won't help much when the AC supply goes out. Admittedly, when you're sitting there in the dark, the work you were doing might not be your first concern, but it's likely to be something you worry about later. Nor is a widespread power failure the only threat. We've seen computers taken out by plugging a vacuum cleaner or coffee pot into the same circuit.

You don't have to put up with losing your work. Once found only in major computer installations or alongside mission-critical systems, an *uninterruptible power supply (UPS)* is now an inexpensive addition that can easily pay for itself by saving hours of work.

A UPS consists of a power supply, a battery, and a reverse power supply. Figure 21-9 shows how this works. The incoming power supply — similar to what's in your computer — creates the DC the battery needs whenever utility AC power is available. The outgoing power supply does the same thing in reverse: It converts battery DC to AC that your computer's power supply can use. The source of the DC power the outgoing supply receives is the incoming AC supply (if it's operating) or the battery. Either way, the AC output is stable, with no interruption in output power as the input AC comes and goes.

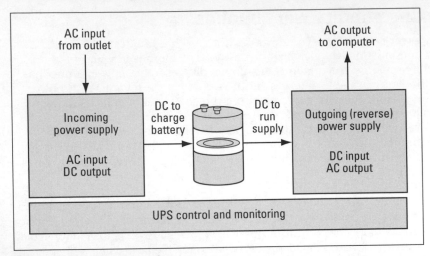

Figure 21-9: UPS schematic

The need to both charge the battery and run the output supply increases the load on the input supply, so it needs to be larger and more expensive. Commercial UPS technology introduces a switch inside the UPS so the output supply runs only when the input power fails, but also introduces a short gap in the output power during switchover.

> **Tip** The capacity of the output power supply inside the UPS determines how big a computer (and how many other devices) it can support. The size of the batteries in the UPS determines how long it can provide power during an outage. You can't exceed maximum ratings, so don't buy a UPS that's too small and be sure to have extra capacity for expanding your systems. The bigger battery in a larger UPS can hold up over extended outages. Figure 21-10 shows the time/power tradeoff for two UPSs from American Power Conversion (APC).

A UPS can be very inexpensive protection. Units that will keep a small computer running for 15 minutes retail for less than $100. Putting your own computer on a UPS protects your local data. Putting your file server on a UPS protects your organization's data. Putting the LAN equipment (hubs and switches, for example) on a UPS protects your ability to connect from one computer to another. Putting your communications gear (for example, routers and modems) on a UPS protects your ability to interact with the Internet. Think about asking your Internet service provider if all their equipment — servers, modems, routers, everything — is on a UPS. If it's not and you must have reliable access to the Net, get another provider.

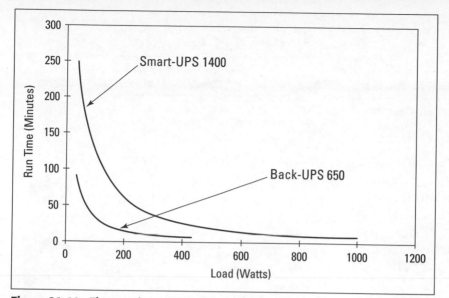

Figure 21-10: The run time a UPS gives you after a power failure depends on the size of the UPS battery and the load the computer puts on the UPS.

External Connectors

It can be traumatic to connect or disconnect all the cables at the back of your PC if you're not familiar with what each one is for and to what it connects. Typical PC connectors have three important properties — type, gender, and number of pins — that let you distinguish one from another.

✦ **Type** is the kind of connector. The ones used for serial, parallel, and video monitor ports are called D subminiature connectors. The one for the keyboard is called a DIN connector and comes in two sizes (regular and mini-DIN).

✦ **Gender** specifies whether the connector has sockets or pins. Serial ports are male D subminiature connectors; parallel ports are female.

✦ **Number of pins** is simply how many connections there are in the connector. Serial ports have 9 or 25 pins. Parallel ports have 25.

Table 21-2 shows the characteristics of some of the more common connectors you'll encounter.

Table 21-2
Common External PC Connectors

Connector Purpose	Type	Gender	Number of Pins	Picture
10Base-2 Ethernet	BNC	Female	1	
10/100/1000Base-T Ethernet	RJ-45	Female	8	
Baseband or composite video	RCA	Female	1	
DVI monitor	DVI	Female	28	
Game	D subminiature	Female	15 (2 rows)	
Keyboard	Mini-DIN	Female	9	
Mouse	Mini-DIN	Female	9	
Parallel communications (LPT1:)	D subminiature	Female	25	
Phone (modem)	RJ-11	Female	4	
Radio frequency (RF) video	F	Female	1	

Connector Purpose	Type	Gender	Number of Pins	Picture
Serial communications (COMx:)	D subminiature	Male	9	
Sound	Mini headphone or RCA	Female	1	
USB	USB	Female	4	
VGA monitor	D subminiature	Female	15 (3 rows)	
S-Video	Mini-DIN	Female	7	

Photos in Table 21-2 ©2004 Barry Press & Marcia Press

It's easiest to apply Table 21-2 as you disconnect wires, but if you have an unknown connector, the table is a starting point. The connectors in the table are the ones at the computer — the ones at the other end of the cable might be very different. For example, the connector at the printer end of a parallel printer cable looks more like an old-style SCSI connector (they're both Centronics-type connectors; the printer connector has fewer pins). Here's a little more information if some of those connectors seem unfamiliar:

✦ **D subminiature** connectors are most common for cables to external modems, but you'll see them for printer ports, game controller ports, monitor video ports, and Ethernet ports, too. They typically have two or three rows of pins. They always have an odd number of pins so that the connector outline is a trapezoid and fits only one way.

✦ **DIN** connectors are the round ones you typically find on keyboards and some mice. DIN stands for *Deutsches Institut für Normung*, which in English is the German Institute for Standardization. DIN connectors come in two basic sizes: the normal size you find on older AT keyboards and the small (mini-DIN) size you find on PS/2 keyboards and mice now universal on ATX-style motherboards. Little plugs in the connector and the pin layout limit the connector orientation to the correct position. Don't force it.

✦ **RCA** connectors are the unthreaded kind you typically find on the back of your stereo, television, and VCR. Female RCA connectors are about ¼ inch in diameter, with a relatively large hole in the middle.

✦ **Mini headphone** connectors are the small round connectors found on headphones and on boom boxes and other audio equipment (for connecting the headphones). Typical mini headphone connectors have two or three wires connected through the one pin — if you look closely, you'll see rings of metal on the pin separated by thin rings of insulation.

✦ **RJ-11** and **RJ-45** connectors are the small modular telephone jacks found all over North America since the old boxy four-pin connectors went away.

✦ **F** connectors are the threaded connectors used with coaxial cable for televisions.

✦ **Centronics** connectors are the ones found on printer parallel port connections.

Summary

✦ A well-designed case improves the maintainability, upgradability, reliability, and serviceability of your computer.

✦ Heat is the worst enemy your computer has. Excessive heat reduces the life of every component in the machine.

✦ Extra capacity in the power supply is inexpensive, creates reserve for expansion, and helps the supply run cooler.

✦ An uninterruptible power supply can save you hours of work when the power goes out.

✦ Knowing what each type of connector on your PC is for helps you identify the components you're working with and helps you connect cables to the back of the system.

Laptops and Handheld Computers

✦   ✦   ✦   ✦

In This Chapter

Choosing mobility
requires compromise

Examining laptop
technology and
components

Examining batteries

✦   ✦   ✦   ✦

Laptops — and now tablet PCs — are a breed apart. The added constraints of minimum size and extended battery operation change the design decisions engineers make for mobile PCs, and raise the cost. The convenience of using the same computer for both desktop and portable situations may save you some time, but it may not save money, and indeed may not save time. The problem is that when you're traveling, you typically want very different capabilities from those you prefer in your home or office.

Table 22-1 shows the problem — weight and size matter most in a laptop. The farther you carry your laptop, the more its weight approaches 20 tons. It's reasonable to make compromises in your laptop's features and performance to get the size and weight down because most people don't do things with a laptop that are as complex as they might do with a desktop computer, and they don't do as many things at once.

Because your laptop's portability is paramount, the compromises you're likely to make may limit its suitability as a desktop machine — it may be short on memory or disk, have a limited display, and may have a lesser processor than you might want.

What's in Your Laptop?

Like any other personal computer, a laptop or tablet PC has the usual processor, disk, memory, display, and communications. Some tablets now even have a keyboard, as do all laptops. Where these systems differ from desktop machines is in the specifications for these components to cope with limited size, weight, and power. Reducing the power requirement is not only a way to extend battery life, but also a way to limit the heat generated inside the laptop case. This is a vital need because protecting the computer from shock and damage requires that the electronics be tightly enclosed, which limits how much heat can be dissipated.

Table 22-1
Size and Weight Count for Mobile Devices

Requirement	Traveling	Desktop
Connectivity	Wireless on the go; modem or Ethernet in the hotel.	Ethernet or modem if you don't have broadband.
Interruptions	You're relatively isolated, so you are interrupted less often (takeoffs and landings notwithstanding).	You're a sitting duck.
Power	You'll carry it with you, so in addition to needing enough batteries to keep running on transcontinental or transoceanic flights, all those batteries are weight you have to carry.	It comes from the wall.
Security	Protection not only against network intrusion, viruses, worms, Trojans, and spam, but against theft (data and system loss are both concerns).	Network intrusion, viruses, worms, Trojans, and spam.
Weight and size	Every ounce and cubic inch matters after you've carried your laptop from one end of the Delta Airlines terminal in the Dallas-Fort Worth airport to the other.	Size may matter, but only in terms of fitting in your office (not your briefcase or pack). Weight is less of a concern.
Workload	Notes, electronic mail, small proposals, calendars, entertainment, communications.	Reports, electronic mail, major proposals, calendars, entertainment, communications.

Processor, memory, and bus

It's difficult to blow air through a laptop to cool it, which further limits heat dissipation. The limited cooling capability restricts how much heat any one device in a laptop can generate, because if the rate at which heat builds up exceeds how fast it dissipates, the device temperature will increase until the laptop fails. Because the heat a processor generates is directly proportional to its clock speed, designers commonly limit processor speed to control heat generated in the chip.

Evolution of the Laptop PC

Laptop PCs — notebooks — have changed substantially since the first clumsy systems. Initial offerings were slow, with tiny screens and floppy disk drives. Later systems added hard drives and bigger screens, but were large, heavy, and slow. More recently very thin, very lightweight notebooks were popular because they're easier to travel with than more fully featured but larger and heavier units.

Relentless increases in capability — well beyond what's required for a portable secondary PC — opened up the possibility of using a laptop as your primary computer. Manufacturers have supported that idea for many years with docking stations that let you park the PC at your desk and hook into a keyboard, monitor, and the LAN, but it's only in the past few years the machines had enough power to make that realistic for all but the most forgiving users.

Reduction in size of the communications chipset has also led to laptops with IEEE 802.11 networking integrated into the machine, with no external card or antenna. Notebooks with integrated networking are literally useful while you walk around, an application once the exclusive domain of *Personal Digital Assistants (PDAs)*.

The combination of thin, lightweight notebooks and embedded communications led designers to create tablet PCs, which were initially the electronic equivalent of a pad of paper. You write and draw on the display surface; your input is either captured directly or interpreted and converted to text. Electronically, tablet PCs were initially laptops with a touch-sensitive screen and no keyboard.

PDAs using the Palm operating system owned virtually the entire handheld computer market. Like first generation tablet PCs, the Palm handhelds had no keyboard, using the "Graffiti" writing system to let users write directly on the display surface with a stylus. Windows PCs have had software support for handwritten input for many years, but it's been clumsy and not terribly useful.

The failings of handwritten input drove both PDAs and tablet PCs to add keyboards. The Research in Motion Blackberry PDAs have had a keyboard from the beginning; Palm PDAs added them as third-party and later first-party accessories. Tablet PCs added fold-away keyboards in later models. The most recent models show the future of notebook PCs may be versions of tablets with keyboards. Many notebooks now have displays that pivot axially, allowing the display to fold down on the back of the keyboard. Users of such machines can use them as writable tablets in that mode or can unfold the keyboard and use them as conventional notebooks.

Nevertheless, the reduced power consumption made possible by advances in chip-manufacturing technology means that current generation laptop and tablet processors, running at full speed, clock at over a gigahertz, with the fastest ones clocking over 3 gigahertz and including the same hyperthreading technology found in the fastest desktops. Power management typically steps down the clock rate when the added speed isn't necessary to reduce heat dissipation.

Intel targets two specific technologies at the mobile PC market:

✦ **Pentium M** — A processor family distinct from the Celeron and Pentium 4 (which you'll also find in laptops and tablets), the Pentium M specifically targets low power consumption instead of maximum performance to give much longer battery life.

✦ **Centrino** — Intel markets a combination of the Pentium M processor and an IEEE 802.11b wireless adapter internal to the notebook or tablet as the Centrino product. (IEEE 802.11g will be added to the product line.) The advantage Centrino brings, beyond lower power consumption and wireless access, is good integration of the hardware and software, making it simple to make the system connect in almost any situation.

AMD has similar products but emphasizes performance in its mobile line with versions of its 64-bit Athlon processor.

The memory and buses in laptop computers are typically somewhat different from those in desktop machines; the highly constrained space in a laptop doesn't leave room for conventional packaging. Most common now is for the electrical interfaces to be standard, such as use of the PCI bus, but the physical form to be smaller than the desktop version of the standard. The resulting designs often don't conform to any widespread industry standard, so production volumes and sources of supply are less and upgrades are more expensive. If you're willing to pay the price in size, weight, power consumption, and cost, however, you can get desktop-equivalent performance. For example, you can get more memory than you'll need for virtually anything you would do — laptops that can handle up to 2GB of memory are available.

PC Card and PC CardBus

The exception to proprietary components in laptop computers is a standard created specifically to allow modules to plug into laptops — the PC CardBus and PC Cards. This standard was formerly known as *PCMCIA (Personal Computer Memory Card International Association)*. As is noted in Chapter 5, PC Cards support read/write and read-only memory, hard disk drives, modems, wired and wireless network adapters, sound adapters, GPS receivers, and more.

PC CardBus isn't a cure-all. It's limited to 2 Mbps, which is acceptable for all these applications, although it's not what you'd really want for disk or memory. The success of the PC Card is reflected in the variety of devices you can buy. The most popular are communications interfaces and disks. The cards have most of the features you'd expect in full-size units — the most likely reason to compromise is that they're expensive.

Tip

Be careful about cables or connectors for PC Cards. Because the card is thin, the connectors can be fragile. (So can the card — more than one has been destroyed when someone left it in their wallet and sat on it.) Check with the manufacturer before you buy — we've seen situations in which replacement cables were either not available or were so expensive that it was cheaper to buy another card.

Laptop displays

All laptops use *liquid crystal displays (LCDs)*. Plasma panels competed in the market for a while, but the much lower power consumption of LCD doomed plasma. Current generation laptops and tablets use active matrix *Thin Film Transistor (TFT)* panels, backlit by very bright LEDs, which offer lower power consumption than fluorescent lights. Active matrix is bright, sharp, and viewable at almost any angle.

The largest laptop and tablet LCDs are over 15 inches diagonal with 1,280×1,024 resolution available. Video chips include full 3D acceleration, although not as fast as what you'll find in the most powerful desktops.

Disk

Laptop disk drives, like desktop drives, have increased in size. You no longer have to struggle to make all your applications fit — you can get 20 to 80GB drives, along with a DVD writer.

Besides capacity, the two biggest differences between laptop disk drives and desktop disk drives are transfer rates and more aggressive power management. Laptop disks are typically slow compared to desktop drives, and get powered down after a short period of inactivity. The motors in the disks consume a significant amount of power, so this is an important measure. When your laptop wants access to the disk, you'll wait while the disk spins up to operating speed.

You have to make an important trade-off between memory and disk in a laptop computer. If you have too little memory, your computer will go to the disk relatively often for fragments of programs, requiring the disk to keep running (or spin up) to satisfy the request. That activity keeps the disk running, drawing power, and slows down operation. If you have enough memory in the laptop (say, at least 256MB if you'll be running only one program at a time), Windows will use the extra memory as a large cache, reducing disk access and letting the disk stay powered down. Your laptop runs faster and longer on each battery.

Few laptops or tablets include internal floppy disks any more (get a USB floppy drive if you need to use floppies), but nearly all include CD-ROM drives, and many include CD-RW or DVD±RW drives. Optical drives are particularly useful if you take along programs such as DeLorme's Street Atlas with a GPS receiver — we print maps for the destination before flying on business, but with software and a GPS in your laptop, you have a navigator alongside you.

Communications and ports

Laptop computers commonly come with a serial port, parallel port, video port, and docking-station port; far more useful, however, are USB and Ethernet ports. You'll want both a modem and a network interface because communications requirements with your laptop depend on where you are. If you're in your office or a hotel with broadband access, you'll probably want to tie the computer into the *local area network (LAN)* and may need a wireless

IEEE 802.11b connection for that. If you're on the road with only a phone line, you'll want a modem to dial in with.

> **Tip** Be careful with built-in modems. It's more common than you might think to plug a modem into a wall jack in a hotel room, only to find out that the hotel's telephone system is digital (or otherwise incompatible). You can easily burn out the interface circuits in a modem this way. If the entire computer has to go in for repair, you're out of business.
>
> You can have other modem problems traveling, too. We've encountered telephone switches in hotels that wouldn't deliver a dial tone to the laptop modem (although they would to an analog phone) and needed a different cable to connect to the phone jacks in the United Kingdom.

Batteries

Power management evolved in laptops to extend their battery life. The technology transferred into desktop machines only when people noticed that reducing the power consumption of hundreds of millions of desktop computers could significantly reduce worldwide power consumption.

Beyond power management (and low power consumption), the key power issue for laptop computers is the battery. Tremendous progress has been made in battery technology to power camcorders, laptops, and other portable electronics, resulting in several competing battery technologies:

✦ **Nickel-cadmium** — Nickel-cadmium (NiCad) batteries are being phased out because of memory problems — the batteries "remember" when they're only partially discharged and don't recharge to full capacity. Recharging a nickel-cadmium battery that's not fully discharged can keep the battery from ever being fully charged again unless you go through a special discharge/recharge cycle.

✦ **Nickel–metal hydride** — Nickel–metal hydride (NiMH) batteries have an advantage over NiCad because they are not subject to the memory effect when being recharged. The newest versions of nickel–metal hydride batteries are claimed to have higher energy-density levels than lithium-ion batteries and at less cost. Nickel–metal hydride batteries have a short shelf life (they discharge in a few days), so be sure to recharge them completely before you go traveling.

✦ **Lithium-ion** — Lithium-ion batteries are a recent development, but are now widely available. You can expect 20 to 30 percent longer performance than with the older versions of nickel–metal hydride (possibly as long as 7 hours' operation) with a good shelf life. A lithium-ion battery provides three times the voltage of a nickel-cadmium battery, which lets designers reduce the number of batteries required. There is no memory effect, and the battery has a life cycle of 1,200 charge/discharge cycles. (Some sources dispute that lifetime estimate, suggesting you'll only get 300–500 cycles.) Lithium-ion batteries don't require environmentally polluting material (such as cadmium, mercury, or PVC).

✦ **Zinc-air** — Rechargeable zinc-air batteries can last up to 15 hours. The battery is large (nearly the size of the laptop itself), heavy, and expensive.

✦ **Lithium-polymer** — Lithium-polymer batteries are still in development. The battery looks like a sheet of plastic about the size of a playing card, and can be wrapped around other components. Projections are that the technology will weigh 75 percent less and run four times longer on a single charge than a nickel-cadmium battery of similar weight. Lithium-polymer batteries can be molded into any shape. The batteries support high-energy densities, do not have memory-drain problems, and use environmentally safe materials. However, lithium-polymer batteries presently have a limited life cycle (about 175 hours) and may not be viable for several years.

Lithium-ion batteries are the technology of choice in laptops today because of their high energy storage for the weight and lack of recharging memory effects. Be careful how you store systems with lithium-ion batteries, though, because the batteries go into thermal runaway above 60 degrees C (140 degrees F) and can burn or explode. (For example, you probably shouldn't leave a laptop, tablet, or cell phone in a car trunk out in the sun.) Whichever battery technology you have in your laptop, be sure to recycle any battery at the end of its useful life. Some battery components are explosive in fires, while others are toxic and difficult to remove from the environment. Check with your local recycling company to find out about safe battery disposal.

If you drive with your laptop a lot, or if you fly a lot and can either upgrade into first class or book it directly, you can use a car/plane adapter from the laptop manufacturer or a third party such as iGo (`www.igo.com`). (Check the front of the seats on the airline you fly for power connectors.) A setup like that enables you to run your laptop indefinitely off car or plane power, regardless of how long your batteries would run by themselves.

Docking Stations

You may find it unacceptable to have two computers (one for travel and one for your desk). For example, if you use your laptop with a wireless network to work while you walk around, having to switch constantly between a laptop and desktop machine is really an inconvenience. If so, you may want to look at what are called docking stations — boxes that sit on your desk and into which you can plug your laptop. The docking station provides additional resources, such as power, a monitor, full-size keyboard, network interface, disk, hard disk, or CD-ROM. The idea is that you don't need those extras while you're mobile, but the docking station makes them available when you're at your desk. The added resources could be enough to let the one computer meet your fixed and mobile requirements while keeping the laptop itself small and light.

Don't assume you'll save money with a docking station. The electrical interface between laptop and docking station is a proprietary connector, and the physical fit of the laptop into the docking station is unique to the specific model. You're likely to have only one source for the docking station, and you pay for the privilege.

Handheld Computers

Not everyone needs a computer of heroic proportion to carry around with them — it may well be you only need something that tracks your address and telephone book, reminds you of appointments, lets you check e-mail, or plays music. If that lesser list covers your needs, a handheld PC — a unit literally about the size of your hand — may be sufficient. In return for limited capability, you get the advantages of a small, lightweight machine (also called a PDA, or personal digital assistant) that runs for tens of hours on small batteries.

A wide range of options in handheld computing exists with greater or lesser compatibility and interoperability with PCs:

✦ **Entertainment** — You can get handheld music (MP3) and video players, storing songs and movies on a compact hard drive. You'll download content from your PC or, for some units, compress directly on the player from a video source.

✦ **E-mail, calendar, and communications** — The stereotypical PDA includes at least a calendar and e-mail client. More useful ones include a wireless data connection and may include a cell phone, too. Ones using the Palm or Blackberry software typically provide Web browsers, but won't run Windows or Linux software, while ones from HP and others run a variety of Windows tailored for the smaller hardware environment. All have some way to interact with the calendar and e-mail software on your PC, and possibly with your Internet service provider (ISP).

✦ **Scaled down laptop equivalents** — Handheld laptops do exist, full PCs sized to fit your hand. You sacrifice a lot in screen size and keyboard usability, and your finger isn't very good as a mouse on the small screen, but you can run any software that fits on the hardware.

With a Web browser and the capabilities available through Web pages, you can get at an enormous range of information including news, stock quotes, and street maps. With e-mail software, you can connect to your Internet service provider and both send and receive messages. A wireless cell phone or IEEE 802.11b interface lets you communicate on the go, while a GPS receiver lets you navigate from stored maps.

> **Note** Devices you plug into the PC Card slot can consume a lot of power, and there's little to be had. The batteries in handheld devices can be drained quickly by power-hungry devices.

Global Positioning System

Some of the most interesting applications of a PC are to navigate and to create maps, survey property, and plot the location of pipes, roads, buildings, and other objects. These applications are made possible by an inexpensive portable receiver for the Global Positioning System (GPS). GPS works by measuring the distance from you to a constellation of satellites, as in Figure 22-1. Your GPS receiver can accurately measure the time it takes for a radio signal to travel from each of the satellites to you (which, as a side benefit, means that a GPS receiver always knows the current time accurately). It uses that time — and an accurate knowledge of the satellite's position — to compute the distance you are from the satellite. After doing those computations for the signals from a number of satellites, it can compute the point that is simultaneously the right distance from all the satellites, and that's where you are.

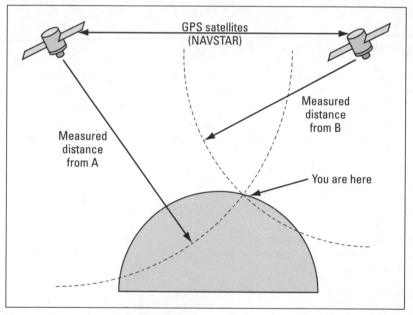

Figure 22-1: GPS calculates the location that puts you at the right distance from all the satellites your receiver can see.

In Figure 22-1, the dashed-line arcs are (in two dimensions) the places at the right distance from each satellite. The point labeled "You Are Here" is the point at the right distance from both satellites. (Actually, there's a point above the top of the figure where the two arcs meet again. Factoring in measurements from more satellites lets your receiver decide which of the two points is your location.)

There are three spread spectrum signals transmitted from every GPS satellite — the C/A code signal (for civilian users), the P code signal (much more accurate, but restricted to military users), and the Y code signal (restricted to military users with the right decryption key). The position error in three dimensions for the C/A code signal can be as great as 93 meters, although it's typically far less. Because mapping and other applications need accuracy better than that, though, people have devised ways to get around the errors introduced into the civilian C/A signal. In North America, the accuracy enhancement approach of choice is the *Wide Area Augmentation System (WAAS)*, which uses a signal from another, geosynchronous satellite to correct errors in the GPS calculations.

A GPS receiver is a good traveling companion for your laptop computer. The DeLorme Earthmate USB receiver is the size of a matchbook and runs off power supplied by the USB port. With the addition of a GPS receiver and GPS-aware street map software, your laptop computer becomes a portable navigation system. If your mapping software lets you record positions, you can create your own maps. A version of the software on a handheld computer makes an ideal walk-around solution.

Communications Security

Your communications options traveling with a mobile computer are far more restricted than in an environment you control, but the security challenges are no less. You're not likely to have a router with network address translation, or a firewall, between you and the Internet, and any wireless networks you join are unlikely to use any form of encryption. If you've shared any drives on your PC, they're exposed to attack on public networks. Worse yet, simple theft of your mobile computer can leave all your data open for exploitation.

You should evaluate the threats you face and your security practices before you travel. The following guidelines can help you build a good set of practices:

✦ **Share nothing** — A mobile PC should have no shared disks or printers. If you need to share data with someone, use a USB flash disk to transfer the data.

✦ **Keep current on patches** — Windows, and to a lesser extent other operating systems, have had many security vulnerabilities that can leave your PC open to compromise. Keeping your mobile PC current with security patches can reduce your exposure.

✦ **Use a software firewall** — Software firewalls, such as ZoneAlarm or the firewall built into Windows XP, can help lock out attacks.

✦ **Don't leave the PC on and connected when not in use** — You're more exposed to attack the longer you stay connected to an insecure network. Shut down your PC or disconnect it from the network when you don't need the connection.

✦ **Password the BIOS and your Windows account** — A password in the BIOS keeps the PC from booting without the password unless the attacker guesses the password or resets the BIOS, something casual thieves may not be able to do. Using the NT File System (NTFS) and passwording your Windows account keeps attackers out of the PC and out of the file system unless they know how to either boot from a CD-ROM and use the NTFSDOS utility, or disassemble the computer and hook the drive to another PC.

✦ **Use secure communications protocols** — Many ISPs offer secure Web pages to let you read your e-mail remotely. Use those services rather than an unencrypted connection through Outlook, Outlook Express, or other e-mail client. Similarly, use only secure protocols to connect into your corporate LAN.

✦ **Encrypt your disk or individual files** — Windows XP provides an encrypted file system capability for that purpose, although you'll need to get a public key certificate to enable it, and must be using NTFS. Strong encryption will keep all but the most sophisticated attackers out, but it will keep you out too if you lose the key.

Upgrades

You need to recognize that there are upgrades you can reasonably do to a laptop, and upgrades you can't. You can add memory, storage, and anything hooked to a PC Card or USB port. You can add batteries (at least as spares you carry, if not in the machine). You're not going to change the processor speed or make the bus faster, and you're not likely to change the display (although we've seen manufacturers offer trade-in programs to improve the overall machine).

Assuming the upgrade you need falls in the doable category, you've got two options. You can upgrade with a PC Card or USB device, which means you can buy in a competitive market with multiple manufacturers, or you can buy specialized devices designed for your specific laptop. The latter are likely to be more expensive with fewer options available, but in the case of internal large disks or CD-ROMs, high-speed memory or internal batteries may be your only choice. They may be your best choice, too, because the software in the laptop will be tailored to know how to adapt to the new devices.

Summary

✦ You'll get fewer features in exchange for the reduced size and weight of a laptop, tablet, or handheld device.

✦ Limited battery power and the limitations of rugged, small packaging constrain how fast your mobile computer can be and how much it can store.

✦ Battery technology will continue to improve.

✦ You should consider both physical and communications security with mobile computing devices.

✦ Upgrades using standard interfaces, such as USB and PC Card, are less expensive and give you more options.

You're Going to Put That Where?

✦   ✦   ✦   ✦

In This Chapter

Examining sensors and alerts

Working with TrackerPod and TrackerCam

Setting up surveillance

Extending your system

✦   ✦   ✦   ✦

Note   What follows is the chapter "Home Surveillance with Internet Remote Access" from our book *PC Toys: 14 Cool Projects for Home, Office, and Entertainment* (Wiley 2003). Prior editions of the *PC Upgrade and Repair Bible* included descriptions of interesting uses people have for PCs, but those applications have become so diverse and interesting that they deserved a book in their own right. Hence, we wrote *PC Toys* and encourage you to give it a look. We reprint this chapter here both to illustrate the diversity of what you can do with a PC and to show you that you can often implement your ideas with products already on the market.

> You don't put kids under surveillance: it might frighten you. — Garrison Keillor, "Easter," *Leaving Home*

Friends of ours built a retirement home some years ago and became concerned about theft and vandalism while they waited in another city to sell their old house and move in. Being the sort to use technology to solve problems, they installed a Black Box VueMate Hub (`catalog.blackbox.com`), to which they connected closed-circuit television cameras. A long-distance call from their PC to the hub gave them access to the cameras, letting them monitor the site whenever they chose.

The unfortunate part of this story is that the VueMate Hub goes for close to $700, plus the cost of cameras. The long-distance phone bills to actually *use* the system seem like chump change in comparison, and despite spending all that money, they could access the cameras only from a PC with the necessary software loaded.

Never Be Out of Reach

As with seemingly everything else, the Internet has revolutionized what you can build for remote surveillance and security. Low-cost video cameras, driven by the market for desktop video conferencing and webcams, have improved to where they generate reasonably high-quality video and provide embedded video compression. Broadband Internet access offers both speed advantages and a permanent connection to the Net, making it suitable for remote monitoring. The global reach of the Internet means that you can monitor your home from Abu Dhabi, if you happen to be there.

One of the things that tends to raise the initial cost of the Black Box unit is its ability to multiplex four separate cameras. This is an important feature because it's impossible to monitor your entire home from just one camera unless that camera is quite a way above the house. You can also increase the coverage you get from each camera with a motion sensor and tracking camera base. You'll see how to set up these features in this project, along with how to integrate your surveillance system with the Internet and access it from any computer with a Web browser.

Sensors and Alerts

Figure 23-1 shows the organization of the overall surveillance system. We used video cameras because they are inexpensive and widely available and also because video cameras are easier to interface to a PC than a still camera. Most video cameras can take still images, too. The system looks simple, consisting of only the camera(s), PC, and broadband modem, but is difficult to implement because of the mismatch between the data rate from the video camera and the uplink rate through the broadband connection. You could see as much as 4 MBps (32 Mbps) from each camera, yet a typical uplink rate is only 128 Kbps. That's roughly a 30:1 differential, which means you're not going to be pumping broadcast-quality video out to the Internet.

You have many options for using the available Internet bandwidth. For example, if you're working with still photos, you can:

✦ Transmit on command

✦ Transmit at set intervals

✦ Transmit at set intervals whenever there's motion

The still photos can be large or small, and can be compressed with lossless or lossy compression — such as JPEG — if you really need to make them small.

Video is much like a rapid succession of still images, so choosing your resolution still matters. The video *frame rate* is similar to the interval between still photos, with *slow scan* video referring to video at only a few frames per second. If you get the frame rate high enough so that *motion compensation* can compactly encode object motion differences between successive frames, video compression technologies — such as MPEG 1, MPEG 2, or MPEG 4 — are useable.

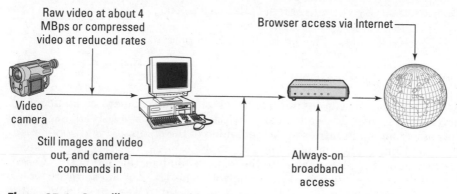

Figure 23-1: Surveillance system block diagram

Building and Using Your Surveillance System from Kits

Our baseline design for the surveillance system solves the bandwidth problem by using compressed still images triggered by motion in the camera field of view, and minimizes the number of cameras needed by following moving objects with the camera. A tracking camera detects movement at a distance, then keeps the moving object in the field of view as it gets closer; the result is that you need fewer cameras to cover the surveillance area.

Parts list

We expected this to be a difficult project when we started to design it, largely because when we had last looked at webcams they did nothing but capture a small video image — no zoom, no tracking base, and no triggering when there's motion. However, our Google search for *pan/tilt camera mount* turned up nearly 18,000 hits. SmartHome was the first hit (www.smarthome.com/7742.html), but at $399.99 for just the camera mount, their equipment was impractical for this project. More refined searching (*pan/tilt camera mount motion tracking*) turned up the TrackerPod robotic camera base and TrackerCam software from Eagletron that, together with a webcam like the Logitech QuickCam Pro 4000, gave us a low-cost system with strong capabilities. The parts we used are shown in Table 23-1.

Table 23-1
Home Surveillance Parts List

Part	Manufacturer and Model Number
Motion Base and Software	Eagletron TrackerPod and TrackerCam Software ($174.99) www.pantiltcam.com/TCamWeb/productdes.htm
Camera	Logitech QuickCam Pro 4000 ($70 and up; see www.shopper.com) www.logitech.com/index.cfm?page=products/ details&CONTENTID=5042

Figure 23-2 is an overview of how the TrackerPod and a camera combine into a surveillance system. The camera and TrackerPod both have USB connections. The camera interface carries audio and video to the computer, and zoom, resolution, and image adjustment commands to the camera. The TrackerPod interface carries position information to the camera and pan, tilt, and LED commands to the servo base. Under control of the TrackerCam software, you can point the camera, record video and stills, upload to Web sites, and monitor or control the camera remotely.

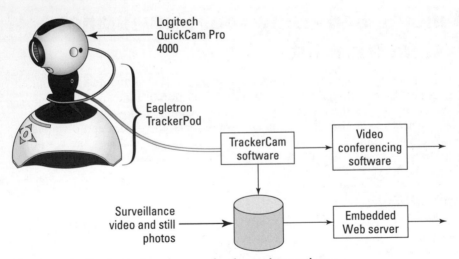

Figure 23-2: TrackerPod, camera, and software integration
Logitech® and QuickCam® are registered trademarks of Logitech.

The Logitech QuickCam Pro 4000 (Figure 23-3) provides surveillance images and sound, offering video resolution up to 640×480 pixels at up to 30 frames per second and still photos at resolutions up to 1,280×960 pixels.

Figure 23-3: Logitech QuickCam Pro 4000
*Logitech® and QuickCam® are registered trademarks
of Logitech.*

Dismount the camera from the base, then use a screw-in mount supplied with the TrackerPod to attach the camera to the motion base, and form the assembly shown in Figure 23-3. Be sure to install the software before connecting the camera and base to the computer because the software installation supplies the necessary USB drives.

Powering the TrackerPod

The TrackerPod requires power from the USB port to drive the motors in the base. The Dell 4550 computer we used couldn't supply as much power to the USB port as our model of the TrackerPod wanted, causing the TrackerPod to constantly reset and the TrackerCam software to lose control. Eagletron has auxiliary power supplies for the early TrackerPods to work around this problem and added current limiters to the motor base circuits in a revised version to reduce the peak draw. The TrackerCam software detects when there's a power problem, giving you this dialog box:

You'll need an auxiliary power supply if your computer can't supply enough power at the USB port.

Click on the first button to bring up a Web page from which you can order the necessary power supply.

Working with the TrackerCam software

Once you install and start the TrackerCam software (you'll have to work through several configuration dialog boxes; the one to go online/offline can be canceled for now) and connect the camera and TrackerPod, you'll see the display on the right of Figure 23-4 labeled Initial TrackerCam window.

Initial TrackerCam window

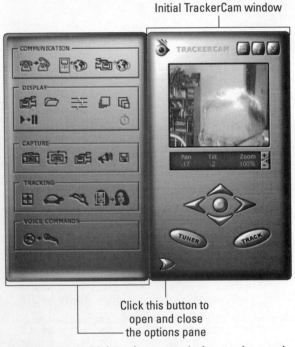

Click this button to
open and close
the options pane

Figure 23-4: Initial TrackerCam window and controls window

Click the button in the lower left to open the options window and use the button next to the right edge of the display pane to make the display window larger (see Figure 23-5).

The window that opens when you click on Tuner in the TrackerCam window (lower left of Figure 23-5) is the interface you use to set up the enormous number of settings for TrackerCam. The defaults are reasonable, for the most part, with the exception of left/right directions. If TrackerCam is set up correctly, clicking on a point in the video window should slew the camera to make that point the center of the image. If the base goes the wrong way, reverse the control direction. Do that by bringing up the tuner (not to be confused with the Configuration Wizard, which is what TrackerCam opens as the tuner when it first starts up and asks if you want the tuner) and then in the Display and Camera section selecting Specify Field of View. On that page, make the existing value for Horizontal FOV negative, and the controls will reverse direction. Click on Enter FOV Values, and then test your work in the video window.

Figure 23-5: Expanded TrackerCam window

Live Internet surveillance

The easiest way to set up surveillance with TrackerCam is to enable the embedded Web server and access live video with a Web browser. Figure 23-6 shows what TrackerCam video looks like in a browser. The video display updates at the rate shown in the lower left; you can use the tuner to adjust the update rate. Using TrackerCam across a LAN permits the full 30 frames per second (fps), while you'll have to throttle down the rate across the Internet. The requirement to run at slow frame rates across the Internet rules out video compression like MPEG-1 or MPEG-2, so TrackerCam uses JPEG compression on individual frames.

JPEG compression outputs variable image sizes depending on the image resolution, scene complexity, and compression quality setting. A typical 320×240 image shrinks to 3KB after JPEG compression (24 Kb), so you'd need 24 Kbps for 1 fps. The bandwidth requirement scales with frame rate, so you need 48 Kbps for 2 fps, 72 Kbps for 3 fps, and so on. You might get 2 fps through a 56K modem if you get a good connection; the 128 Kbps uplink common to ISDN, DSL, and some wireless systems may support 5 fps. You're using 720 Kbps for 30 fps at 320×240 resolution.

The Communication pane in Figure 23-4 lets you access the controls to turn on the embedded server for live video. Click on the rightmost icon in the pane to get the dialog box in Figure 23-7 and turn on Put Me Online and, optionally, Guests Allowed. After you make sure the IP address in the lower right is correct, the URLs at the bottom can be copied and pasted into Web browsers for remote access. Disable guests and create user accounts unless you want the camera images open to everyone or unless you've taken other access security measures.

Figure 23-6: See what's going on from anywhere with slow scan video.

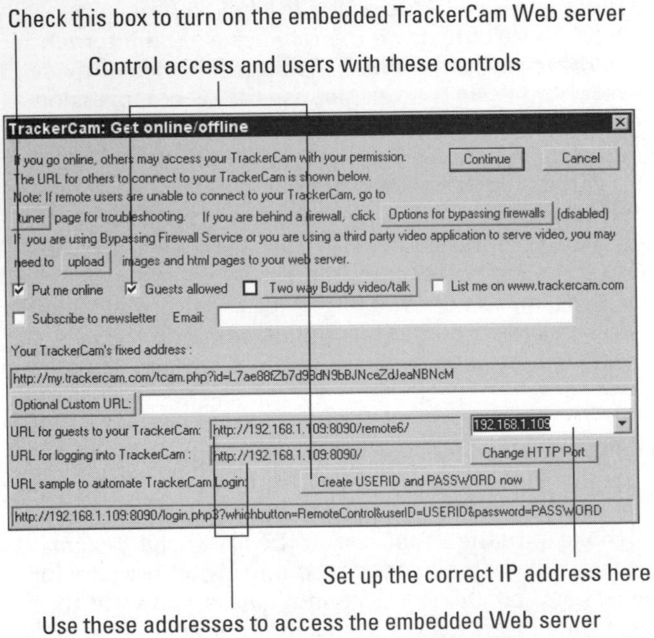

Check this box to turn on the embedded TrackerCam Web server

Control access and users with these controls

Set up the correct IP address here

Use these addresses to access the embedded Web server

Figure 23-7: The Get Online/Offline dialog box gives you controls for remote access to TrackerCam.

Cable/DSL Router Security and TrackerCam

You already know that you're vulnerable to attack any time your computers are connected to the Internet. One of the best ways to protect your computers from attack is to use an external hardware router providing Network Address Translation (NAT) because most of those routers can be set up to allow no unsolicited access to your computers from outside your LAN. That's the approach we use (which is why our IP addresses you see in this chapter are sequences like 192.168.1.109), and the logs we get from our router make it evident we're being probed constantly. The problem with routers like the Linksys we use, though, is that it takes some work to permit outside access when you want it.

This screen shot from the browser interface to our router shows how we set it up for remote access to both TrackerCam and HomeSeer. The idea is that anytime an external network request to access one of the indicated ports or port ranges arrives at our router, it's diverted to the internal address shown. We turned on both TCP and UDP access rather than researching whether UDP is needed in addition to TCP, but if you're even more paranoid than we are you'll try the software with only TCP enabled and see what happens.

Use port forwarding on your router to direct incoming requests to a specific computer.

In practice, though, we don't leave any of those ports open on a regular basis — we open them when external access is required and close them again when the need goes away. We get from tens to hundreds of probes of our network every hour, so it's just prudent to keep the ports closed if they don't need to be used.

Recorded Internet surveillance

The problem with live surveillance is that if something happens when you're not looking, you miss it. TrackerCam lets you record surveillance images on disk and access those images either locally from a computer with local or shared network disk access, or across the Internet using a Web browser. Set up surveillance through the tuner (click on the Tuner button in the main TrackerCam window, Figure 23-5, then pick Surveillance — Capture Stills, found under Communications. The configuration page (see Figure 23-8) lets you choose how often you save an image, how much disk space surveillance may use, and when surveillance is active.

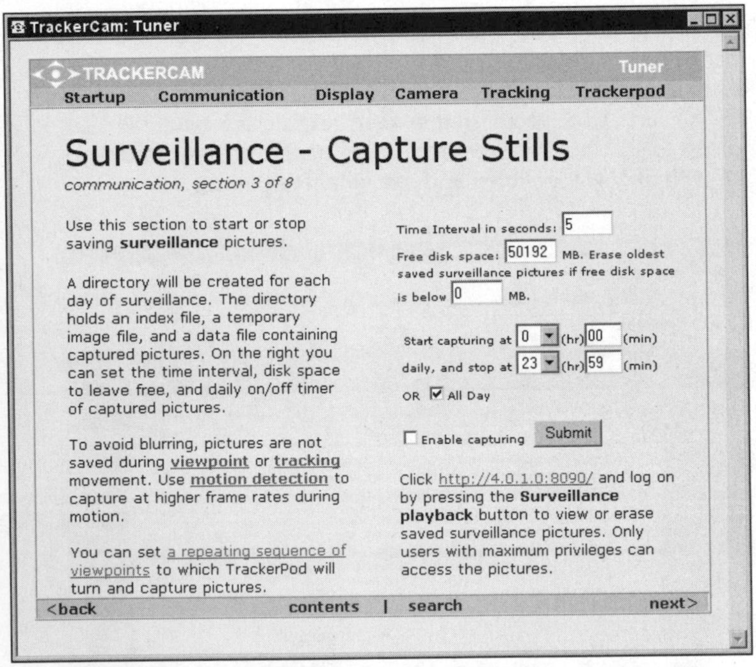

Figure 23-8: Use the Surveillance — Capture Stills page to enable still photo surveillance, define how often to capture an image, control disk use, and set times.

You can do more than simply position the camera and have it snap images. For example, from the tuner contents section, choose Viewpoint Order in the Tracking section. Define a sequence of viewpoints (places at which the camera points) on this page (see Figure 23-9), and let surveillance visit the viewpoints in sequence. The grid you see is a plane in front of the camera, so by choosing a box, you specify both pan and tilt. Define viewpoints by clicking in the box where the camera should point; if you clear all existing points, you can simply click all the viewpoint positions in sequence to create the path. If you name them using the pane on the right, those names will show up in the remote browser window and can be selected to point the camera. You can define the times at which viewpoints are active, too.

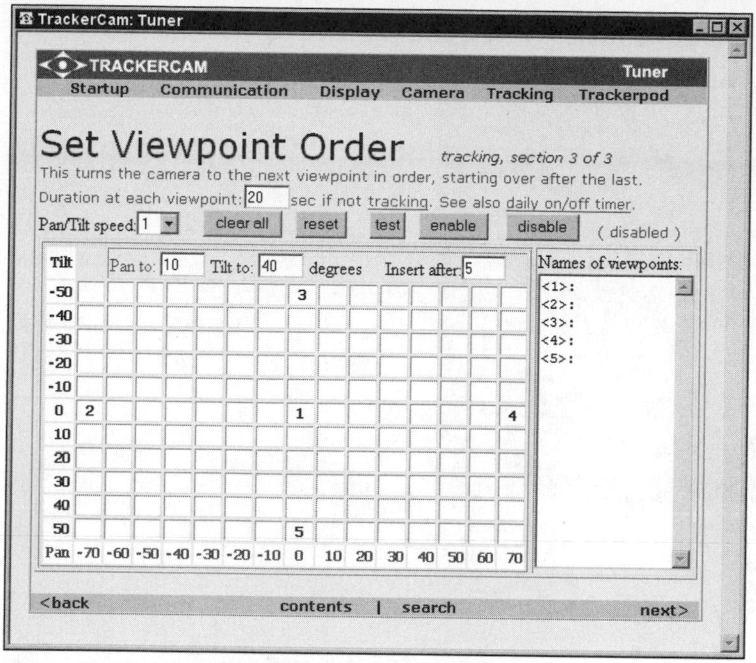

Figure 23-9: Set up viewpoints to have the camera scan an area under surveillance.

Motion detection and tracking

You can also set up your system to recognize motion and start collecting images when motion is present. The TrackerCam software has algorithms built in to detect and follow motion in the frames received from the camera. Figure 23-10 shows the motion detection algorithm in operation. The white bounding box in the figure shows the area of the image in which it has identified motion, in this case because the dog had just turned around. You can set the threshold for motion detection to be more or less sensitive, depending on the size and speed of the motion you want to see or exclude.

Once TrackerCam detects motion and establishes a bounding box, it can use that detection to trigger snapping a still image or motion clip. Basing your surveillance on motion detection helps eliminate recording useless images. TrackerCam can also slew the TrackerPod to follow the bounding box, keeping in the field of view as the object in the box moves. Test the motion tracking not only for sensitivity, but to check the speed at which the TrackerPod slews — too slow, and it can't keep up.

Detailed settings for tracking and motion capture are in the Capture Motion page under Communication, shown in Figure 23-11. The top part of the right column lets you enable or disable motion tracking (which is the same as the Track button in the main window), and set the detection threshold. The rest of the right column sets the parameters for motion-based video capture.

Figure 23-10: A bounding box in the camera view shows the area TrackerCam identified as containing motion.

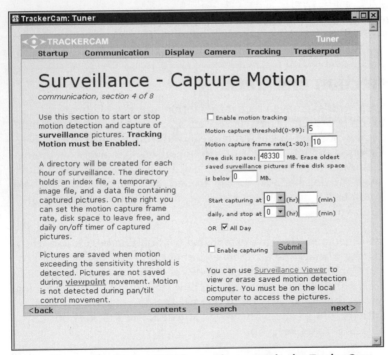

Figure 23-11: The Capture Motion settings page in the TrackerCam Tuner

Videoconferencing

One of the problems with desktop video conferencing is that the camera is so close that if you move to one side to do something you're out of the picture. The TrackerPod solves the basic problem by being able to track your movements, but because there are so many videoconferencing applications (including CUseeMe and Microsoft NetMeeting), it's impractical for the TrackerCam software to include the equivalent of all those programs. Instead, TrackerCam implements a "pseudo camera," interposing itself between the actual camera and any application wanting access to video from a camera. This feature makes the motion tracking functions that are available invisible to the other application, which simply thinks it's getting a video stream from a fixed camera.

The left-hand icon in the Communication pane in the options window starts your videoconferencing application. The first time you click on the icon you'll get a dialog box used to identify the application; after that, the application simply starts. Figure 23-12 shows how this works. TrackerCam is running behind NetMeeting, while the identical image in both the NetMeeting and TrackerCam windows shows you that they're getting the same video feed.

Figure 23-12: Configure NetMeeting to use the TrackerCam Capture camera, and you'll have motion tracking from within NetMeeting.

Building a Surveillance System to Your Own Design

There's really no end to what you can do with a home surveillance system. You can start with the basic system we describe and enhance it to meet your specific requirements, or you can start with entirely different equipment and software. The driving factors are what you want to accomplish and how much you're willing to spend.

Multiple cameras

You will need more than one camera if your objective is to watch your entire house. You can easily tie multiple cameras to your PC if they're webcams with USB interfaces, but if you're using standard composite video, you'll need a PC interface able to accept and digitize the analog video signal. One possibility is the Webcam Corporation Model WCSP100-4, a PCI board accepting four NTSC or PAL analog video signals. The board includes software to monitor the cameras and give you a combined quadrant display of all four (see Figure 23-13). You can watch the video remotely with a Web browser, and you can set up the software to initiate video recording when it detects motion and to send you an e-mail alert.

Figure 23-13: Simultaneous quadrant display from four cameras

Long cables and wireless cameras

For the same reason that it's hard to put full-motion video onto the Internet — it's hard to transmit lots of bits a long distance — the camera's data rate makes it difficult for you to set up your cameras a long way from your PC. You don't always have a choice, though, so you may need to design remote cameras into your surveillance system. The following sections discuss some of your options.

Long cables

Many webcams use a USB interface into the PC, which would normally limit you to keeping the computer in the same room as the PC. Eagletron, the maker of the TrackerPod we used in the baseline design, makes an adapter that will extend USB cables as far as 200 feet. At $160 for the 150-foot version, those adapters (secure.eagletron.com/TCam/purchase/cart.php?Item=H2002E150) are expensive, so you'll want to be careful where you use them.

Wireless

One possibility is a wireless pan/tilt camera, but these are expensive too. The X10 Vanguard is representative ($799.99 list; $499.99 special offer in early 2003; see www.x10.com/products/vanguard_sg1.htm). Equivalent cameras we researched were even more expensive.

You also have the option of a stationary wireless camera, such as the X10 Xcam2 ($79.99 at www.x10.com/products/x10_vk45a.htm). It's an order of magnitude cheaper, but you'll need more cameras to get full area coverage.

If you already have cameras that produce standard composite video, RadioShack makes wireless audio/video senders (catalog number 15-2572 at www.radioshack.com) for under $100. These units transmit the composite video plus stereo to the paired receiver; if your requirements are within their range, which is affected by walls, metal, people, and other interference, they're small and simple.

Integrated home automation

You can combine video surveillance with home automation. The X10 Floodcam is an example (www.x10.com/products/x10_vt38a.htm); it combines a wireless camera, floodlights, and a motion sensor, and transmits the motion indication to your X10 system for further response. The camera can be turned on and off from the X10 system, too.

On a simpler level, the power supply for the stationary X10 Xcam2 will respond to your X10 controls, turning the camera on and off.

Archiving to removable storage

Security installations in which permanent storage of what's recorded is necessary often record the video to videotape. You could do that, but it's difficult to do if you're using the motion tracking features of the TrackerPod. Instead, if you have a CD-RW or DVD writer, you could dump the captured files to optical disk. You could use one of the many available programs to make your optical drive work like a read-write drive, then either write a program to dump directories to disk or use something like the Unison file synchronizer (`www.cis.upenn.edu/~bcpierce/unison`). If you need control over the times at which the application runs, consider using a Windows scheduled task.

Summary

✦ The essence of surveillance is making images of interesting events available remotely. As you dig into building a surveillance system, you'll grapple not only with the camera issues of resolution, image quality, and field of view, but also system control and communications bandwidth.

✦ You'll need to strike a balance among those characteristics if you want to keep costs within reason.

Diagnosis and Repair

T his might well be the chapter you turned to first because one of the most common reasons people want computer hardware help is to fix problems. You can certainly find no shortage of people with broken or unreliable computers. No magic prescription for fixing broken computers exists, though — just plodding, methodical analysis to eliminate what is working right until what's left is the problem. Nor are all the methods we look at in this chapter painless. Some involve stripping all your data and programs off the disk and starting over from scratch; others involve substituting components (which gets expensive if you're wrong about what the trouble is). If you don't have good backups plus the master copies of your software, you could be in trouble when — not if — your computer goes down.

Repair isn't a very pleasant subject. Unless the problem is as simple as cleaning dust out of the machine (fairly common, actually) or reseating cards and cables, you're going to be swapping components and working with low-level software.

Don't be misled by the term *repair*, either. Actually repairing a broken motherboard, adapter card, or drive in a personal computer is beyond the tools and skills of most people. If there's really been a hardware failure, repairing a personal computer requires that you *replace* the broken part. You can sometimes test your diagnosis by swapping in replacement parts from another computer, but if you have only one computer, swapping components means buying components.

The good news, if you can call it that, is that most often problems in running computers are due to software problems. Once you get things set up properly and are past the first few months of operation, personal computer hardware is quite reliable. Failures happen, but nowhere nearly as often as software conflicts and crashes. We've focused on hardware problems in this book, but the isolation techniques we'll cover can help you with software problems as well.

In This Chapter

Diagnosis and repair techniques

Using isolation procedures on dead machines

Using isolation procedures on functioning machines

Diagnosing networks

There's a lesson in that last observation — the most reliable personal computers are ones that people *use*, not ones that people fiddle with. Once you get a computer to where it's stable, it's likely to stay that way unless you install new software or hardware, or change settings on software you already have installed. We're not saying you should never install new things or make system changes — we simply want to warn you that it's those things that are most likely to create problems.

Basic Techniques

You have to do three things if you're going to work on computer hardware without doing more damage than good:

✦ **Control static electricity** — You absolutely must eliminate static electricity — electrostatic discharge (ESD). Voltages you can't see or feel can kill the chips in your computer.

✦ **Follow careful, well-defined procedures** — You get nowhere ripping hardware (or software) apart, making random changes in the hope something will work. You must have in mind a carefully thought-through sequence of tests and changes. You'll want to change only one thing at a time, so you can isolate what causes different results.

✦ **Use the proper tools** — We're as guilty as anyone of using a vise grip as the universal tool, but that's not the right way to go about working on computer hardware (we usually reserve the Vise Grip for plumbing). The parts are relatively small and fragile, so you must have tools appropriate to the job.

Cross-Reference We discussed both static electricity and tools in Chapter 1 because they're terribly important — we wanted to make sure you didn't miss them. If you *did* skip that part, please go back and read about them now.

Mechanical Procedures

With the exception of blowing dust out of the case (see Figure 24-1), or out of optical or floppy drives, or connecting and disconnecting peripherals, hardware work involves taking the case of your computer apart. We don't recommend taking apart monitors (because of the severe high voltage safety hazards and because there aren't any parts inside replaceable without specialized training, parts, and tools) or other external devices (because there usually aren't any user-replaceable parts inside). You might want to avoid taking apart a laptop computer, too (again due to lack of replaceable parts inside).

Figure 24-1: Dust accumulates quickly.
©2004 Barry Press & Marcia Press

You have to judge for yourself whether or not you think you can take apart and reassemble your computer. If you're reasonably skilled at mechanical disassembly and reassembly, you have a good chance of being able to put the machine back together in no worse condition than when you started, even if you've never taken one apart before. Here are some guidelines to consider:

✦ **Power supplies** — You can do no repairs inside a power supply without a good understanding of power conversion electronics. You can create a safety hazard by doing the wrong thing inside a power supply, so unless you're trained to do electronics repair, don't disassemble or stick anything inside the power supply. The voltages in there can kill you.

Power supply replacement, however, is one of the easiest repairs you can do.

✦ **Disk drives** — Don't ever take a disk drive apart (floppy disk, hard disk, CD-ROM, DVD, or any other kind). Removing one from a computer (or adding one in) is a possibility, but you can damage a disk drive irreparably by taking it apart. Not even the manufacturers repair disks — Seagate tests failed disks to see what happened, records the results for future quality-control analysis, and then scraps them.

✦ **Processor** — Replacing a processor is easy because they're all installed in sockets. The most complicated parts of replacing a processor are getting the right part, making sure it's aligned properly in the socket, and making sure it's properly sealed to the heat sink and fan.

✦ **Memory** — Memory is on plug-in modules and is straightforward to insert or remove.

✦ **Adapter boards** — Boards that plug into your motherboard are straightforward to remove and replace. *Accelerated Graphics Port (AGP)* video cards have a unique retention mechanism you have to disengage to remove the card.

✦ **Motherboards** — Physically replacing a motherboard is largely a mechanical job. The hard part is figuring out how to reconnect all the cables that used to go on the old board onto the new board and how to set up the new board to work with your adapter cards and with your software. Have a motherboard replacement done for you unless you understand why these points are issues and know how to go about solving them.

✦ **Monitor** — There's nothing you can do inside a monitor, LCD, or CRT, and the voltages in a CRT monitor can kill you well after you've disconnected the power. The only repair you're likely to make is to repair bent pins on the data cable or degauss the CRT.

Disassembly tips

In all cases, be sure to follow good ESD protection practice and make a drawing or take photos of the assembly as you disassemble. The drawing has to be good enough to enable you to put the machine back together exactly as you found it. The following sections cover some details you'll want to be careful to note.

Which slot is the board in?

Not all slots are equivalent. Some old PCI motherboards require you to designate which PCI slots are bus masters, which ends up differentiating one slot from another. The sequence of boards in slots can matter for PCI cards because of cross-board compatibility problems. Cable length limitations may restrict the slots a card can go in. Cables may be required between two cards.

What cables connect to the card?

You can't depend on cables inside a computer being capable of plugging into only one place because cables for different purposes sometimes have the same connectors. If you plug a cable into a socket other than where it came from (and is designed to go), the best you can hope for is that things won't work right. If you're unlucky, you can destroy a drive, adapter card, or motherboard.

Some cables connect to more than one device. The cable from the floppy disk controller can connect to two floppy disks. A cable from an IDE host adapter can connect to two disks, a disk and a CD-ROM, a CD-ROM and a tape drive, or other combinations of two devices. Make sure you know which connector goes to which device.

It doesn't generally matter which power cable connects to which drive, as long as you're careful not to stretch them beyond their length. No cables should be under tension.

Where is pin number one?

Connection orientation is vitally important. Not all connectors have notches or irregular shapes to ensure correct insertion, so cables can often plug in either of two (or more) ways. The same results are likely if you orient something the wrong way as if you plug something into the wrong place: Either the connection won't work, or you'll destroy something.

Caution It's extraordinarily important that you get the orientation right if you have a motherboard that uses an internal cable from the motherboard to USB connectors on the front or back of the case. Get the orientation wrong, and you can destroy the motherboard the first time you connect a USB device.

Problems like these are why everything that disconnects inside your computer is marked, and sometimes keyed. Data cables — usually flat, wide ribbons of wires — have the wire at one edge marked with a stripe, a different color (usually red), or some other distinguishing feature. The marked wire goes to pin one on the connector. The printed circuit card should have numbering on the face near the connector. Sometimes only pin one is numbered, sometimes pins at both ends are numbered, sometimes all pins are numbered, and sometimes there's an obscure mark for pin one. Don't take the connection apart without being sure you can identify how to put it back together. The technical manual for your motherboard — check the manufacturer's Web site — will usually diagram the connections.

Power supply cable orientation matters, too. ATX power supply connections to the motherboard are keyed. Connections to disk drives (other than serial ATA) use a standard four-wire connection that is keyed, but sometimes difficult to make fit. Connections to 3.5-inch floppy drives are smaller, and keyed only by skirts that descend from the side of the power cable connector. The skirts on those smaller connectors are easy to defeat if you happen to insert the connector upside down, leading to misorientation and drive failure.

Processor chips have a unique mark in one corner, and usually one pin that's different in the array of pins on the bottom. Processors will only go in the socket one way, and you'll bend pins trying to force one in any other way. Memory module orientation is keyed by keys on the socket and corresponding notches on the module.

A number of twisted-pairs of wires run from the chassis to the motherboard and sometimes to adapter cards. These wires connect to the speaker, keylock, reset button, disk activity indicator, ATX power and sleep switches, and other controls on the front panel. The twisted pairs will have one color that's common to all of them, and another color that's unique. Some (but not all) of the pairs have to be oriented the right way when plugged in; these include the pairs that connect to indicator LEDs and that supply power to the front panel. A lot of different schemes for marking the connectors that the wires plug into exist, so you'll need to make a very careful drawing (and check it twice) before you unplug anything.

Top-level disassembly

Be sure to disconnect your computer from the wall outlet before you start taking it apart. Power line voltages are dangerous, and you don't want to risk coming in contact with them. You may see other sources (including some versions of the A+ Certification exams) that recommend you turn the power off but leave the cord connected so you maintain a ground path. This is a really bad idea because ATX power supplies aren't ever really off if they're connected to a power source — they provide a low power 5 V supply to the motherboard even when the system is turned off. You don't want to be working on the system with any power present because in addition to the safety issue, you could damage components when you connect or disconnect them.

Cases open in many ways. Some require you to remove screws and take off the cover; others simply snap or slide open. However the case opens, open it slowly so you can watch for cables or other components inside the case that might catch on the cover. (For that matter, be equally careful putting the case back on when you're done. Crimped wires can result in damaged insulation and shorted connections.) When you're working inside the computer, be careful not to dislodge connectors by accidentally pushing or pulling on cables.

Familiarize yourself with what's inside once you open the case; take detailed, close-up photos of all the connections if you want a good, permanent record. You can identify most of the adapter cards from what plugs into them. For example, the monitor plugs into the video card, your disk drives plug either into the motherboard or a host adapter, external speakers usually plug into the sound card, and the telephone line plugs into a modem. A CD-ROM or DVD can plug into the motherboard or a host adapter.

There's no completely general procedure for disassembly. Adapter cards usually have one screw at the top of the bracket, and you'll need to disconnect any attached internal or external cables before you remove the card. Disk drives typically have screws at the side.

Caution Use the same screws when you re-assemble the machine, without mixing them up. Disk drives in particular often have limitations on how long the screws into the side of the drive can be. If you use a longer one, you risk cracking a printed circuit board, damaging a component, or shorting out wires inside the drive. Don't expect that to be covered by warranty.

Put circuit boards and disk drives in anti-static bags after you remove them. It's a good idea to keep the bags the boards were shipped in for this purpose.

As a matter of practice, use a minimalist approach to taking things apart. Disassemble what you must, but leave everything else alone.

Isolation Procedures

The most irritating thing we ever hear from tech support representatives is when we're told — without having explained the problem and the steps we've taken to isolate it — to remove and reinstall Windows and see if the problem's still there. The most annoying case of this we had was when we'd called merely to ask if the company's Web server had moved to another address. It had, but the tech support representative had to work from a preset script and couldn't believe that it wasn't our computer's problem.

Nevertheless, an important concept underlies that standard silliness, which is that because PCs are complex, it's hard to isolate problems. You make it easier to find the problem by simplifying the situation as far as possible. Removing those files and reverting to a brand-new Windows installation accomplishes that, so it's part of many standard tech support diagnostic scripts.

We're going to restrict the isolation and diagnosis procedures in this book to hardware-related issues because adding in software problems would expand what we need to look at to another complete book.

Rules of thumb

Here are the three concepts we suggest should guide you when you're working on computer hardware:

✦ **Occam's Razor** — Named after the 14th-century English philosopher William of Occam, Occam's Razor says, "Do not proliferate theoretical entities unnecessarily." In the context of PC repair, that means the simplest explanation that accounts for all the evidence is the one to try first.

✦ **Be observant and precise** — Look carefully to see everything that's going on, and don't jump to assumptions or generalizations that aren't warranted by what you observe. Know the details of the error messages you see, and look around the point of failure for other indications. Look for patterns, including what events trigger the failure.

✦ **Have specific failures in mind** — When you try to explain the problems you see, remember that usually only one piece of hardware will fail at a time. If your analysis requires two failures, you're likely to have violated Occam's Razor.

Something else to keep in mind is to try to identify the last thing you changed, be it hardware or software. That change has a high likelihood of being part of the problem.

Observation and low-level isolation

The first thing to do is to simply step back and look at what's going on. Does the computer light up as if it has power into it? What about the monitor? Personal computers have a typical set of sounds they make as they start to boot, including the memory test count up, noises from the floppy disk, and a beep right before the operating system starts. Different or missing sounds can be a clue as to what's malfunctioning.

If the computer or monitor seems completely dead, check to make sure that it's plugged in, turned on, and that there's really power at the outlet. We've fixed more than a few "broken" computers that way. Remember that the outlet might have a wall-mounted switch, a power strip might be between the wall and the computer, extension cords can be disconnected, and power strip switches might be turned off or circuit breakers might be popped.

While you're at it, check that the computer cables themselves are all plugged into the right places and are seated securely. We've seen computer systems that color-coded the cables and sockets. You can write on the back of the computer with a fine-point Sanford Sharpie marker to label what goes where, or can use masking tape to write on (so you can change things when you upgrade the computer).

The first thing you see on the monitor as the system boots might be the version and copyright of the video card basic input-output system (BIOS), or it might be the initial display from the motherboard BIOS. Two other alternatives are:

✦ **Error codes** — You may see an error code on the screen. A common one is the number 103, which usually means a keyboard problem. (You can generate a 103 error code on many systems just by pressing a key before the computer finishes resetting.) Check with your system (or motherboard or BIOS) vendor for the meaning of the error codes.

✦ **Beeps** — If not enough of the computer is working to allow a screen display (such as a memory failure in the first bank) or if the video card isn't working, you'll get a series of long and short beeps. The meaning of the beep sequence is specific to the system, motherboard, or BIOS vendor. Some motherboard manuals include the explanation of beep codes in an appendix; if yours doesn't, you can try the Ultra-X Web site at `www.uxd.com/postcodes.shtml`, the manufacturer's Web site, or the manufacturer's technical support line.

System unresponsive

If there's no video and no beep from the system during boot (and — if it's separate — you're sure the speaker is plugged into the motherboard), check to see if there's power from the power supply. If you can hear the disk drives and fans start to spin and can see LEDs lit on the front panel, it's likely that the power supply is working. If you're skilled with a multimeter, you can check this at the connectors where the power cables come into the motherboard. Relative to any of the black wires, the red wire should be at 5 V, the yellow at 12, the blue at −12, and the white at −5. You can do a simpler check on a disk drive connector: Relative to either of the two middle ones, the yellow wire should be +12 V, while the red one should be +5 V. You have to have a load such as the motherboard or a disk connected to the power supply to do these measurements with the power supply connected to the motherboard or a hard disk.

If there's no output from the power supply, and you know the power line is feeding power to the system, check these items:

✦ **Fuse** — Some power supplies have externally replaceable fuses accessible from the back of the computer. After unplugging the computer, check if the fuse has blown, and replace it if so. If the replacement fuse blows, something's drawing too much power inside the computer. You might need to replace the power supply, but you equally well might have a short circuit in the power wiring within the computer.

✦ **Power switch** — A signal from the motherboard turns on an ATX power supply. That signal in turn derives from the power switch connected to the motherboard, but is also conditioned by tests for processor and memory compatibility on the motherboard. Check the connection to the power switch. Check for additional power switches, too — some power supplies have a power switch on the back in addition to the system power switch on the front.

✦ **Memory and processor** — The power supply won't start up without the processor seated in its socket, and in some cases won't appear to start up with a processor incompatible with the motherboard, or with memory incompatible with either the motherboard or processor. If this is a new system or an upgrade — and has never started up before — check compatibility again, and check that the processor is in the socket properly.

If the power supply appears operational, try (with the power supply disconnected from the power source) removing all the adapter cards from the motherboard, disconnecting power from all the drives, removing the memory modules, and disconnecting the keyboard and mouse. Only the motherboard (with the processor) should remain connected to the power supply. The point of disconnecting everything is to simplify the test — in that configuration, only three replaceable components (power supply and power switch, motherboard, and processor) could have failed. We've assumed that the problem here isn't a conflict between two cards; such conflicts rarely cause the system to be completely unresponsive.

If the system still generates no beeps to indicate the processor is running once you apply power and start the system, you have a failed motherboard, failed processor, or a relatively subtle problem in the power supply. Substituting a known-good power supply or processor are the simplest tests; unless the system has been subject to overheating, the power supply is the most likely culprit.

If the motherboard does respond with beeps, however, the problem is in one of the components you disconnected. You can isolate which one by adding them back one by one and retesting each time. The last one you added before the system stops responding again is the culprit. Remember to disconnect the power before removing or adding cards. Once you find the failed component, replace it.

Monitor unresponsive

If the system seems to be responding properly (such as the right sounds as it boots, disk activity, and the Windows start-up sound) but there's no video, look at the screen closely with the brightness and contrast turned up all the way. A completely dark screen could indicate no power to the monitor or a failure within the monitor. A scrambled image on the screen (or no image but a visible background raster present) could indicate a damaged cable or connector, or a failure in either the monitor or the display card. In either case, you can isolate the problem between the monitor and the computer by trying another monitor. If that fixes the problem, you'll need to either replace the monitor or have it fixed. Check the cost of fixing the monitor before you decide to have the repair done; the cost of CRT monitors is so low that the repair cost might not be much different from the replacement cost, if you can find someone to do the repair at all.

Video operational during boot

If you can get video during boot, the system can help you figure out what's wrong. If you get an error message before the actual operating system start-up sequence, then you need to identify what component the message refers to. You figure that out by seeing where in the boot sequence the message occurs in addition to reading the text of the message. The typical boot sequence goes like this:

1. **Video BIOS start-up** — Even though the motherboard BIOS is active before video BIOS start-up, nothing can show up on the screen until the video adapter BIOS initializes the card. A message from the BIOS might identify the card and date of the video BIOS.

2. **Motherboard BIOS sign on** — The motherboard BIOS identifies itself, including version, and may provide some configuration information about the system.

3. **Peripheral device initialization** — The BIOS initializes the devices it controls. This includes the IDE disks and CD-ROM, keyboard and mouse, and the floppy disk.

4. **Adapter card initialization** — There's a BIOS on some other adapter cards (such as network adapters). The motherboard BIOS calls the

adapter BIOS for each card. Adapters might display a message identifying the product and the BIOS version. Some, such as disk controller adapters, search for and identify devices attached to the card, too.

5. **Operating system start** — This is signaled by the initial message from the operating system (such as "Starting Windows 98") or a graphical splash screen.

6. **Hardware configuration check and device driver load** — As the operating system loads, it checks the hardware configuration to see if it matches what's expected, and loads drivers to control the hardware.

> **Tip**
>
> You can get an idea of where the problem lies from what's going on in the boot sequence when the problem happens. For example, if the BIOS expects to find an IDE disk but the disk is not responding, the boot might hang (or stop for a long time) after the motherboard sign-on message. Some versions of the AMI BIOS display a "WAIT..." message at that point; your BIOS might be different. Similarly, if an adapter card sign-on message is followed by an error code, you know that the problem lies with that adapter or something else in the boot sequence after that adapter but prior to the next message you normally see. It really helps in troubleshooting to know precisely what normal behavior should be!

If the machine initializes normally but won't boot, saying that it found no operating system and that you should insert a bootable floppy, you have one of three problems:

✦ **Failed disk or host adapter** — On some systems, the boot sequence continues even if the disk drive is inoperative. At the point when the BIOS tries to find an operating system, you get the message that no operating system was found because the BIOS can't read the disk. Problems with the power supply or data cables to the disk could cause this, too.

✦ **Corrupted disk** — If the contents of the disk have been scrambled, the BIOS might not be able to find what looks like an operating system. This is one of the situations in which you'll either be thankful for good backups or wish you had them. (Before you panic, though, try a reset or power off/on cycle — we've seen a number of cases where the hardware, which was in a bad state, was easily cured this way.)

✦ **No active partition** — Among the information that the disk partition table keeps are an indicator of what type of file system each partition contains and an indicator whether or not a partition is active (that is, bootable). A common mistake when you initially partition a disk is to forget to mark the first partition as bootable. After you format the disk and try to make it boot, you get the "No operating system" error, even though you just put it there.

If you can boot from a floppy or CD-ROM, you can start trying to find out why the hard disk won't boot. Check if you can hear the drive spinning and if there's an activity light on the disk. Be sure to check the activity light directly on the disk if there is one, and not the one on the machine front panel, because the light on the front panel sees status from the host adapter, not individual disks. If the front panel light isn't working, you know the disk isn't seeing commands. If the disk is broken or the cable damaged, though, the front panel light can be on while nothing is happening at the disk. If the disk is operational, look for software-related problems such as a scrambled file system.

Memory failures

Another possibility is that either the Power-On Self-Test or parity testing hardware detects a bad memory location. If you have more than one memory bank, such as if your motherboard can accept one to three SDRAM modules, you might have some options, as is discussed in the list that follows. Some higher performance Pentium 4 motherboards (such as the Intel D875PBZ you'll see in Chapter 25) have two banks of modules, however, and if they're used in parallel, both parallel modules will have to work.

✦ **Failed bank zero** — The computer won't boot if the first bank of memory (that's either bank zero or one, depending on how your motherboard is numbered) is bad. If you have two banks, you can swap bank zero and bank one (or bank one and bank two if your numbering starts at one). If the memory was in fact the problem, swapping the two banks should move the problem to a higher address (corresponding to the higher-numbered bank) and allow the computer to boot.

✦ **Failed other bank** — If other than the first bank of memory has failed, you might have two choices: leave it in or take it out. Many systems detect the failed memory, complain (and possibly require you to go into setup and confirm the new limit), and run. If yours is one of those, you can leave the failed memory in; otherwise, take it out. If your computer has more than two banks of memory, you can relocate the removed bank to the end, making the most of the memory you have left.

Diagnostics

Observation and replacement only go so far unless you have a really well stocked parts bin. Ultimately, you'll want the ability to run a comprehensive set of diagnostics to help isolate what's wrong. We prefer to run diagnostics without the full operating system loaded (such as from DOS) so there's no interference from device drivers and other software in Windows. You'll want to make sure you have an emergency boot disk so you can start the machine without a hard disk running. We like bootable CD-ROMs for this purpose, because if you have CD-ROM drivers in the boot sequence, you can load megabytes of diagnostics and other tools on the CD-ROM well beyond what fits on a floppy.

You have a surprising number of choices for PC diagnostics, including AMIDiag Suite by AMI, QA+Win32 by DiagSoft, and QuickTech PRO by Ultra-X. All three will locate and diagnose most problems associated with the major components of your PC.

Problems in Functioning Machines

It's much harder to fix problems in machines that mostly work because, in many ways, a dead machine is the easiest to troubleshoot. The range of things that can have failed in a dead machine is limited, it's easy to replicate the problem, and it's easy to tell when you've fixed it.

Ignoring software-related problems, you'll face three other kinds of problems in partly functional machines, all of which can be much harder to solve:

✦ **Configuration** — You may encounter conflicts among devices for resources (interrupts, direct memory access channels, memory addresses, or bus slots).

✦ **Incompatibilities** — Some hardware simply doesn't work properly with other hardware, even if both are installed correctly and no resource conflicts exist. Incompatibilities can lead to instability and crashes.

✦ **Something doesn't work right** — Even if the machine is stable, sometimes the hardware doesn't work the way it should.

The next sections suggest how to approach repairs.

Configuration problems

Much of what goes wrong in hardware is the result of two or more devices wanting the same resources. The conflict can be over an interrupt, a direct memory access channel, a reserved memory address, or a physical bus slot (or combinations of these). Autoconfiguration in the PCI bus helps avoid these conflicts. Your best tool for finding conflicts, assuming you can get Windows to come up, is the Windows Device Manager. The device drivers in Windows 9X and NT/2000/XP report the resources they have assigned. Cross-checking the assigned resources lets Windows find out about conflicts, reporting the results in the Device Manager. When the Device Manager finds a conflict, it flags the device with a yellow or red warning symbol. You'll want to check what problem Windows is reporting (it might be something besides a conflict) and resolve it if you can.

The reverse of the conflict problem is the case where a card doesn't have the resources it needs. For example, without realizing what we had done, we once installed a PCI network card into an older motherboard that was incapable of assigning interrupts automatically to the PCI bus. Until we realized that the card didn't have an interrupt, we had the odd situation where Windows automatically recognized the card and installed the necessary software, but the network wouldn't work. The card worked in another machine (one with a BIOS that assigned PCI interrupts automatically). We discovered the problem by noticing that the Device Manager had no interrupt assigned to the card; after we assigned an interrupt to the right PCI slot, everything worked properly.

Some other configuration problems and troubleshooting assets are under the Windows 9X Performance tab (to the right of that for the Device Manager) or the Windows 2000/XP Performance Options (on the Advanced dialog box tab in System Properties):

✦ **Virtual memory** — You don't want to disable virtual memory in Windows. You don't even want to run out of space for the swap file Windows uses to implement virtual memory.

✦ **Graphics** — The accelerators (or their drivers) on some graphics cards can cause trouble. You can progressively disable more and more of the accelerator functionality using the dialog box behind the Graphics button on the Performance tab of the System Properties sheet. If this fixes an unreliable system, see if the card manufacturer can help you restore accelerated functionality. If the vendor won't help, or can't, consider another manufacturer.

It doesn't work right

The ultimate simplification of your Windows installation is to format the disk and reinstall Windows from scratch. As obnoxious as that is, an unstable system is really a prime target for such drastic treatment. Make sure you have complete backups — and test the backup — before you reformat, and make sure you have the installation master disks and installation keys (if required) for all your software. At the point you've rebuilt Windows (but before you start reloading software), you're assured you won't have software-related problems due to conflicts among third-party programs or due to incorrect old settings for hardware. If the system becomes stable at that point, you can reinstall the rest of your software (not from the backup — from the original versions) and reload your data from tape. Try to exercise the system carefully after adding back each application so you'll be able to identify a problem as soon as it happens.

> **Tip** It's difficult to carry out a from-scratch rebuild if you intermix data files with application programs because it's hard to know which files belong to the program and which to you. We recommend trying to keep the files you create and work with in a place separate from programs for just that reason.

Most often, a malfunctioning machine won't have the grace to simply fail outright. Instead, just certain things won't work, and either won't work at all or will work randomly or erratically. This category is an enormous catchall, of course, but in a lot of cases what seem to be hardware problems are really issues with device drivers.

Another of the most important lessons in trying to troubleshoot complex malfunctions is to get the people using the computer to be as precise as possible when describing the problem. A complaint of "the modem's broken" might more precisely be described as "I can't get e-mail, and when I try I don't hear the modem dial." That more precise description should lead you to initially check the phone line, cable, and modem.

Observation is still a powerful tool when you're trying to isolate specific failures in functioning machines. For instance, if the CD-ROM doesn't work, try putting a disk in the drive, waiting a while, and then ejecting it. If the disk hasn't turned from its initial position, the drive didn't spin. If the drive has power and doesn't spin, you'll have to replace it.

Network Diagnosis

Just as your computers will fail periodically, you can expect your network to fail, too. Many network problems are due to misconfiguration of the protocols, routing tables, or other configuration data. Although TCP/IP configuration and troubleshooting is a book entirely to itself, troubleshooting your network hardware is fairly simple (although potentially tedious if you have a large network). If you have a small network, the manual procedures we'll look at in this section are sufficient.

Tip

Don't overlook that network problems can cause machines to seem to malfunction, and machine failures can take down a network.

The fundamental problem with broken network hardware is that some sections of your network become inoperative or unreachable. The strategy for finding the failure is to identify the point in the network that can cause the symptoms you see. If necessary, you can isolate down to finer-grained symptoms by partitioning the network in half, dividing the broken half into smaller and smaller halves until you isolate the failed component. You may have to disconnect parts of the network physically to isolate halves, or you may be able to get the insight you need by using the `ping` and `traceroute` programs.

By far, the majority of network failures are due to cabling problems — bad connectors, and shorted or open cable.

✦ **10Base-2** — The terminators and tee connectors in a 10Base-2 network are particularly vulnerable to damage. A cracked, shorted, or open resistor inside a terminator is rarely visible, but can be caused by things like whacking the terminator against a wall while you're pulling cable, or by kicking the cable. Cracked insulation in tee connectors can be equally bad and might not be apparent even if you remove and inspect the connector. It's easy to destroy a tee just by pushing the computer back into a wall. The only certain way to check a tee or connector is to replace it with a known good one and see if that fixes the problem you're having.

✦ **10/100/1000Base-T and other hub-based wiring** — The hubs and switches in your network usually provide indicators on their front panels to indicate operational and faulted status of connections, as do the ports on your PCs. Between those indicators and selective disconnection to isolate suspect subnetworks, you shouldn't have much problem isolating what's wrong. That and speed are really the big advantages of 100/1000Base-T.

Poor modem performance caused by a noisy telephone line can cause your network to appear to have failed. If you can hear noise on your phone line (pick up the receiver and dial one number — other than zero — to stop the dial tone), so can your modem. If you're using a local Internet service provider, they might be able to tell you how many retransmissions you're getting, and if the number is higher than usual for your area. As with all other problems, the troubleshooting approach is to think through how the components related to the problem work, list the ways in which their operation could fail, and test those ways one by one.

Viruses

The onslaught is so great that at some time you're likely to have to clean up a machine infected with a virus. The key to doing that is to have a boot disk — we recommend a CD-ROM — you can use to start the machine, load antivirus scanning and disinfection software, and clean up the infected disk. Your antivirus software is likely to come with directions on how to prepare an emergency disk, but there are three issues you should think through in advance:

✦ **Virus definition updates** — The virus definition files you scan with are likely to be somewhat out of date because those definitions change rapidly and no one has the time to keep remaking emergency disks. Instead, you need a way to get the current version and load it on demand. A second, clean computer can do that for you.

✦ **Windows NT File System** — We recommend using the Windows NT File System (NTFS) with Windows NT/2000/XP because it's more efficient, more reliable, and handles bigger drives than the Win9X FAT and FAT32 file systems. You must not boot the infected hard drive because you could be spoofed by the virus, so you must boot from removable media. Unless your antivirus software vendor provides the necessary tools, you'll likely boot DOS from floppy or CD-ROM. DOS-based boot disks can't read NTFS, but if you have NTFSDOS (NTFSDOS Professional works from DOS and is at `www.winternals.com/products/repairandrecovery`) you can.

✦ **Test** — It's too late to test your emergency disk and find out it doesn't work when you need it. Test it when you make it.

No standard way to remove a virus from your system exists — check what your antivirus software vendor says to do for the specific virus the antivirus scanner says you have.

Case Study: A Dead Machine

At one point, an older machine of ours failed. We've described the sequence of events leading up to the failure in this section, along with the steps for troubleshooting and recovery. Every failure is different in some way, so it's not our intent to define a cookbook troubleshooting sequence here. Instead, this section is here to provide some insight into the thought processes that can help you repair machines.

Well before the time of the failure, we'd upgraded the system motherboard in the generic mini-tower chassis. The system had been in operation for about a year following the upgrade and was very stable. The first indication that something was wrong was that the machine started to lock up randomly, with the lockups happening infrequently at first, but then more often. We made copies of critical files at that point — we weren't convinced that the machine was stable enough to back it up entirely, but wanted to make sure that the most volatile files were safe.

One of the first things we tried to isolate the problem between hardware and software was to reinstall Windows on top of itself. That kind of reinstallation (as opposed to an install on a reformatted disk) is a pretty benign operation — it doesn't take too long, little gets changed, and in many cases the operation restores altered or corrupted dynamic link library (DLL) files and fixes problems in the Registry. It's a reasonable thing to try when you can't pin down a problem to any set of programs or operations before you progress to more drastic measures.

It's not an easy analysis whether lockups are due to hardware or software problems — particularly with Windows — but since we knew that the software on the machine hadn't changed, it was worth looking into hardware issues when the problem persisted through a reinstall of Windows. One of the first hardware issues we look for when a computer starts to act up randomly is excessive heat. Fans that stop working or blocked airflow can raise the temperature inside chips to beyond their rated limits. When that happens, the least that's likely to happen is that the chip will operate incorrectly — signals take longer to propagate through hot chips, so critical timing is more likely to be missed.

The first hardware check we did was to check the power supply air outlet temperature. Do this with the back of your hand close to the air outlet for the fan in the power supply. Use the back of your hand simply because it's more sensitive to temperature and air movement than the skin on your fingers. We noticed that there was relatively little airflow, and that the air was warmer than we expected. Looking at the fan showed it was running, so we went looking for clogged air vents.

We'd never looked closely at the air inlets in that chassis. What we found when we looked was both surprising and disturbing — the *only* air inlet was a single very narrow slit across the front of the case. That meant that under the best of circumstances, only a restricted amount of air could get through the case. What was worse was that the slit was almost completely blocked with dust, so there was almost no air at all moving. Vacuuming the slit clean restored reasonably cool airflow, so we started the system running a looping series of diagnostics to exercise it, and after it remained stable for a day, we put it back in operation.

After two weeks of stable behavior, the system failed to boot one morning. We were making coffee as it started, but when we returned to the machine,

Windows had started partially and then hung. We couldn't see anything else remarkable, so we reset the machine and let it reboot. Operation resumed normally, but we left a note for people to watch the machine more carefully again. Nothing out of the ordinary happened for a few days, but then the machine failed completely. Powering on the system resulted in the usual disk spin up noises, the fan ran in the power supply, and with one exception, the lights on the front panel looked normal. Nevertheless, the machine did not even start to boot — no video, no beep codes, no nothing.

The one exception to the front panel lights looking normal is that the power light blinked rather than remaining on steady, with the blink at a reasonably constant rate. Nothing in the documentation for the motherboard described this behavior, so beyond noting the difference, we had no diagnostic information. (In retrospect, we're suspicious that the blink is indeed a diagnostic indication Intel's built into the motherboard logic.) Using the approach we described previously in this chapter under the "System unresponsive" heading, we concluded that at some level the power supply was working, since we had lights on the front panel and could hear the disks spin. We removed all adapter cards and memory from the motherboard, disconnected the disks, and tried the system. We received the same response — lights, but nothing else. Given that, the problem had to be the power supply, the motherboard, or the processor.

We had a spare power supply in stock, but not a spare processor or motherboard. We therefore temporarily replaced the power supply and tested the system. Nothing changed — the system continued to be inoperative. That test showed the problem was either the motherboard or the processor — it's unlikely both would have failed. We had to make some choices about how to proceed — we could either start exchanging parts with another machine, taking it down for the duration of the test, or else take our best guess as to which had failed and order a replacement part. We chose to disassemble the other, working machine and swap processors. The machine wasn't busy at the time, so we didn't inconvenience anyone, and making the test allowed us to be sure which component had failed. The processor from the failed machine did not work in the good machine; the processor from the good machine brought the failed machine to life. That was conclusive evidence that the processor itself had failed. In the process, we had the opportunity to power up the failed machine with no processor whatsoever, and noticed that the front panel power light continued to flash. With a working processor, the light remains on steadily.

Processors that have been in operation for as long as this one had are very reliable, so we thought some about why the chip had failed before we reassembled the system (including changing the processor speed setup on the motherboard). The most likely causes of computer failure are static electricity, overvoltage, overclocking, and heat. Since we hadn't disassembled the machine, we could most likely rule out static electricity. We run computers on a UPS and within clock specifications, so we could rule out overvoltage and overclocking. That left only heat as a likely suspect, and we knew that the machine had cooling problems sufficient to cause random lockups only a few weeks before the failure. We couldn't prove the cause of failure without sophisticated analysis of the chip, which we're unequipped to carry out, but we believe we had sufficient evidence to draw a conclusion safely.

An implication of the argument that heat killed the old processor is that there might have been enough heat buildup to damage other components. For that reason, we didn't return the machine to service immediately — we set it running an endless series of motherboard tests, logging the results, and left the machine alone for a period of a week. When it completed that time with no failures, we checked the file system for corruption, reloaded the one bad file we found from backup, and returned the machine to service.

Summary

✦ Your best troubleshooting tool is a planned, methodical approach and careful observation.

✦ You'll want a good (small) set of tools, including protection from static electricity.

✦ You shouldn't have to force anything. The bigger hammer approach doesn't apply to computer disassembly and reassembly.

Building an Extreme Machine

◆ ◆ ◆ ◆

CHAPTER 25

In This Chapter

Mechanical assembly

Installing the processor

Configuring the motherboard

Configuring the BIOS and disk drives

Installing Windows

◆ ◆ ◆ ◆

Building a computer from components — building a desktop computer — proceeds in three phases. You need to plan what you'll put in the machine, assemble these components, and then install software.

Hardware Planning

Planning which components you'll use in your computer helps you develop a parts list. You'll choose each of the components based on what you'll use the machine for, what you want to pay for the components, and how long you expect the machine to be in service. The machine we describe building in this chapter has the parts list shown in Table 25-1.

Our design goal was to build a very high performance PC, one suitable for intense first-person shooter gaming and DVD production, as well as more general applications, that would be quiet enough to be in the room where people are watching TV or talking. The parts list for the machine is significant for what it doesn't include — there's no modem and no floppy — as well as what's in there.

> ✦ **No modem** — It used to be we recommended every machine have a modem, but the real significance of that recommendation was that it's valuable to be connected to the Internet. Unless you just can't get a broadband connection, we now recommend you use broadband to connect to the Internet, using an Ethernet port in your PC and a hardware router. That combination makes a modem useless in a PC unless you need it to receive faxes.

✦ **No floppy** — There's really little value to floppy drives anymore, particularly with the inexpensive availability of USB flash drives, other than perhaps for system setup and repair. Although we did need a floppy temporarily to set up the RAID drivers for this system, we chose not to include a drive in the case.

✦ **Quiet case, power supply, and CPU cooler** — The main sources of noise in a PC are fans moving air and the case conducting vibrations from fans and disks. Using larger, slower fans reduces the air noise, while rubber bushings between vibrating parts and the chassis surfaces suppress vibration noise. The Antec P160 case includes vibration-damping mounts for the rear fan and hard disks, while the Antec TrueControl power supply includes a control to reduce the fan speed to just what's needed to keep the supply within acceptable temperature limits.

When the system is idle, the Zalman CPU cooler (they call it a CPU noise reduction system) keeps the processor under 40 degrees C (104 degrees F) with the system in 21 degrees C (about 70 degrees F) ambient air without creating significant noise. Under load, the processor still remains at about 50 degrees C (122 degrees F). The motherboard itself contributes to reducing the noise, making do with entirely passive cooling for the chipset and voltage regulator.

The liability of the Zalman cooler is that it significantly exceeds the maximum CPU cooling system weight specification for the Intel Pentium 4 processor and motherboard. You should not move the PC when it will be subjected to shock or vibration without taking precautions to prevent motherboard damage from the weight of the cooler.

✦ **Power supply capacity** — At 550 W, the Antec power supply is large as well as quiet, giving you the capacity to drive the auxiliary power connection on the video card along with a full complement of disks and memory. The supply lets you adjust the output voltages to set them precisely or, if you know what you're doing, to overclock a system. (We strongly recommend against overclocking because overclocked systems are likely to be less stable than ones run within specification.)

✦ **Huge monitor** — The Sony LCD is huge, and ridiculously expensive, costing more than the rest of the PC, but it's crisp and has a large image.

The more general issues guiding our choices were these:

✦ **Chassis and motherboard form factor** — Few useful alternatives to the ATX form factor exist. The new form factors emerging for small PCs limit the heat dissipation, and so aren't ideal for a very high performance machine.

✦ **Processor** — As of January 2004, the 3.2 GHz Pentium 4 is the fastest Intel processor available with the exception of the Pentium 4 Extreme Edition (which has a much larger cache but is far more expensive). The processor was expensive when initially introduced; you might choose to save money by picking a processor a notch or two slower than the fastest available. We chose the Intel processor both as much because of the reliability and speed of the D875PBZ motherboard as because of the processor itself.

✦ **Memory** — We consider 256MB of memory a floor for new machines, but suggest at least 1GB for high-end PCs. We used two matched DDR SDRAMs, one in each channel, to enable the fastest memory access by the motherboard. The 800 Hz system bus requires PC3200 memory.

✦ **Disk and interface** — We used a pair of serial ATA disks to exploit the RAID 0 striping capabilities of the motherboard, using the parallel ATA ports only for the DVD writer connection. We used a large pair of drives at that — 160GB each — to create a large disk for video work.

✦ **Video** — As of January 2004, the ATI Radeon 9800 XT was the fastest video card available. There's a constant battle for performance supremacy between ATI and nVidia, with all the benefits coming to the gamer.

We chose the manufacturers of all these components based on reliable past experience. There's no question it's possible to assemble a machine with equivalent specifications at lower cost using other components; we'll simply note that in our experience, quality components pay off in better reliability and fewer problems.

The following sections describe and illustrate how to build the PC. Key photos are in the text, while the color section at the end of the book includes those photos plus additional photos of intermediate steps.

Table 25-1
The Desktop Parts List

Component	Manufacturer	Model
Chassis	Antec	P160 Aluminum mid tower www.antec-inc.com
Disk	Seagate	Barracuda 7200.7 160GB SATA drive (quantity 2) www.seagate.com
DVD Writer	Sony	DRU510a internal 4X DVD±RW drive www.sonystyle.com
Keyboard/Mouse	Logitech	Cordless Comfort Duo www.logitech.com
Memory	Crucial (Micron)	CT6464Z40B 512MB DDR PC3200, CAS latency 3, unbuffered, non-parity, 5ns, 2.5 V (quantity 2) www.crucial.com

Continued

Table 25-1 *(continued)*		
Component	**Manufacturer**	**Model**
Monitor	Sony	SDM-P232W/B 23" Flat Panel LCD (1,920×1,200) www.sonystyle.com
Motherboard	Intel	D875PBZ, with gigabit Ethernet and 8 USB 2.0 ports, without onboard audio www.intel.com
Power Supply	Antec	TrueControl 550 www.antec-inc.com
Processor	Intel	3.2 GHz Pentium 4 with hyperthreading and 800 MHz system bus www.intel.com
Processor Cooling	Zalman Tech.	CNPS7000A-Cu heat sink and fan assembly www.zalman.co.kr/english
Sound	Turtle Beach	Santa Cruz www.turtle-beach.com
Speakers	Acoustic Authority	A-3780 Pro Series speakers www.cyberacoustics.com
Video	ATI	Radeon 9800 XT www.ati.com

Preliminary Mechanical Assembly

First off, we're going to remind you again about the importance of an anti-static wrist strap — *any* time you touch a board with electronic devices on it, you need to use effective anti-static protection. If you don't, you could end up with some very useless equipment.

The first step in assembling a computer is to perform the gross mechanical assembly, mounting the disk drives into the chassis. You mount the power supply at the same time if you received it separately from the chassis.

Chassis layout and assembly

The Antec P160 chassis follows the standard ATX layout, with the power supply at the top rear, external bays at the top front, internal bays at the bottom rear, and motherboard at the bottom rear. The back of the case includes a noise-isolated fan, and there are provisions for another fan on the front. The motherboard mounts on a separate, removable tray to simplify installation and maintenance.

Figure 25-1 shows the drive mounting bays from the inside. External 5.25-inch drives mount on slide rails, while internal 3.5-inch drives mount on grommets in vibration-isolated carriers. The screws you use to attach internal 3.5-inch drives have a longer unthreaded shank to space the drive away from and avoid crushing the rubber grommets.

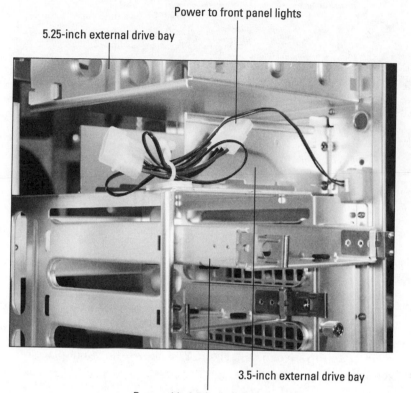

Power to front panel lights

5.25-inch external drive bay

3.5-inch external drive bay

Removable 3.5-inch disk carrier

Figure 25-1: Antec P160 disk drive bays
©2004 Barry Press & Marcia Press

Remove the front panel from the chassis before you start working. It removes from the bottom towards the top and might be difficult the first few times. The wiring to the front panel lights goes to the connector visible on the right in Figure 25-1; the connector at the end of the front panel wires can be removed from the chassis front so you can set the front panel aside.

The power supply mounts in the back of the case, as shown in Figure 25-2. The rails and sheet metal forming the case are designed to cradle the power supply while you screw it in place, but you have to watch that you don't accidentally crimp an output wire between the supply and the chassis. The TrueControl power supply has a voltage adjustment control panel you mount in a 5.25-inch external bay; we used the bottom one and left the cover plate in place to keep curious fingers from making unfortunate adjustments.

Input voltage selector

Input power shutoff

External drive power connector

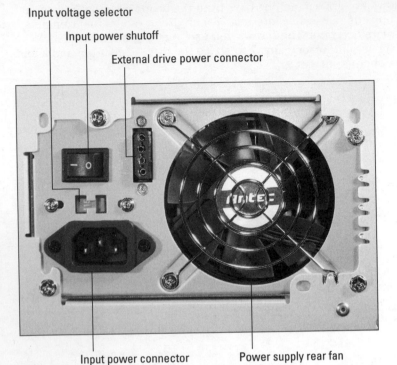

Input power connector   Power supply rear fan

Figure 25-2: TrueControl power supply mounted in chassis

©2004 Barry Press & Marcia Press

The chassis rear fan mounts differently than most fans, in that it uses flexible plugs to secure it to the chassis instead of hard mount screws, reducing the vibration transmitted to the sheet metal. Figure 25-3 shows the fan in place on the chassis back panel.

Mounting the drives

The next step is to install the DVD writer and the power supply control. We put the writer in the topmost external 5.25-inch bay, but you can use any of the available bays in the chassis. You attach slides to the drive and then ease the assembly into the chassis from the front.

After that's complete, mount the disk drives in the vibration-isolating carriers (make the screws snug in the grommets but not overly tight) and snap the carriers into the chassis (see Figure 25-4). We placed the drives in the middle two slots so the airflow from the front of the chassis would flow right over the drives for cooling. The label on top of the drive may have important information — for parallel ATA drives, for example, it's likely to have all the information you need to configure jumpers and figure out which end of the data connector has pin 1 (it's often the one closest to the power connector).

Flexible fan mounts

Power connector

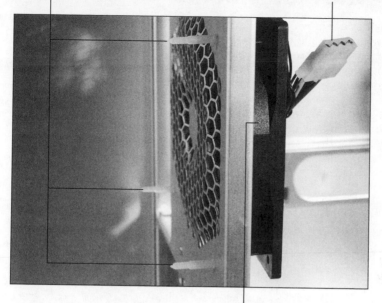

Low-speed 120 mm fan

Figure 25-3: Fan mounted on back panel
©2004 Barry Press & Marcia Press

Figure 25-4: Disk drives mounted in chassis
©2004 Barry Press & Marcia Press

Installing the Motherboard

The chassis provides a removable tray for mounting the motherboard. Take the tray out of the chassis and then replace the generic ATX I/O panel supplied with the chassis with the custom one that comes with the motherboard. The removable motherboard tray really simplifies assembling and maintaining the system because you can get to the mounting positions without having the chassis box in the way. ATX chassis secure the motherboard with threaded metal clips or (better) solid metal standoffs that attach to holes in the tray. You want to use a standoff in each hole in the tray that lines up with one of the metal-rimmed holes in the motherboard (see Figure 25-5) — the Intel D875PBZ motherboard uses 10 of them.

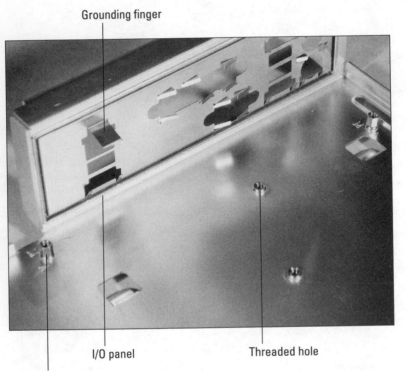

Grounding finger

I/O panel   Threaded hole

Brass standoff

Figure 25-5: I/O panel and standoffs on motherboard tray

©2004 Barry Press & Marcia Press

Figure 25-6 is an outline drawing of the Intel D875PBZ motherboard showing the processor location and the internal power, data, and control interfaces. There are no jumpers to set on the board because it detects and sets processor speed and voltage automatically. As it is, there is only one jumper on the board to cause the BIOS to boot into a special configuration mode, from where you can set any of the BIOS parameters.

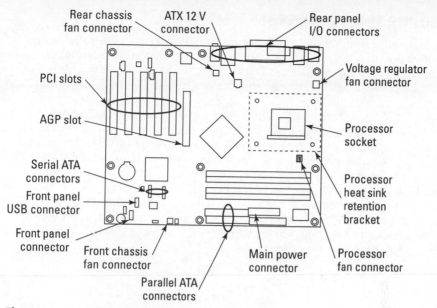

Figure 25-6: Intel D875PBZ motherboard layout
Drawing courtesy Intel Corporation

The connectors for the ATX I/O panel are at the upper left of Figure 25-6 and are detailed in Figure 25-7.

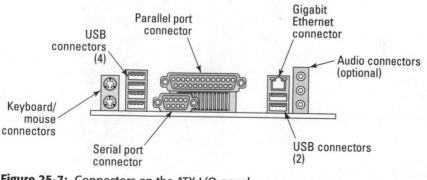

Figure 25-7: Connectors on the ATX I/O panel
Drawing courtesy Intel Corporation

Set the motherboard onto the tray, being careful to align the I/O connectors into the I/O panel. The fingers sticking out of the I/O panel push against the connectors to make sure the outside connector shield grounds to the chassis. Some of the fingers have to slide onto one side of the connector, such as the one sticking out from the upper-left part of the panel in Figure 25-5.

Installing the processor

We recommend installing the processor on the motherboard after mounting the motherboard in the chassis. For the Antec case, that recommendation translates to mounting the processor after attaching the motherboard to the tray, but before sliding the tray into the chassis.

The Intel D875PBZ motherboard comes with the heat sink bracket and processor socket attached. Figure 25-8 shows the processor socket — note specifically the two missing pinholes in the upper-left corner of the photo. The processor (see Figure 25-9) has corresponding missing pins so you know which way to orient the processor when you place it in the socket. Installation consists of raising the lever just visible at the top of Figure 25-8 so it's straight up, dropping in the processor, and closing the lever. The processor should drop in with no force, and should be flush against the socket on all sides. If not, then either the lever's not all the way up, you've turned the processor the wrong way, or there's a bent pin on the processor.

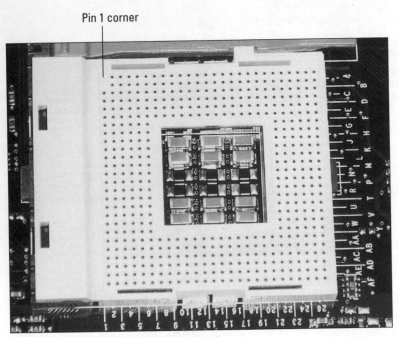

Pin 1 corner

Figure 25-8: Pentium 4 processor socket
©2004 Barry Press & Marcia Press

Mount the processor heat sink and fan after installing the processor. Figure 25-10 shows the Zalman cooler; one of the bracket ends you use to secure the cooler to the heat sink mounting bracket is visible in the lower right of the photo.

Pin 1 corner

Figure 25-9: Pentium 4 processor, bottom view
©2004 Barry Press & Marcia Press

Figure 25-10: Zalman processor cooler
©2004 Barry Press & Marcia Press

Prepare the processor by spreading a very thin layer of thermal grease on the top of the processor, as in Figure 25-11. Use a flat, stiff edge, such as the edge of a credit card, to spread and thin the thermal grease. Your goal is to have a very thin, smooth layer — the grease just fills holes that block heat transfer. If you get more than a very thin layer, or leave gaps, and you're likely to impede heat flow and cook the processor.

Figure 25-11: Thermal grease on processor
©2004 Barry Press & Marcia Press

Slide the spanning brackets supplied with the cooler in place between the posts on the motherboard heat sink attachment bracket, then place the Zalman cooler on the processor, and screw it down onto the spanning brackets (see Figure 25-12). Use the inner two holes on the cooler itself to feed the screws to the spanning brackets and tighten the screws on either side of the cooler alternately until they're snug.

We oriented the cooler so its fan wires pointed towards the edge of the motherboard, then ran the wires counterclockwise around the base of the cooler, and plugged them into the processor fan connector.

Spanning bracket

Mounting bracket on motherboard

Processor fan power
connector

Figure 25-12: Mounted Zalman cooler

©2004 Barry Press & Marcia Press

Inserting the memory

The last step before installing the motherboard tray back in the chassis is to
insert the DDR DIMM memory strips. The Crucial Web site has tools to help
you find compatible memory, but you'll nevertheless want to read your motherboard documentation to see if there are restrictions on the order in which
you populate memory sockets and to make sure you use a memory configuration that gives you maximum performance. In the case of the Intel 875 chipset
on the D875PBZ motherboard, using matched pairs of DIMM strips in both
memory banks takes advantage of the dual channel memory interface and
enables what Intel calls dynamic addressing mode, which gives you faster
memory access. Installing the pair of 512MB DIMMs we showed in the parts
list, one per channel, meets both criteria.

Figure 25-13 shows the DIMM strips installed in the D875PBZ motherboard, one in slot zero of each bank. The sockets and DIMM strips are both keyed, so you can insert the memory only one way into the socket. Be gentle inserting the strips to minimize the stress on the motherboard itself.

DIMM in bank 0, slot 0

Retention clips

DIMM in bank 1, slot 0

Figure 25-13: DIMM strips in the memory sockets

©2004 Barry Press & Marcia Press

Once you insert the DIMM into the socket, you'll be able to close the latches completely. If you don't get the memory in the socket properly, the BIOS won't see it when you boot the computer. The latches should fit all the way into the notches on the DIMM strips.

Secure the motherboard tray back into the chassis. Fit an adapter card into the motherboard as a pathfinder, and screw it to the card bracket panel — the card helps set the fine position of the motherboard before you tighten the motherboard mounting screws. We typically mount two cards, one at either end of the slots, to avoid misalignment due to pivoting around a single card. Once you've inserted the adapter cards and tightened up the card brackets, gently tighten all the motherboard mounting screws.

Cabling in the power supply

Next, wire the power supply to the connectors on the motherboard. Figure 25-14 shows the main ATX power supply cable in place (the photo is not of the D875PBZ motherboard). Plug in the ATX auxiliary 12 V cable, too, and then route them both temporarily in the chassis to keep them out of the way while you work.

Figure 25-14: Main ATX power supply cable
©2004 Barry Press & Marcia Press

The power supply includes — separate from the 12 V cable to the motherboard — a fan output cable that has only 12 V (yellow and black) wired. Don't use it for anything but fans because disk drives, the video card, and other items require the 5 V supply, too. The power supply also connects to the disks, the chassis front panel via a disk-like connector, and (because it came equipped with a disk drive–style power connector) the rear panel fan. The Antec power supply doesn't have serial ATA disk drive power connectors, so you have to use adapters like the one shown in Figure 25-15.

The Antec TrueControl power supply includes a fan-like three-pin output connector you can plug into the motherboard to let its fan speed sensors measure the power supply fan speed. We connected it to the rear panel fan connector on the motherboard.

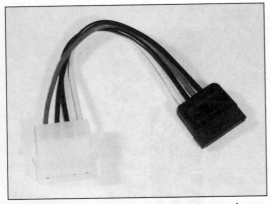

Figure 25-15: Serial ATA disk drive power adapter
©2004 Barry Press & Marcia Press

Having made all the power supply connections, dress the wires out of the way and secure them with cable ties. It's mandatory that you keep the wires out of the airflow paths, and highly desirable that you keep the wires away from where you need to be working. If you're using a chassis with a transparent side panel, you'll want to make the wiring as invisible as possible.

Wiring the chassis to the motherboard connectors

Now, wire the chassis to the motherboard connectors. Figure 25-16 shows part of the motherboard, with callouts showing the front panel connectors. You'll wire up the power switch, reset switch, hard disk activity LED, and power LED to the pairs of pins shown in the photo (the information about which pin does what is stenciled on the motherboard near the header and is in the motherboard manual). For each pair, the colored wire is usually the one to install closest to pin 1, although the orientation matters only for LEDs and not for switches. You won't hook up a speaker because there's already a speaker-like device mounted on the motherboard.

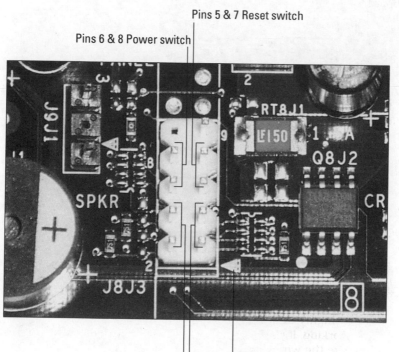

Figure 25-16: Intel D875PBZ motherboard front panel header

©2004 Barry Press & Marcia Press

The wires from the front panel tie to connectors in pairs corresponding to the pairs in Figure 25-16. Figure 25-17 shows the completed connections, along with the USB front panel cable. The USB cable connector is one piece, laid out to match the header on the motherboard, and keyed to keep you from turning it the wrong way. If you're using a different motherboard or case, check the front panel USB wiring carefully because if you get it wrong you can damage the motherboard.

Figure 25-17: Completed front panel and USB wiring

©2004 Barry Press & Marcia Press

Final Cabling

At this point, you've built up the chassis and drives, installed the processor and memory, mounted the motherboard in the chassis, and cabled the chassis to the motherboard. The only wiring that's left is to hook up the data cables. Figure 25-18 is a close-up of the floppy disk and IDE connectors on the D875PBZ motherboard. If you look at the photo closely, you can see the labels on the motherboard, such as the one for the primary IDE port. Pin 1 is on the left for all three connectors. Set the jumper on the DVD writer to be the master and then cable the primary IDE connector to the drive.

Secondary parallel IDE connector

DIMM sockets, bank 0 and 1

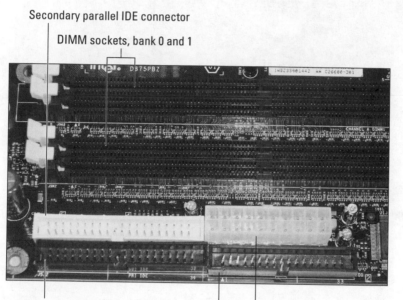

Primary parallel IDE connector

Main ATX power connector

Floppy disk connector

Figure 25-18: IDE drive connectors

©2004 Barry Press & Marcia Press

The serial ATA drives each connect directly to a port on the motherboard — one drive ties to each port. It doesn't matter which drive goes to which port, since they're the same. The serial ATA connectors are keyed so that you can't put them on backwards. Figure 25-19 shows the completed power and data cable wiring near the motherboard.

Figure 25-19: Power and data wiring

©2004 Barry Press & Marcia Press

Installing Adapter Cards

The ATI Radeon 9800 XT video card and Turtle Beach Santa Cruz sound card get installed next (unless you already installed them both before as pathfinders). The video card can go only in the AGP slot (see Figure 25-20). We installed the sound card in the PCI slot farthest away from the video card to minimize heat issues from the video card.

Figure 25-20: Motherboard slots
©2004 Barry Press & Marcia Press

Figure 25-21 shows the completed system.

Figure 25-21: Completed system internal view
©2004 Barry Press & Marcia Press

Planning Your Software

You have four steps to accomplish to install software on your desktop computer once it's built. Here are the steps:

1. **BIOS update and configuration** — You need to set up the BIOS to reflect your hardware and OS and might need to update it to the manufacturer's latest version.

2. **Disk configuration** — You then enable the RAID capability to increase performance and make the pair of drives appear as a single device.

3. **RAID drivers** — You install Windows from CD-ROM, but the disk doesn't contain the driver you need for the RAID array, so you need to have them ready to load separately.

4. **OS installation** — After all those preliminaries, you can install the operating system.

We installed Windows XP Professional on this PC. We detest Microsoft's Windows Product Activation — and all Digital Rights Management (DRM) schemes in general — because DRM assumes the consumer is a criminal and takes away legal consumer rights. Nevertheless, we show you how to install Windows XP on this PC because it manages the hyperthreaded processor and RAID array better than prior Windows versions.

Configuring BIOS

Hook up a keyboard, mouse, and display; plug in the computer and display and power them on. We suggest you power the display on a minute before the computer so you'll see everything on the display output by the computer. Listen carefully to the computer as it powers up. Normal sounds include the power supply and other fans, disks spinning up, and the starting beep from the speaker. Abnormal behavior includes the absence of those sounds or the presence of beep codes from the speaker. Follow the instructions in Chapter 24 if you don't get the normal sounds, or if you don't get a normal BIOS startup display on the monitor.

Once the BIOS shows onscreen, quickly push the F2 key to get the BIOS setup screen. Other motherboards use different keys; Del (Delete) is common on boards using the AMI BIOS. We've also seen systems using Control+Alt+S or some other combination. The documentation that came with the computer or motherboard should tell you the combination if it's not apparent onscreen. Check the BIOS version, and if it's not the current version from the manufacturer, update it now before you start configuring and installing software. You'll have to use the standalone BIOS update (and a temporary floppy disk drive) since you don't have Windows running yet.

The Intel D875PBZ BIOS has fewer manual configuration settings than many other boards. Once you enter the BIOS, the top-level menu has choices for Main, Advanced, Security, Power, Boot, and Exit. We describe the key BIOS settings using notation like *Main ⇨ Hyper Threading Technology* to indicate the path through the menus to the setting we're describing. Here are the most important settings:

✦ **Main ⇨ Hyper Threading Technology** — The 3.2 GHz processor implements hyperthreading, which lets it appear like two processors and gives you as much as a 25 to 30 percent performance boost. This setting has to be enabled to turn the second processor appearance on.

✦ **Advanced ⇨ Boot Configuration ⇨ Plug & Play O/S** — Turn this on unless you're running Windows NT 4 or another operating system that does not support Plug and Play (PnP) device configuration. The difference the option makes is to control whether the BIOS sets up resources for PnP cards or leaves the work for the operating system.

✦ **Advanced** ⇨ **Drive Configuration** — On other motherboards, this is where you'd configure IDE (parallel ATA) drives, although in nearly all situations you'll just use automatic configuration. More important for this machine is the Advanced ⇨ Drive Configuration ⇨ ATA/IDE Configuration setting, which you have to set to Enhanced to enable the serial ATA ports, and the Advanced ⇨ Drive Configuration ⇨ Intel Raid Technology setting, which you must enable to set up the two serial ATA disks as one striped set. Once you enable that last setting, a reboot will show the RAID configuration BIOS screen.

✦ **Advanced** ⇨ **Video Configuration** ⇨ **AGP Aperture Size** — AGP video boards get an address space allocated to them of up to 256MB, the size of which is independent of the actual memory on the board. Some boards give better performance with one setting than another. The best way to determine the right setting is to check the video card manufacturer's recommendation. If you can't find one (check the Web site, too), set it to the closest value to the actual video memory on the card. If you have to guess, test video performance in several 3D applications or games for different aperture sizes and choose the fastest one.

✦ **Advanced** ⇨ **USB Configuration** — You'll want to make sure *High-Speed USB* is enabled so you can use USB 2.0 devices. Also under here is *Legacy USB Support*; be sure to enable that option if you have a USB mouse or keyboard, so they'll work if you boot into the BIOS, an emergency recovery disk, or an operating system without USB support. We left the *USB 2.0 Legacy Support* option at *Full-Speed* to make sure the USB 1.1 keyboard and mouse we use have no configuration issues.

✦ **Advanced** ⇨ **Fan Control Configuration** ⇨ **Fan Control** — Enable this to let the system control fan speed as it manages temperatures.

✦ **Boot** ⇨ **Silent Boot** — By default, the D875PBZ BIOS displays a graphic logo instead of the more useful BIOS startup messages, even though the F2 key still works to enter BIOS setup. Change this setting to *Enabled* to see the boot messages.

Once you've finished setting up the BIOS, save your settings and exit. The system will then reboot.

Configuring the Disk and Installing Windows

Upon reboot, you'll see a new BIOS screen giving you the ability to configure the serial ATA RAID capability. Press Ctrl+I to enter the RAID BIOS and then choose to create a RAID volume. We simply chose to use all of both installed serial ATA disks and took the recommendation for 128K blocks as being suitable for a workstation. Save the settings and exit, and the system will reboot again.

You're ready to boot the CD-ROM and start the Windows XP install at this point with one exception, which is that Windows XP does not include the device driver required to use the RAID array. Windows XP does, however, provide a mechanism to load additional drivers as the installation CD-ROM starts up, but is so brain dead that it can load those drivers *only* from a floppy. Because we didn't want a floppy drive in the machine, we temporarily cabled in one until Windows XP finished installing and then disconnected it the next time we turned off the machine. You tell Windows XP Setup to load the driver by pressing F6 (watch the message bar at the bottom for when), so Intel calls the driver file you need the *SATA RAID: F6 Driver Disk*. You can download the file from the Intel D875PBZ motherboard site, and specifically from `www.intel.com/design/motherbd/bz/bz_drive.htm`. Download the file and run it on another PC (one with a floppy) — the program unpacks the data, wipes the floppy you gave it clean, and writes the necessary files. Insert that disk in your temporary floppy drive when Windows XP Setup asks for it.

You'll partition and format the hard disk as part of Windows XP Setup. Partitions divide the space on the drive into areas where you can place file systems, most always corresponding to drive letters for Windows. (UNIX doesn't use drive letters because it collects file systems on various partitions into named branches rooted into a tree.) Windows NT/2000/XP work best using NTFS (NT File System), so choose that when Windows XP Setup asks you what type of partition you want to create. Continue to follow the rest of the Windows XP setup instructions to complete OS setup.

Checking Your Configuration

Select the Device Manager tab in the System applet, and look for yellow or red icons that indicate problems. If you find problems, check under the properties of that device for clues as to what the problem is and what corrective action you need to take. Devices you find shown as unknown indicate that you probably need to install a manufacturer-supplied driver. Start with drivers unique to your motherboard and then add drivers for adapter cards and other peripherals as required.

For each of your devices, check the manufacturer's Web site for more current drivers for your operating system. You'll want to do that periodically, but be sure to evaluate new drivers before putting them on machines used for productive work.

Installing Applications

Once Windows is up and stable, you can go ahead and install applications, the first of which should be a good antivirus program. We usually let programs install to their default directories unless that's `\windows`, in which case we force the installation elsewhere to keep the application files separate. We strongly recommend that you set up your applications (or discipline yourself while you work) so that your data files are *not* in the same directory as the application, because when you go to upgrade or uninstall a program, you may find that having the files intermixed with the application makes it hard to figure out which files are yours and which are part of the program.

The first thing to do once you have the bulk of your software installed is to defragment the disk. You can access this function by choosing Start ⇨ Programs ⇨ Accessories ⇨ System Tools ⇨ Disk Defragmenter. Windows will likely complain that the disk doesn't need to be defragmented, but force it to run anyway. If you look at the detailed display from the disk defragmenter program while it runs, you'll see that a lot of empty space is interspersed with your files. Although Windows is telling you that the files themselves are not fragmented, which is probably true, it isn't looking at how fragmented free disk space is. By running the defragmenter now, you close up that empty space and help keep the work you do later from fragmenting.

Summary

✦ Assembling a computer in the right order makes things simpler and avoids damage to more fragile components. Assemble the chassis, drives, motherboard, processor, memory, and internal cables in that order.

✦ Depart from most computer users' standard practice — read the documentation for your hardware components carefully, looking for detailed steps you need to accomplish and for limitations on what you can do.

✦ Assembling a computer isn't really that hard — planning what you're going to build, having a basic understanding of the components, and taking a careful approach to component selection are the keys to success.

✦ Check the Internet to be sure your device drives are the latest ones.

✦ When things go wrong, use the basic troubleshooting pattern — simplify and isolate.

Glossary

μM Micron (or micrometer). A unit of length equal to one millionth of a meter.

μS Microsecond. One millionth of a second.

10Base-2 Also known as "cheapernet" and "Thinnet." Another name for Ethernet using thin (0.2-inch) coaxial cable and BNC connectors.

10Base-T, 100Base-T, and 1000Base-T The group of proposed IEEE 802.3 physical layer specifications for 10, 100, and 1,000 Mbps Ethernet over twisted-pair wiring. Recognizable by its characteristic RJ-45 connectors.

802 A set of IEEE standards for local area networks (LANs) and metropolitan area networks (MANs).

- ✦ .1 — For general management and internetwork operations such as security and bridging
- ✦ .2 — Logical link control sublayer of the data link layer
- ✦ .3 — For the CSMA/CD (carrier sense multiple access with collision detection) network access method used by Ethernet networks
- ✦ .11 — For wireless local area networks

AC-3 The audio standard for DVDs distributed in North America. Dolby Laboratory's AC-3 is an audio format that uses five independent sound channels (left front, right front, center front, right rear, and left rear) plus a nondirectional subwoofer. Due to the use of five channels plus a subwoofer, this system is often referred to as a 5.1 system. In Europe, DVDs use the MPEG-2 audio format as a standard.

Acceptable Use Policy (AUP) A policy that defines allowable conduct using network resources. You'll usually see an Acceptable Use Policy defined by Internet service providers and other entities providing Internet access.

access time The average time interval between a storage peripheral (usually a disk drive or semiconductor memory) receiving a request to read or write a certain location and returning the value read or completing the write.

ACPI Advanced Configuration and Power Interface. The power management standard succeeding APM (Advanced Power Management) to support operating system control and management of device power consumption.

adapter A board installed in a computer system, usually a PC. Adapters provide a variety of functions, including disk interface, video, sound, and network communications.

ADSL Asymmetric digital subscriber line. A DSL technology that allows more bandwidth from the network to you than from you to the network.

AGP Accelerated Graphics Port is a bus interface for graphics accelerators providing fast, high-throughput direct access to system memory. As PC applications became more graphics intensive (as with multi-player 3D games and advanced CAD programs), the bandwidth required to display each screen rose dramatically. AGP graphics addressed this bandwidth bottleneck with a high-bandwidth pipeline between the graphics accelerator and system memory.

amplitude The magnitude of a signal, often in units of decibels (dB).

analog signals Signals that can vary over a continuous range (for instance, the human voice over conventional telephone lines). Analog circuitry is more subject to distortion and noise but can often more easily handle complex signals than can digital signals, which can have only discrete values. Analog signals connect through the VGA port to a monitor, while digital ones connect through a DVI port.

anonymous FTP The facility that enables you to log into an FTP server without having your own account on that server. You log in with "anonymous" as your user ID and (by convention) your e-mail address as the password. Some sites enforce the convention, and some do not.

ANSI American National Standards Institute.

anti-static Materials that help dissipate static electricity and therefore prevent damage to electronic devices through electrostatic discharge.

antivirus Software to detect and intercept computer viruses transmitted via networks, e-mail, or removable storage.

ARP (Address Resolution Protocol) A protocol for dynamically mapping Internet Protocol addresses to physical hardware addresses on LANs. Limited to LANs that support hardware broadcast. Required to permit computers to discover the physical addresses of other computers on the same network.

array The part of a RAM that stores the bits. The array consists of rows and columns, with a cell at each intersection that can store a bit.

ASCII American Standard Code for Information Interchange. A method of encoding text as binary values. The standard ASCII character set consists of 128 decimal numbers (0–127) for letters of the alphabet, numerals, punctuation marks, and common special characters.

aspect ratio The relationship between width and height of a computer monitor or television set. Standard-definition (conventional) television products provide a 4:3 aspect ratio. High-definition television uses a 16:9 aspect ratio.

AT command set The name of the commands used to control most personal computer modems, taken from the characters *AT* that precede most commands. Originally developed by Hayes Computer Products.

ATA AT Attachment. The most common standard for disk drive interfaces to PCs. ATA typically refers to parallel disk interfaces; the term SATA (Serial ATA) is used explicitly for the newer serial interface.

ATAPI ATA Packet Interface. An extension of the ATA specification to support devices such as CD-ROMs.

attenuation The decrease in magnitude of the power of a signal transmitted over a wire. As attenuation increases, signal power decreases.

ATX A form factor specifying the size and layout of desktop computers. The specification extends to the definition of the power supply and its interface to the PC. A variant of the ATX power supply, ATX12V, is used with Pentium 4 processors.

authentication An exchange to ensure that users are who they say they are and are authorized to access remote resources. A common example is the sequence requiring you to enter a user name and password to access the Internet through your Internet service provider.

autodetect The ability to automatically recognize hardware and install the appropriate drivers.

autorun A capability built into Windows that lets CD-ROMs launch software when inserted in the PC.

back door A preprogrammed hole in an otherwise secure system that compromises its defenses, allowing intruders access.

backup Copying information from a hard disk onto another data storage device.

bandwidth Measure of the information capacity of a transmission channel. Strictly speaking, bandwidth is the difference, expressed in hertz (Hz), between the highest and lowest frequencies of the channel. For a given modulation and power level, the data rate you can transmit down the channel is proportional to the bandwidth.

bank A slot or group of slots populated with memory modules.

baseband A transmission scheme in which the entire bandwidth, or data-carrying capacity, of a medium (such as coaxial cable) is used to carry a single digital pulse, or signal, between multiple users. Because digital signals are not modulated, only one kind of data can be transmitted at a time.

bay The brackets in a chassis that hold disk and tape drives. External bays have an opening to the outside; internal bays do not.

BER Bit error rate. A measure of the number of incorrect bits per bit transmitted. Usable communications channels have a BER far less than one.

b-frame An MPEG-2 bidirectional frame, which uses both past and subsequent frames as a reference to calculate compressed frame data. For a given data rate, b-frames improve video quality as compared to MPEG-2 streams with just i-frames or i- and p-frames.

binary A method of encoding numbers as a series of bits. The binary number system, also referred to as base 2, uses combinations of only two digits: 0 and 1.

BIOS Basic input-output system. Provides fundamental services required for the operation of a computer. Permanently present in the machine, these routines are now generally stored in flash memory (early PCs used read-only memory). The motherboard contains a BIOS to support all of its standard functions. Adapter cards can carry additions to the BIOS for their own unique functions.

bit The smallest unit of information a computer processes. A bit can have a value of either 1 or 0.

blind dialing An automated process whereby the modem goes off-hook and dials without waiting for a dial tone. This is prohibited in many countries.

BNC connector BNC jacks and plugs connect 10Base-2 network hardware via coaxial cable. A BNC barrel connector joins two lengths of cable. A BNC tee connector joins two lengths of cable to the back of a device. A BNC terminator closes off an unused end of a BNC tee or a coaxial cable.

bonded disk DVD video discs are 1.2 mm thick and consist of two 0.6 mm layers permanently bonded together. This procedure produces a disc that is more resistant to warpage and offers improved tilt margins, making it possible to use both sides of the DVD disc.

bonding An international standard for aggregating multiple data channels into a single logical connection. Commonly applied to dial-up lines.

boot drive The drive from which the operating system loads (usually A: or C: in Windows).

booting The process by which a computer starts and loads the operating system.

bottlenecks Traffic slowdowns that result when too many network nodes try to access a single communications path or node, often a server node, at once.

bps Bits per second.

Bps Bytes per second.

bridge A device that interconnects local or remote networks no matter what higher-level protocols (such as IPX or TCP/IP) are involved. Bridges form a single logical network, centralizing network administration. They operate at the physical and link layers of the Open Systems Interconnect (OSI) Reference Model.

bridge/router A device that can provide the functions of a bridge, router, or both concurrently. A bridge/router can route one or more protocols, such as TCP/IP and/or IPX, and bridge all other traffic.

broadband Internet access connections faster than are available through dial-up analog modems, so faster than 56 Kbps.

broadcast A message forwarded to all network destinations.

buffer An area in a device or computer memory for temporary storage of data. Badly written software that fails to check for data streams overflowing the buffer size may be vulnerable to attack.

bus A pathway for data in a computer system. All PCs have a bus, which is able to host add-on (expansion) devices, such as modems, adapter boards, and video adapters. Expansion devices use the bus to send data to and receive data from the PC's CPU or memory. Essentially all PCs made today use the PCI bus; future PCs are likely to migrate to the newer PCI Express bus.

byte A unit of information made up of 8 bits. The byte is a fundamental unit of computer processing; almost all aspects of a computer's performance and specifications are measured in bytes or multiples thereof (such as kilobytes, megabytes, and gigabytes).

cache memory A small, fast memory holding recently accessed data and designed to speed up subsequent access to the same data. Most commonly refers to high-speed memory located between the CPU and the main memory, or a memory between a disk drive and the PC itself. Two levels of cache are typical next to the CPU: Level 1 and Level 2. Level 1 cache sits next to the processor and is smaller and faster than Level 2. Level 2 sits between Level 1 cache and main memory. Both are likely to be physically inside the CPU chip.

caching The process by which data requested by the operating system is retrieved from a cache instead of from some slower source (for example, main memory for a CPU cache or a hard disk for a disk cache).

CAS Column address strobe. The signal that tells the DRAM to accept the given address as a column address. *See* RAS.

CCITT (Consultative Committee for International Telegraph and Telephone)
An international organization that developed communications standards known as *Recommendations* for many forms of analog and digital communication. Now superseded by the ITU-TSS.

CD Compact disk. A standardized optical disc holding approximately 650 or 700MB whose contents can be set only at manufacturing time.

CD quality Recording quality similar to that of a compact disc player. Requires that 16 bits of information per channel be recorded for every sample taken, and that each channel be sampled 44,100 times per second.

CD-R CD recordable. A form of CD-ROM that can be written. Any specific part of the CD-R media can be written to only once, but provisions in the CD-R specification allow multiple tracks to be written on the same media at separate times.

CD-ROM CD-read only memory. A form of CD adapted to hold computer files.

Centronics interface A 36-pin connection that became the standard way to attach printers to a PC parallel data port. Also called a parallel printer interface.

CERT Computer Emergency Response Team. An organization tasked to facilitate response to Internet computer security events. The CERT Web page is at www.cert.org. Their security issue archive is at ftp.cert.org and includes information about how to defeat attacks. Their e-mail address is cert@cert.org. The 24-hour telephone hotline is (412) 268-7090.

chipset A group of integrated circuits to perform a specific function. Most commonly refers to the chips on the motherboard supporting the CPU, or to the chip(s) providing graphics display functionality.

client The user-end software supporting specific functions, such as Telnet or FTP. The other end of the connection is the server.

client/server A distributed system model of computing that brings computing power to the desktop, where users (clients) access resources from servers.

clock A source of digital timing signals.

clock rate The number of pulses emitted by a computer's clock in one second; it determines the rate at which operations are performed.

CMOS Complementary Metal-Oxide Semiconductor. Outside of digital design, a term used to refer to the device in personal computers that holds configuration data while power is turned off.

CO Central office. A local telephone company office that connects to all local loops (subscriber lines) in a given area and where circuit switching of customer lines occurs. Your distance from the CO can limit the DSL speed (or availability) you receive.

coaxial cable A data transmission medium with a single-wire conductor wrapped by an insulator and an outer metal shield.

codec Coder/decoder. A hardware or software device to encode and decode audio or video signals.

cold boot Starting a computer by applying power.

column Part of the memory array. A bit can be stored where a column and a row intersect.

COM port The DOS and Windows name for a serial port.

command.com The command processor for Windows systems. It provides the C> prompt. Renamed cmd.exe in Windows NT, 2000, and XP. bash is one of the more common command processors (shells) for Linux systems.

communications protocol A set of procedures that controls how a data communications link or network operates.

Compact Flash One of several flash memory form factors used for storage in cameras and other portable electronic devices.

component video An interface providing the elements of a video signal as separate components, consisting of luminance, which is brightness in the video image, and separate red and blue (Y, R-Y, B-Y) signals.

compression Reversibly reducing the size of data to lower the bandwidth or space required for transmission or storage.

contention A network access method where devices compete for the right to access the physical medium.

CPU (central processing unit) The chip in a computer that has primary responsibility for executing program instructions. The basic components of a computer are the processor, memory, display, storage, and input/output devices.

CRC Cyclic redundancy check. A mathematical method (related to checksums) used to check that data is error-free.

crossover cable An Ethernet cable that reverses the transmit and receive pairs between the connectors.

CSMA/CD Carrier sense multiple access with collision detection. Channel access method used by Ethernet in which devices transmit only after finding the data channel clear for some period of time. When two devices transmit simultaneously, a collision occurs and the colliding devices delay their retransmissions for a random length of time.

cylinder The set of tracks at one specific radial distance, spanning multiple platters and platter sides on a disk.

data compression A reversible data transformation that exploits statistical characteristics of the data to produce a more compact representation. Data compression may be lossless, in which case the exact original data can be reconstructed from the compressed form, or (for audio, pictures, or video) lossy, in which case an approximation that contains some differences is reconstructed.

datagram A logical block of data sent as a unit without prior establishment of a network connection. Contains source and destination address information as well as the data itself.

DDR *See* dual data rate.

decibel (dB) A unit of measure for analog signal amplitude.

decoding The process that decompresses encoded video and audio information for playback.

degauss To remove residual magnetism, leaving the device in a magnetically neutral state.

demodulation Opposite of modulation; the process of retrieving data from a modulated carrier wave.

denial-of-service attack A network attack in which a server or communications channel is made unavailable, typically by either overloading the server or flooding the communications channel.

device driver A software module that enables other software in a computer to communicate with hardware devices such as disk drives, sound cards, video cards, or mice. Each kind of device typically requires a different driver.

DHCP Dynamic Host Configuration Protocol. An Ethernet protocol computers use to receive network addresses and other LAN configuration data.

dial-up Communication established by a switched-circuit connection using the telephone network. The term comes from the fact that one of the connections dials up the telephone at the other end.

die An individual cell — a "chip" — on a semiconductor wafer that contains the complete circuitry to perform a specific function. The wafer itself contains many copies of the chip.

digital recording A recording technique in which sounds and/or images are converted into groups of electronic bits for storage.

digital signal A discrete signal that can take on only one of several (usually only two) discrete levels. In contrast, analog signals can take a continuous range of levels.

DIMM Dual inline memory module. A printed circuit board holding memory devices. Similar to the older SIMM, but with more independent contacts.

DIN connector A German connector standard. DIN connectors are commonly used for keyboards, PS/2-style mice, and audio/video interfaces.

DirectX A group of technologies designed by Microsoft to let Windows-based computers run applications with multimedia elements such as full-color graphics, video, 3D animation, and surround sound.

DLL Dynamic link library, a Windows software module typically shared among multiple programs.

DMA Direct memory access. DMA provides peripheral devices direct access to system memory without adding to CPU overhead. DMA allows hardware control of the transfer of streams of data to or from the main memory of a computing system.

DNS Domain Name Service and Domain Name System (one refers to the service your PC uses; the other refers to the overall combination of software, servers, and protocols). A distributed Internet-wide database used with TCP/IP to associate host names and IP addresses. DNS lets you specify computers by name rather than numerical IP addresses, simplifying access and making changes of IP address relatively transparent.

dongle An electronic "key" typically attached to a parallel port to verify access to protected software.

DOS partition A section of a disk storage device, created by the DOS FDISK program, in which data and/or software programs are stored. Computers have a primary DOS partition that contains the special files needed to boot the computer. A computer's disk devices may also have extended DOS partitions. Each DOS partition is assigned a unique drive letter, such as C: or D:. A single disk device can have multiple partitions. *See also* NTFS.

DRAM Dynamic random access memory. The most common system memory technology, DRAM can hold a charge (that is, data) for only a short period of time. Therefore, to retain the data, it must be refreshed periodically. If the cell is not refreshed, the data is lost. *See also* RAM and SRAM.

DSL Digital Subscriber Line. A technology for transmitting data across a telephone line at rates faster than possible with dial-up analog modems.

DSP Digital signal processor. A specialized microprocessor designed for high performance while computing the mathematical functions used to manipulate waveforms. Useful in processing audio, video, and communications signals.

dual data rate Used to refer to how information is clocked between the CPU and memory or graphics cards.

DVD A high-density digital format consisting of a 4.7" (120 mm) disc, 1.2 mm in thickness, featuring two bonded layers, each measuring 0.6 mm. DVD-ROM substantially improves upon the storage capability of conventional CD-ROMs, providing 7 to 13 times the current storage capability on a single side of the disc.

DVD-R, DVD+R Write-once recordable DVD discs with 4.7GB storage capacity.

DVD-RAM A rewritable DVD disc format. First-generation DVD-RAM disks hold 2.6GB of data per side (5.2GB on a double-sided disc). Second-generation DVD-RAM disks hold 4.7GB of storage per side, or 9.4GB per disk.

DVD-ROM A DVD disc for data storage in computers.

DVD-RW, DVD+RW Rewritable versions of DVD-R and DVD+R, respectively.

DVD-Video A DVD disc intended for playback on a consumer DVD player or PC.

DVI Digital Video Interface. A digital standard for connecting high-resolution, high-color flat panels, monitors, and projectors to video sources. DVI avoids the ghosting and other problems of analog connections.

ECC Error-correcting code. A mathematical extension of the checksum idea. ECC is used to discover and repair corrupted data in memory, on disk, and over communications links. ECC is a more elaborate error detection method than parity; the sort used with memory can detect multiple-bit errors and can locate and fix single-bit errors.

EDO Extended Data Output. An obsolete form of DRAM technology that shortened the read cycle between memory and CPU by holding the data on the bus longer, which allowed overlapped operation.

encoding A process by which redundant signal information (typically audio or video) is identified and removed.

encryption Applying a specific algorithm to data so as to alter the data's appearance and prevent other devices from reading the information without the appropriate knowledge. Decryption applies the algorithm in reverse to restore the data to its original form.

EPROM Erasable programmable read-only memory. A version of a ROM that is programmable multiple times using special erasure and programming devices.

ESD Electrostatic discharge. The dissipation of static electricity. ESD can easily destroy computer electronics.

Ethernet A 10 Mbps to 1 Gbps baseband, CSMA/CD network technology. Ethernet specifies protocols for connection and transmission in local area networks.

FAQ Frequently asked questions. Files on a variety of topics to make answers to common, widely asked questions available.

Fast Ethernet A (now disused) term for 100Base-T Ethernet.

Fast Page Mode An obsolete form of dynamic RAM (DRAM).

FAT File allocation table. Also, FAT32, a variant for larger disks. A DOS data structure, kept on the disk, that shows which clusters are in use for files, and which are available for use. *See also* NTFS.

feature connector A connector provided on graphics adapters to allow attaching other video-related devices (such as TV tuners).

fiber-optic cable A transmission medium that uses glass or plastic fibers, rather than copper wire, to transport data or voice signals. The signal is imposed on the fibers via modulated light from a laser or a light-emitting diode (LED). Because of its high bandwidth and lack of susceptibility to interference, fiber-optic cable is used in long-haul or noisy applications.

file server A device on a network that provides mass storage of files. A file server can be dedicated (performs network-only service functions) or non-dedicated (where user applications can coexist while the network is available).

firewall A router, workstation, or other computer with multiple network interfaces and software that controls and limits specific protocols, types of traffic within each protocol, types of services, and direction of the flow of information. Used to improve the security of a network.

FireWire A computer interface following the IEEE 1394 standard. Typically used for camcorders and other video applications.

flash memory A nonvolatile memory device that retains its data when the power is removed.

flat panel display A computer display using plasma or LCD technology to produce an image.

form factor A specification of the shape and interfaces of a device, including mechanical size and mounting, cooling, shock and vibration, power, and electrical signals.

FPM *See* Fast Page Mode.

fragmentation Breaking a packet into smaller units when transmitting over a network medium that cannot support the original size of the packet. Also, disjoint storage of files on a disk, which degrades performance.

FTP File Transfer Protocol (TCP/IP). The Internet application and protocol used to send complete files over TCP/IP services.

full-duplex The capability of a device or line to transmit data simultaneously in both directions. Contrast half-duplex.

gateway A device that can interconnect networks using different communications protocols. The gateway may perform a protocol conversion to translate one set of protocols to another. Contrast bridge and router.

Gbps Gigabits per second.

General MIDI A table of 128 standard sounds or instruments for MIDI cards and synthesizers.

gigabit Approximately 1 billion bits: 1 bit × 1,024³ (that is, 1,073,741,824 bits).

gigabit Ethernet An IEEE standard for 1,000 Mbps Ethernet.

gigabyte Approximately 1 billion bytes: 1 byte × 1,024³ (that is, 1,073,741,824 bytes).

GPF An error-detection trap within the processor when a program performs an illegal operation (such as accessing restricted spaces in memory).

GPS Global Positioning System. A system to compute the distance from you to each of the visible satellites by measuring the time it takes for a radio signal to travel from each of the satellites to you and then computing the distances.

GUI Graphical user interface.

half-duplex Data transmission that can occur in two directions over a single line, but only one direction at a time. Contrast full-duplex.

heat sink A structure that dissipates heat from a device to the surrounding environment to cool the device.

hop A unit that equates to the passage of a packet through one router.

hop count A routing metric used to measure the distance between a source and a destination.

horizontal scan rate The frequency in KHz (kilohertz) at which the monitor is scanned in a horizontal direction; high horizontal scan rates produce higher resolution.

HTML Hypertext Markup Language. The underlying syntax for Web pages.

HTTP Hypertext Transfer Protocol. The Internet protocol for communicating Web pages from a Web server to a Web client.

HTTPS Secure Hypertext Transfer Protocol. An encrypted version of HTTP used to secure Web communications across the Internet.

hub A concentrator or repeater in a star topology at which node connections meet.

hyperthreading Enhancements to the CPU that make one physical processor appear to be multiple ones, permitting more of the CPU electronics to be used at one time.

IANA Internet Assigned Numbers Authority. The central registry for various Internet protocol parameters, such as port, protocol, and enterprise numbers.

IC Integrated circuit. An electronic circuit built as a semiconductor chip packaged for mounting on a printed wiring board.

ICMP Internet Control Message Protocol. The collection of messages defined as part of TCP/IP to detect and exchange information about errors, problems, and operating parameters. You interact through ICMP when you use the ping command.

IEEE Institute of Electrical and Electronics Engineers. A professional organization that defines standards such as Ethernet.

IETF Internet Engineering Task Force. The technical body that oversees the development of the fundamental Internet suite of protocols.

i-frame MPEG-2 frames that transmit the entire video frame using compression similar to that for JPEG images. i-frames are the reference for bidirectional and p-frames.

Industry Standard Architecture *See* ISA.

Internet The worldwide internetwork. Uses the Internet protocol suite.

Internet address A 32-bit address assigned to hosts using TCP/IP. A newer version of TCP/IP increases the size of these addresses, but is not widely used yet.

Internetwork A series of networks interconnected by routers or other devices that functions as a single network. Sometimes called an internet, which is not synonymous with the Internet.

I/O An operation, program, or device that enters data into or extracts data from a computer.

I/O port A data path between the CPU and external devices such as a keyboard, display, or reader; it may be an input port or an output port, or it may be bidirectional.

IP Internet Protocol. Associated with TCP and UDP, IP is a set of communications protocols developed to internetwork dissimilar systems.

IP address The sequence of numbers that identify your computer on the Internet. IP addresses are currently 32 bits.

IP address mask A sequence of numbers (for example, 255.255.255.0) that divides your IP address into the network portion (for example, 255.255.255) and the host number portion (for example, 0).

IPX Internetwork Packet Exchange. A Novell NetWare communications protocol used to route messages from one node to another. Novell's version of IP (not directly interoperable with IP).

IR An abbreviation for infrared.

IRC Internet Relay Chat. An Internet service that allows multiple users to converse in real time on different subjects (each subject is called a channel). Similar to instant messaging, but non-proprietary.

IRQ Interrupt request. The identifier of a signal that a device can send to the processor to indicate it needs service.

ISA Industry Standard Architecture. The bus used in the original IBM PC. Now obsolete, replaced by PCI.

ISP Internet service provider. A company that sells dial-up (or other) access to the Internet.

ITU International Telecommunications Union.

ITU-TSS International Telecommunications Union-Telecommunications Standardization Sector.

Kbps Kilobits per second (multiples of 1,024 bits per second).

keys Notches on a memory module or other connector that prevent it from being installed incorrectly or into an incompatible system.

kilobit Approximately 1,000 bits: 1 bit $\times$ 2^{10} (that is, 1,024 bits).

kilobyte Approximately 1,000 bytes: 1 byte $\times$ 2^{10} (that is, 1,024 bytes).

LAN Local area network. A data communications network confined to a limited geographic area, with moderate to high data rates (10 to 1,000 Mbps, for example). The area served may consist of a single building or a campus-type arrangement. A LAN is typically owned by its users, includes some type of switching technology, and does not use common carrier circuits (although it may have gateways or bridges to other public or private networks).

latency Delay between two events, such as the time delay between when the first bit of a packet is received and the last bit is forwarded.

LCD Liquid crystal display. Two thin transparent surfaces (usually glass), with grooves full of a liquid crystal substance that are then polarized and electrically charged to reorient the crystal and selectively allow light to pass through.

leakage Undesirable conductive paths in components, subsystems, and systems; also the current through such paths.

LED Light-emitting diode.

Line In A connector on audio equipment to which a device such as a CD player or tape cassette player may be attached. *See also* Line Out.

Line Out A connector on audio equipment to which audio components such as stereo speakers can be attached. *See also* Line In.

link A physical connection between two nodes in a network. It can consist of a data communication circuit or a direct channel (cable) connection.

LISTSERV An automated mailing list distribution system. LISTSERVs are organized by topic of interest and maintained on an ad hoc basis.

local loop The line from a telephone customer's premises to the telephone company CO (central office).

MAC Media Access Control. A method of controlling access to a transmission medium, for example, Ethernet.

master/slave Used to refer to the relationship of devices (especially ATA disk drives) on a communications channel. Discouraged as offensive in Los Angeles.

Mb Megabit.

MB Megabyte.

Mbps Megabits per second (one million bits per second), a measurement of data transmission rate.

MBps Megabytes per second (one million bytes per second).

megabit Approximately one million bits: 1 bit × $1,024^2$ (that is, 1,048,576 bits).

megabyte Approximately one million bytes: 1 byte × $1,024^2$ (that is, 1,048,576 bytes).

memory A computer system's high speed, random access storage. Memory stores data electronically in integrated circuits.

memory bank A unit of memory in a computer, the size of which is determined by the computer's CPU.

memory cycle The minimum amount of time required for a memory to complete a cycle such as read, write, read/write, or read/modify/write.

memory types *See* DRAM, EPROM, PROM, RAM, ROM, and SRAM.

microATX A form factor specifying the size and layout of desktop computers. The specification extends to the definition of the power supply and its interface to the PC.

micron A unit of measure equivalent to one-millionth of a meter; synonymous with micrometer.

MIDI Musical Instrument Digital Interface. A standard that allows for the exchange of data between two music synthesizers or a synthesizer and a computer.

MIME Multipurpose Internet Mail Extensions. An Internet standard for converting multiple file formats to ASCII text prior to transmission in e-mail.

MIPS Million instructions per second. A measurement of processor speed.

MMC Multimedia Card. One of several flash memory form factors used for storage in cameras and other portable electronic devices.

modulation A process by which signal characteristics are transformed to represent information.

motherboard Also known as logic board, main board, or system board; your computer's main electronics board, which in most cases either contains all CPU, memory, and I/O functions or has expansion slots that support them.

MPEG Moving Picture Experts Group. MPEG-1, -2, and -4 are types of lossy data compression for storage and playback of combined video and audio data. MPEG-3 (MP3) is a standard for lossy audio compression.

MTBF Mean time between failures.

MTTF Mean time to failure.

MTTR Mean time to repair.

MTU Maximum transmission unit. The largest possible unit of data that can be sent on a given network medium.

Multilink PPP A variant of PPP for channel aggregation, used by connections over multiple 56 Kbps dial-up lines. Outlined in IETF RFC 1717.

multimedia A combination of media used for entertainment, education, and communication.

multitasking The execution of commands in such a way that more than one command is in progress at the same time. *See also* hyperthreading.

nano Literally, one-billionth (10^{-9}).

nanometer A measurement equal to one-billionth of a meter. The shorter-wavelength thinner-beam red laser incorporated in DVD players measures 650 nanometers, compared to 780 nanometers for a conventional CD player laser.

nanosecond (ns) One-billionth of a second. Memory data access times are measured in nanoseconds. For example, memory access times for typical 30- and 72-pin SIMM modules range from 60 to 100 nanoseconds. Light travels approximately 8 inches in 1 nanosecond.

NetBIOS Network Basic Input/Output System. Standard interface to networks on IBM PC and compatible systems.

network layer The protocol layer responsible for routing, switching, and subnetwork access.

network topology The arrangement of nodes usually forming a star, ring, tree, or bus pattern.

NFS Network File System.

nibble Usually 4 bits or half a byte.

NIC Network interface card.

NNTP Network News Transfer Protocol. The Internet protocol supporting Usenet newsgroups.

node Any device connected to a network, including servers and workstations.

nonvolatile memory Memory that retains information if power is removed and then reapplied.

ns *See* nanosecond.

NTFS NT file system. This alternative to the DOS FAT file system is used by Windows NT, 2000, and XP to provide increased performance and enhanced security.

NTSC National Television Standards Committee. They devised the NTSC television broadcast system in 1953. Supports vertical resolution of 525 horizontal lines stacked on top of each other. There are 59.94 fields displayed per second. A field is a set of even lines, or odd lines. The odd and even fields are displayed sequentially, interlacing to form the full frame. One full frame is displayed every $\frac{1}{30}$ of a second.

open source Computer software for which the source code is made available for public examination and modification. *See* www.opensource.org.

operating system Software controlling the overall operation of a multipurpose computer system, including memory allocation, input and output, interrupt processing, and scheduling.

OSI Open Systems Interconnection. *See* OSI Reference Model.

OSI Reference Model A seven-layer network architecture model of data communication protocols developed by ISO and CCITT. Each layer specifies particular network functions such as addressing, flow control, error control, encapsulation, and reliable message transfer.

packet A collection of bits comprising data and control information formatted for transmission from one node to another.

packet filtering Examination of en-route packets by a router to decide whether or not to allow transmission of each packet.

packet switching A type of data transfer that occupies a communication link only during the time of actual data transmission. Messages are split into packets and reassembled at the receiving end of the communication link.

packetization Information that, instead of being transported as a constant stream of information, is transported as blocks.

packet-switched network A network in which data is transmitted in units called *packets*. The packets can be routed individually over the best available network connection and reassembled to form a complete message at the destination.

page One unit of information from a Web server. Also, the bits that can be accessed from one memory row address.

page mode A now-obsolete memory mode in which if RAS is kept low and the DRAM is given a column address without being given a new row address, the chip will remember which row it was on the last time and automatically stay on that row.

PAL Page Alternation Line. A European standard for television signals having 625 horizontal lines of vertical resolution. Fifty interlaced fields are displayed per second, or 25 frames per second.

palette In 256-color modes, the palette defines the range of colors you can display simultaneously. Also, the hardware in a video board that stores the available colors.

parity A method of data-integrity checking that adds a single bit to each unit (typically a byte) of data. In odd parity mode, the parity bit is set if the checked data contains an odd number of ones; in even parity mode, the parity bit is set if the checked data contains an even number of ones.

parity bit A bit added to a group of bits to detect the presence of an error.

patch cable An Ethernet cable with male RJ-45 connectors on either end.

PCI Peripheral Component Interconnect. A type of high-speed computer bus.

PCI Express A high-speed computer bus intended to replace PCI. PCI Express typically uses fewer data lines and can operate at higher speeds and over longer distances than PCI.

PCMCIA Personal Computer Memory Card International Association. Now called PC Card. A standard for small, flat credit-card-sized devices used in notebook computers.

peer-to-peer communications A type of communications and data exchange between peer entities (for example, two user PCs) on two or more networks. Contrast with client/server.

peripheral A device installed on a computer system.

p-frame MPEG-2 frames constructed by analyzing previous frames and estimating where objects will be in the next frame.

ping A program used to test reachability of destinations by sending them an ICMP echo request and waiting for a reply. Ping is also used as a verb: "Ping the site to see if it is available."

PIO Programmed Input/Output. A method of data transfer in which the host microprocessor transfers data to and from memory via the computer's I/O ports. PIO is not as fast as direct memory access (DMA) and imposes a significant load on the processor.

pits and lands Marks on the surface of a CD-ROM or DVD disc that are read by a laser as the series of ones and zeros.

pixel A single dot on a display. Derived from the words *picture* and *element*.

pixel shader A programmable graphics operation implemented on the video card to create custom lighting, coloring, and other effects on a per-pixel basis.

Plug and Play A standard intended to overcome the configuration problems inherent in the ISA bus by letting adapters self-configure and automatically resolve system resources such as interrupts (IRQ), DMA, port addresses, and BIOS addresses. Largely obsolete *per se* with the advent of the PCI bus, but co-opted to refer to any device that automatically configures itself (for example, PCI, USB).

polling A method of controlling the sequence of transmission by devices on a multipoint line by requiring each device to wait until the controlling processor requests it to transmit.

POP Post Office Protocol. An Internet standard protocol for reading mail from a server. The commonly used version is POP3.

port I/O address The number of the I/O port through which the processor communicates with a peripheral.

POST Power-On Self-Test, a set of diagnostic routines that run when a computer is first turned on.

POTS Plain Old Telephone Service. Really. POTS refers to the existing analog telephone lines, and is the universal term in the telecommunications industry.

power down To turn the system's power off.

power up To turn the system's power on.

PPP Point-to-Point Protocol. Provides Internet protocol connections over serial circuits.

PROM Programmable read-only memory. A version of a ROM that is programmable once using special devices.

protocol A standardized set of rules that specify the format, timing, sequencing, and/or error checking for data transmissions.

PTT Public Telephone and Telegraph. A generic term for European telephone companies. Most are (currently) state owned and operated. The *Deutsche Bundespost* is one example of a PTT.

pulse dialing Dialing a telephone line as if using the older-style rotary dial wheel.

QoS Quality of service. Describes the delay, throughput, bandwidth, and other performance characteristics of a network connection.

RAM Random access memory. A configuration of memory cells that holds data for processing by a computer's CPU. The term *random access* means the CPU can retrieve data from any individual location at any time.

Rambus Rambus DRAM is a memory standard capable of transferring 1.6 GB per second.

RAS Row address strobe. The signal that tells the DRAM to accept the given address as a row address. Used with CAS and a column address to select a bit within the DRAM.

refresh An electrical process used to maintain data stored in DRAM. The process of refreshing electrical cells on a DRAM component is similar to that of recharging batteries. Different DRAM components call for different refresh methods; and some (such as SDRAM) perform refresh automatically.

refresh rate Also called vertical scan rate, the speed at which the screen is repainted. Typically, color displays must be refreshed at 60 times per second to avoid flicker. Also, a specification determined by the number of rows on a DRAM component that must be refreshed.

register-level compatibility Complete compatibility at the hardware level from the software point of view.

remote user A user who needs client access to a server over WAN links.

removability A feature where the media in a removable media disk drive, or the entire drive, can be removed and then replaced while the computer remains in operation, without causing problems to the hardware or operating system.

repeater Used to extend the network topology, allowing a cable's segments to be lengthened beyond normal specification limits. *See also* hub.

RGB Red/green/blue, a color model typically used with monitors.

RISC Reduced instruction set computing. RISC chips, such as in the PowerPC processor used in Apple computers, implement simpler instructions than CISC chips, such as the x86 processors used in Windows machines.

RMA Return Material Authorization. Required if a customer desires to return products to the manufacturer or supplier.

ROM Read-only memory. Generally a chip on a computer or I/O card with software programmed inside of it that controls some function.

router A protocol-dependent device that connects subnetworks together. It is useful in breaking down a very large network into smaller subnetworks.

routing protocol A protocol that accomplishes routing through the implementation of a specific routing algorithm.

routing table A table stored in a router or some other internetworking device that keeps track of routes (and, in some cases, metrics associated with those routes) to particular network destinations.

routing update A message sent from a router to indicate network reachability and associated cost information. Routing updates are typically sent at regular intervals and after a change in network topology.

row Part of the RAM array; a bit can be stored where a column and a row intersect.

RS-232 A serial data transmission interface specification.

RTFM Read the Manual. Acronym suggesting a response to an easily answered question. Sometimes found on automotive license plates.

sample A measurement of sound taken during a certain duration. In digital recording, sampling means recording voltages that make a sound as a sequence of numerical values representing the sound's amplitude.

scan rate The frequency in hertz (Hz) at which the monitor is scanned horizontally. Generally, the higher the scan rate, the higher the resolution.

SCSI Small Computer System Interface. A bus interface standard that defines standard physical and electrical connections for devices. SCSI provides a standard interface that enables many different kinds of devices, such as disk drives, magneto-optical disks, CD-ROM drives, and tape drives to interface with the host computer.

SD Secure digital. One of several flash memory form factors used for storage in cameras and other portable electronic devices.

SDRAM Synchronous dynamic random access memory. Delivers bursts of data at very high speeds using a synchronous interface.

sector The smallest storage access unit on a hard drive.

seek time The average time it takes for a hard drive to position its heads to a specific sector.

self-refresh A memory technology that enables SDRAM and some other memory technologies to refresh on its own, independent of the CPU or external refresh circuitry.

semiconductor An element, such as silicon, that has intermediate electrical conductivity between conductors and insulators, and in which conduction takes place by means of holes and electrons.

Serial ATA A higher speed modification of the parallel ATA disk drive interface to use fewer, faster wires between drive and PC.

serial interface An interface that requires serial transmission, or the transfer of information in which the bits composing a character are sent sequentially. Implies only a single transmission channel.

serial port A connection for a serial device like a mouse or a modem.

serial presence detect Indicator memory and pins on SIMMs and DIMMs that provide size and timing information to the PC.

server A computer that provides shared resources, such as files, printers, and servers, to the network.

SIMM Single in-line memory module. A printed circuit board with contacts and memory devices that plugs into a computer's memory socket.

SMTP Simple Mail Transfer Protocol. A protocol governing mail transmissions defined in RFC 821. The associated message format descriptions are in RFC 822.

SNMP Simple Network Management Protocol. A network management system for TCP/IP-based internets. One of the most egregious uses ever of the word *simple*.

SODIMM Small outline dual inline memory module. A smaller and thinner version of a standard DIMM. The small outline DIMM is about half the length of a typical 72-pin SIMM. SODIMMs are typically used in laptop computers.

soft error In memory components, a correctable data error made by a device not having anything physically wrong with it.

sound file Any file that holds sound data, including MIDI (.mid), wave (.wav), and MPEG-3 (.mp3).

SPD *See* serial presence detect.

spoofing The use of a forged network source address to circumvent a firewall or mask the sender.

SRAM Static random access memory. An integrated circuit similar to a DRAM (dynamic random access memory) with the exception that the memory does not need to be refreshed.

star topology A network topology in which nodes are connected to a common device such as a hub or concentrator.

storage A medium designed to hold data, such as a hard disk or CD-ROM.

storage capacity The limit to the amount of information that can be recorded on any recording medium. In DVD, this varies from 4.7GB on a DVD-5 disc to 17GB on a DVD-18 disc.

STP Shielded twisted-pair. A common transmission medium that consists of Receive (RX) and Transmit (TX) wires twisted together to reduce crosstalk. The twisted-pair is shielded by a braided outer sheath.

surround sound A multiple-channel sound system that produces an audio ambience similar to the cinema sound experience.

S-video An interface between video source and display providing higher-quality signal transmission than the more common RCA video connector because it separates the chrominance and luminance signal components.

switched Ethernet An Ethernet hub with integrated MAC layer bridging or switching capability to provide each port with full LAN bandwidth; separate transmissions can occur on each port of the switching hub, and the switch filters traffic according to the destination MAC address.

synchronous DRAM A DRAM technology that uses a clock to synchronize signal input and output on a memory chip. The clock is coordinated with the CPU clock so the timing of the memory chips and the timing of the CPU are coordinated.

system board *See* motherboard.

T-connector A T-shaped device with two female and one male BNC connectors.

TCP Transmission Control Protocol. *See also* TCP/IP and IP.

TCP/IP Transmission Control Protocol/Internet Protocol. A set of protocols developed by the U.S. Defense Department's Advanced Research Projects Agency (ARPA) during the early 1970s. Its intent was to develop ways to connect different kinds of networks and computers.

Telnet The Internet standard protocol to connect to a computer as a remote terminal.

timbre How the ear identifies and classifies sound. Example: The timbre of the same note played by two different instruments (flute and tuba) will not be the same.

topology The physical layout of a network. The principal LAN topologies are bus, ring, and star.

Trojan From Trojan horse. A malicious computer program posing as some other program or image that, when run, compromises the security or integrity of the PC.

true color Video displays and scanners operating with 24- or 32-bit color.

TWAIN A programming interface for scanners.

twisted-pair Cable consisting of two 18 to 24 AWG (American Wire Gauge) solid copper strands twisted around each other. The twisting provides a measure of protection from electromagnetic and radio-frequency interference. Twisted-pair cable typically contains multiple sets of paired wires. *See* STP (shielded twisted-pair) and UTP (unshielded twisted-pair).

UART Universal Asynchronous Receiver/Transmitter chip, used to implement the communications (COM) port in personal computers. Often integrated with other functions in a single chip.

UDP User Datagram Protocol. An Internet standard protocol that allows an application on one machine to send a datagram to an application program on another machine. No confirmation of arrival is supplied, and order of arrival is not guaranteed, so UDP is faster than TCP.

Universal Disk Format Defines data structures such as volumes, files, blocks, sectors, CRCs, paths, records, allocation tables, partitions, character sets, time stamps, and so forth; and methods for reading, writing, and other operations. A format used on CD and DVD.

URL Uniform Resource Locator. A form of Internet address used by World Wide Web browsers. Each browser-accessible resource on the Internet has a unique URL (for example, `http://www.wiley.com`).

USB Universal Serial Bus. A high-speed serial interface expected to connect keyboard, mouse, speakers, monitor, and other devices to your computer.

Usenet More commonly known as newsgroups, Usenet is a worldwide bulletin-board system incorporating tens of thousands of groups on thousands of servers around the world.

UTP Unshielded twisted-pair. Twisted-pair wiring like STP, but without the outer shield. More common than STP. *See also* STP.

V.42bis The CCITT analog modem data compression standard. Provides a theoretical maximum of 4:1 compression, although 2:1 or less is more commonly experienced.

VESA Video Electronics Standards Association. Sponsors efforts to set graphics and video standards.

VGA Video Graphics Array. An analog display interface standard introduced with the IBM PS/2 series.

virus A malicious computer program that replicates itself from one PC to the next through e-mail and infected removable disks.

WAAS Wide Area Augmentation System. A system of satellites and ground stations transmitting GPS signal corrections for better position accuracy.

WAN Wide area network. A network that uses common carrier–provided lines; contrast with LAN.

warm boot Rebooting a computer without turning the power off (for example, Ctrl+Alt+Del).

wave file A standard Microsoft file format for storing waveform audio data.

waveform A graph showing the amplitude of a sound over a particular interval of time. Any portion of that interval is a sample.

worm A malicious computer program that replicates itself from one computer to the next using security vulnerabilities reachable across networks.

write-back cache Cache memory that holds data written by the processor until the bus and main memory have time to perform the write.

write-through cache Cache memory that executes processor writes to main memory immediately, requiring the processor to wait until the operation is complete.

WWW World Wide Web. The Internet-based hypertext system.

ZIF socket Zero-insertion force socket. A mechanism for a processor socket supporting simple replacement of chips.

Index

SYMBOLS & NUMERICS

µM, 421

µS, 421

3COM OfficeConnect 56K LAN Modem, 163–164, 174

3D video accelerator, 83–86

3D viewing and rendering pipeline, 85–86

10Base-T, 100Base-T, and 1000Base-T, 421

10Base-2, 179–180, 389, 421

103 error code, 382

16550 chip, 162, 309–310

802, 421

A

AC-3, 421

Accelerated Graphics Port (AGP)

    connector, 73, 74

    description of, 422

    slot, 52

    video and, 83

accelerator

    3D video, 83–86

    video card and, 41

Acceptable Use Policy (AUP), 421

access time

    description of, 422

    disk and, 38, 114

    memory and, 36

acknowledgment, 202

Acoustic Authority A3780 speakers, 266–267

ACPI (Advanced Configuration and Power Interface), 62, 422

active matrix technology, 94, 95

ad hoc mode, 186

adapter

    car/plane, 353

    description of, 422

    Ethernet, 184

    video, 285–286

    wireless notebook, 189, 190

    Xbox wireless, 189–191

adapter board, removing and replacing, 378

adapter card

    case and, 329–330

    heat pocket and, 336, 337

    installing, 415–416

    mounting, 409

Ad-aware (Lavasoft) Web site, 244

adding disk drive, 122–127

additive color mixing, 322

address lease expiration, 216–217

Address Resolution Protocol (ARP), 215, 422

Adobe PostScript, 316

ADSL (Asymmetric Digital Subscriber Line), 164–165, 422

Advanced Configuration and Power Interface (ACPI), 62, 422

Advanced ➪ Boot Configuration ➪ Plug & Play O/S, 417

Advanced ➪ Drive Configuration, 418

Advanced ➪ Fan Control Configuration ➪ Fan Control, 418

Advanced ➪ USB Configuration, 418

Advanced ➪ Video Configuration ➪ AGP Aperture Size, 418

AGP (Accelerated Graphics Port)

    connector, 73, 74

    description of, 422

    slot, 52

    video and, 83

air mouse, 305

airflow and heat buildup, 333, 340, 391–393

all-in-one unit, 318, 325–326

AMD processor, 54, 60–62, 350

American Standard Code for Information Interchange (ASCII), 423

AMIDiag Suite (AMI), 386

amplitude, 422

analog audio, 254–255

analog joystick, 297

analog signal, 422

analog-to-digital (A/D) converter, 256, 257

analyzing upgrade options, 6

anonymous FTP, 422

ANSI, 422

Antec

P160 case, 396, 398–400

TrueControl power supply, 396, 399, 410, 499

Web site, 397

anti-adware software, 242–244

antiglare treatment on monitor, 99

anti-static, 422

anti-static bag, 381

anti-static wrist strap, 398

antivirus software

overview of, 235, 242–244, 422

Trojan protection and, 240

updating, 236

application

client as, 219

installing, 419–420

security of, 240

application layer, 205

arbitrary address, 217

archiving to removable storage, 374

arithmetic-logic unit, 47

ARP (Address Resolution Protocol), 215, 422

ARPANET, 212

array, 422

ASCII (American Standard Code for Information Interchange), 423

aspect ratio, 40, 423

assigned address, 217

assigning drive letter, 127

Asymmetric Digital Subscriber Line (ADSL), 164–165, 422

AT command set, 423

ATA, 423

ATA drive, installing, 125–126

ATA master/slave, parallel, 124

ATAPI, 423

Athlon processor (AMD), 60, 350

ATI

hardware, 91

Radeon 9800 XT video card, 397, 415

Web site, 92

attachment to electronic mail, 236

attack part of note, 253

attenuation, 423

ATX

connector panel, 73, 74

description of, 423

form factor, 337–339

power connector, 73, 74, 380

audio compression, 259–261

AUP (Acceptable Use Policy), 421

authentication, 423

autodetect, 423

autorun, 423

avoiding choke point, 52

B

back door, 423

backing up

attacks and, 242

external hard drive and, 151–153

removable disk and, 145

removable storage and, 150–151

video clips, 286

backlight of LCD panel, 94

backplane, 67

backup, 423

bandwidth

description of, 423

maximum video, 101

memory and, 36

surveillance system and, 360, 361

bank, 424

base station, 185, 189

baseband transmission, 175, 177, 424

basic input-output system (BIOS)

automatic detection and configuration settings of, 124

boot sequence controls, 235–236

configuring, 417–418

description of, 424
Legacy USB Support feature, 306
password in, 356–357
battery
for digital camera, 281, 282
for handheld computer, 354
for laptop, 352–353
bay, 331, 424
beep sequence, 382
BER (bit error rate), 424
B-frame, 89–90, 424
binary, 424
BIOS (basic input-output system)
automatic detection and configuration
settings of, 124
boot sequence controls, 235–236
configuring, 417–418
description of, 424
Legacy USB Support feature, 306
password in, 356–357
bit, 424
bit error rate (BER), 424
bitmap, 163, 319
Black Box VueMate Hub, 359–360
Blackberry PDA, 349, 354
blind dialing, 424
blocking
macro virus, 236–237
spam, 247
suspect sites, 244
blue laser diode, 142
BNC connector, 424
bonded disk, 424
bonding, 424
boot drive, 424
boot sequence, 384–385
booting
from CD-ROM drive, 135–136, 386
description of, 424
from external media, 151
video operational during, 384–386
Boot ⇨ Silent Boot, 418
bottleneck, 425
Bps, 425
bps, 425

branch prediction, 55
bridge, 425
bridge/router, 425
brightness and monitor, 99, 104
broadband
description of, 425
Internet access, 170–172
security issues with, 165
usage of, 157, 395
broadcast, 425
browser, security options for, 240
buffer, 425
building
extreme machine
adapter card, installing, 415–416
application, installing, 419–420
BIOS, configuring, 417–418
cabling in power supply, 409–410
checking configuration, 419
disk, configuring, and installing
Windows, 418–419
final cabling, 413–414
hardware planning, 395–398
memory, inserting, 407–409
motherboard, installing, 402–403
preliminary mechanical assembly,
398–401
processor, installing, 404–407
software planning, 416–417
wiring chassis to motherboard
connectors, 411–412
surveillance system
from kit, 361–371
to own design, 372–374
bus
description of, 28, 29, 32, 425
external, 75–76
hyperthreading and, 59
interconnections, 33
ISA, 67–69, 71
laptop computer, 350
PCI, 68, 69–70
types of, 32–33
video, 83
waveform audio, 258

bus connection, 66–67
bus interface, 71
Butchart Gardens Web site, 213
buying new computer, 6–7
byte, 425

C

cable
  checking, 382
  coaxial, 427
  crossover, 194, 196, 427
  data, 379, 413–414
  fiber-optic, 431
  long, for webcam, 373
  network diagnosis and, 389
  patch, 438
  for PC Card, 350
  twisted-pair, 180–182
cable TV Internet service, 165–167,
  170–172
cache buffer size, 113
cache coherence problem, 58–59
cache memory, 48–49, 425
caching, 425
camera. *See also* TrackerCam software
  digital
    choosing, 281–283
    image resolution and memory,
      277–280
    overview of, 276–277
    quality of images from, 275
    resolution for, 280–281
    storage and, 149
  webcam, 361–363, 372–373
Canon
  EOS 1D camera, 277
  MultiPASS 730, 326
  recycling ink jet cartridge from, 314
capacitance, 158
capacity
  of DVD, 138, 140
  of floppy disk, 145–146
  of hard disk, 112, 125–126

of memory, 50–51
of memory module, 35
of network, 193
of Zip drive, 147
capturing digital video, 284–285
carrier sense multiple access with
  collision detection (CSMA/CD), 177,
  178, 427
CAS (column address strobe), 425
case
  airflow and heat buildup, 333
  ATX form factor, 337–339
  choosing, 339–340
  cooling, 333–337
  for desktop PC, 332
  dust in, 376, 377, 391
  opening, 380
  overview of, 329–331
  parts of, 331–332
  taking apart, 376–378
cathode ray tube (CRT) monitor
  color balance, tracking, purity, and
    saturation, 99–101
  dot pitch, 106
  focus and convergence, 97–99
  geometric distortion, 102
  ghosting, 101–102
  replacement of, 93
CCITT (Consultative Committee for
  International Telegraph and
  Telephone), 160, 426
CD, 426
CD Plus format, 136
CD quality, 426
CDMA (Code-Division Multiple Access),
  178
CD-R, 137, 426
CD-ROM
  audio and line interfaces, 263
  backup and, 151
  bootable, 386
  coding data onto, 131
  data storable on, 138
  description of, 129–130, 426

disk formats, 136
disk longevity, 142
DVD compared to, 139–140
mastering process, 130–131
reading, 131–133, 134, 135
recordable, 137
CD-ROM drive
booting computer from, 135–136, 386
constant linear velocity, constant
angular velocity, and, 135
performance of, 133–134
port for, 135
CD-ROM/XA format, 136
CD-RW (CD-Rewritable), 137
Celeron processor (Intel), 53
central office (CO), 426
central processing unit (CPU), 4, 427. *See
also* processor
Centrino processor, 350
Centronics connector, 346
centronics interface, 426
CERT (Computer Emergency Response
Team), 426
charge-coupled device, 276
charging roller, 314
chassis, 27. *See also* case
chassis layout and assembly, 398–400
children and Internet use, 171
chip. *See also* processor
inside processor, 31
Northbridge and Southbridge, 33,
69–70, 73, 74
number of transistors in, 14
signal and power level operating
conditions for, 8
16550, 162, 309–310
chipset
description of, 426
design of, 33
front side bus and, 32
history of, 70–71
PCI bus and, 71–72
choke point, 51–52, 171

choosing
approach to support and maintenance,
25–26
case, 339–340
components for extreme machine,
395–398
digital camera, 281–283
Internet access, 170–172
modem, 172–174
monitor, 106
network technology, 191
operating system, 5–6, 19
power supply, 341
printer, 317–319
processor, 43
sound system, 271–272
speakers, 264–267
video card, 91
circuit board, 65, 330
cleaning
dust in case, 376, 377, 391
inside of mouse, 303
keyboard, 290
machine infected with virus, 390
client, 197, 219, 426
Client for Microsoft Networks, 220–221
client/server, 426
clock, 29, 426
clock rate, 13–14, 426
CMOS (Complementary Metal-Oxide
Semiconductor), 426
CMOS (Complementary Metal-Oxide
Semiconductor) array, 276
CMYK (cyan, magenta, yellow, black) color
model, 322
CO (central office), 426
Coalition Against Unsolicited Commercial
Email Web site, 245
coaxial cable, 427
codec, 427
Code-Division Multiple Access (CDMA),
178
cold boot, 427

color
balance, tracking, purity, and
saturation, 99–101
scanner and, 321
settings for, 81–83
color ink jet printer, 313–314
color models, 322, 440
color temperature control, 103
column, 427
column address, 50
column address strobe (CAS), 425
COM port, 427
command.com (Windows system), 427
commands, comparable UNIX and
Windows, 232
communications protocol, 427
Compact Flash, 427
compatibility with Intel products, 60–62
Complementary Metal-Oxide
Semiconductor (CMOS), 426
Complementary Metal-Oxide
Semiconductor (CMOS) array, 276
component video, 427
components
choosing for extreme machine, 395–398
inside computer, 27–28
outside computer case, 42
repairing compared to replacing, 375
surveillance system, 361–363
compression
audio, 259–261
data, 428
description of, 427
digital camera and, 279
JPEG, 87, 88, 89, 279
video, 87–90, 140
configuration problems, 387–388
configuring
BIOS, 417–418
disk, 418–419
dual screen, 18
file sharing
overview of, 219–220
Windows 98, 222

Windows 2000 and Windows XP,
220–222
printer sharing, 222–223
TCP/IP, 218–219
connecting modem to computer, 163
connection orientation, 379
connector
AGP, 73, 74
BNC, 424
case and, 330–331
Centronics, 346
D subminiature, 344, 345
DIN, 345–346, 429
external, 343–346
F, 344, 346
feature, 431
gender of, 343
headphone, 345, 346
IDE, 413
I/O port, 339
pins in, 343
PS/2 mouse and keyboard, 73, 74,
305–306
RCA, 344, 346
RJ-11, 344, 346
RJ-45, 180–182, 184, 344, 346
constant angular velocity and CD-ROM
drive, 135
constant linear velocity and CD-ROM
drive, 135
Consultative Committee for International
Telegraph and Telephone (CCITT), 160,
426
contention, 427
contrast and monitor, 99, 104
controls on monitor, 102–104
convergence, 97–99
cookie, 244
cooling internal disk drive
desktop, 122–123, 333–337, 340
laptop, 348
Zalman CPU cooler, 396, 404, 405–407
copier, 325–326
copyright and copy protection, 260–261

CPU (central processing unit), 4, 427. *See also* processor
cracking, 204, 235, 241–242
CRC (cyclic redundancy check), 427
crossover cable, 194, 196, 427
CRT (cathode ray tube) monitor
　color balance, tracking, purity, and
　　saturation, 99–101
　dot pitch, 106
　focus and convergence, 97–99
　geometric distortion, 102
　ghosting, 101–102
　replacement of, 93
Crucial Web site, 397, 407
CSMA/CD (carrier sense multiple access
　with collision detection), 177, 178, 427
current, 340
cursor, 304
cycle time, 36
cyclic redundancy check (CRC), 427
cylinder, 111, 427

D

D subminiature connector, 344, 345
data
　coding onto CD-ROM, 131
　transferring, 113–114
data cable, 379, 413–414
data compression, 428
data link layer, 198–199
datagram, 428
DCT (Discrete Cosine Transform), 87–89
DDC (Display Data Channel) interface, 95,
　105–106
decay part of note, 253
decibel (dB), 428
decoding, 428
default gateway, 216
default route, 213
defragmenting disk, 420
degauss, 428
degaussing coil, 100–101, 104
degrees per watt, 333

Dell Web site, 5
DeLorme Earthmate USB receiver, 356
demilitarized zone (DMZ), 208–209
demodulation, 159, 428
denial-of-service attack, 204, 428
design of PC and ATX form factor,
　338–339
designing small local area network,
　193–195
desktop system, preconfigured, 16–19
device driver, 428
devices, sharing wires among, 65–67
DHCP (Dynamic Host Configuration
　Protocol), 215–218, 428
diagnostics, running, 386
dial-up, 428
dial-up analog modem, 159–164, 172–174
die, 428
digital audio sampling, 256
digital camera
　choosing, 281–283
　image resolution and memory,
　　277–280
　overview of, 276–277
　quality of images from, 275
　resolution for, 280–281
　storage and, 149
Digital Display Working Group, 95
digital joystick, 298
digital recording, 428
Digital Rights Management (DRM),
　260–262, 268
digital signal, 428
digital signal processor (DSP), 429
Digital Subscriber Line (DSL), 164–165,
　170–172, 429
digital video
　capturing and editing, 284–286
　making DVD from, 286–288
　overview of, 283–284
Digital Video Interface (DVI), 430
Digital Visual Interface (DVI) specification,
　95–96
digital-to-analog (D/A) converter, 39, 81

DIMM (dual inline memory module)
   description of, 428
   installing, 407–409
   memory socket, 73, 74
DIN connector, 345–346, 429
direct memory access (DMA), 429
direct sequence, 185, 187
DirecTV Internet access, 169–170
DirectX technology, 91, 285, 429
disassembly
   tips for, 378–380
   top-level, 380–381
disconnecting power supply, 380
Discrete Cosine Transform (DCT), 87–89
disk
   accessing full capacity of, 125–126
   backup and, 151–153
   capacity of, 37
   configuring, 418–419
   defragmenting, 420
   description of, 28
   digital video and, 283
   editing digital video and, 285
   external, 150, 151–153
   geometrical layout of, 111–112
   Microsoft recommendations for, 24–25
   storage requirements, 112–113
disk cache, 114–115
disk capacity, 37
disk drive
   adding, 122–127
   cooling internal
      desktop, 122–123, 333–337, 340
      laptop, 348
      Zalman CPU cooler, 396, 404,
         405–407
   corrupted, 385
   description of, 36
   failed, 115–116, 385
   IDE, setting up, 125
   laptop, 351
   mounting, 400–401
   performance of, 113–115
   reliability of, 115–116
   size of, 331
   stacking, 335–336
   taking apart, 377
disk drive connector, 73, 74
disk mirroring, 119–120
display. *See also* monitor
   description of, 28
   laptop, 351
   Microsoft recommendations for, 25
   minimum display memory, 39–40
   updating, 41
Display Data Channel (DDC) interface, 95,
   105–106
DisplayMate software, 96, 102
DLL (dynamic link library), 391, 429
DMA (direct memory access), 429
DMZ (demilitarized zone), 208–209
DNS (Domain Name Service and Domain
   Name System), 203–204, 215, 429
docking station, 353–354
domain name server, 203
Domain Name Service (DNS), 203–204, 215,
   429
Domain Name System (DNS), 429
dongle, 429
DOS drive letter assignment, 127
DOS partition, 429
dot clock, 80, 81
double data rate SDRAM, 50
download site reviews, 244
DRAM (dynamic random access memory),
   50, 429
drawing motions and tablet device,
   308–309
drive letters, assigning, 127
driver
   impulse, 312–313
   for mouse, 304–305
   printer-specific, 316
   for scanner, 324
   socket, 10
   video, 92
driving simulator, 297
DRM (Digital Rights Management),
   260–262, 268
drum, photoconductor, 314–315

DSL (Digital Subscriber Line), 164–165, 170–172, 429

DSP (digital signal processor), 429

dual data rate, 429

dual inline memory module (DIMM)
description of, 428
installing, 407–409
memory socket, 73, 74

dual screen configuration, 18

duplex printing, 317

dust in case, 376, 377, 391

DVD
CD-ROM compared to, 139–140
disk longevity, 142
making from digital video, 286–288
overview of, 137–138, 429
recordable, 140–141
storage capacity of, 138, 140

DVD drive, cost of, 139

DVD writer, installing, 400

DVD-R and DVD+R, 430

DVD-RAM, 430

DVD-ROM, 430

DVD-RW and DVD+RW, 430

DVD-video, 430

DVI (Digital Video Interface), 430

DVI (Digital Visual Interface) specification, 95–96

Dvorak keyboard layout, 293

dynamic branch prediction, 54–55

dynamic execution, 55–56

dynamic field, incident, 101

Dynamic Host Configuration Protocol (DHCP), 215–218, 428

dynamic link library (DLL), 391, 429

dynamic random access memory (DRAM), 50, 429

E

Eagletron Web site, 373

ECC (error-correcting code), 430

editing digital video, 285–286

EDO (Extended Data Output), 430

Eidos, 91

802, 421

El Torito Bootable CD-ROM Format Specification, 135–136

electromagnetic interference, 329

Electronic Industries Alliance specification RS-232C, 162, 305

electronic mail (e-mail), 229–231, 236. *See also* spam

electronics system, building, 65

electrostatic discharge (ESD), 8–9, 376, 430

emergency boot disk, 386

EMI (electromagnetic interference), 329

encoding, 430

encryption
description of, 430
of file system, 357

enlarging digital image, 278–279

envelope shaper, 253–254

erasable programmable read-only memory (EPROM), 430

ergonomics and keyboard use, 293–295

error code, 382

error-correcting code (ECC), 430

ESD (electrostatic discharge), 8–9, 376, 430

Ethernet. *See also* gigabit Ethernet
description of, 430
network and, 179–184
switched, 443

Ethernet card, 201

Ethernet connector, 73, 74

Ethernet switch, 195–196

evaluating speakers, 265

exclusive or (XOR), 187

Expanded TrackerCam window, 364, 365

expanding
case and, 332
network, 196–198

expansion bus, 33

Extended Data Output (EDO), 430

external bay, 331

external bus, 75–76

external connection, 42

external connector, 343–346

external disk drive, adding, 122

external USB storage, 149–150

F

F connector, 344, 346
failure
    of disk drive, 115–116, 385
    of optical drive, 134
fan, mounting, 404–405
FAQ, 430
Fast Ethernet, 430
Fast Page Mode, 430
FAT (file allocation table), 431
fax machine, 325–326
fax transmission, 163
FDMA (Frequency Division Multiple
    Access), 178
feature connector, 431
fiber-optic cable, 431
file allocation table (FAT), 431
File and Printer Sharing for Microsoft
    Networks, 220–221
file extension, showing, 239–240
file server, 220, 431
file sharing
    configuring, 219–220
    Windows 98, 222
    Windows 2000 and Windows XP,
        220–222
File Transfer Protocol (FTP), 228–229, 431
firewall
    cable modem technology and, 167
    cracking protection and, 242
    description of, 205, 431
    laptop and, 356
    on-computer, 209–210
    satellite technology and, 170
    standalone, 207–209
    3COM OfficeConnect 56K LAN Modem
        and, 174
    Trojan protection and, 240
    worm protection and, 239
FireWire (IEEE1394)
    description of, 75, 431
    digital video camera and, 286
first node address, 218

first-in, first-out queue, 162
fixing large drive problems, 126
Flash Disk, 149
flash memory
    BIOS code and, 74
    description of, 37, 431
    digital camera and, 149, 279
flashlight, 10
flat panel display, 94–97, 431
flatbed scanner, 320
flight simulator, 296
floppy connector, 73, 74
floppy disk, 145–147
floppy drive
    external, 150
    installing, 396
FM (frequency modulation) synthesizer,
    253–254
focus and CRT monitor, 97–99
form factor, 431
fragmentation, 431
frame rate, 361
framing information on CD, 133
free e-mail address directory, 247
FreeBSD, 20, 231
Freebyte, 242
frequency, 340
Frequency Division Multiple Access
    (FDMA), 178
frequency hopper, 185
frequency modulation (FM) synthesizer,
    253–254
frequency response, 255
front panel light, 385–386
front side bus, 32, 52
FTP (File Transfer Protocol), 228–229, 431
full-duplex
    description of, 176, 177, 431
    LAN and, 194–195
    waveform audio and, 258
functioning machine, problems in, 387–388
fuse, 383

G

game controller, 296–300
game pad, 299
games
    display update performance and, 41
    Internet service and, 171
    matching video hardware and software, 91
    modem and, 172–173
    multi-player, 203
    Quake, 232
    sound system for, 271
    3D video accelerator and, 83–86
    USB mouse and, 306
gateway, 431
Gbps, 431
gender of connector, 343
general MIDI, 432
geometric distortion onscreen, 102
ghosting, 101–102
GHz (gigahertz), 13
Gibson Research Corporation Web site, 239
gigabit, 432
gigabit Ethernet, 183, 184, 432
gigabyte, 432
glare off screen, minimizing, 106
G.Lite technology, 164–165
Global Positioning System (GPS), 351, 355–356, 432
GoldWave Web site, 269
Google, 233
Google toolbar, 244
GPF, 432
GPS (Global Positioning System), 351, 355–356, 432
graphics bus, 33
graphics card, 388
Graphire3 tablet (Wacom), 308, 309
grayscale, 317
Green Book CD-ROM format, 136
grounding, 9
GUI, 432

H

half-duplex
    description of, 176, 177, 432
    LAN and, 194–195
halftoning, 317
handheld computer, 349, 354
handwritten input, 349
hard disk
    accessing full capacity of, 125–126
    backup and, 151–153
    capacity of, 37
    configuring, 418–419
    defragmenting, 420
    description of, 28
    digital video and, 283
    editing digital video and, 285
    external, 150, 151–153
    geometrical layout of, 111–112
    Microsoft recommendations for, 24–25
    storage requirements, 112–113
hardware. *See also specific devices*
    planning for extreme machine, 395–398
    waveform audio, 257–259
    working on, 376
harmonic distortion, 255
head, 37
headend facility, 166
headphone connector, 345, 346
headset, 273
heat buildup and airflow, 333, 340, 391–393
heat pocket, 335–336
heat sink, 333–335, 404–405, 432
heuristic scanning, 243
Hewlett Packard
    Deskjet 5850 printer, 318
    LaserJet 1012 printer, 318–319
    LaserJet 3300mfp, 326
    PCL, 316
    recycling ink jet cartridge, 314
    Scanjet 3970, 319, 320
High Color pixels, 81, 82
home automation, 373
hop, 432

hop count, 226, 432

horizontal scan rate, 432

horizontal size and position control, 103

HTML (Hypertext Markup Language), 227, 230, 432

HTTP (Hypertext Transfer Protocol), 227, 432

HTTPS (Secure Hypertext Transfer Protocol), 432

hub
  description of, 432
  LAN and, 195
  network and, 180
  powered and unpowered, 148
  uplink port, 196

hypertext link, 227

Hypertext Markup Language (HTML), 227, 230, 432

Hypertext Transfer Protocol (HTTP), 227, 432

hyperthreading, 57–60, 417, 432

I

IANA (Internet Assigned Numbers Authority), 215, 217, 432

IC (integrated circuit), 433

ICMP (Internet Control Message Protocol), 433

IDE (Integrated Drive Electronics)
  connector, 413
  drive, setting up, 125
  overview of, 72

IEEE 802.11 wireless LAN standard, 169, 186, 188

IEEE 1394
  description of, 75, 431
  digital video camera and, 286

IEEE (Institute of Electrical and Electronics Engineers), 160, 433

IE-SPYAD, 240, 244

IETF (Internet Engineering Task Force), 212, 433

I-frame, 89–90, 433

iGo , 353

image, digital, enlarging, 278–279

image-processing software, 283

impulse driver, 312–313

Industry Standard Architecture (ISA)
  bus, 67–69, 71
  description of, 434

infrastructure mode, 186

Initial TrackerCam window, 364

ink jet printer, 312–314

input device
  game controller, 296–300
  keyboard, 289–296
  mouse, 302–306
  overview of, 301–302
  tablet, 308–309
  trackball, 306–307
  troubleshooting, 309–310

input pre-amp, 256

inside of computer, 27–28

installing
  adapter card, 415–416
  application, 419–420
  motherboard, 402–403
  processor, 404–407
  Windows OS, 418–419

instant messaging, 234

Institute of Electrical and Electronics Engineers (IEEE), 160, 433

instruction execution cycle, 30–32, 45–48

instruction pool, 55–56

integrated circuit (IC), 433

Integrated Drive Electronics (IDE)
  connector, 413
  drive, setting up, 125
  overview of, 72

Intel
  compatibility with products of, 60–62
  D875PBZ motherboard, 184, 386, 402–403, 404
  processor
    Celeron, 53
    Centrino, 350
    dynamic execution, 55–56
    extensions to instruction set, 56–57

hyperthreading, 57–60
  Pentium 4, 53, 396–397, 405
  Pentium M, 350
  performance and, 53
  Web site, 398
interface for scanner, 324
interleaving, 49
internal bay, 331
internal disk drive, adding, 122
Internet
  description of, 433
  live surveillance via, 365–366
  recorded surveillance via, 368–369
  reliability of, 230–231
Internet address, 433
Internet Assigned Numbers Authority
  (IANA), 215, 217, 432
Internet Control Message Protocol (ICMP),
  433
Internet Engineering Task Force (IETF),
  212, 433
Internet Packet Exchange (IPX), 433
Internet Protocol (IP), 201, 433
Internet Relay Chat (IRC), 234, 434
Internet service
  cable TV, 165–167, 170–172
  choosing, 170–172
  electronic mail, 229–231
  file transfer, 228–229
  games and, 171
  instant messaging, 234
  newsgroup, 232–233
  overview of, 225
  ping, 225–226
  satellite, 169–170
  Telnet, 231–232
  time, 233
  wireless, 168–169
  World Wide Web, 226–228
Internet Service Provider (ISP), 231, 434
Internetwork, 433
interpolated resolution, 322–323
interrupt request (IRQ), 434
I/O, 433

I/O bus (I/O channels), 28, 37
I/O panel on motherboard, 338, 402
I/O port, 52, 433
I/O port connector, 339
Iomega Zip drive, 146–147
IP address, 206–207, 433
IP address mask, 433
IP (Internet Protocol), 201, 433
IPv4, 213
IPX (Internet Packet Exchange), 433
IR, 433
IRC (Internet Relay Chat), 234, 434
IRQ (interrupt request), 434
ISA (Industry Standard Architecture)
  bus, 67–69, 71
  description of, 434
ISDN, 157, 160
ISO 9660 format, 136
isolation procedures
  memory failure, 386
  observation and low-level isolation,
    382–384
  overview of, 381
  rules of thumb, 381–382
  video operational during boot, 384–386
ISP (Internet Service Provider), 231, 434
ITU, 160, 434
ITU-TSS, 434

J

joystick, 297–298
JPEG compression, 87–89, 279

K

Kbps, 434
keyboard
  ergonomics and repetitive stress,
    293–295
  impaired access and, 296
  layout of, 293
  split design of, 294
  switches and tactile feedback, 289–291
  wireless, 294–295, 305

keyboard controller, 291–292
keys, 434
kilobit, 434
kilobyte, 434
Kodak DX4530 camera, 277, 278

L

L1 and L2 cache memory, 49
LAN (local area network)
    description of, 434
    designing small, 193–195
laptop
    battery, 352–353
    communications and ports, 351–352
    disk drive, 351
    display, 351
    docking station, 353–354
    evolution of, 349
    overview of, 347–348
    PC card and PC CardBus, 350
    portability of, 347, 348
    processor, memory, and bus, 348–350
    security issues, 356–357
    upgrading, 357
laser printer, 314–315
last node address, 218
latency, 434
layer, 198
LCD, 434
LCD panel
    active matrix technology and, 94, 95
    keeping image sharp, 94–97
    laptop and, 351
    pixels and, 79–80
    Samsung line of, 96–97
leakage, 434
LED, 434
lens for digital camera, 281
Line In, 434
Line Out, 434
linearity, 102
link, 227, 435
Linux, 20–21, 148

Linux Router Project, 209
liquid, spilling on keyboard, 290
LISTSERV, 435
lithium-ion battery, 352–353
lithium-polymer battery, 353
local area network (LAN)
    description of, 434
    designing small, 193–195
local loop, 435
logical address, 214
Logitech
    Cordless Comfort Duo, 294–295
    Cordless Optical TrackMan, 306–307
    Cordless RumblePad, 299
    Formula Force GP wheel, 299–300
    Freedom 2.4 Cordless Joystick, 298
    mouse, 304
    QuickCam Pro 4000, 361–363
    Web site, 362, 397
longevity of CD-ROM and DVD disks, 142
lossless compression, 259
lossy compression, 259
low-pass filter, 256
low-power mode, 62
LS-120 format floppy disk, 146, 147

M

μM, 421
MAC address, 199, 213
MAC (Media Access Control)
    description of, 435
    restrictions, setting, 189
magnetic shielding, 265
mailing list on security, 238–239
Main ⇨ Hyper Threading Technology, 417
maintenance
    choosing approach to, 25–26
    tools for, 7
Maltron keyboard, 296
Master Boot Record (MBR), 235
master/slave, 435
maximum transmission unit (MTU), 436
maximum video bandwidth, 101

MB, 435
Mb, 435
MBps, 435
Mbps, 435
MBR (Master Boot Record), 235
Mean time between failures
    description of, 436
    disk drive and, 115
mechanical mouse, 303
mechanisms of scanner, 320–321
Media Access Control (MAC). *See also*
    MAC address
    description of, 435
    restrictions, setting, 189
medium, 175
megabit, 435
megabyte, 435
memory. *See also specific types of memory*
    cache, 48–49, 425
    description of, 27, 34–36, 435
    digital camera and, 282–283
    digital image and, 277–280
    disk capacity compared to, 37
    editing digital video and, 285
    failure of, 386
    growth in capacity of, 50–51
    inserting or removing, 378, 407–409
    laptop computer, 350, 351
    laser printer and, 315
    Microsoft recommendations for, 22–23
    minimum recommendations for, 24
    motherboard and, 52
    operating system and, 5
    wiring modules, 34
memory bank, 435
memory bus, 32–33
memory chip, 14–15
memory cycle, 435
memory key, 149, 151
memory location, 35
memory module, 35–36
MHz (megahertz), 13
mickey, 303–304
microATX, 435

Microhouse EZ-Drive, 125
micron, 435
microphone
    overview of, 268–269
    speech recognition, 269–270
    voice annotation, 269
    Voice over IP and Internet phone,
        270–271
microphone jack, 273
Microsoft
    base station model MN-700 IEEE
        802.11g, 189
    DirectX technology, 91, 285, 429
    Intellimouse, 304–306
    Internet Connection Sharing, 209
    NetMeeting, 203, 284, 371
    Office, 236–237
    Outlook, 241
    recommendations
        for hard disk, 24–25
        for memory, 22–23
        for processor, 22
    security patch, 238
    Windows Media Audio, 260
    Windows operating system
        commands comparable in UNIX, 232
        configuring file sharing on, 220–222
        Device Manager, 387, 419
        editing digital video and, 285
        Image Color Matching, 321
        installing, 418–419
        minimum requirements for, 21–25
        network properties dialog box, 218
        reinstalling on top of itself, 391
        TCP/IP Properties dialog box, 219
        versions of, 19–20
        Windows 9X, installing, 127
        Windows XP, 357
    Windows Product Activation, 261–262
    Wireless Intellimouse Explorer, 306
    Wireless Notebook Adapter, 189, 190
    Xbox wireless adapter, 189–191
MIDI file, 255

MIDI (Musical Instrument Digital Interface), 262–263, 435

MIME (Multipurpose Internet Mail Extensions), 230, 436

mini headphone connector, 345, 346

minimum requirements to run Windows OS, 21–25

MIPS, 436

mIRC software, 234

mirror, 10

mixer, 263

MMC (Multimedia Card), 436

MMX technology, 57

mobile device. *See* handheld computer; laptop

modem

    cable, 165–167

    characters per second, 161

    choosing, 172–174

    description of, 158

    dial-up analog, 159–164, 172–174

    DSL, 164–165

    internal compared to external, 173–174

    laptop and, 352

    latency comparison, 173

    maximum data rate for, 158–159

    network diagnosis and, 390

    standards, 160

    transmission times for connection speeds, 172

modulated transmission, 176–177

modulation

    definition of, 436

    modem and, 159

    network and, 175

monitor. *See also* display

    brightness, contrast, and, 99, 104

    choosing, 106

    color settings, 81–83

    controls, 102–104

    CRT (cathode ray tube)

        color balance, tracking, purity, and saturation, 99–101

        dot pitch, 106

        focus and convergence, 97–99

        geometric distortion, 102

        ghosting, 101–102

        replacement of, 93

    DDC-compatible, 105–106

    editing digital video and, 285–286

    flat panel (LCD) display, 79–80, 94–97, 351

    multimedia, 104–105

    pixels and, 79–80

    placing to minimize glare, 106

    repairing, 378

    technical characteristics of, 93

    television compared to, 79

    television in window of, 90–91

    unresponsive, 384

    video card and, 39

    video data path, 81

Moore's Law, 14

motherboard. *See also* chipset

    AMD processor and, 60

    ATA drive and, 125–126

    built-in Ethernet adapter and, 184

    bus and, 67

    case and, 329–330

    checking, 383–384

    components of, 51–52, 73–74

    description of, 72, 436

    form factor, 337–339

    installing, 402–403

    Intel D875PBZ, 72–73

    mounting, 331

    parallel and serial ATA and, 124

    replacing, 4, 378

    security tray in chassis, 409

motion compensation, 361

motion detection and tracking, 369–370

mounting

    adapter card, 409

    drives, 400–401

    heat sink, 404–405

    internal disk drive, 122–123

    power supply, 399, 499

mouse
creation of, 301
cursor, 304
Microsoft Intellimouse, 304–306
overview of, 302–304
troubleshooting, 309–310
wireless, 294–295, 305
MP3, 260
MP3 player, 267–268
MPEG 2 video compression, 140
MPEG (Moving Picture Experts Group)
description of, 436
video compression and, 87–90
MTBF (Mean time between failures)
description of, 436
disk drive and, 115
MTTF, 436
MTTR, 436
MTU (maximum transmission unit), 436
multilink PPP, 436
multimedia, 436
Multimedia Card (MMC), 436
multimedia monitor, 104–105
multimeter, 10, 383
multiprocessing, 57–60
Multipurpose Internet Mail Extensions
(MIME), 230, 436
multitasking, 436
Musical Instrument Digital Interface (MIDI)
description of, 262–263, 435
file, 255

N

name server address, 216
nano, 436
nanometer, 436
nanosecond, 436
NAT (Network Address Translation),
206–207, 209, 218, 367
National Television Standards Committee
(NTSC), 437
NetBIOS, 436
netmask, 216

NetMeeting (Microsoft), 203, 284, 371
network
characteristics of, 176–178
editing digital video and, 286
expanding, 196–198
hardware for, 175–176
laptop and, 349, 351–352
local area, 193–195, 434
protocols for, 211–212
resources needed for, 5
router, 198–201
technologies
choosing, 191
Ethernet, 179–184
wireless, 179, 184–191
troubleshooting, 389–390
wide area, 215, 445
network address, 200, 206–207, 213–214
Network Address Translation (NAT),
206–207, 209, 218, 367
network layer, 198–199, 205, 437
Network News Transfer Protocol (NNTP),
232–233, 437
network sniffer, 204
Network Time Protocol (NTP), 233
network topology, 437
networking. See network
newsgroup, 232–233, 244
NFS, 437
nibble, 437
NIC, 437
nickel-cadmium battery, 352
nickel-metal hydride battery, 352
Nigerian spam, 245
NLS (On-Line System), 302
NLX form factor, 339
NNTP (Network News Transfer Protocol),
232–233, 437
node, 437
noise
modem and, 158
in PC, 396
power supply and, 340
telephone lines and, 165

nonvolatile memory, 437
Northbridge chip, 33, 69–70, 73, 74
note, shape of amplitude of, 253
notebook computer. *See* laptop
NTFS (NT File System), 356–357, 390, 437
NTFSDOS Professional, 437
NTP (Network Time Protocol), 233
NTSC (National Television Standards
 Committee), 437
nVidia
 hardware, 91
 Web site, 92

O

observation and low-level isolation,
 382–384, 389
Occam's Razor, 381
OCR (optical character recognition), 324
octet, 213
Ogg Vorbis, 260, 268
103 error code, 382
16550 chip, 162, 309–310
On-Line System (NLS), 302
Ontrack Disk Manager, 125
open relay server, 245–246
open source, 437
Open Systems Interconnection Reference
 Model, 198–199, 204, 212, 437
operand, 30
operating system
 CD and DVD drives and, 142
 choosing, 5–6, 19
 description of, 437
 drive letter assignment, 127
 editing digital video and, 285
 error message regarding, 385
 Linux and UNIX, 20–21, 148, 232
 Palm, 349, 354
 unstable, 388
 USB support and, 148
 Windows
  commands comparable in UNIX, 232
  configuring file sharing on, 220–222
  Device Manager, 387, 419
  editing digital video and, 285
  Image Color Matching, 321
  installing, 418–419
  minimum requirements for, 21–25
  network properties dialog box, 218
  NTFS, 356–357, 390, 437
  reinstalling on top of itself, 391
  Sound Recorder, 269
  TCP/IP Properties dialog box, 219
  unstable, 388
  versions of, 19–20
  Windows 9X, 127, 388
  Windows 2000/XP, 388
  Windows XP, 357
Opteron processor, 61
optical character recognition (OCR), 324
optical drive
 laptop, 351
 troubleshooting, 143
optical formats, 129
optical mouse, 303–304
optical resolution, 321
Orange Book CD-ROM format, 136
OSI Reference Model, 198–199, 204, 212,
 437
output power, 255

P

packet, 437
packet filtering, 205–206, 208, 437
packet switching, 438
packetization, 438
packet-switched network, 438
page, 438
page description languages, 315–317
page mode, 438
PAL (Phase Alternating Line), 79, 438
palette, 438
Palm operating system, 349, 354
Parallel ATA, 52
parallel ATA channels, 124
parallel port connector, 73, 74

parallelogram distortion, 102
parity, 438
parity bit, 438
partitioning disk, 385
patch cable, 438
patch cord, 182
PC Card, 75–76, 350
PC CardBus, 350
PC Toys: 14 Cool Projects for Home, Office, and Entertainment (Barry Press & Marcia Press), 359
PCI Express, 70
PCI (Peripheral Component Interconnect) bus
    chipset and, 71–72
    description of, 69–70
    ISA bus compared to, 68
    bus slot, 52
    connector, 73, 74
    description of, 438
PCL (Hewlett Packard), 316
PCMCIA, 438. *See also* PC Card
PDA (Personal Digital Assistant), 349, 354
peer-to-peer communication, 199, 438
Pentium 4 processor (Intel), 53, 396–397, 405
Pentium M processor (Intel), 350
performance
    all-in-one unit, 325–326
    of CD-ROM drive, 133–134
    cooling comparison, 333
    of disk drive, 113–115
    games and display update, 41
    of hard disk, 135
    of LAN, 194
    of memory key, improving, 151
    3D rendering and, 86
peripheral, 438
Peripheral Component Interconnect (PCI) bus
    chipset and, 71–72
    description of, 69–70
    ISA bus compared to, 68

bus slot, 52
    connector, 73, 74
    description of, 438
Personal Digital Assistant (PDA), 349, 354
P-frame, 89–90, 439
Phase Alternating Line (PAL), 79, 438
phoneme, 269
photography. *See* digital camera
physical address, 199, 214
physical layer, 198–199
physical location of added disk drive, 122
piezoelectric crystal, 312–313
pincushion control, 103
pincushion distortion, 102
`ping` utility, 225–226, 439
Pinnacle Systems
    PCTV Deluxe, 284, 285
    Studio 8, 284, 285, 286, 287–288
    Studio Deluxe PCI video capture card, 283, 284
pins in connector, 343
PIO (Programmed Input/Output), 439
pipelining, 53–54, 55
pits and lands, 439
pixel
    description of, 439
    LCD panel and, 79–80
    video card and, 39
pixel shader, 439
Plain Old Telephone Service (POTS), 271, 439
planning for extreme machine
    hardware, 395–398
    software, 416–417
platter, 37
pliers, 10
Plug and Play, 105, 417, 439
pointing device
    game controller, 296–300
    keyboard, 289–296
    mouse, 302–306
    overview of, 301–302

Continued

pointing device *(continued)*
  tablet, 308–309
  trackball, 306–307
  troubleshooting, 309–310
point-to-point connections, 66, 175, 176
Point-to-Point Protocol (PPP), 439
polling, 439
polygon drawing, 86
polyphony, 263
POP (Post Office Protocol), 229, 439
pop-up window blocker, 244
port
  for CD-ROM drive, 135
  COM, 427
  I/O, 52, 433
  laptop, 351–352
  serial, 162, 305, 442
  Universal Serial Bus (USB), 147, 286
  uplink, 196
port I/O address, 439
port number, 214
Post Office Protocol (POP), 229, 439
POST (Power-On Self-Test), 439
PostScript (Adobe), 316
POTS (Plain Old Telephone Service), 271,
  439
power, 340
power amplifier, 265–266
power down, 439
power management
  desktop, 62–63
  laptop, 351, 352
power supply
  air outlet temperature, checking, 391
  Antec TrueControl, 396
  ATX system, 339
  cable orientation, 379
  checking, 382, 383
  choosing, 341
  disconnecting, 380
  mounting, 399, 499
  overview of, 27, 329, 340
  repairing, 377
  TrackerPod robotic camera base, 363
  uninterruptible, 341–343
  wiring to motherboard, 409–410

power switch, 383
power up, 439
Power-On Self-Test (POST), 439
PPP (Point-to-Point Protocol), 439
preconfigured systems, 16–19
presentation, sound system for, 271–272
Press, Barry and Marcia, *PC Toys: 14 Cool
  Projects for Home, Office, and
  Entertainment,* 359
printer
  all-in-one unit, 325–326
  choosing, 317–319
  ink jet, 312–314
  laser, 314–315
  overview of, 311
  page description languages, 315–317
printer sharing, configuring, 222–223
private TCP/IP network addresses, 207, 217
processor. *See also* CPU (central
  processing unit)
  AMD, 54, 60–62, 350
  checking, 383–384
  choosing, 43
  clock rates for, 13–14
  connecting to memories, 65–67
  description of, 4, 27, 29
  digital signal, 429
  dynamic branch prediction, 54–55
  dynamic execution, 55–56
  editing digital video and, 285
  failure of, 392–393
  increasing volume of data available to,
    48–49
  installing, 404–407
  instructions and, 30–32, 45–48
  Intel
    Celeron, 53
    Centrino, 350
    dynamic execution, 55–56
    extensions to instruction set, 56–57
    hyperthreading, 57–60
    Pentium 4, 53, 396–397, 405
    Pentium M, 350
    performance and, 53
  in laptop, 348–349
  machine instructions to, 46

Microsoft recommendations for, 22
Opteron, 61
picture of, 30, 31
positioning of, 338
raster, 315
replacing, 378
signal processing, 56–57
speed of operation of, 47–48
superscalar instruction execution, 53–54
processor cooling fan, 333–335
processor socket, 73
programmable read-only memory (PROM), 439
Programmed Input/Output (PIO), 439
proprietary design, needless, 339
proprietary messaging, 234
protocol. *See also specific protocols*
description of, 32, 440
network, 211–212
URL and, 227
protocol stack, 199
PS/2 mouse and keyboard connector, 73, 74, 291, 305–306
Public Telephone and Telegraph (PTT), 440
pulse dialing, 440

Q
QA+Win32 (DiagSoft), 386
quality
CD and, 426
of image from digital camera, 275
of manufacturer, focusing on, 16
of sound, 271
quality of service (QoS), 440
QuickTech PRO (Ultra-X), 386
QWERTY keyboard layout, 293

R
Radio Shack Web site, 373
RAID (Redundant Array of Inexpensive Disks), 117–122
RAM (random access memory), 440

Rambus, 440
RAS (row address strobe), 440
raster processor, 315
raw resolution, 321
RCA connector, 344, 346
read the manual (RTFM), 441
reading CD, 131–133, 134, 135
read-only memory (ROM), 441
Real Audio, 260
recordable CD-ROM, 137
recordable DVD, 140–141
recording Internet surveillance, 368–369
recycling ink jet cartridge, 314
Red Book CD-ROM format, 136
reduced instruction set computing (RISC), 440
Redundant Array of Inexpensive Disks (RAID), 117–122
refresh, 440
refresh rate, 440
register-level compatibility, 440
release part of note, 253
reliability
of disk drive, 115–116
of Internet, 230–231
remote surveillance
building to own design, 372–374
live Internet, 365–366
motion detection and tracking, 369–370
overview of, 359–360
parts list, 361–363
recorded Internet, 368–369
sensors and alerts, 360–361
TrackerCam software, 364–365
remote user, 440
removability, 440
removable storage
archiving to, 374
backup and, 150–151
external USB, 149–150
floppy disk, 145–147
overview of, 145
repairing compared to replacing component, 375
repeater, 440

repetitive stress and keyboard use, 293–295

resolution
all-in-one unit, 325–326
digital image and, 277–281
ink jet printer, 313
laser printer, 315
LCD panel, 95–96
live Internet surveillance, 365
Logitech QuickCam Pro 4000, 362
monitor, 79–80
performance and, 86
scanner, 321–323
surveillance system, 361
video data path and, 81

response time, 226
Return Material Authorization (RMA), 441
RGB (red-green-blue) color model, 322, 440
RISC (reduced instruction set computing), 440
RJ-11 connector, 344, 346
RJ-45 connector, 180–182, 184, 344, 346
RMA (Return Material Authorization), 441
ROM (read-only memory), 441
rotation control, 103
rotation rate of disk, 38, 113
rotational distortion, 102
rotational latency, 114
router, 198–201, 367, 441
routing protocol, 441
routing table, 213, 441
routing update, 441
row, 441
row address, 50
row address strobe (RAS), 440
RS-232C standard, 305, 441
RTFM (read the manual), 441

S
μS, 421
sample, 441
sampling clock, 257
sampling rate, 258

satellite Internet access, 169–170
sawtooth wave, 252
scalability of network, 193
scan rate, 441
scanner
all-in-one unit, 325–326
characteristics of, 319–320
interfaces, 324
mechanisms, 320–321
number and accuracy of colors, 321
resolution, 321–323
software, 324–325
screen
brightness, contrast, and, 99, 104
choosing, 106
color settings, 81–83
controls, 102–104
CRT (cathode ray tube)
color balance, tracking, purity, and saturation, 99–101
dot pitch, 106
focus and convergence, 97–99
geometric distortion, 102
ghosting, 101–102
replacement of, 93
DDC-compatible, 105–106
editing digital video and, 285–286
flat panel (LCD) display, 79–80, 94–97, 351
multimedia, 104–105
pixels and, 79–80
placing to minimize glare, 106
repairing, 378
technical characteristics of, 93
television compared to, 79
television in window of, 90–91
unresponsive, 384
video card and, 39
video data path, 81
screwdriver, 10
screws, 380, 399
SCSI (Small Computer System Interface), 441
SD (secure digital), 441

SDRAM (synchronous dynamic random access memory)
  chipset and, 72
  description of, 50, 441
Seagate
  Barracuda, 113
  BounceBack Express software, 152, 153
  Disk Wizard, 125
  external hard drive, 150, 152
  Web site, 397
sector, 37–38, 111, 441
secure digital (SD), 441
Secure Hypertext Transfer Protocol (HTTPS), 432
security issues
  attacks and threats, 204
  broadband, 165
  cable modem technology, 167
  cable/DSL and TrackerCam, 367
  cracking, 204, 235, 241–242
  Ethernet network, 183
  mobile device, 356–357
  network, 193
  packet filters, 205–206
  remote surveillance, 359–360
  Trojan, 204, 235, 240–241, 444
  virus, 204, 232, 235–237, 390, 445
  wireless network, 188
  worm, 204, 235, 238–240, 445
security patch, 238, 242
seek time, 114, 441
selecting
  approach to support and maintenance, 25–26
  case, 339–340
  components for extreme machine, 395–398
  digital camera, 281–283
  Internet access, 170–172
  modem, 172–174
  monitor, 106
  network technology, 191
  operating system, 5–6, 19
  power supply, 341
  printer, 317–319
  processor, 43
  sound system, 271–272
  speakers, 264–267
  video card, 91
Self-Monitoring Analysis and Reporting Technology, 116
self-refresh, 442
semiconductor, 442
sendmail program, 245
serial ATA, 72, 442
serial interface, 442
serial port, 162, 305, 442
serial port connector, 73, 74
serial presence detect, 442
server
  description of, 20, 197, 442
  open relay, 245–246
  setting up, 197–198
  URL and, 227
service set identifier (SSID), 188
shadow mask, 97, 98, 100–101
sharing wires among devices, 65–67
shield for keyboard, 290–291
shielded twisted-pair (STP), 180, 443
shooter, first and third person, 296
signal processing, 56–57
Simple Mail Transfer Protocol (SMTP), 229–230, 442
Simple Network Management Protocol (SNMP), 229, 442
sine wave, 251–252
single in-line memory module (SIMM), 442
Single Instruction Multiple Data (SIMD) technology, 57
size of sound recording, 257
slow scan video, 361
Small Computer System Interface (SCSI), 441
small outline dual inline memory module (SODIMM), 442
SmartHome webcam, 361
SMTP (Simple Mail Transfer Protocol), 229–230, 442

SNMP (Simple Network Management Protocol), 229, 442
Sobig.F virus, 243
socket driver, 10
Socket Watch, 233
SODIMM (small outline dual inline memory module), 442
soft error, 442
software. *See also* driver; *specific software*
    anti-adware, 242–244
    antivirus
        overview of, 235, 242–244, 422
        Trojan protection and, 240
        updating, 236
    as cause of problem, 375
    hard disk space required for, 24–25
    image-processing, 283
    matching video hardware and, 91
    memory requirements for, 23
    multiprocessing and, 59–60
    operating system and, 8
    planning for extreme machine, 416–417
    printer management, 316–317
    scanner, 324–325
    support for, 25
soldering iron, 10
Sony
    DRU510a, 140, 141
    LCD monitor, 396
    Web site, 397
sound. *See also* microphone; speakers
    analog audio, 254–255
    overview of, 251–254
    surround sound, 266, 443
    troubleshooting, 272–273
    USB audio, 264
    waveform audio, 255–262
sound card
    CD audio and line interfaces, 263–264
    controls for, 258
    quality of sound and, 255
    Turtle Beach Santa Cruz, 258–259
    wiring to stereo, 265
sound file, 442

sound system, choosing, 271–272
Southbridge chip, 33, 69–70
spam, 245–247
Spam Gourmet, 247
SpamAssassin, 247
SpamCop, 247
spanning brackets, 406
speakers
    Acoustic Authority A3780, 266–267
    choosing, 264–267
    CRT monitor and, 100–101
    monitors and, 104–105
    troubleshooting, 272–273
speech recognition, 269–270
speed of scanner interface, 324
spilling liquid on keyboard, 290
spiral track on CD, 130
spoofing, 206, 442
spread spectrum technology, 185, 187
SpywareBlaster, 244
SRAM (static random access memory), 442
SSE (streaming SIMD extensions), 57
SSID (service set identifier), 188
stacking drives, 335–336
standby mode, 62, 339
standoff, 330, 331, 402
star topology, 443
Start ➪ Programs ➪ Accessories ➪ System Tools ➪ Disk Defragmenter, 420
static electricity, 8–9, 376
static magnetic field, 100
static random access memory (SRAM), 442
steering wheel, 299–300
stereo, wiring sound card to, 265
storage
    CD-ROM and, 138
    definition of, 443
    digital camera and, 279
    digital video and, 283
    hard disk space required for, 112–113
    removable
        archiving to, 374
        backup and, 150–151
        external USB, 149–150

floppy disk, 145–147
overview of, 145
video compression and, 87
storage capacity, 443
STP (shielded twisted-pair), 180, 443
streaming SIMD extensions (SSE), 57
string, 34
subcarrier, 165
subnet, 216
subtractive color mixing, 322
subwoofer, 273
summer, 253–254
superscalar instruction execution, 53–54
support
choosing approach to, 25–26
evaluating, 7
surround sound, 266, 443
surveillance, remote
building to own design, 372–374
live Internet, 365–366
motion detection and tracking, 369–370
overview of, 359–360
parts list, 361–363
recorded Internet, 368–369
sensors and alerts, 360–361
TrackerCam software, 364–365
sustain part of note, 253
sustained transfer rate of disk, 38, 39
S-video, 443
switch, 180, 195–196, 289–292
switched Ethernet, 443
switching fabric, 195, 196
synchronous dynamic random access
memory (SDRAM)
chipset and, 72
description of, 50, 441
system board. *See also* chipset
AMD processor and, 60
ATA drive and, 125–126
built-in Ethernet adapter and, 184
bus and, 67
case and, 329–330
checking, 383–384
components of, 51–52, 73–74

description of, 72, 436
form factor, 337–339
installing, 402–403
Intel D875PBZ, 72–73
mounting, 331
parallel and serial ATA and, 124
replacing, 4, 378
security tray in chassis, 409

T

tablet, 308–309, 310
tablet PC, 349. *See also* laptop
T-connector, 443
TCP (Transmission Control Protocol),
201–203
TCP/IP (Transmission Control
Protocol/Internet Protocol)
configuring, 218–219
description of, 212, 443
TDMA (Time Division Multiple Access),
177, 178
telephone, frequency response of, 158–159
television
cable, and Internet service, 165–167
in window, 90–91
Telnet, 231–232, 443
10Base-T, 100Base-T, and 1000Base-T, 421
10Base-2, 179–180, 389, 421
texels, 86
texture mapping, 83–86
thermal grease on processor, 406
Thin Film Transistor panel, 351
3COM OfficeConnect 56K LAN Modem,
163–164, 174
3D video accelerator, 83–86
3D viewing and rendering pipeline, 85–86
throughput, sustained, 113
tilt control, 103
timbre, 253, 263, 443
Time Division Multiple Access (TDMA),
177, 178
Time to Live (TTL), 226
toner, 314, 315

tools for working on computer hardware, 9–10

topology, 443

total harmonic distortion, 255

traceroute utility, 213–214

traces, 65

track, 111

trackball, 301–302, 306–307

TrackerCam software (Eagletron)
    Capture Motion page, 369–370
    Capture Stills Page, 368
    configuring, 361, 364–371
    Live Video, 366
    Online/Offline dialog box, 366
    Set Viewpoint Order Page, 369
    Web site, 362

TrackerPod robotic camera base, 361, 363, 371

TrackerPod Web site, 362

transferring data, 113–114

transistor density, 14

Transmission Control Protocol (TCP), 201–203

Transmission Control Protocol/Internet Protocol (TCP/IP)
    configuring, 218–219
    description of, 212, 443

trapezoid distortion, 102, 103

tree architecture, 196, 197

triangle wave, 252

Trojan
    description of, 204, 235, 444
    protecting against, 240–241

troubleshooting. See also isolation procedures
    cache coherence, 58–59
    case study, 390–393
    configuration, 387–388
    description of problem and, 388
    diagnostics, running, 386
    input device, 309–310
    network, 389–390
    optical drive, 143
    processor cooling fan, 334
    sound problems, 272–273

true color, 444

True Color pixels, 81

TTL (Time to Live), 226

Tucows, 247

Turtle Beach Santa Cruz sound card, 258–259, 415

TV tuner, 90–91

TWAIN, 324, 444

twisted-pair, 180–182, 444

type of connector, 343

"Typing Injury FAQ," 295

U

UART (Universal Asynchronous Receiver/Transmitter), 444

UDP (User Datagram Protocol), 203, 444

Ultra DMA IDE interface, 72

Ultra-X Web site, 382

Uniform Resource Locator (URL), 227–228, 444

uninterruptible power supply (UPS), 341–343

Unison File Synchronizer, 152–153, 374

Universal Asynchronous Receiver/Transmitter (UART), 444

Universal Disk Format, 444

Universal Serial Bus (USB)
    connector, 73, 74
    description of, 75, 444
    motherboard and, 52
    port, 147, 286
    sound system and, 254
    upgrades and, 7

UNIX, 20–21, 232

unresponsive monitor, 384

unresponsive system, 383–384, 392

unshielded twisted-pair (UTP), 180, 444

upgrading
    analyzing options for, 6, 15
    being hardnosed about, 4–5
    future costs of, 7–8
    laptop, 357
    video card, 92

uplink port, 196

UPS (uninterruptible power supply), 341–343

URL (Uniform Resource Locator), 227–228, 444

USB audio, 264

USB mouse, 306

USB (Universal Serial Bus)
   connector, 73, 74
   description of, 75, 444
   motherboard and, 52
   port, 147, 286
   sound system and, 254
   upgrades and, 7

Usenet, 444

User Datagram Protocol (UDP), 203, 444

user-user encoding (UUE), 230

uses for computer, 4–5

UTP (unshielded twisted-pair), 180, 444

UUE (user-user encoding), 230

V

V.42bis, 444

V.90 modem, 161, 172

vertical size and position control, 103

VESA (Video Electronics Standards
   Association), 444

VGA (Video Graphics Array), 79, 444

video amplifier in monitor, 101

video bus, 83

video camera and surveillance system, 360

video card
   ATI Radeon 9800 XT, 397
   choosing, 91
   description of, 39–41

video compression, 87–90, 140

video data path, 81

video, digital
   capturing and editing, 284–286
   making DVD from, 286–288
   overview of, 283–284

video driver, 92

Video Electronics Standards Association
   (VESA), 444

Video Graphics Array (VGA), 79, 444

video memory, 39–40

video operational during boot, 384–386

videoconferencing, 203, 284, 371

virtual memory, 388

virus
   cleaning up machine infected with, 390
   description of, 204, 235, 445
   newsgroup and, 232
   protecting against, 235–237

virus hoaxes, 243

vision impairment and monitor choice, 106

VisualRoute, 213

voice, 253–254

voice annotation, 269

Voice over Internet Protocol (VoIP), 271

voltage, 340

volume control for speakers, 272

Vonage, 271

W

WAAS (Wide Area Augmentation System),
   356, 445

Wacom graphic tablets, 308–309

WAN (wide area network), 215, 445

warm boot, 445

wave file, 255, 445

waveform, 251–252, 445

waveform audio
   compression and, 259–261
   hardware, 257–259
   overview of, 255–257

waveform generator, 253

wavelength division multiplexing, 178

Web browser, security options for, 240

Web sites
   Acoustic Authority, 398
   Ad-aware (Lavasoft), 244
   Antec, 397
   ATI, 92, 398
   Black Box VueMate Hub, 359
   broadband service, 171

Continued

Web sites *(continued)*
Butchart Gardens, 213
CERT (Computer Emergency Response
Team), 426
Coalition Against Unsolicited
Commercial Email, 245
Crucial, 397, 407
Digital Rights Management, 260–261
DisplayMate software, 96
domain names, 203
download site reviews, 244
Eagletron, 373
free e-mail address directory, 247
FreeBSD, 231
Freebyte, 242
Gibson Research Corporation, 239
GoldWave, 269
Google, 233
IE-SPYAD, 240
iGo, 353
Intel, 398
Internet Assigned Numbers Authority
(IANA), 215
Linux and USB, 148
Linux Router Project, 209
Logitech, 362, 397
Maltron keyboard, 296
mIRC software, 234
Nigerian spam, 245
NTFSDOS Professional, 437
nVidia, 92
Ogg Vorbis, 260
Radio Shack, 373
for recycling ink jet cartridge, 314
Seagate, 397
Socket Watch, 233
Sony, 397
Spam Gourmet, 247
SpamAssassin, 247
SpamCop, 247
TrackerPod and TrackerCam, 362
Tucows, 247
Turtle Beach, 398
"Typing Injury FAQ," 295

Ultra-X, 382
Unison File Synchronizer, 152–153, 374
virus hoaxes, 243
VisualRoute, 213
Vonage, 271
X10 Xcam2, 373
XFree86 X Window system, 92
Zalman Tech, 398
webcam, 361–363, 372–373
Webcam Corporation Model WCSP100-4,
372
WEP (Wired Equivalent Privacy), 188
white screen, viewing, 101
Wide Area Augmentation System (WAAS),
356, 445
wide area network (WAN), 215, 445
width of memory module, 35
WiFi Protected Access (WPA), 188
WiFi (Wireless Fidelity), 186
Windows Media Audio, 260
Windows operating system
commands comparable in UNIX, 232
configuring file sharing on, 220–222
Device Manager, 387, 419
editing digital video and, 285
Image Color Matching, 321
installing, 418–419
minimum requirements for, 21–25
network properties dialog box, 218
NTFS, 356–357, 390, 437
reinstalling on top of itself, 391
Sound Recorder, 269
TCP/IP Properties dialog box, 219
unstable, 388
versions of, 19–20
Windows 9X
installing, 127
Performance tab, 388
Windows 2000/XP, Performance
Options, 388
Windows XP, 357
Windows Product Activation, 261–262
Wired Equivalent Privacy (WEP), 188
wireless access point, 186

Wireless Fidelity (WiFi), 186
wireless technology
    Internet service and, 168–170
    mouse and keyboard, 294–295, 305
    network and
        advantages of, 186
        overview of, 179, 184–185
        specifications for, 186, 188
    webcam, 373
wiretap, 204
wiring
    chassis to motherboard connectors,
        411–412
    color coding of, 380
    hub-based, 389
    power supply to motherboard, 409–410
    sharing among devices, 65–67
    sound card to stereo, 265
wiring specifications for twisted-pair, 182
word processor, origins of, 302
working on computer hardware
    static electricity and, 8–9
    techniques for, 8, 376
    tools for, 9–10
workload on computer, 4–5
WorkPace software, 295
World Wide Web (WWW), 226–228, 445

worm
    description of, 204, 235, 445
    protecting against, 238–240
WPA (WiFi Protected Access), 188
write-back cache, 49, 445
write-through cache, 49, 445
WWW (World Wide Web), 226–228, 445

X

X10 Xcam2 and Floodcam, 373
XFree86 X Window system, 92
XOR (exclusive or), 187

Y

Yellow Book CD-ROM format, 136

Z

Zalman CPU cooler, 396, 404, 405–407
Zalman Tech Web site, 398
ZIF (zero-insertion force) socket, 445
zinc-air battery, 353
Zip drive, 146
ZoneAlarm (Zone Labs), 210, 239
zoom feature of digital camera, 283

Color Photographs

Understanding what you're looking at inside a PC is fundamental to being able to upgrade and repair the machine. The details of what's inside often depend on color, and on small characteristics not readily visible in black-and-white photographs. We've included color photographs here from throughout the book, and Chapter 25 in particular, along with additional photos to give you more detail on how to build the system you read about in that chapter. Your PC is likely to be somewhat different in overall layout than the one we show, but the standardization throughout PCs ensures that the individual components inside yours will look similar in most ways to the ones you see in the photos.

We've also included prints of several photos to help you visualize the capabilities of digital cameras. Consumer-grade digital cameras can produce excellent photos, ones good enough that, within the limits of the consumer unit, you have to look closely at a comparable photo taken with a professional-grade camera to find the differences in quality.

Intel D875PBZ Pentium 4 motherboard.

The Kodak DX4350 is capable of excellent quality photographs.
© 2004 Barry Press & Marcia Press

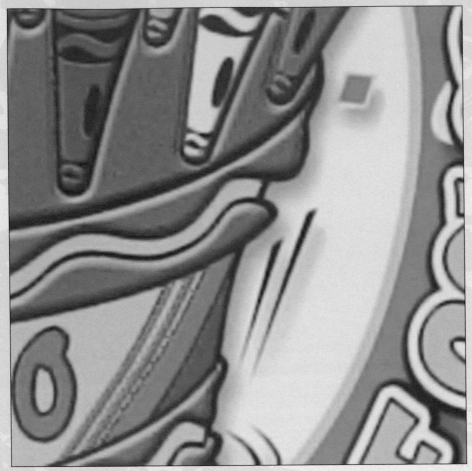

This image was taken with a Canon EOS 1D professional digital camera.
Photo by Jansen Gunderson

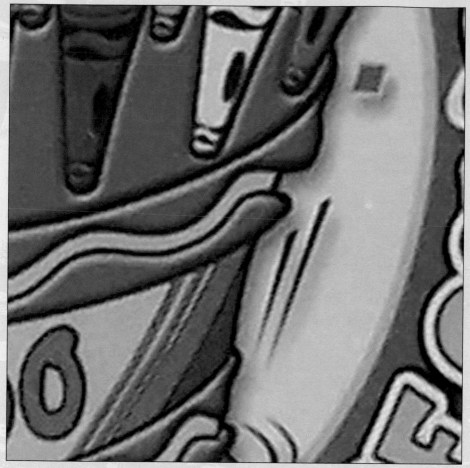

This image was taken with a Kodak DX4350 consumer digital camera.
Photo by Jansen Gunderson

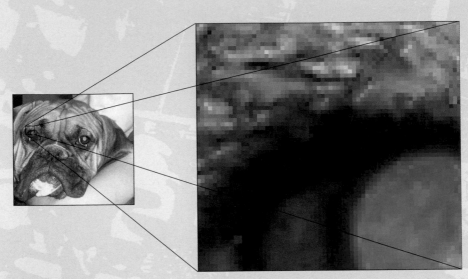

Pixelization can result from not fitting the image to the camera sensor.

Optional front fan bay.

External 3.5 bays.

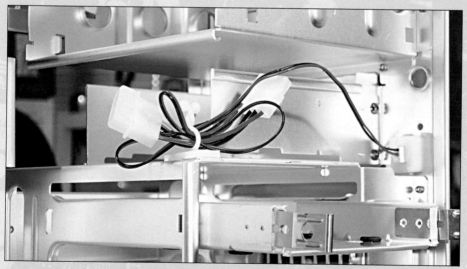

Antec P160 disk drive bays.

Antec TrueControl 550 (bottom side up).
© 2004 Barry Press & Marcia Press

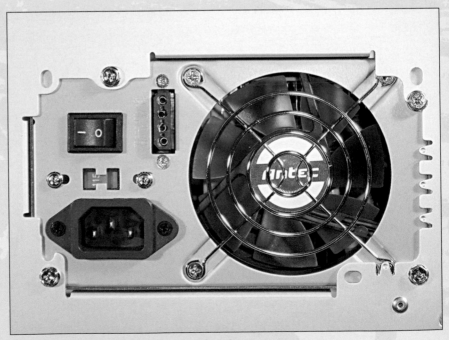

Antec TrueControl 550 mounted in chassis.
© 2004 Barry Press & Marcia Press

Antec vibration-isolated 120 mm fan.

Fan mounted on back panel.

Slide rail mounted on DVD writer. Use the alternate hole if you want the front of the drive flush with the front of the chassis rather than recessed behind the drive cover panel.

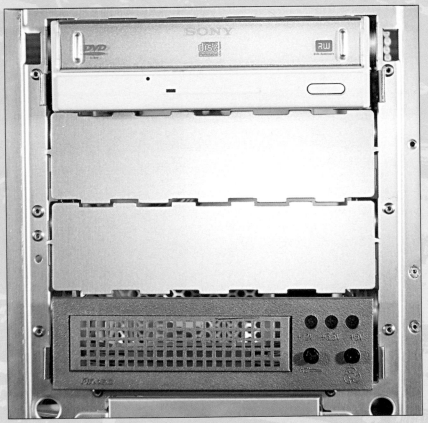

We installed the Sony DRU510a in the top 5.25-inch external bay and the power supply control in the bottom one. The control is hidden behind a blank cover plate once the chassis front panel is installed.

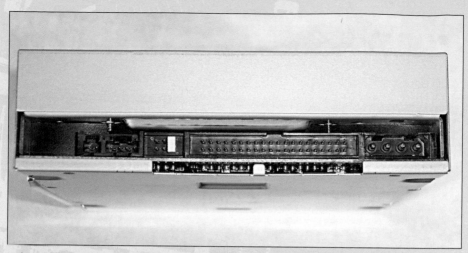

Left to right: audio connectors, master/slave jumpers, IDE connector, power connector.

© 2004 Barry Press & Marcia Press

The Seagate SATA drives mount one each in the drive carriers using the screws and grommets visible in the view on the right.

© 2004 Barry Press & Marcia Press

The SATA connectors are on the left in this view of the disks mounted in the Antec chassis. The larger one is the power connector; the smaller one is for data.

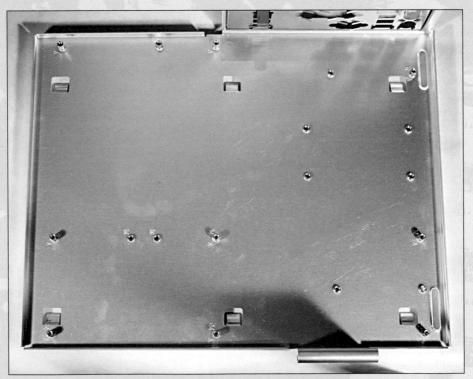

Take the motherboard tray out of the chassis for assembly. The Intel D875PBZ motherboard uses 10 brass threaded standoffs. Check you have the correct mounting screws before inserting the standoff and make the standoffs snug but not so tight the threads strip. Cyanoacrylate glue will keep the standoffs secure if necessary.

Replace the generic I/O cover plate with the one supplied with the motherboard.

The Pentium 4 socket on the motherboard requires no force to insert the processor so long as you line up pin 1 and the rest of the pins properly. Lift the lever to open the socket, insert the processor, and then close the lever.

Pin 1 on this 3.2 GHz Pentium 4 processor is in the upper left of the photo, marked both by the small triangle in the corner and by the two missing pins in the same corner. The missing pins must line up with the missing holes in the processor socket on the motherboard.

This Zalman CNPS7000A-Cu heat sink and fan assembly (cooler) exceeds the Intel weight specification, but is very quiet and in a room temperature environment has kept our processor at about 36 degrees C (96.8 degrees F).

The Zalman cooler includes a tube of thermal grease. Spread the contents over the socketed processor and then use the edge of a credit card to smooth it out, leaving just a very thin layer on the processor surface. Excess past the edges of the processor doesn't matter, but too much grease on the top of the processor reduces the heat transfer from the processor to the cooler rather than increasing it.

Mount the Zalman cooler on the motherboard heat sink retention bracket using the spanning brackets included with the cooler. The curved part of the spanning brackets points down, and the screws go through the inner holes on the tabs sticking out from the cooler itself. Alternate tightening the screws down on either side a few turns until both are snug so that the cooler remains flat on the processor as you work. Once the cooler is tightened down, route the wires around the cooler and plug them into the processor fan connector on the motherboard.

DIMM sockets, such as those in this photo, have retention clips at the ends to secure the DIMM strips, and keys in the bottom of the sockets to ensure the strips only go in one way.

© 2004 Barry Press & Marcia Press

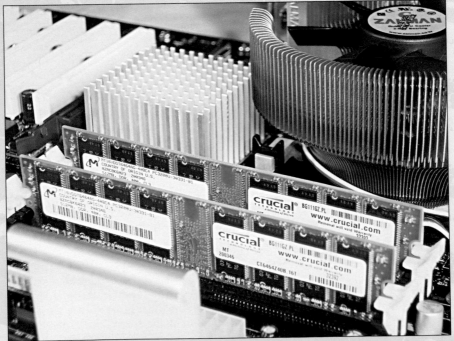

The DIMM strips mount one per memory bank on the motherboard.

© 2004 Barry Press & Marcia Press

The main ATX power cable is keyed and has a retention clip to keep it attached to the motherboard.

© 2004 Barry Press & Marcia Press

The ATX auxiliary 12 V connector is keyed and has a retention clip much like the main power connector, but fewer wires. All the wires on the power supply cable will be yellow or black.

© 2004 Barry Press & Marcia Press

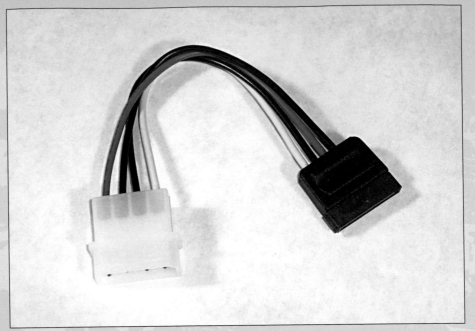

This serial ATA power cable adapter transforms the conventional disk drive connectors from the power supply to the different shape and pinout required on the back of the serial ATA disk drives.

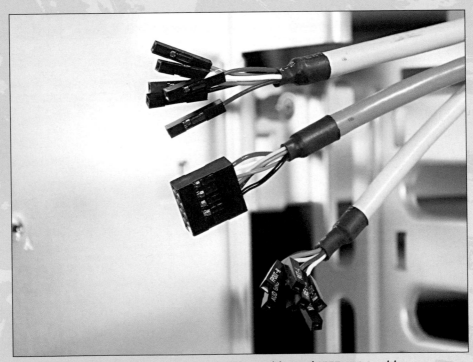

Top to bottom: Front panel audio cables, USB cable, and IEEE 1394 cable.

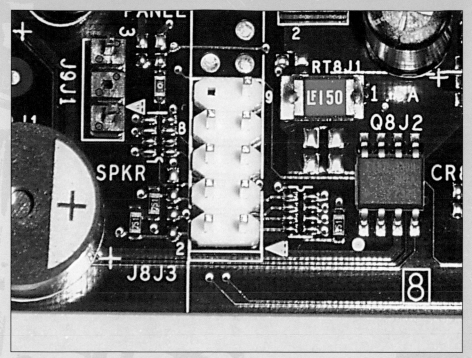

Individual wire pairs from the front panel LEDs and switches connect to this header. Follow the header pinouts from the manufacturer's motherboard documentation. (The Intel D875PBZ motherboard also includes a table of pinouts on the motherboard itself.)

© 2004 Barry Press & Marcia Press

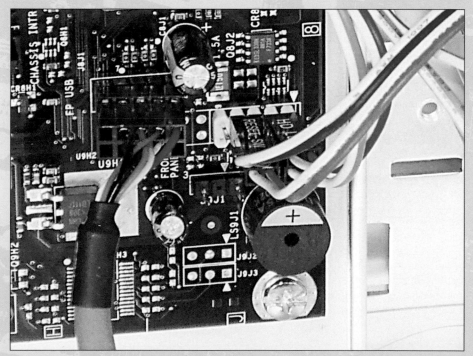

Completed front panel USB cable and LED/switch wiring.

© 2004 Barry Press & Marcia Press

Front panel temperature sensor probes and LED/switch connectors (middle).
© 2004 Barry Press & Marcia Press

You'll use only the parallel ATA connector (bottom left) of these data connectors
because there's no floppy disk drive in this machine and no need to connect any
parallel ATA drive other than the DVD writer. The ATX main power connector is at the
upper left of the group of four connectors, while the memory banks are above the
data connectors.
© 2004 Barry Press & Marcia Press

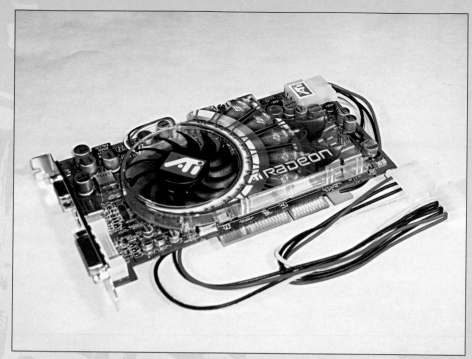

Insert the auxiliary power connectors from the Radeon 9800 XT into a power supply connector with all lines wired.

Keep other cards as far away from the Radeon 9800 XT as possible, and make sure the card is securely in the AGP slot.

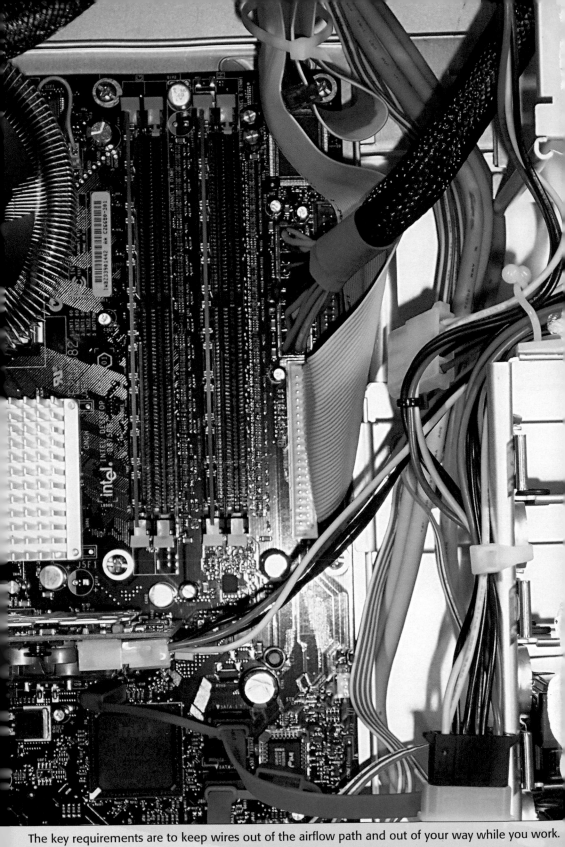

The key requirements are to keep wires out of the airflow path and out of your way while you work.

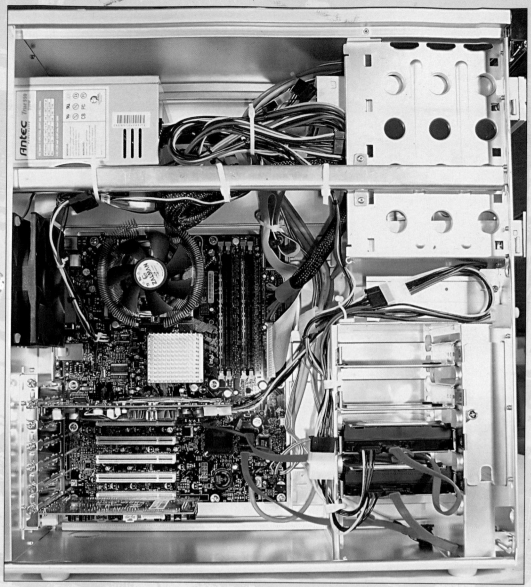

The completed PC.

Slots on the motherboard.